REACHING HIGHER

Rhona S. Weinstein

Reaching Higher

The Power of Expectations in Schooling

HARVARD UNIVERSITY PRESS

Cambridge, Massachusetts, and London, England   2002

Library of Congress Cataloging-in-Publication Data

Weinstein, Rhona S.
  Reaching higher : the power of expectations in schooling / Rhona S. Weinstein.
    p. cm.
  Includes bibliographical references (p.) and index.
  ISBN 0-674-00919-3 (alk. paper)
  1. Academic achievement.   2. Expectation (Psychology).   3. Motivation in education.
I. Title.

LB1062.6 .W45 2002
370.15′4—dc21   2002069084

For my husband, Harvey,
with love

Ah, but a man's reach should exceed his grasp
Or what's a Heaven for?

—Robert Browning, 1855

If we just take people as they are, . . . we make them worse;
but if we treat them . . . as they should be, we help them
become what they can become.

—Johann Wolfgang von Goethe, 1795

Contents

REACHING HIGHER

Introduction

The academic expectations of teachers and parents, educational institutions, and society at large can shape children's lives in school and beyond through self-fulfilling prophecies. Yet the workings of such expectancy effects are far more complex than are commonly understood or than are implemented in current educational reforms that mandate "higher" expectations and high-stakes accountability. To harness its power in positive ways requires a deeper understanding of how such social influence processes unfold and change in real-world settings. This book describes these complex pathways and charts a direction for the promotion of positive educational prophecies, so that all children can develop fully in environments that are both challenging and supportive across their school years.

Our capacity to learn is nourished in the context of human relationships. Most critical here are the beliefs about learning that we bring to our relationships with children. The expectations we hold—about the capability or lack of capability of those we teach—have deep and interwoven roots. These differential expectations guide sharply different educational practices. All too often, under certain conditions, these expectations are confirmed in children's own attitudes and behaviors, thereby creating self-fulfilling prophecies.

Sadly, our system of education is largely built upon beliefs and practices on the negative side—about differences in and limits to ability. Our expectations of ability are too low, too narrowly construed, too bound to time and speed, and too differentiated (high for some, low for others) by social status factors that are irrelevant to the potential to learn. So too are our educational methods narrowly conceived. Guided largely by repetition rather than compensatory and enriched methods, our teaching strategies minimize effort, fail to overcome blocks in learning, and limit what can be learned.

When we respond to the individual differences among students by lowering our expectations and providing inferior educational opportunities, we underestimate the capacity for all children to grow intellectually and we fail to provide adequate tools for learning. In these ways, we confirm our own predictions. To prevent such educational tragedies—a particularly urgent goal given the growing diversity of children attending our schools—we need to both embrace and support pedagogically a vision of *possibility* regarding the educational achievement of *all* our children.

The Gap between Research and the Real World

As a longtime scholar in this field, I have contributed my share of empirical studies to the journals. Yet as I read the findings, I feel the distance that comes from our scientific study of this phenomenon. So much of what has been learned fails to capture the complexity of such effects in the real world. My early professional experiences first fueled my curiosity. In my graduate training at the Yale University Psycho-Educational Clinic, I came upon a vivid example of what I later came to call a self-fulfilling prophecy in my work with a child who had a reading problem. While providing mental health consultation services to a small rural school district near the university, I was referred a ten-year-old boy whom I will call Eric. Eric had never. learned to read and he was seriously behind his peers in fourth grade. Years of tutoring had not alleviated the problem and psychological testing failed to reveal a learning disability. Instead, the test results depicted an anxious performer who blocked on so many tasks that it was impossible to obtain a valid estimate of his ability. My assessment of the child, his siblings, and his parents provided little explanation for the genesis or persistence of this reading problem.

A visit to his classroom, however, provided more of the story. Eric was a member of the lowest reading group, which was called the "clowns." Among its members were the sole ethnic minority child, a nonreader, an overweight child, and so on. Comparing the climate of the highest and lowest ability reading groups was exceedingly painful. In the highest group, the pace was lively, the material interesting, and the children active. In the lowest group, the work was repetitive, remedial, and dull. Upon following the children out to recess, I found that the friendship patterns matched the reading group assignments, but the members of the lowest reading group stood alone and isolated, even from each other.

So I suggested changing the context for learning instead of trying to change the child—that is, that Eric be moved up to the middle reading group. I also insisted on a contract specifying that he remain there for a three-month trial and that I would provide extra tutoring and psychological help to support his learning. A lengthy battle ensued. In a classic catch-22, both Eric's teacher and the principal asked for proof that Eric was capable of handling the material in the middle reading group. I argued that we would not have proof until the educational context was changed and Eric's anxiety about learning was relieved. I finally won approval. Eric was promoted to the middle reading group and slowly but surely began to read and partici-pate in classroom life. By the end of the school year, he had reached grade level in his reading skills and he had friends. He proudly showed them off to me, his arms linked with theirs, as I walked the school halls. One of his greatest moments came when he and his new friends were hauled down to the principal's office to be chastised for chattering in class.

This case was a pivotal one for me. A child who could not read at the start of fourth grade had become a grade-level reader by year's end. The interven-tion was relatively simple given the severity of the reading problem: a belief in the child's capacity to learn, a more challenging and motivating educa-tional climate, and support through tutoring, play therapy, and the friend-ship of peers.

But I kept thinking about the other Erics left behind in the lowest reading groups, where nothing had changed about their daily lives at school. Indi-vidual treatment models took me only so far. This case, then, cemented my shift from clinical to community psychology and to preventive work with populations of children. It alerted me to the larger institutional context in which this problem was embedded—the school's unwavering belief in the accuracy of psychological tests for predicting ability and the sanctity of reading-group assignments. And this case sent me scurrying to the scientific literature. I was curious about the evidence for a causal link between expec-tations and achievement in schooling, and it was here that I first stumbled upon the research on self-fulfilling prophecies.

Years later, I continue to see too many examples of limiting perceptions of human potential, similar to those I described for Eric. I am certain that somewhere in this book, readers might also catch glimpses of themselves. The following examples highlight our tendency to underestimate the poten-tial to learn:

- In a workshop I conducted on racism in a high school, a number of African American and Latino students recounted the raised eyebrows of

teachers as they entered class the first day of advanced placement courses—signals that they were not expected to achieve and were not welcome. In this same school, a parent told of the difficulties that her attractive blond daughter had in being taken seriously for a career in mathematics.

- At another high school, each year a cohort of low-achieving ninth graders, largely members of ethnic minorities, was routinely assigned to remedial classes that did not qualify them for college admission upon the completion of high school, regardless of how well they performed.

- A parent approached our clinic with the concern that his child's ability was being underestimated. A teacher had accused the child of faking the parent signature on a summer reading list because the list was "too long" to have been accomplished.

- Another parent came for help when told that her child, then only in kindergarten, was recommended to repeat the year because of a suspected learning problem. The child described her teacher as forcing her "to work at her level" and to avoid tasks that "would be too hard for her." This parent had always taught her child to approach any challenging task with persistence and alternative strategies.

- Another parent raged about how her child was handled in an evaluation for a suspected learning disability. After testing, the parents were told that their child was mentally retarded and would be recommended for special education. Shocked, the parents demanded an investigation and sought an independent testing from our clinic. During the investigation, it was discovered that an error had been made in the addition of the scores and that indeed, the child had demonstrated above-average intelligence. Just think how much information had to be dismissed for a teacher, principal, and school psychologist to deliver a verdict of "mental retardation" on the basis of an erroneous test score.

These examples reflect, first, beliefs about what children and youth are and should be capable of and second, actions that follow from such beliefs. Such judgments about capability often apply stereotypes about social groups such as about race and gender, reflect myths about development and behavior, confuse what is with what could be, and put too much weight on test scores rather than daily performance as evidence of ability. The actions taken in response to these judgments often determine very different learning opportunities and convey strong messages about capability. The effect of these social processes is heightened because they occur in the context of significant relationships between learners and teachers and because the power is unequal. We accord schools the role of defining ability for society at large. As one parent lamented after a long history of educational placements outside the classroom that left her child far behind academically, with poor self-esteem and few peer relationships: "I never questioned their authority. I thought the school would know better than I what my child needed in order to learn."

It is human nature to reduce the complexity of social stimulation by categorizing people, events, and settings (Macrae and Bodenhausen 2000). Such categorization enables us to sift quickly through complex experiences, identify core defining features, predict possible outcomes, and plan courses of action. Without such guiding schemas, appraising each new situation would be an impossibly time-consuming task. Yet while our categories enable us to see more clearly, they can also blind us. Herein lies the opportunity for limiting or even biased perceptions based upon the application of faulty or stereotyped beliefs (Allport 1954; Marx, Brown, and Steele 1999). Gordon Allport (1954) described prejudice as reflective of man's "normal and natural tendency to form generalizations, concepts, categories, whose content represents an oversimplification of his world of experience" (p. 27). Further adding to the complexity, as the studies of Mahzarin Banaji and her colleagues have demonstrated, some of this categorizing goes on automatically without conscious awareness (Banaji and Bhaskar 2000).

What we see is what we *believe to be* the reality. The sociologist Robert Merton recognized the inherent difficulty of disproving these beliefs once they have been formed. In the classic paper that named this phenomenon, Merton (1948) wrote: "The specious validity of the self-fulfilling prophecy perpetuates a reign of error. For the prophet will cite the actual course of events as proof that he was right from the very beginning" (p. 195). Since we spend most of our day-to-day lives with people who share our assumptions, the categorizations that guide our actions are too seldom challenged.

Can the beliefs and actions of powerful others actually cause outcomes that confirm the original prophecy? What are the characteristics of individuals and environments in classrooms, schools, families, and societies that accentuate or mitigate such self-fulfilling prophecies? What are the conditions that harness positive rather than negative prophecies and that render some individuals more resilient and less susceptible in the face of limiting beliefs and closed educational doors? Can negative self-fulfilling prophecies be pre-vented? These are the questions that frame this book.

Revitalizing a Stagnating Field of Study

There has been a long history of both literary and scientific interest in expec-tancy effects—that is, if and how beliefs about the other (and about the self) can become fulfilled in reality. One can say our interest began with the Greco-Roman myth of the sculptor Pygmalion and his love for the statue Galatea. It was because of the strength of his love that the goddess Venus brought Galatea to life. This legend also appeared in George Bernard Shaw's play *Pygmalion* (1912/1940), which recounted a successful experiment to train a cockney flower girl to pass as a lady. Expectancy effects were formally defined by two sociologists, W. I. Thomas (1931) and Robert Merton (1948) and had their first empirical test in the classic *Pygmalion in the Classroom* study (1968) by psychologist Robert Rosenthal and principal Lenore Jacobson. To-day there exists a vast research literature exploring its workings.

It is of interest that our earliest depiction of expectancy effects, in Galatea, focused on positive rather than negative and limiting beliefs—a positive per-spective we have yet to fully explore and capitalize upon. There is also a negative side of expectancy effects—where because we expect little or less of others, we provide negative, inferior, or different treatment and ultimately receive little in return. These negative processes have been named "Golem" effects based on the Hebrew slang word for dumbbell (Babad, Inbar, and Rosenthal 1982). Aldous Huxley, in his 1932 novel *Brave New World,* de-scribed the workings of negative self-fulfilling prophecies in a society that decides to not only breed but also condition certain individuals for a lower-class future. Huxley described the conditioning rooms where infants of the Delta caste who approached brightly colored books were exposed to loud noises and electric shocks until they "shrank away in horror . . . safe from books all their life" (1932/1946, pp. 28–29).

Research interest in expectancy effects in schooling, once a booming en-terprise and long a hotbed of controversy, has greatly lessened in recent years in response to continued skepticism about the power and importance of such effects. Few investigators persist in such research; fewer still imple-ment interventions (Babad 1993; Brophy 1998b). Further, the research that is done has an exceedingly narrow focus that fails to do justice to the com-plexity and institutional embeddedness of the phenomenon in schooling, to the variation in individual and environmental conditions that may moderate outcomes in children, and to the design and evaluation of preventive action. I will argue here that expectancy effects in schooling have been largely misunderstood and underestimated. And I suggest that this is a critical time to revisit research on self-fulfilling prophecies in schooling—with new perspectives, broader evidence, and a commitment to the design and evaluation of interventions that will harness positive expectancy effects for the benefit of all children.

The power of expectancy effects lies not in momentary beliefs, brief teacher-student interactions, and single outcomes but rather in the cumulative consequences of entrenched beliefs about ability over the course of a school career. Our research methods have too long prioritized the viewpoint of observer over the perspective of participant, largely neglecting insights gleaned from children, the recipients of expectations in schooling. Further, in our concern for experimental rigor, our studies have captured primarily the narrow and the short-term rather than the broad and the entrenched view of the phenomenon. This prevailing paradigm has reinforced our preoccupation with the proof question (do self-fulfilling prophecies exist?) and stifled interest in the conditions question (under what circumstances can expectancy effects be found?).

Thus we have become blind to the fact that, while expectancies are expressed in educational opportunities and interpersonal interactions between teachers and students, they are reinforced by institutional arrangements in the classroom, school, family, and larger society. Further, these layers of institutional arrangements, and their interdependence or lack thereof, enhance or minimize the probability of self-fulfilling prophecies. We have also ignored what can be learned from naturally occurring variations as well as planned interventions. Simple behavioral and linear models are grossly inadequate for the complexity of the task. The need to specify conditions, to link psychological factors with institutional elements, to capture the interactive effects of these processes over longer periods of time, and simply, to humanize the problem requires a shift toward an ecological model of explanation.

Ecological theory, the study of the interrelationships of organisms and their environments, reminds us that individual and collective behavior both reflect as well as influence the context in which they occur (Bronfenbrenner 1979; Bronfenbrenner and Morris 1998). An ecological perspective widens the sources of evidence and the time period of consideration, allowing us to bring together somewhat disparate and disaggregated features of the problem into a dynamic and integrated whole (Kelly 1969, 1979; Vincent and

Trickett 1983). An ecological framework of understanding underscores the importance of (1) the perceived and lived experience of students, teachers, principals, and parents, (2) the interaction of person and environment, (3) the interdependent and nested layers of institutional, family, and community beliefs and practices that link classrooms, schools, homes, and universities, and (4) processes over time, such as history, natural transitions, and planned interventions. Integrating this kind of information helps us to learn what over the course of a schooling career magnifies the effects of negative self-fulfilling prophecies and what can save or buffer children from poor consequences. By shifting the prevailing theoretical paradigm toward an ecological perspective, I hope to provide a richer and more contextualized understanding of self-fulfilling prophecies in schooling than we can glean from a single research literature.

I draw upon material culled from multiple vantage points: as a researcher, clinician, and consultant to schools; as a university professor serving both as a teacher and as an eternal student under peer review; and as a parent guiding my own children through schooling. At the core are findings from a long-standing research program on the dynamics of self-fulfilling prophecies in elementary and high school classrooms. My research has examined the perceptions and understandings of children about teacher expectations and explored if and how awareness of differential treatment by teachers results in differential achievement by students—a question that addresses the mediation of expectancy effects. I have also applied what we learned from children about the communication of expectations in the classroom to the design and evaluation of school-based and collaborative preventive intervention programs.

By articulating the voices of children in their role as students, I bring forth an often ignored perspective about schooling and broaden the model of expectancy processes to include the target of academic expectations—his or her understanding of the school experience. I also illustrate the experiences of multiple players—teachers, principals, parents, and university faculty—in myriad contexts and across time, enabling a look at natural variations in the expectancy process, as well as planned interventions to interrupt the cycle of lowered expectancies.

How the Book Is Organized

Part 1 sets forth the reasons for taking a broader look at self-fulfilling prophecies in schooling. In this Introduction, I have described the gap between the research and the real world of expectancy effects—a disconnect that leads me to press for a change in explanatory theory. Chapter 1 presents a case study of educational expectancy processes in real-world conditions, a complex scenario that any new theory must explain. It documents a twenty-two-year history of a child with a learning disability as his parents and the schools disagree over what to expect and how best to support his academic achievement. The case depicts the institutional proclivity of schools for limiting and low expectations when faced with learners who are different, as well as the often overlooked role of buffering influences—alternative interventions implemented by family, other schools, and teachers that can break the cycle of negative self-fulfilling prophecies.

Chapter 2 provides a historical overview of research about how expectations can become self-fulfilling prophecies and how prevailing paradigms greatly limit our understanding. I make the case for a shift to an ecological model that examines all players in expectancy processes in varied and interdependent contexts over time. Ecological theory can synthesize our knowledge in ways that better reflect the experience, the institutional embeddedness, and the interactive features of expectancy processes in schooling. In Chapter 3, I highlight the urgency of reexamining what we know about negative expectancy effects during an era of increasing diversity in the student population and of failing schools that are largely ill-prepared to deal effectively with such diversity. Despite the rhetoric of current educational reform, the risk for negative effects may be heightened and differential expectations and self-defeating educational practices persist untouched.

In Part 2, an ecological perspective is applied to illustrate what is learned by taking seriously the perspectives of students. In Chapter 4, the voices of elementary school children are used to capture their sophisticated awareness of the different lives lived within classrooms as a function of how smart students are perceived to be by teachers. Chapter 5 in turn highlights differences among classrooms in the culture of achievement expectations communicated to students. Learning from the reports of children and from interviews and observations of teachers, I highlight the different theories and practices of two fifth-grade teachers. Teachers, and the classroom environments they create, differ in the degree to which they emphasize differentiated treatment (the selection of talented children for different pathways) or equitable treatment (the development of talent in all children).

Chapters 6 and 7 speak to the risks for children of negative expectancy processes, reflected in both immediate and more enduring outcomes. Chapter 6 illustrates what happens to children in the short term in these contrasting classroom environments. Interviews with four fourth-grade students, both top-ranked and bottom-ranked, reveal how in contrasting classrooms children think differently about students' potential to learn. Empirical studies also show that the more differential treatment that children report in their classroom, the greater the gap between children on a range of critical competencies, not only academic but also social and emotional. Yet individual, social, and developmental differences among children also affect how much children are placed at risk and how susceptible they are to the expectations of teachers. Chapter 7 explores retrospective accounts of university students as they reflect upon critical incidents in their own achievement history. Here we see that the differential responses of teachers are long remembered and perceived to have enduring consequences for interest in subject matter, motivation, self-esteem, and achievement, unless self-reflection or positive support from significant others helps to reframe and buffer these negative experiences.

Part 3 moves beyond individual classrooms to educational systems as educators see them. I examine both planned interventions and natural variations in school-wide achievement cultures. I also illustrate parallel features and critical interdependencies between the culture of the school and the culture of the classroom, with implications not only for students but also for teachers. Indeed, all are learners. Such interdependencies can be mutually reinforcing, deepening the institutional embeddedness of expectancy effects or contrarily undermining such effects, be they positive or negative. Targeting and aligning these cultural features at multiple levels prove critical in any effort to promote more equitable learning that will filter down into classrooms.

Chapter 8 examines the transformation of an existing achievement culture in a high school as it shifts from a highly stratified system to a more equitable and development-focused system of high expectations for all students. I use a case study of a collaborative intervention that targeted ninth-grade students in the lowest academic track. This cultural shift (in beliefs, instructional strategies, and institutional policies) was as much about what happened to and for teachers as it was about what happened between teachers and students. While Chapter 8 illustrates possibility in the face of constraint, Chapter 9 speaks to the ideal, in an elementary school where positive expectations are already in place and fully aligned. I identify the qualities of school culture and principal leadership that articulate and maintain this culture—an equitable and development-focused learning community for all players, teachers as well as parents. Children are not sifted by ability for scarce opportunities; rather, seemingly limitless and diverse opportunities demand student engagement and thus develop the talents of many.

Chapter 10 turns to the university setting, where the student pipeline is directed, teachers are taught, disciplinary knowledge is discovered, and faculty are developed as scholars and teachers. Akin to the variation seen earlier in K–12 education in both classrooms and schools, universities differ in their achievement cultures, with varying commitments to differentiation (the selection of faculty stars) versus equity and development (the growing of faculty stars). Universities, in the achievement culture they adopt, have a critical leadership role to play both within academia and beyond. They can shape the reform of K–12 education by either exacerbating negative prophecies or by promoting positive expectations that can broaden and diversify the talent pool.

Finally, the Conclusion speaks to the implications for research and intervention. How a problem is defined frames our inquiry and actions taken. Children struggling to overcome the effects of their teachers' and schools' low expectations usually have to contend with multiple, multilayered risk factors, both across levels of the educational system and across domains, such as family, school, and community. These risks, and the positive steps that caring adults take to buffer these risks, determine in large part how vulnerable or resilient those children will be. Interventions must be framed around decreasing the risks, increasing the positive influences that protect children, and creating and transforming educational settings that promote positive prophecies.

With this book, I hope to pave the way for a broadened look at for whom, where, when, and how expectancy effects take place and what consequences they have for children. It is my hope that these new perspectives might guide more effective strategies for school reform and preventive intervention. While the methods adopted here are informed by theory and by a critical look at the evidence, they also press beyond the limitations of existing scientific paradigms and raise questions about the philosophical and moral dimensions of this problem in schooling.

Let me also note at the outset that in addressing expectations and their expression in the practices of schooling, I do not place blame. Expectations about ability, and the instructional practices that follow from these expectations, are institutionalized in the very roots of educational theory and societal beliefs. Teachers and administrators put into practice what they themselves have learned as sound pedagogical knowledge, and what they themselves have faced as learners and continue to face in their work lives in schools. And so, too, do parents take action or fail to take action on the basis of what they know and have experienced.

The capacity for change, however, does lie with us: teachers and administrators can take responsibility for children's school failure and turn it around toward success. Doing so requires a radical shift in assumptions about children's ability and the practices that will motivate and support student learning. The capacity for change also lies in the hands of parents, who, if informed and believed, can better advocate for and support their children in ensuring their access to and success with the highest levels of pedagogical challenge. Finally, the capacity for change lies in the hands of faculty (as scholars and educators) and universities (as the last station in the pipeline), because they frame the national debate about what constitutes intellectual achievement and how it is best nurtured.

The breadth of the topics considered and the multiple perspectives drawn upon are intended to humanize a problem whose influence on children has been underestimated in the language of discrete variables and averaged numbers. An important aspect of our children's lives—their schooling—is at stake, and now is the time for stretching the capacities of all children's minds. All children who pass through our schools must be helped to reach higher if we are serious about excellence and equity in education.

PART I

Reframing the Debate:
What Children Can Become

CHAPTER 1

Colliding Expectations of Family and School

> What the best and wisest parent wants for his own child, that the community must want for all its children. Any other ideal for our schools is narrow and unlovely; acted upon, it destroys our democracy.
>
> —John Dewey, 1899

A single case study—here, a child with a learning disability—when seen across a twenty-two-year schooling history, illuminates the complex and dynamic interplay of factors that frame the development of "accurate" academic expectations and the implementation of "appropriate" instruction. In this chapter, I examine how parental expectations about children's ability emerge in the context of evolving interactions between home, school, and the helping professions, which in concert or in conflict come to shape both the definition and the development of ability in children. The expectations developed and instructional actions taken are especially critical when a child is identified as different from his or her normative group. In such cases, the danger is very great that ability will be underestimated and underdeveloped. One could substitute any kind of difference—race, culture, language, poverty, gender (females with regard to achievement in math and science, males with regard to reading), learning style, or disability—for the characteristics of the child written about here and see many similarities in the experiences depicted.

By focusing on varying contexts and across time, this case study captures both the institutional reinforcement of negative expectancy processes and how a child's fate can be rewritten. That is, even in the face of negative expectations, the potential for resilience instead of vulnerability exists when the beliefs and actions of some significant adults—parents, teachers, and administrators—create another, more beneficial educational context for the child. This kind of interactive complexity, across the domains of home and school, and across time, is precisely what a theoretical model of expectancy effects must ultimately explain.

The case material examined here is derived from the parental perspective. Why begin there? First, parents are frequently overlooked in studies of academic achievement, although there is substantial evidence of a relationship between the family environment, the nature of parental involvement in school, and children's developing competence (see Coleman 1987; Conners and Epstein 1995; Cowan et al. 1994; McCaslin and Good 1996b). When we do explore parental contributions to school achievement, we look largely at static relationships. For example, in the simple linking of socioeconomic background to achievement, we know on average that children whose parents earn more and have higher levels of education show higher achievement in school. Yet these static numbers tell us little about the underlying mechanisms of such effects (Bronfenbrenner 1986). They tell us nothing about the conceptions held, the opportunities available, the transactions engaged in, or the contexts in which they occur, all of which ultimately contribute to student achievement both inside and outside of schooling. Nor do they tell us about the myriad of exceptions—evidence that, despite obstacles of poverty, discrimination, or child disability, some parents, through their beliefs and actions, help their children achieve far beyond the expectations of schools and society (Clark 1983; Hrabowski, Maton, and Greif 1998).

Most critical are parents' own relationships with achievement, their beliefs about and responses to academic success and failure. In an interview published in the *New York Times Magazine,* Toni Morrison talks about such parental teaching, which helps children, despite obstacles in their path, learn to feel extraordinary and to do good work—regardless of how such efforts are evaluated by others or even whether they are noticed. Morrison is quoted as saying:

> Interestingly, I always felt deserving. Growing up in Lorain, my parents made all of us feel as though there were these rather extraordinary deserving people within us. I felt like an aristocrat—or what I think an aristocrat is. I always knew we were very poor. But that was never degrading. I remember a very important lesson that my father gave me when I was twelve or thirteen. He said, "You know, today I welded a perfect seam and I signed my name to it." And I said, "But Daddy, no one's going to see it!" And he

said, "Yeah, but I know it's there." So when I was working in kitchens, I did good work. (Dreifus 1994, p. 73)

Second, parents have a unique and potentially more positive view of the strengths and individuality of their children. Further, they have a long-term stake in their children's development. Most parents hope for the best for their children and the best is what the community must provide for all its children, as the educational philosopher John Dewey (1899) warns. All who have seen children grow from seemingly helpless infants into competent youngsters—capable of mastering the intricate tasks of language acquisition, toilet training, feeding themselves, riding a bicycle, and engaging in social exchange—have seen ample evidence of their strivings for achievement, their sustained effort amid multiple false starts, and the joy they feel when they accomplish their goal. In the context of unabashed mastery, parents have also noted the unique and endearing special attributes of their children that reflect wonderfully individual talents, interests, and personalities. They cherish their children's capacity and embrace their individuality.

Such parental perceptions collide rudely with the worldview of formal schooling, where family-derived and unique notions of achievement are re-placed with rigidly applied normative comparisons tied to age, peer group, or standardized test performance. In her 1978 book *Worlds Apart: Relation-ships between Families and Schools,* Sara Lawrence Lightfoot poignantly de-scribes the sometimes unhappy divide between parents' homegrown views of their children's capabilities and the schools' views, which are usually based on normative and comparative standards of the mainstream culture. This divide is made even sharper by any difference from the mainstream—in cultural beliefs and practices, in disability, in language, and so on. The per-spective of schools likely rules the day, since families look to the school for "information about their children's abilities and likelihood of success—both in the present and the future" (McCaslin and Murdock 1991, p. 232). By de-sign, given current conceptualizations of ability and its measurement, fully two-thirds of our children fall short in this comparison. Thus, it is not sur-prising that parents can appreciate Garrison Keillor's (1985) description of all the children in Lake Wobegon as "above average."

Further, by design, schools offer little sustained opportunity for teachers to come to know and value the individual strengths of children and, most importantly, to capitalize upon such qualities by encouraging mastery of difficult challenges, such as those that the developing child confronts as an infant and toddler (Noddings 1992; Sarason 1990). Instead, differences in children's preparation, learning style, language, and customs unlock a self-perpetuating cycle of lowered and limiting academic expectations that change children's experiences in school. Here is one example of these processes in action.

Parenting and Schooling a "Learning-Disabled" Son

The Early Years: An Emerging Problem

BIRTH COMPLICATIONS.   Not surprisingly for twins, the boys' birth was marked by complications. One month premature, they were delivered by emergency cesarean section, and both came into this world with underdeveloped lungs. The diagnosis was hyaline membrane disease, a disorder that at that time in 1975 required treatment in an incubator in an intensive-care nursery. One twin, whom I will call Adam, was more severely ill because he had suffered the collapse of both lungs and required high levels of oxygen. The parents were warned of the possibility that he would not survive and, if he did, that he might be blind due to the high levels of oxygen administered. But he was a fighter; he struggled to live and succeeded.

The parents felt blessed to bring both sons home. Of course, they were vigilant, looking for clues to any disabilities that might have resulted from the twins' high-risk prematurity. As the years passed, they dealt first with Adam's visual problems. He had been diagnosed with strabismic amblyopia (a condition in which the eyes are misaligned and the brain suppresses the image from the nondominant eye); he needed eye muscle surgery, a patch, and glasses to correct his vision. Yet despite these interventions, the parents reported that Adam showed little interest in visual stimuli of any kind—books, signs, or letters. He was a hands-on, spatially oriented child who took apart and put together everything he could touch. The ophthalmologists consulted could not explain Adam's relative lack of interest in visual stimuli.

FAILURE TO LEARN TO READ.   After a positive Montessori preschool and kindergarten experience, the problems appeared early in first grade, as the twins made the change to a new school. The first-grade teacher hesitated when she began her conference about Adam in the second month of school.

She asked the parents, "How do you feel Adam is doing in school?" The mother reported knowing that the teacher was looking for the parents' perception of the problem before she framed it herself. The teacher did not want to be the first to say that Adam was not learning to read.

The parents were aware that all was not well at school, but they had not understood why. Although Adam had been happy in his kindergarten year at the previous school, he was now reluctant to get up in the morning. He came home from school angry. He was prone to throwing things around the house and picking fights with his brother. His liveliness and sociability were waning. He complained that he had no friends, that no one wanted to play with him at recess, and he described himself as wandering along the corridors of the school, alone and unhappy. He did not have anything to share about what he learned at school. When his parents asked, he shrugged his shoulders and turned away. He cried with little provocation, complained of stomachaches, and begged to be allowed to stay home from school.

After that first critical conference, Adam's behavior grew worse and worse. How to handle Adam became the only topic of conversation between husband and wife. Adam became able to verbalize that he felt dumb and stupid at school; in fact, he said that he knew that he was the dumbest kid in the entire school. On three separate occasions, he expressed that he felt so stupid that life was not worth living. Once he grabbed a knife to show his parents that he was serious about the depth of his feeling.

LABEL APPLIED.   The first conference with the teacher was immediately followed by a meeting with the principal. There, in the second month of first grade, the parents were told that they had one bright son and one not-so-bright son. They were warned of the danger of having expectations for Adam that were too high. The principal told the parents, "I'm afraid that Adam is not college material like his brother, and you will do him a great disservice if you expect the same from him." Stunned, they replied, "But how can you predict college capability on the basis of the first two months of first grade?"

Adam was apparently not learning to read at the same rate as others in his class—others who had been exposed to a reading-readiness program that he had not experienced in his previous school. His current school was in a small (three-school) district of families of primarily high economic means. The principal told the parents that Adam was eligible for special education monies, which would enable psychological testing, and, if he qualified, placement in a special education class by the middle of first grade. He strongly advised the parents to act immediately.

TREATMENT REFUSED.   Before responding to the principal's suggestion, the mother asked whether she could observe in Adam's class and in the special education class as well. She reported shock and dismay at what she saw in a number of visits to his regular classroom. The teacher worked with four ability-based reading groups, and the lowest group consisted of Adam alone, sitting at his own table for the entire reading period. This fact Adam had not reported to his parents, although it was probably why he had decided that he was the dumbest kid in the school and felt a lack of connection with the other children in the class.

The mother's observations of the special education class of six students revealed a mix of student problems from apparent but not convincing mental retardation to emotional difficulties, with a curriculum that surely would set behind any youngster who stayed too long in that setting. Perhaps Adam's parents knew too much to follow blithely the principal's recommendation. In addition, these parents had experienced another school setting—the Montessori kindergarten—where according to the teachers Adam had proceeded well in his reading-readiness skills, and most importantly, he had been happy.

Against the principal's wishes, the parents chose not to have Adam tested by the school. They also asked to have him remain in his regular class. They argued that they did not want labels to follow him around throughout his school career and that they did not want him exposed to a watered-down curriculum. Once the decision was made, the parents began trying to get to the root of Adam's reading problem and attempting to change the conditions that he had experienced at school. But in rejecting the principal's recommendation, they were challenging the authority of the school itself.

INTERVENTIONS OUTSIDE OF SCHOOL.   Three actions were taken. First, the parents asked a reading expert at the local university to evaluate Adam's reading, as a check for their own perceptions and those of the school. After working with Adam over a two-hour period, the expert described Adam as having a lively intellect, reading skills largely at grade level, and some scattered problems with visual memory skills—but little that suggested an inability to learn to read. Second, they consulted several experts for an assessment of Adam's vision. After many puzzling reports, one expert ophthalmologist, using experimental techniques, prescribed highly magni-fied bifocal glasses, which radically improved Adam's ability to see symbols and may have contributed to a greater readiness for reading. This difference was immediately apparent when Adam, with his new glasses on, noticed billboard signs for the first time and began to show interest in words. Finally, the parents also found a skilled learning disabilities teacher who agreed to work after school with Adam and to help move along his reading.

UNCHANGING LOW EXPECTATIONS.   The mother met with Adam's first-grade teacher regularly to try to change her perceptions about his ca-pacity to learn and to modify her methods of instruction. The parents asked that Adam become part of a regular reading group, and he was moved to the third, now lowest, group. The tutor called the teacher, and they shared strat-egies for teaching Adam. The parents also shared information with the teacher about Adam's strengths and interests.

Despite these efforts, and despite improvement in his reading skills (he scored at the forty-fourth percentile in reading and completed primer mate-rials by the end of first grade), Adam's motivation and his feelings about himself underwent little change. It seemed that each week there were new assaults to his self-image and new limits placed on his exposure to chal-lenging curricula. First grade passed into second grade, and even with a new teacher there was very little change in the school's perceptions about Adam's ability to learn. The parents later learned that the second-grade teacher was a roommate of the first-grade teacher, which may well have been a factor in the transfer of perceptions about Adam.

DIFFERENT SCHOOL CAREERS FOR TWINS.   Having fraternal twins meant that the parents confronted comparative sibling issues head-on. One twin was placed in the highest reading group and the other in the lowest reading group, and even though they were in separate classes, each child was fully aware of this distinction. Adam's twin brother was recommended for an enrichment program in reading (a great books program) with a spe-cial teacher and wonderful classics to read. It pained Adam to no end that he could not participate. The parents wondered why, with his bright mind, he was reading only about Dick and Jane. How was this to be explained at the dinner table when the family gathered to share the experiences of the day?

Adam's twin brother was also recommended for enrichment math, which highlighted problem-solving skills, while Adam was recommended for remedial math classes. In response, the parents asked for access to the test scores that had determined the different placements. They discovered that the twins had scored within one point of each other, the ninety-sixth and ninety-fifth percentiles. Additional conferences were held, first with the teacher and next with the principal, about how this differential assignment could have been made, despite virtual equivalence of test scores. The parents were told that Adam was assigned to remedial math because of his reading problem. "He wouldn't be able to handle word problems," the principal informed them. "It didn't stop him on the test," the parents retorted. Even after a detailed letter arguing the case, the most that could be accomplished was to get Adam out of remedial math; he was still not admitted to enrichment math.

What these parents faced was having two siblings, both of them bright in their view, although admittedly with different strengths and weaknesses—sent along two different curricular routes in school, with one labeled "smart" and one "not-so-smart," and with the gap between them in exposure to knowledge and in self-esteem growing rapidly. And the twins were still only in second grade. It is important to note for the record that, by the end of second grade, Adam had completed grade-level materials in both reading and mathematics. When the parents' attempts to change the school situation failed, they made a decision to leave this school and to seek out another, more positive educational environment.

Mid-Elementary Years: A Change of Schools

A BRITISH PROGRESSIVE SCHOOL. The first four months of third grade were spent in a progressive school in London, where the parents were on sabbatical. Once Adam was exposed to alternative teaching practices, the parents saw enormous improvement in his performance and his self-esteem. Happily, in their view, reading was not taught using ability-based reading groups. Instead, the teacher worked with the class as a whole, with individuals, and with student-directed groups. The classroom contained a wonderful library that was replenished from time to time with visits to and exchanges from the school's larger library. In combination with teacher-directed reading material, children chose the books they would read. There was much reading aloud, much sharing of books, and trips to community settings to see a play or to visit a historical site related to a book that the class was reading.

Adam flourished in such a stimulating and accepting environment, and it was here that his passion for reading developed for the first time. He made enormous progress in his reading, and he felt exceptionally good about himself. His parents simply marveled that this teacher saw their son as a bright, eager learner with much talent—a perception in stark contrast with the view of the teachers and the principal in his previous school.

AN ALTERNATIVE PRIVATE SCHOOL. Following the sabbatical, the parents found a remarkable private school to take both sons through elementary school. There, from the moment both sons walked in the door and were welcomed with individual interviews with the principal and assigned student mentors, they faced high expectations and multiple, diversified demands for involvement and challenge. So much so that, despite their differences, they were able to survive as twins in the same classroom and both were able to succeed.

Adam continued to struggle with his reading, particularly with spelling and other rote skills in math and Spanish. Yet, as was the school's explicit policy, these struggles never kept Adam from moving forward with his studies. He was always exposed to challenging and enriched subject matter regardless of the unevenness of some of his skills. In this setting, given the diversity of the opportunities provided to students and the demand for their involvement, Adam developed a passion for the theater, as well as for literature, writing, and science. The lines blurred daily between what was learned in the classroom, on the set in rehearsals, in the production room for the school newspaper and literary magazine, or on the coastal science trip.

Adam continued to work hard on the basic skills because the larger picture was exciting, stimulating, and worth pursuing. Further, his part in it and his accomplishments were valued and appreciated, despite his need to work harder than some of the other students. The miracle for these parents was that twin brothers could feel equally challenged and equally valued in the same classroom in the same small school, not despite their differences but because of them. One was a struggling learner in certain subjects, the other a quick study in most, yet this distinction was only a part of what they were about to the school, the teachers, and their peers. The challenge ahead for Adam was, as the parents described it, to continue to expend the effort necessary to keep all of his options open once the protective environment of this unusual elementary school could no longer shield him from the harsher realities of the larger world.

PSYCHOLOGICAL TEST PREDICTIONS. There were times when Adam's basically upward trajectory hit rock bottom—when the extra tutoring and the many hours spent on homework (when his brother committed far fewer hours and everyone else was outside playing basketball) seemed too much to bear. There were times when the unevenness in Adam's grades seemed to prove that perhaps he was not capable, perhaps his parents and the school were pushing too hard. At one of these low moments, at the end of third grade when Adam was nine years old, Adam's parents decided to obtain a formal psychological assessment of his learning disabilities outside of the school context so that the test results would be private. The test report summary read:

> Adam has a learning disability in visual-motor and visual-spatial skills and in rote visual and auditory memory and sequencing. His impulsivity, poor organization, and weak attention exacerbate his problems. Thus, in school Adam has trouble processing instructions. He finds spelling and the mechanics of written language hard to master and he has some difficulty learning number facts and retaining certain kinds of information. Despite his difficulties, Adam has made tremendous gains in reading . . . In the emotional area, Adam's air of bravado is a facade to compensate for his insecurity. As he improves academically and continues to develop friendships he should continue to become more confident . . . Adam is an endearing, precocious little boy with good learning potential. With the appropriate academic support and remedial help, there is every reason to expect continuing progress in school and a growth in personal confidence and self-esteem.

Although the report ended on a positive note, underscoring Adam's potential to learn, the parents were left with lots of questions as well as ambivalent feelings. In part, they felt validated that indeed Adam demonstrated observable learning difficulties, difficulties that fell under the diagnostic category of dyslexia. On the other hand, they felt overwhelmed by the extent of these difficulties and the potential for rough waters ahead, wondering if, in fact, they had expected too much, as the first school principal had suggested.

The ongoing question about expectations that were perhaps too high was reflected in Adam's sixth-grade teacher's evaluation of his work, shared with Adam and his parents. His teacher wrote: "I see Adam growing as a person, acquiring more depth, self-awareness, and finesse. Adam has won the respect of many of his peers for his outstanding ideas and thoughtful judgments. Sometimes Adam has such high standards for himself, particularly in the finished products of his creative zeal, that I feel he is not being realistic. He needs to get more practical about some of his dreams. And yet, oh, aim for the stars, Adam! Who would have thought in September that you would come in glowing with a long, well-crafted story written in one night? But you did!"

THE QUALITIES OF TUTORING.   The outside-of-school tutoring continued and proved enormously helpful. This exceptionally talented teacher of students with learning disabilities worked privately with Adam from the third grade until well into high school. They met once or twice a week and worked across multiple subjects. In an interview with this teacher about her teaching methods, she described her approach, beginning with the purpose of diagnostic assessment as she saw it: "Before diagnostic work, I talk to a child and explain what testing is and how it helps. Diagnostic work shows me why there is trouble, where it is, and how we can fix it. I only test as far as is necessary. Once there is trouble, I stop. I don't want to frustrate the child. I want the child to leave feeling good. I show the child where he did well, where he had difficulties, and how I can help—the child needs to anticipate success."

The learning disabilities teacher underscored the importance of explaining to the child and to his parents what went wrong with his learning and how improvements in learning can be made: "I provide a context for a more positive understanding of learning problems with both the child and the parents. I mention famous people with similar problems (for example, Einstein), that different developmental trajectories may mean a child may not be ready to learn when a specific skill is taught (and that these gaps can be filled in later), that given certain teaching practices, children may have been exposed to limited modalities for learning (perhaps in their weakest areas), and that low scores don't mean low intelligence."

She cautioned that diagnostic work provides the underpinnings for teaching but that the focus must be on the teaching itself: "The testing is adapted for each child (tapping visual, auditory, and motor skills in reading and math) and in contrast to the work of many others, lasts only an hour: I must start the teaching. When you do one-to-one teaching, you continually diagnose and reevaluate. Once I find the level at which the child is reading or doing math, I begin at a lower level so the child immediately experiences success. I work on one skill at a time to know that a child is getting it. I explain to the child what I am doing and when the skill will be used."

Most importantly, the work is highly individualized, and no time limit is set for accomplishment. In each lesson, this teacher builds successful learning experiences and ends with some fun. A hallmark of her approach is caring and consistent communication of progress and teaching strategies with the child, parents, and teachers. "I never set a time limit; each child learns at his or her own pace and that pace changes. I never go to the higher level of skill until the skill is mastered. At the end of each lesson, I make room for fun through oral reading, riddles, and joke books. I keep careful records of what is done with each child—records that can be shared with teachers and parents."

Middle and High School: A Return to the Public Schools

MANAGING MIDDLE SCHOOL. Committed to public education, the parents made a transition back into the public schools. They intentionally moved into what many viewed as a better school district. As anticipated, the adjustment to public middle school was a difficult one—due in part to the large size of the school (more than two thousand students), tracked classes, multiple teachers, and bureaucratic nature of its organization. The parents tried to soften the blow by requesting teachers whose teaching styles would be helpful to Adam—teachers who focused on conceptual rather than rote learning and who stressed interactive and hands-on assignments. And they tried to keep Adam assigned to the higher-track classes. When his grades were uneven, however, there were attempts to have him moved down.

The road was rocky but with bright spots along the way: some teachers believed in Adam and stimulated his involvement in their classes. For his part, Adam periodically asked for conferences with teachers to clarify their expectations and to share how (that is, the conditions under which) he learned best. These contacts with teachers, outside tutoring, and hard work at home facilitated his academic survival.

Adam, an active and friendly student in a largely bureaucratic middle school environment, tended to get into disciplinary trouble, something that had never happened previously. One such incident began when he was sent out of class for talking to his neighbor about the assignment. Outside the classroom door was a chair, so he sat down (he had not been told to stand). When the teacher came out to speak to him and found him seated, he gave him a detention for disrespect. On his way to the afterschool detention, he was stopped by one of his teachers to discuss an assignment. Although Adam said he would be late if he chatted, the teacher persisted. He was late for his detention and hence received a second detention.

Upon hearing this story, the parents and Adam met with the school principal to express concern about this seemingly unfair escalation of disciplinary actions. The principal agreed and said that she would cancel Adam's second detention. Believing it to be canceled, he of course did not attend. As a result, the parents received a warning notice that Adam was facing suspension from school for failure to attend a detention and that they needed to meet with school officials immediately. Adam went to see the vice-principal and explained the circumstances. The vice-principal, however, did not believe Adam's story and insisted that the parents come in to verify the events, which they did.

Two things dismayed the parents about this incident. First, that movement in the classroom and the school was so restricted. The tight orchestration and monitoring of behavior was at odds with the needs of middle school students, particularly an active student like Adam. Second, that Adam's word had not been believed stood in stark contrast to the respect each student had received in his previous school. This lack of trust slowly and insidiously undermined his confidence.

BATTLING THE TRACKING SYSTEM IN HIGH SCHOOL.   After an uneven two years in middle school, the parents offered their sons the choice of public or private high school, although they insisted that the boys apply to and visit two private schools in addition to the local public school. After much careful deliberation, both boys said they would like to go to the public high school because of its larger size and the greater diversity of its student body. The parents set three conditions for them: first, that they get excited about their courses, work hard, and show growth in their learning; second, that they develop good relationships with a number of teachers who would get to know them well; and third, that they become deeply involved in one or more extracurricular activities about which they could develop a passion. If all three conditions were met, the parents felt the twins would be getting an excellent education.

There was still much to negotiate in an 1,100-student high school in a high-achieving, high-socioeconomic-level school district with four tracks (high honors and advanced placement, honors, general, and remedial). Admission into the highest tracked classes was by grades, with relatively few spaces available. The parents intervened as best as they could (it was getting harder as Adam moved up the grade levels) in requesting certain teachers and certain track placements for Adam.

By and large, Adam was in a challenging program and college bound, with a number of honors classes in English and math. But in history, a subject he greatly loved, he could not gain admission to the advanced placement class. His mother called the department head to intervene one last time. It was a B+ that stood in his way. "Adam is simply not capable of handling the advanced material," the teacher said. "Would you meet with, talk with Adam?" Adam's mother asked, adding, "I think that you will find him very capable and very enthusiastic about working hard." "The grade disqualifies him—the proof of the pudding," replied the teacher. As it happened, that same department head was Adam's teacher in an honors history class. It turned out to be an excellent course and Adam did exceptionally well, placing first in the class. Ironically, the teacher, not remembering the parents' request, wrote on Adam's final paper, "You should have been in the advanced placement class; you would have aced it."

Each year of high school, the road was bumpy for Adam as he learned about each teacher's expectations for the course, told each teacher about his own learning style and effective strategies, scheduled conferences, and used tutoring. Eventually he was on his way—excited, working hard, and generally, given some unevenness, doing very well. He also used high school to express his passion for, and to further develop his talents in, theater and sports.

COLLEGE APPLICATIONS AND SUCCESS.   Adam's anxiety grew about the upcoming college applications and the hurdles of the PSAT, SAT, and final exams. Not surprisingly, given his learning disability, Adam did not test well under timed conditions and on multiple-choice examinations. He took private classes with practice sessions to improve his performance; in fact, he took an SAT class twice. His performance did improve, and he achieved good scores on the timed version of the test. College applications, which require multiple essays and countless forms, are a challenge for any student and the process is an emotionally trying one. His parents wondered, "Where will Adam's accomplishments be appreciated? Where will be the best fit for him?" Not surprisingly, he chose a small, highly regarded liberal-arts college. He had been accepted at eleven of the twelve colleges to which he had applied.

POSTSCRIPT: COLLEGE.   Adam's parents worried about the transition to college—would Adam be able to sustain his strategies in a faraway college without their immediate support? But such worries proved groundless.

Adam's coping strategies were now internalized and very much his own. Every semester was a touch rocky at the start, as Adam got to know the professors and the new material. But the exciting news was that he was enjoying the challenge of courses in the Greek classics, English literature, drama, and philosophy; he was growing by leaps and bounds; and he loved college. He graduated with a double major, successfully completed an honors thesis, and won several fellowships to help him through the next stages of career preparation.

When Adam's parents think about the principal's prediction early in first grade ("not-so-bright, not college material"), they are grateful that they refused to listen. All they wanted was to keep doors open for Adam so that he could continue to develop academically, choose a stimulating path for himself, and feel good about his accomplishments. Keeping doors open in school systems that operate to close doors is no small accomplishment for parents. No small accomplishment indeed—even if one of the parents is a researcher who studies this same process as it happens to other people's children. Adam, his name a pseudonym, is my son.

Reflections

A Comparative Perspective

Sending two children with different learning styles through school in the same grade and at the same time gave our family a comparative, illuminating, and very personal perspective on how institutions constrain educational opportunity. That Adam's performance was appraised more favorably in the Montessori kindergarten and the British progressive classroom than in the district elementary school (the former schools allowed for different developmental trajectories) and by the reading expert than by the first-grade teacher (the reading expert focused on national rather than local norms for grade-level skills) helped to clarify the nature of his learning problems and to nurture a more hopeful picture of his capability.

That there was an identifiable problem, a visual problem as well as a learning disability, was never at issue. What was contested was its intractability and its implications for learning opportunities across the curriculum. The limiting expectations for Adam prescribed a course of action that labeled him as deficient and limited his exposure to challenging curricula. There was much at stake, and the consequences began to accumulate quickly:

growing differences in content coverage both in reading and in math, a diminishing self-esteem as well as sense of belonging, and a loss of interest in school and in learning. And there was little room for disagreement.

As parents, we too felt the pain of our son being found deficient, and we reeled under the unequal power relationship as the school became the defining agent. Yet we had the professional background to question the judgment of the school, as well as the financial means to fight back—with tutoring, a change of schools, and pressure for assignment to challenging classes. For parents with fewer informational as well as fiscal resources for problem resolution, the possibility of losing such a battle greatly increases.

The school's role in defining ability and the parallel role of the health and helping professions in predicting human potential are critical influences as parents develop and adapt expectations for their growing children. Daily, these professions predict for parents what children are likely to achieve—especially children born with a host of disabilities, children sustaining disabilities from illness or accident, and children whose race, behavior, and progress are simply different from what is perceived as normative at each school. How do we determine whether such predictions are accurate only because they limit what parents and schools are willing to try in educating these youngsters? This empirical question must be tested by raising the bar of expectations and providing appropriate and sufficient educational supports for children to meet such expectations.

Since we were not willing to follow the advice of the school system, we were accused of having unrealistically high expectations for our child and of demanding too much—a view with which some readers may agree. Yet our child's academic life and self-image were at stake. While we were unsure of our position, we questioned the certainty of the school's position. We were reluctant simply to write off our son as not being college material, especially at the very start of schooling. We were convinced that, given a better match between his needs and the learning environment, the observed problems had a chance of working themselves out, a chance we thought was well worth taking. We were skeptical of labels and educational placements that would take him ever further from the normative experience children should have in school.

Our strategy was to seek alternative educational conditions that could ultimately resolve the difficulties. That these difficulties were resolved, that our son became an avid reader and successfully handled the challenges of a rigorous college curriculum, suggests that our expectations were not out of line with his capabilities. Indeed, one may reasonably ask whether, except for a very small percentage of children with severe mental retardation, in fact all children could meet the challenge of higher-order learning if they were given appropriate supports and the precious gift of time.

Limiting Expectations and Practices

Many false premises undergird the predictions made about Adam's capacity to learn. His lack of exposure to the school's readiness program, for example, was not taken into account in appraising his performance level. Adam's performance was judged solely in relative terms, against the particular school population instead of against national norms, where his achievements placed him just below average for his age group. Few saw capability beyond the clear deficits that did exist. The problems that stemmed from his visual impairment and learning disability became all that he was in the eyes of others. Deficits in reading became generalized to presumed deficits in mathematics, even to the point of disregarding test scores. Finally, what existed at one point in time was confused with what could be in the future. Difference became deficit, deficit overruled strength, and assessment dominated intervention.

Similarly, false premises abound in the educational strategies that were embraced. Instruction was not linked to diagnostic assessments of where the problems in learning actually lay. Instead, it focused on remediation alone, offering largely repetition and leaving behind enrichment and higher-order learning. In addition, Adam's assignment as the lone member of the lowest reading group and a proposed special-class placement eroded a sense of community within the school and among peers. Further, the challenging curriculum was mostly reserved for those students in the "great books" and "math enrichment" programs, the highest reading groups and tracks, and advanced placement classes. Children's voices were not believed, children's interests were not honored, and children's agency was not encouraged. These limiting perceptions of capability and limiting educational pathways, which began as fleeting impressions and tentative actions, all too quickly became institutionalized. Limited exposure to educational content made it difficult to do better or place higher, the eroding of motivation diminished effort, and a lowly sense of academic self damaged confidence. Even when growth occurred, it was neither seen nor appreciated; instead, only the negative prophecy was confirmed.

Risk and Resilience

This case study underscores the complexity of how academic expectations unfold and instructional opportunities are allocated across a school career—a complexity that begs a theoretical explanation and requires preventive intervention. Examples have been given of some of the institutional roadblocks to equal educational opportunities, roadblocks that are put up in response to differences in what children bring to school and how they learn. Threats to a common and high-challenge educational experience appear early. Small differences between children loom large, dependent upon the mix of students within a classroom and within a school. Similar roadblocks can occur in response to differences of language, financial means, educational exposure, cultural ways, and a variety of disabilities. Where difference spells deficit, expectations are lowered and children's classroom experiences diverge. Problems in one academic area such as reading are quickly generalized to other areas of the curriculum because prevailing views and practices support such generalizations. Failure and differential treatment from others threaten the child's self-esteem, formation of peer friendships, and enjoyment of school.

The false premises that undergird these beliefs and practices are not unique to this case but are routine in many school districts across the country. Experiences like those described in this chapter may lead some to question the rigid systems of special education, bilingual instruction, and ability-based teaching in reading groups and academic tracks. But we must remember that it is also the beliefs about children and their potential to learn, and beliefs about our sense of efficacy in moving children forward, that keep these institutional arrangements in place.

This case study tells of resilience, not defeat, in the face of limiting expectations and practices. What were some of the beliefs that helped this child stay on course, despite the need for great and sustained effort? What actions were taken that shaped his mastery of the academic world and his ultimately positive self-image?

The Interventions

The theory that guided the diagnosis and action in this case was ecological—that is, the learning problems were understood to have resulted from a mismatch between the needs of the child and the qualities of the environment (Cowan 1970; Kelly 1969). Diagnostic appraisals were brief and immediately tied to intervention strategies. Effective intervention required changes in the school environment, a balancing of challenge and remediation, and a recognition of the whole child. It also drew upon the agency of child and parents.

In sharp contrast, most theories that explain human dysfunction are deficit-driven and fail to define corresponding strengths. Problems are viewed as residing in individuals (a form of intrapsychic and biological determinism), while contextual features are largely ignored. As Philip Cowan (1970) notes: "The disease metaphors of psychological and educational diagnosis tend to focus on the child's sickness . . . they give us no information at all about the many ways in which a child with learning disorders does in fact achieve . . . When a child has a 'learning disease,' there is an overwhelming temptation to place him in an isolation ward or a quarantined community (special class). Treatment . . . attempts to get rid of the disease by changing the child so that he can readjust to the original environment from which he was removed" (pp. 48–49).

As Cowan goes on to argue, it is far more productive to look at dysfunction as resulting from a child-environment mismatch. When we change our instructional strategies—for example, by allowing the child to use different sensory modalities in learning—we enable the child to learn. Thus, in order to assess and aid a child's learning difficulties, we must also evaluate and change the learning situations in which a child finds him- or herself. Diagnostic testing needs to be brief, frequent, and immediately tied to teaching strategies.

Today, however, just as during my early training, assessment generally proceeds apart from teaching and testing does not inform instruction. A recent continuing education workshop on learning disabilities taught about 150 discrete intellectual abilities and the tests that psychologists can use to assess them. But when I asked about the implications for teaching, the instructor, a national expert, said that the field still had little to offer regarding effective intervention; it was up to teachers to find their way. This longstanding disconnect between psychology and education (Sarason 2001) continues, despite the model provided by Lightner Witmer, the founding father of clinical, child clinical, and school psychology. Witmer (1907/1996) wrote, "If psychology was worth anything to me or to others, it should be able to assist the efforts of a teacher" (p. 248). Witmer, who discarded formal tests and engaged instead in diagnostic teaching, is still ahead of his time almost one hundred years later (Routh 1996).

While Adam's visual perception problems were aided by highly magnified bifocal glasses and his visual memory problems were addressed with specific remedial and compensatory strategies, these interventions were not enough: Adam continued to face low expectations and remedial teaching at school. We had to change the expectations that were in place through communication with teachers and principals, requests for higher group and higher track placements, and requests for certain teachers whose conceptual rather than rote style of teaching better matched Adam's ways of learning. Sometimes we were successful. But there were times when we felt forced to change schools to find what was needed—to select school environments whose philosophy and policies would continue to challenge and appreciate Adam, turning him into a reader, a writer, a scientist, a student with a true love for learning. In selecting different educational environments, our son's educational opportunities broadened and his experiences became more positive. Adam was more than his grades and his test scores. The opportunities he had to develop all aspects of himself were critical because they allowed him to counterbalance the hard work and rocky passages of certain kinds of academic learning with the smoother sailing of other kinds of learning and doing. The Montessori classroom, British primary school, and alternative private school, because of their educational philosophies, proved more successful than the high-achieving small school district in making sure that a variety of challenging and supportive experiences awaited each child and that the uniqueness of each child was appreciated.

In my work with parents, I urge them not to accept, without careful examination, any ceiling placed on what their child can learn. I also encourage them to explore different teaching environments in order to find out how their child best learns. Since some of the supports illustrated in this case study (tutors, private school, SAT classes) are dependent upon financial means, our efforts at educational reform must be directed first toward preventing such limiting expectations, and second, toward creating effective built-in supports in every public school. Regardless of parents' options for alternative educational environments, they can pressure school districts for real choices: transfers between classrooms and between schools, placement in higher groups or tracks, and the use of special education resources within the classroom and without the damaging effects of labeling.

Gloria S. Boutte (1992) writes movingly about her frustrations as an African American parent and educator concerned about the low expectations for her daughter in an integrated kindergarten class. It was her persistent actions, in telling teachers that she did not want her daughter "tracked as below average" that helped her daughter have more successful school experiences. She notes: "If students are placed in ability groups, then parents have a right to be informed . . . My professional background made me more aware of these problems than most parents, who tend to assume that all children at a particular grade level are learning the same content" (p. 787). Similarly, Claude Goldenberg's (1989) case study of Hispanic first graders provides an excellent example of how more support from parents proved critical in boosting children's achievement and enabling promotion into a higher-level reading group.

Indeed, a parent who heard me speak about these issues years before came back recently to tell me that she tried these interventions with great success. Her son, who at the time was a member of the lowest reading group, showed little interest in school. She met with the teacher and asked how she could help him prepare to move into the highest reading group. Perhaps because this parent was an immigrant with limited proficiency in English, it took three visits and an entire school year before the teacher sat down with the parent to provide extra materials to improve her child's reading skills. That summer and into the next year, she worked steadily with her son. Over time, he grew both in interest and skills and eventually graduated to the top reading group. Approximately ten years later, she told me that her son had just been admitted as an undergraduate student at the University of California, Berkeley, an accomplishment that she was sure had resulted from her intervention.

Not only was parental action essential to Adam's success; drawing him in as a full partner in his education, engaging his effort, and teaching him self-monitoring and self-evaluative strategies were also critical to his progress. Listening to and learning from his experiences in school as early as that first-grade year proved pivotal to enlisting his aid and his wisdom. That he had a voice, that his concerns were alleviated with helpful information from his learning disabilities tutor, and that there was a plan—one that as he grew older he could put in place himself with predictable success—gave him a sense of control over his own ways of learning. Indeed, this set of beliefs and strategies became internalized and could be successfully generalized to new situations. Critical was the unwavering belief that academic ability was indeed malleable, not inborn and fixed at birth. Thus, while performance levels and error patterns proved informative, they were not definitive: there was always a focus on improvement. Operating under an incremental rather than entity theory about ability, as described by Carol Dweck (2000), mobilizes active coping rather than passive helplessness in the face of learning problems.

Also critical to our strategy was a focus on effort, evaluation, and strategy change. Working hard became a sign of strength of purpose, not lack of ability. Progress or lack thereof was the marker for a pat on the back or for a re-evaluation of the appropriateness of the strategy and the time frame. Most importantly, we were tenacious in not giving up, despite the appearance of new obstacles around the corner. This accountability for progress, for widening Adam's options, and for nurturing positive attitudes was shared by development-focused teachers who held themselves accountable for the nurturing of each of their students.

All Should Struggle

Because of his disability, Adam felt that he learned substantially more. One of his college application essays was about growing up learning disabled. This essay was later published in the *Journal of Learning Disabilities*. In it, he wrote about the surprising benefits of his learning disability:

> Dyslexia. It is a long word. It conjures up very mixed feelings inside me. The word dyslexia has been a shield I've hidden behind, a barrier I've vehemently tried to conquer, and a bullet that many times in my life has dug into my soul . . . But things have changed. I've learned to read and write. I've learned to love history, philosophy, and the sciences. And yet, however hard I've tried to lose the label, its grip has only held solid. It has taken me the last four years to finally acknowledge that I will always be dyslexic. But instead of ignoring it, I have finally learned to use dyslexia to my advantage. It has become a tool to define who I am. By making me a very focused learner, dyslexia has given me a zest for solving problems that is applicable in all areas where I've wished to focus my attention . . . I have compensated for difficulties with rote learning by identifying problems early, by learning conceptually, and by determining when I need help and seeking this help in the form of tutoring . . . This has not always been easy, but I believe that because of my learning disability, I have learned substantially more. (J. A. Weinstein 1994, p. 142)

Adam became a better and more persistent learner because he had to actively secure the conditions and help he needed.

Given that the expenditure of effort is a sign in most classrooms of a lack of ability, how did Adam's struggles affect his twin brother whom I described earlier as a quick study? In fact, Adam's twin had never been challenged enough by his schooling experiences. One day in his junior year of high school, he asked for my feedback on a draft of a history paper. After a serious reading of the piece, I concluded that this was another example of getting by—a light treatment of the topic without evidence of intellectual struggle. I asked whether he was serious about getting feedback; he acknowledged that he was. With trepidation, I told him as gently as I could what I thought. His thunderous response stunned me: he stormed out, accusing me of applying university standards to a poor high school boy. Two long hours passed before he reappeared to ask, "Can you show me what you mean?"

So began a process on his part in which he stretched himself, exposed his vulnerabilities, looked into contradictions, read across multiple sources, and let out his curiosity. It was a risk worth taking, and I have always felt that the disjunction between serious university study and K–12 schooling rests on this: students are not taught that the prize is in the struggle. One can ask whether those who slide through school without effort, without failure, and perhaps, without passion are also the disabled ones. Should we not ultimately expect *all* to struggle, to learn from failure, and to persist in overcoming obstacles to solving challenging problems? Is that not what achievement is really about—instead of finishing work fast, without error, and alone (without access to resources), as we will learn from children's reports is what "smartness" has come to mean in school? When uneven performance and the use of help are stigmatized by schools, we create a world in which striving for mastery on complex tasks is rarely attempted unless success is assured.

Central to any discussion of academic expectations must be what parents want for their *own* children—a personal perspective that is too often ignored. The journalist Ellen Goodman (1994) powerfully articulated the power of a personal stake in an op-ed piece on the debate by policy makers about health care reform. Goodman called for a denial of health benefits to legislators and their own families comparable to the 95 percent coverage they were willing to approve for the population at large. In doing so, she named individuals who would lose their coverage due to disqualifying pre-existing conditions. This same perspective (is it good enough for your own child?) must be a part of any discussion of achievement expectations for children and the implications for school reform.

CHAPTER 2

Turning Points in Research on Expectations: Toward an Ecological Paradigm

Operations and measurements are paradigm-determined. Science does not deal in all possible laboratory manipulations. Instead, it selects those relevant to . . . the immediate experience that the paradigm has partially determined. As a result, scientists with different paradigms engage in different concrete laboratory manipulations.

—Thomas Kuhn, 1962

Despite its earliest beginnings in sociology, the research on self-fulfilling prophecies has been dominated by a behavioral and positivist paradigm, drawing much of its theory and empirical findings from psychology. Anomalous findings that could not be easily explained moved the explanatory paradigm toward a social-cognitive model, shifting the inquiry from a positivist or law-seeking one toward one using interpretivist or meaning-seeking principles. This shift, however, was never fully embraced. Nor have these sociocognitive perspectives proven sufficient to fully capture the contextual, interactive, and cumulative features of expectancy effects in schooling. An ecological approach is urgently needed.

Within prevailing research paradigms, thin slices of the problem have been selected for study, certain evidence has been favored over other evidence, and many findings have been ignored. The voices of children have been largely neglected as a source of evidence about the nature and influence of expectancy processes. Much relevant knowledge remains untapped, and there is much to learn about for whom, where, when, in what ways, and with what effects self-fulfilling prophecies about ability operate in schooling. There is also much to question about the basic assumptions underlying what we call the accuracy of our perceptions of children's ability and the appropriateness of our prescribed educational treatments. As a result, expectancy effects have been roundly misunderstood as well as severely underestimated—conclusions that have limited the vigorous development and evaluation of applied efforts designed to prevent the occurrence of negative self-fulfilling prophecies in education.

How did we get to this place and how might we move forward? Since much has been written about educational self-fulfilling prophecies (see Brophy 1998b for a recent review), my treatment here will be necessarily selective, focused on critical turning points in the history of research studies. I noted earlier the long history of interest in the proposition that to "expect" can set into motion events that ultimately create the foreseen reality. Virtually every subfield of psychology has explored one or more aspects of the role of beliefs or expectancies and the consequences that flow from such perceptions (Kirsch 1999; Zuroff and Rotter 1985). Further, social psychology and sociology have had as a core theme the relationship between social perception and social reality, be it causative or reflective (Merton 1948; Snyder and Stukas 1999).

But the application of expectancy theory to education is exceedingly complex and carries with it special ethical considerations. In education as in other healing professions, "the prophets are charged by society to bring about beneficial changes in the people about whom they must make professional prophecies" (Rosenthal and Jacobson 1968, p. 11). Not surprisingly, as Jerome Dusek (1985) warns in the very first sentence of *Teacher Expectancies,* "The study of teacher expectancy effects on children's learning and school performance is a volatile pursuit" (p. xiii). This volatility in part reflects the enormous implications that findings pose for the conduct of teachers and administrators. It also stems from the very different suppositions and allegiances that researchers bring to the study of these effects—cross-purposes that have often led to little exchange of concepts and findings. Elisha Babad (1993) describes the differences between the theoretical and laboratory-oriented perspective of the social psychologist, who is interested in the controlled experiment, and the practical and classroom-based perspective of the educational psychologist, who values naturalistic field investigation. Salient differences also emerge in the disparate allegiances of basic science versus applied science and among the diverse disciplines of psychology, anthropology, sociology, and political science.

Early Definitional Roots
of Self-Fulfilling Prophecies

Donald Campbell (1993) points to the philosopher Francis Bacon as among the first of scientists to write about the cognitive biases of the human mind in the 1620 *Novum Organum:* "For the mind, darkened by its covering the body, is far from being a flat, equal, and clear mirror that receives and reflects the rays without mixture, but is rather . . . an uneven mirror which imparts its own properties to different objects . . . and distorts and disfigures them" (quoted in Campbell 1993, p. 30). The potential for such distorted beliefs to become self-fulfilling at least as perceived was also suggested in Bacon's observation that "when any proposition has been laid down, the human understanding forces everything else to add fresh support and confirmation" (p. 33). Robert Rosenthal and Lenore Jacobson (1968) provide early anecdotal examples of self-fulfilling prophecies, such as the curing of hysterical paralysis at times when beliefs about a cure were in evidence (Moll 1898), the case of the Hollerith tabulating machine at the U.S. Census Bureau, where workers informed of "expected" output rates performed at lower levels than uninformed workers (Jastrow 1900), and the case of the horse Clever Hans, in which experiments showed that Hans's knowledge of the answer depended upon the knowledge and subtle movements of the questioner (Pfungst 1911/1965).

As described by David Zuroff and Julian Rotter (1985), the "expectancy" construct played a critical role in early psychology research on animal and human learning, on expectancy-value theories, and on theories of interpersonal perception. The basic assumption was that we bring a set—that is, a preparedness—to perceptual processes and "we perceive that which we are expecting to see" (p. 27). Expectancies continue to be among the most highly studied constructs in psychology, and their description varies widely across different theories, domains of behavior, and applications to self or to others (Bandura 2001; Maddux 1999). In sociology, Bruce Biddle (1979, 1986) traces the history of expectancy concepts to role theory, where they have been used to "account for behavioral uniformity, for influence attempts, for conformity, for the organization of instrumental efforts, [and] for the persistence of social systems" (1979, p. 133).

The work of two sociologists, W. I. Thomas and Robert K. Merton, provided the theory for subsequent research on self-fulfilling prophecies. In 1931, Thomas wrote a highly influential essay in which he argued for the importance of social perception and its consequences: "A paranoiac person, at present in one of the New York institutions, has killed several persons who had the unfortunate habit of talking to themselves on the street. From the movement of their lips he imagined that they were calling him vile names and he behaved as if this were true. If men define those situations as real, they are real in their consequences" (p. 189). Merton (1948) drew upon the Thomas theorem and argued its relevance "to many, if not most social processes" and as a key to "the workings of our society" (p. 193). Merton provided the field with the name and definition of self-fulfilling prophecy: "a false definition of the situation, evoking a new behavior which makes the original false conception come true" (p. 195). He distinguished between the beliefs about a situation, the behaviors that bring about a confirming response, and the confirming response itself—charting a model of the processes underlying self-fulfilling prophecies that could be empirically studied.

Merton also underscored the *false* nature of beliefs, in a declaration about cognitive bias that mirrored Bacon's observations about the distortions of the mind but deviated from Thomas's conception about the importance of both objective as well as subjective reality. Thomas noted in his classic passage that "[man's] immediate behavior is closely related to his definition of the situation, which may be in terms of objective reality or in terms of subjective appreciation—'as if' it were so" (p. 188). Despite Thomas's broader view, subsequent research emphasized the inaccuracy of beliefs and largely overlooked the role of accurate perceptions in prophecies that maintain reality or what have been called sustaining effects (Jones 1977; Krishna 1971).

Also largely ignored in subsequent psychological research was the study of institutional and societal self-fulfilling prophecies that were so provocatively illustrated by examples in the Merton essay. One of these examples included Merton's economic parable about a bank failure rumor that led to citizens' withdrawal of funds and the destruction of the previously solvent bank. In another example, Merton described the perceptions of "fair-minded" white citizens that Negroes were strikebreakers. He argued: "Our unionist fails to see, of course, that he and his kind have produced the very 'facts' which he observes. For by defining the situation in which Negroes are held to be incorrigibly at odds with principles of unionism and by excluding Negroes from unions, he invited a series of consequences which indeed made it difficult if not impossible for many Negroes to avoid the role of scab. Out of work after World War I, and kept out of unions, thousands of Negroes could not resist strikebound employers who held a door invitingly open upon a world from which they were otherwise excluded" (p. 197). It is also telling that Merton turned to institutional policies and legislation as the means by which the vicious cycle of self-fulfilling prophecy effects could be prevented.

In stark contrast to Merton's examples, the empirical research in psychology largely targeted intra- or interpersonal rather than societal and institutional self-fulfilling prophecies. Psychological research was to invest heavily in proving this phenomenon, not only in education but also in the social psychology laboratory and in work organizations. Meanwhile other social sciences, such as sociology, anthropology, and political science, turned their attention to the broader study of the stratification of the opportunities in society, particularly in schooling—an important piece of the puzzle but one less clearly tied to proving the influence of such prophecies.

Thomas's essay about the importance of social perception appeared in a slim volume that bemoaned a situation still true today: the inability of social science research to transform our society. In the introduction to this volume, the Committee on Training for the Brookings Institution (1931) described the problem:

> This difference in the reception accorded to the natural and the social sciences undoubtably results in part from a difference in subject matter. The natural scientist is dealing with material that is helpless in his hands . . . Quite the reverse is true of the subject matter of the social sciences. Their subject matter is man; and man does react emotionally to the findings of the investigator . . . He is full of preconceived notions, prejudices and unverified beliefs . . . There is no general conviction that the social sciences are sciences at all . . . There is doubt whether such social forces can be revealed, isolated, and recombined by the human intelligence, so that it will be possible to prophesy events in the social firmament as the astronomer may prophesy with confidence the appearance of the celestial sphere a century hence. (pp. 4–5)

Thus, social perception is argued both to cause social phenomena as well to deny their results—an irony that foretold the future ambivalent, often skeptical response of researchers to evidence that self-fulfilling prophecies exist in schooling.

The Effects of Teacher Expectations on Student Performance

Experimental Studies: The Rosenthal Effect

The first empirical test of the self-fulfilling prophecy phenomenon targeted the question of proof. Does it exist? As Peter Blanck (1993) explains in the preface of the tribute volume *Interpersonal Expectations,* the systematic study of interpersonal expectations in a variety of social contexts "took root in 1956 when Robert Rosenthal set forth a hypothesis in his doctoral dissertation regarding a phenomenon he labeled unconscious experimenter bias" (p. xi). Having to explain why his three groups of subjects performed differently on pretreatment ratings, Rosenthal wrote: "The implication is that in some subtle manner, perhaps by tone, or manner, or gestures, or general atmosphere, the experimenter, although formally testing the success and failure groups in an identical way, influenced the success subjects to make lower initial ratings and thus increase the experimenter's probability of verifying his hypothesis" (Rosenthal 1956, p. 44). This observation began a program of research demonstrating that unintended beliefs of researchers did indeed influence the results of their studies with both animals and humans. Rosenthal was to make three major contributions to the field of expectancy effects: this research on experimenter effects; the application of this research to classroom teachers; and the use of meta-analysis to statistically aggregate findings across research studies in many domains.

These controversial findings shook the faith of scientists in the truth of psychological results and heralded a new field of study, the social psychology of the experiment. Rosenthal continued to experimentally produce bias in the laboratory through introducing false beliefs to experimenters—for example, about maze-bright and maze-dull rats. As Rosenthal (1993) recalls, these findings of experimenter expectancy effects were exceedingly difficult to publish in the psychological literature. They were ultimately summarized in a 1963 *American Scientist* paper with a query about their broader applicability to the work of physicians, psychotherapists, employers, and teachers. Indeed, subsequent research has demonstrated such effects in these contexts as well as in the courtroom, in business organizations, and in social interactions (Blanck 1993; Eden 1992; McNatt 2000; Snyder and Stukas 1999). It was the letter of an elementary school principal, Lenore Jacobson, to Rosenthal—with the invitation "If you ever 'graduate' to classroom children, please let me know whether I can be of assistance"—that led to the application of these findings to education (Rosenthal 1993, p. 9).

There were many fascinating elements about the Rosenthal and Jacobson study *Pygmalion in the Classroom* (1968), which was a principal-researcher collaboration well ahead of its time: the use of a randomized experiment in a real school, the implanting of positive beliefs about expected intellectual growth, and the use of psychological tests to convey the false expectation. The experiment involved administering a nonverbal intelligence test to all of the children in the elementary school—in May of the prior school year, January and May of the experimental year, and two years later. Within each of the eighteen classrooms (three at each of the six grade levels), approximately 20 percent of the children were chosen at random to serve as the experimental group. These children were identified to teachers as intellectual bloomers, supposedly on the basis of the first test results. Teachers were told that "they will show a more significant inflection or spurt in their learning within the next year than will the remaining 80 percent of the children" (Rosenthal and Jacobson 1968, p. 66). Given their random selection, any differences existed solely "in the minds of teachers" (Rosenthal 1993, p. 10). At the end of the year, across the school as a whole, children who had been identified as spurters outperformed other students in intellectual gains on this test. Inspection by grade level, however, revealed the major significant findings to be evident in the first two grades only, and a two-year follow-up failed to demonstrate long-term evidence of this experimental manipulation, except among those who had been fifth graders during the experimental year.

Enormous controversy ensued over methodological problems such as the validity of the IQ test, the effects of multiple administrations of the same test, and the differences in findings by grade level (for example, Elashoff and Snow 1971). Scores of studies attempted replication. Over cries of failure to replicate, Rosenthal invested in meta-analyses to determine with statistical precision whether subsequent research lent support to Pygmalion's conclusions.

Indeed, Rosenthal and others found consistent evidence that induced teacher expectations can influence student performance. The Rosenthal and Rubin (1978) meta-analysis of 345 experimental studies of interpersonal expectancy effects across multiple settings found significant evidence for expectancy effects in 39 percent of these studies and in 29 percent of the thirty-four studies that specifically focused on learning and ability. The effect as measured by the "effect size" (the difference between the means of the two comparison groups divided by the within-group standard deviation) was moderate to large: of the five most significant studies the effect size was 1.25 as compared to 0.54 for these thirty-four studies. Mary Lee Smith's (1980) review of forty-seven teacher expectation studies demonstrated stronger effects on student achievement than on student IQ (an effect size of 0.38 versus 0.16). But Stephen Raudenbush's (1984) meta-analytic review of eighteen experimental teacher expectancy studies revisited these IQ results by investigating a possible confounding factor—the credibility of the expectancy information given to teachers as a factor that might influence the magnitude of the expectancy effect on IQ. He found that the less teachers knew their students prior to receiving the false information (that is, the earlier in the school year), the stronger the effect on IQ. He also found stronger expectancy effects in the first and second grades, as well as in the seventh grade (entry into middle school), speculating that these are the points at which teachers have the least prior information about students and are thus most susceptible to false information.

What of the magnitude of these findings? Rosenthal and Rubin (1982) developed the binomial effect size display to describe the practical significance of teacher expectancy effects on the success and failure rates of students. As one example, in the seven credible experiments of expectancy induction highlighted by Raudenbush, an effect size of .29 would significantly improve the rate of favorable outcomes from 43 to 57 percent (Rosenthal 1993). In interpreting the magnitude of these effects, it is critical to note that the size of effects increases dramatically when the conditions that heighten susceptibility are taken into account. With rare exceptions, however, the majority of studies report effects on average across entire samples.

Naturalistic Studies of Expectancy Effects

Although the experimental features of the Pygmalion study and of its many replications enabled stronger claims about what caused expectancy effects, many asked whether these effects could be demonstrated in more ecologically valid contexts—in the natural rather than the induced expectations of teachers. Naturalistic research allowed the study of both negative as well as positive beliefs, since ethical considerations precluded the implanting of negative expectations about students. But here the challenge was to separate teacher effects on students from actual student differences (that is, to control for preexisting student performance differences).

Several examples of such naturalistic studies are described here. Elisha Babad, Jacinto Inbar, and Robert Rosenthal (1982) distinguished between biased and unbiased physical education teachers and compared the treatment and performance of three groups of students—randomly selected and induced high-expectation students, teacher selected high-expectation students, and teacher selected low-expectation students. After controlling for prior grades in physical education, performance differences were documented between these groups in line with expectancy effects and as hypothesized, for biased teachers only. Similarly, we found that beyond preexisting student achievement differences, teacher expectations predicted from 9 to 18 percent of the variance in year-end reading achievement in elementary school classrooms that children described as high in differential treatment as compared to 1 to 5 percent of the achievement variance in classrooms with less differential treatment (Brattesani, Weinstein, and Marshall 1984).

Across all the sixth-grade classrooms in his sample, Lee Jussim (1989) found that teacher expectations about student ability predicted student grades and achievement scores in mathematics after controlling for the effects of prior student achievement differences. Although Jussim argues that the evidence is stronger for teacher accuracy (that is, prior achievement scores proved to be stronger predictors of student performance), the evidence for teacher expectation effects is clear (with path coefficients of 0.12 to 0.19). He also found evidence of bias in teacher expectations that was linked to factors other than student achievement. But most critically, his study did not distinguish between teachers in the degree to which such bias occurred. Other studies have capitalized on naturally occurring experiments where random samples of children are placed in higher level ability-based groups or tracks and are shown to do better than those with similar baseline achievement levels who were not moved up (for example, Mason et al. 1992).

Weighing the Evidence

Has the existence of self-fulfilling prophecies in the classroom been proven? Although causal claims cannot be made in correlational studies due to potential uncontrolled variables (Mitman and Snow 1985), in both field experiments and naturalistic correlational studies, the evidence is consistent and strong: teacher expectations can influence student academic performance, although not in all contexts. Yet controversy about the existence and magnitude of this effect still persists. For some, the proof of the pudding is an all or none question—to the extent that if expectancy effects are not found every time and everywhere, the phenomenon has no significance. Variance in findings is viewed as error rather than as information critical to identifying contextual moderators.

As a result, researchers have rarely asked how the pattern of findings can inform us about the kinds of persons and environments for which self-fulfilling prophecies occur. The heat of the continued debate has narrowed our focus to the proof question and led us to ignore the conditions question. It has also limited interest largely to achievement outcomes and to effects that are measured over relatively short periods of time, such as the course of one school year—thereby sidestepping completely the way that children's motivation and perceptions about ability play into their intellectual and cognitive capacities (as well as ignoring the larger cumulative context of an entire school career). This focus on proof also told us nothing about how teacher expectations influence students—a question about mechanisms that captured the imagination of the next wave of researchers.

Mediating Mechanisms: How Expectations Are Communicated

"Observable Sequences of Behavior"

The 1970 paper by Jere Brophy and Thomas Good was greeted with much excitement. They wrote: "The Rosenthal and Jacobson work remains only a demonstration of the *existence* of expectancy effects: their study did not address itself to any of the events intervening between the inducement of teacher expectations and the administration of the criterion achievement test. The present study focuses on these intervening processes, applying a method of classroom interaction analysis to identify and document differential teacher behavior communicating different teacher expectations to individual children" (p. 365). This classic paper provided an explicit model that explained self-fulfilling prophecies as outcomes of "observable sequences of behavior," launched a powerful new research tool to quantitatively chart differential experience *within* classrooms, and brought to light strong behavioral evidence that teachers did indeed treat students differently, in accord with their naturally occurring expectations (p. 365). It was to greatly influence the research that followed as well as efforts to influence teacher expectancy behavior.

Their model further delineated in six steps Merton's (1948) distinctions about beliefs, the behaviors that bring about the confirming response, and the confirming response:

1. The teacher forms differential expectations for student performance.
2. He then begins to treat children differently in accordance with his differential expectations.

3. The children respond differentially to the teacher because they are being treated differently by him.

4. In responding to the teacher, each child tends to exhibit behavior that complements and reinforces his teacher's particular expectations for him.

5. As a result, the general academic performance of some children will be enhanced while that of others will be depressed, with changes being in the direction of teacher expectations.

6. These effects will show up in the achievement tests given at the end of the year, providing support for the "self-fulfilling prophecy" notion. (pp. 365–366)

Brophy and Good observed teacher-student interaction in four first-grade classrooms targeting the six highest and six lowest students, including boys and girls on the teachers' rank-ordered list of expected achievement. The observation instrument tracked the sequence of interaction patterns, distinguishing between teacher-initiated and student-initiated behaviors as well as capturing different types of teacher behavior. Although the findings documented strong student differences (the highest-ranking students, the "highs," more frequently initiated interactions with the teacher, gave more correct answers, and demonstrated fewer reading problems than did the lowest-ranking students, or the "lows"), after statistically controlling for these differences, teachers were found to systematically favor highs over lows by "demanding and reinforcing quality performance" (p. 373). In the context of reading group instruction, even though highs succeeded more than lows, they were more often praised when they did succeed and less often criticized when they failed. To highs, teachers were also more likely to provide specific feedback about the quality of answers as well as to continue the interaction in the event of failure—for example, by repeating or rephrasing the question and by providing clues. With lows, however, teachers were more likely to ignore the response and to give up by providing the answer or calling on someone else.

Although all four teachers exhibited this pattern of favoring highs over lows, there were classroom differences in the degree of differential treatment. Further, in these first-grade classrooms, gender differences appeared in general but were not related to ability expectations. Boys had both more positive and more negative interactions with teachers, particularly with regard to behavior (they seemed to more frequently disrupt the class than the girls). These findings strongly indicated the presence of that type of differential teacher treatment that could not only maintain but also increase existing student differences (Brophy 1985).

The Culture of the Classroom

Another paper was published in 1970 on the mediation question, one that reflected the traditions of anthropology rather than of psychology. The abstract describes the scope of this work by Ray Rist:

> Many studies have shown that academic achievement is highly correlated with social class. Few, however, have attempted to explain exactly how a school helps to reinforce the class structure of the society. In this article, Dr. Rist reports the results of an observational study of one class of ghetto children during their kindergarten, first and second-grade years. He shows how the kindergarten teacher placed the children in reading groups which reflected the social class composition of the class and how these groups persisted throughout the first several years of elementary school. The way in which the teacher behaved toward the different groups became an important influence on the children's achievement. Dr. Rist concluded by examining the relationship between the "caste" system of the classroom and the class system of the larger society. (p. 411)

Rist described kindergarten seating arrangements by the eighth day of school that were based on family income, education, and size. He documented more teacher contact, more material covered, and more opportunities to respond for children at the higher-status tables and belittling and ridiculing by peers of children at lower-status tables. By first grade, no upward mobility in table assignment was observed; the initial placement had been confirmed by competence testing, which in turn hinged on the materials to which children had been exposed in kindergarten. In second grade as well, no upward mobility into the highest reading group was documented.

During this same year, the mechanism question was addressed in two different ways—by documenting specific teacher behaviors in interpersonal interactions, and by describing how the social organization of classroom life became institutionally reinforced. The behavioral interpretation set forth by Rosenthal and extended by Brophy and Good largely shaped the next generation of mediation studies as well as efforts to educate school staff. Although Rist's study remained frequently cited, other qualitative case studies were rarely considered as evidence for self-fulfilling prophecy effects. Further, research studies in sociology, anthropology, and political science that captured the replication of race and social class differences in the classroom (such as Cohen 1982; Entwisle and Hayduk 1978) were rarely integrated into a growing literature on expectancy effects in schooling. As Monica Harris and Robert Rosenthal (1985) noted: "There is universal agreement among researchers of interpersonal expectancy effects that we need to pinpoint precisely what behaviors mediate expectancy effects" (p. 365). Precision meant being able to count and aggregate findings across behaviors and across studies.

The Need for a More Inclusive Paradigm

In reviews of the mediation studies, Brophy (1983, 1985) identified seventeen behaviors that teachers displayed differentially toward high- and low-expectancy students—and argued that specifying such discrete behaviors is important for teacher education efforts. The 1985 meta-analysis of Harris and Rosenthal demonstrated support across 136 studies for the mediating role of climate (teachers' warmth toward highs, r = 0.37), input (the teaching of ever more difficult material to highs, r = 0.33), and output (greater opportunities for highs to respond, r = 0.20) but far less support for feedback variables (more differentiated and positive performance information to highs, r = 0.07). In practical terms, for example, these effect sizes mean that for student recipients of a positive climate from teachers, 68 percent will score above average on outcome measures as compared to 32 percent of student recipients of a negative climate. Other mediating behaviors with strong support (listed here in order of their effect sizes) include not behaving in a cold manner, maintaining closer physical distances, exhibiting less off-task behavior, having longer interactions, asking more questions, encouraging more, engaging in more eye contact, smiling more, and praising more.

In light of these findings, Rosenthal (1989) reduced the factors in his mediation theory to two orthogonal dimensions—teacher affect, which he argued was communicated largely nonverbally, and teacher effort, which he conceptualized as verbal in nature. Subsequent meta-analytic work has demonstrated that even "thin slices of expressive behavior" lasting less than five minutes are enormously predictive of outcomes in a wide variety of social situations (Ambady and Rosenthal 1992). Studies have shown that judges as young as ten- and thirteen-year-old children who view brief ten-second video clips of teachers talking about and to high- and low-expectancy students can successfully identify negative affect toward low-expectancy students (Babad, Bernieri, and Rosenthal 1987, 1989b, and 1991). These studies also provide evidence of leakage—that is, contradictory messages expressed across different channels of communication (Babad 1993). For example, teachers were less able to control negative affect in facial expression or bodily position than in speech.

What can we conclude about the mediation of classroom self-fulfilling prophecies through differential teacher treatment? Across multiple studies, teachers appear to provide those students for whom they hold high expectations more opportunities to learn, and under more positive conditions than for students for whom they hold low expectations. These differences are also more likely to be teacher-driven effects, not the result of differences in how students interact. These findings suggest that it is not simply beliefs about ability but the actions that follow from these beliefs that bring about self-fulfilling prophecy effects. Most importantly across these studies, not all teachers show this differential treatment to the same degree and not all differentiating behaviors prove significant in each study.

Yet although the prevailing focus on discrete teacher behaviors helps delineate what teachers actually do, it leaves us without a unifying framework for understanding the interrelationships among these behaviors and the conditions under which these behaviors can enhance or diminish student achievement. In our zeal to aggregate findings across studies, we have allowed our fascination with specific teacher behaviors to eclipse the study of classroom culture as identified by anthropologists. We have similarly ignored inquiries by sociologists and political scientists into how institutions allocate curriculum and educational opportunity. This has prematurely narrowed the search for mechanisms that might mediate or bring about expectancy effects.

The Minds and Characteristics of Teachers and Students

Starting in the late 1970s, the climate was ripe for a paradigm shift in studies of self-fulfilling prophecies in the classroom, moving from simpler behavioral models to more complex sociocognitive theories. This shift was fueled in part by the puzzling variability in both the effect findings and the findings about mediating mechanisms, which urgently needed explanation, and in part by the cognitive science revolution which led an interest in thinking to replace the interest in behavior in many fields (Bruner 1990; Mueller 1979). In the early research, teachers and students were treated almost as black boxes: inputs such as expectations were induced, and outputs, such as teacher behaviors and student achievement, were measured. In sociocognitive models, motivated thoughts and actions were instead seen to occur within an interpreted social context, in which children become engaged in subject matter learning in the context of their relationship with teachers, and in comparison to and full public view of their peers. Children's understanding of these conditions proved critical to unraveling the effects of expectancy processes. Thus, explanatory models became increasingly more complex, addressing how teachers formed expectations and how students perceived and responded to expectancy cues. Models also began to explore the potential for differential susceptibility of both teacher and student to such effects (Braun 1976; Darley and Fazio 1980; Weinstein and Middlestadt 1979).

Investigations of personality moderators of self-fulfilling prophecies can be traced to the early "experimenter effect" work, where the expecters, those holding the expectations, were found to differ in their susceptibility to the collection of biased data (Rosenthal and Fode 1963). In a provocative paper entitled "Johnny Reads the Cues: Teacher Expectations," Carl Braun (1973) alerted researchers to the importance of the perceptions of participants as indicative of differential susceptibility in this process. Braun wrote, "Just as teachers differ in acceptance of induced cues about the learner, learners vary in the extent to which they read and internalize cues" (p. 709). Brophy and Good (1974) further delineated their model to highlight how teacher expectations can influence student achievement in ways both direct (through exposure to curricular material) and indirect (through changes in motivation, self-concept, and level of aspiration). The notion of indirect effects, whereby achievement is influenced through eroded or enhanced motivation, requires that students be aware of expectancy cues. Brophy and Good (1974) also proposed a typology of teachers, ranging from reactive (differentiating but not biased), proactive (compensating for student differences), and overactive (holding rigid and harmful expectations).

My own experience of anomalous results began here. Influenced by the case of Eric described earlier and this growing body of research, I chose in my doctoral dissertation to study self-fulfilling prophecies in the evolution of reading group membership in first-grade classrooms (Weinstein 1976). I used the Brophy and Good observation measure to chart teacher-student interactions but applied it in the Rist context—to study reading groups in three first-grade classrooms during the first five months of school. The findings revealed remarkably restricted mobility between groups: no member of a low reading group was able to gain entry into the highest reading group during the five months. Further, at midyear, reading group membership explained a significant proportion of the variance in student reading achievement (25 percent) and peer acceptance (13 percent), beyond preexisting student differences. These findings suggested that a widening gap both in academic performance and in social status accompanied reading group membership, with better outcomes associated with membership in higher groups. Yet contrary to my hypothesis, teachers did not favor children in the highest reading group. Instead, they directed proportionally more critical comments to the top reading group and supported members of the low reading group with praise.

How can we understand the lack of fit between student outcomes and the hypothesized mediating teacher behaviors? Differences in the material taught could certainly explain the growing gap in achievement, but what about peer status? Here, the wise observations of my undergraduate research assistants helped solve the puzzle. These observers pointed out qualitative differences in the kinds of praise given to highs and lows, although these differences were not coded by the observation instrument. Wondering about the cues students were actually reading, I wrote:

> It becomes increasingly clear that the teachers did treat the reading groups very differently. At issue is the perception of these differences and its resultant impact. It is possible that critical comments concerning performance suggest high expectations and that high rates of praise (and as the observers pointed out, for less than perfect answers) convey an indiscriminant "fine, fine, fine" to those from whom less is expected. Tapping student perceptions of various types of teacher feedback might help to clarify how expectations are conveyed in the classroom. (Weinstein 1976, p. 115)

It was also evident from anecdotal observations that, through reading group membership, the teachers were introducing the students to the status system of the classroom. Three observations were particularly revealing:

1. As early as October, one teacher mentioned to her class that "Joey's group has all of this to do because they are very smart and this is more difficult."
2. Teachers used words such as "remedial," "trying," and "painfully

slow" to describe their work with the lowest reading group despite the fact that its members were reading at grade level on tests administered in January.
3. The effect of downward mobility within the reading group structure was most strikingly illustrated by a parent's promise to the teacher that she would punish her daughter daily until she was moved back to the highest reading group.

These observations revealed much about the culture of the classrooms, but to capture fully the critical mediating mechanisms of these expectancy effects, I needed access to different perspectives than those of the observers. So began my own research on child mediating processes in self-fulfilling prophecies, starting with an exploration of children's perceptions of teacher behavior. I, as well as other researchers, began to fill in missing pieces of the expectancy model first to understand the thinking and character of teachers and students, and second, to identify critical differences in teachers and students that might explain where, when, and how expectancy effects occur.

Teachers

Research has explored factors that influence both the formation of teacher expectations and how such expectations play out in differential treatment of students. One contributor to teacher judgments of ability is student performance. Indeed, teacher estimates of children's ability have been shown to be consistent with performance on standardized achievement tests (Hoge and Coladarci 1989). But there are other sources of information beyond student ability that have been found to play a role in the formation of expectations. A meta-analysis of studies about the bases for teacher expectations found that teachers also respond to student qualities such as attractiveness, classroom conduct, race, and social class in forming their expectations (Dusek and Joseph 1983). A second meta-analysis of experimental studies confirmed that even given comparable achievement, teacher judgments about white and middle-class students were more favorable than those for black and lower-class students (Baron, Tom, and Cooper 1985).

Ethnic and socioeconomic bias in teacher perceptions has also been documented in some but not all naturalistic studies (see Alvidrez and Weinstein 1999; Madon et al. 1998). With regard to gender bias in teacher expectations, the evidence provides a more complex picture that varies according to grade level and subject area. Some studies show that teachers rate boys lower than girls on reading ability, even when boys and girls have identical achievement (Ross and Jackson 1991). Other studies have found that teachers overestimate the ability of boys in mathematics (Jussim 1989; Jussim and Eccles 1992), and still other studies show no gender bias in teacher judgments of elementary and junior high school students (Dusek and Joseph 1983, 1985). Indeed, most of the research on gender differences and achievement has focused on charting differential teacher treatment of boys and girls rather than the expectations held. While the evidence for bias in teacher perceptions of ability is stronger for race and socioeconomic class than for gender, long-standing negative achievement stereotypes do persist for African Americans, Latinos, and Native Americans, for girls with regard to math, and for children with special needs (Deyhle and Swisher 1997; Fischer et al. 1996; Sadker and Sadker 1994; Safford and Safford 1996; Steele and Aronson 1995; Valencia 1991). Such findings underscore that certain groups of children are at greater risk for inappropriately lower academic expectations.

Research efforts have also explored personality characteristics that might explain why some teachers are more likely to develop biased appraisals. Two types of personality dimensions have been hypothesized to affect teachers' responsiveness to expectancy effects (Babad 1993): first, an authoritarian cognitive style that may make a teacher more susceptible to accepting biased information and more resistant to alternative information, and second, an expressive and powerful style of communicating expectations to students. Support has been found for the relationship between a dogmatic or controlling cognitive style in perceivers (the first personality type) and stronger evidence of self-fulfilling prophecy effects—with teachers (Babad 1993; Cooper 1979; Cooper and Good 1983), in experimental counseling sessions (Harris and Rosenthal 1986), and across a variety of experimental contexts (Cooper and Hazelrigg 1988), although far less support was found in the Harris Cooper and Pamela Hazelrigg meta-analysis (1988) for expressiveness and likability as factors in the communicability of expectations.

Students

Research on the student role in classroom expectancy effects has proceeded on three fronts. First, researchers have developed instruments to measure children's awareness of differential teacher treatment. Our own studies

(Weinstein and Middlestadt 1979; Weinstein et al. 1987) have shown such awareness in children as young as first graders. As mentioned earlier, the studies of Elisha Babad have documented student knowledge of teacher expectations from even brief glimpses of teacher behavior (Babad, Bernieri, and Rosenthal 1991; Babad and Taylor 1992). Studies that have directly compared students' and teachers' reports of differential classroom interaction have also shown some compatibility of perceptions (Cooper and Good 1983; Mitman and Lash 1988). Yet importantly there is also evidence for striking differences in interpretation: for example, the teacher behavior of "calling on" students is understood differently depending upon the student addressed. Such insights into children's thinking have led to different models of expectancy communication in the classroom—models shaped by student perceptions.

Second, our studies have used student perceptions to identify expectancy-prone teachers and examined how student awareness can lead to confirmation of teacher expectations. These studies have documented greater overlap between teacher predictions about students' abilities and the actual achievement, self-perceptions, and social competence of children in those classrooms where children reported greater differential treatment by teachers (see Weinstein and McKown 1998). And finally, we and other researchers have begun to explore differences in children's susceptibility to teacher expectancy effects. The Cooper and Hazelrigg (1988) meta-analysis of largely experimental studies, for example, used a photo-rating task with adults to look at personality moderators for both the holders of expectations and the targets of expectations. They found a relatively weak link between targets' influenceability and decoding skills and their likelihood to conform to expectations. An experimental study with undergraduates, however, provided support for participants' need for approval as a moderator of expectation conformity (Hazelrigg, Cooper, and Strathman 1991). In an experimental counseling context, Harris and Rosenthal (1986) documented that clients who scored higher in self-monitoring, willingness to change in response to others, and need for social recognition proved more susceptible to counselor bias. Against this backdrop of experimental work with adults, research in naturalistic classroom settings has provided evidence for differential susceptibility of children to teacher expectancy effects as a function of both developmental or grade-level differences and membership in stigmatized groups (Jussim, Eccles, and Madon 1996; McKown and Weinstein 2002; Kuklinski and Weinstein 2001).

Addressing the Moderator Question

Across these studies, the evidence is compelling that teachers and students alike are active players in self-fulfilling prophecies. And most critically, individual differences among teachers and students create conditions that can heighten or minimize these effects—conditions that we are just beginning to understand. Despite the growing importance of sociocognitive perspectives and the moderating factors identified here, surprisingly little empirical work has addressed the moderator question, especially given the abundant effect and mechanism studies. And despite evidence of variation among teachers; differences between students, teachers, and observers in interpretation of expectancy cues; and differences in children's exposure and response to expectancy effects as a function of age and membership in a stigmatized group, our conclusions still rest upon aggregated findings across teachers, populations of students, and grade levels. Further, the importance of the "objective" observer as the primary recorder of classroom reality remains sacrosanct.

A Scholarly War

More than thirty years after *Pygmalion in the Classroom,* there is a serious lull in research about the educational context and a surprising lack of interest in the design of expectancy enhancement interventions, despite a national educational reform effort that places "expectations" at its core. As scholars, we have largely ignored the problem of how to eradicate negative self-fulfilling prophecies and indeed promote positive prophecies in schooling (Babad 1993; Weinstein et al. 1991). This state of affairs likely stems from a continued skepticism about both experimental and naturalistic demonstrations of the phenomenon. A recent chapter titled "Attempts to Raise Intelligence," criticized expectancy research on the basis of the previously named flaws of a single study, the classic Pygmalion experiment (Spitz 1999). Lee Jussim and his colleagues (1998), too, concluded that "expectancy effects are typically neither pervasive nor powerful" (p. 12); "the main reason that teacher expectations predict student achievement is because they are accurate" (p. 7). In revisiting this literature, Brophy (1998b) similarly determined that "the magnitude of these effects is relatively small on the average (making perhaps a 5–10 percent difference in student achievement outcomes)" and that "the majority of teachers develop accurate and reality-based expectations . . . Most differential teacher-student interaction patterns . . . represent either appropriate proactive attempts to meet differential student needs or at least understandable reactive responses to contrasting student behaviors" (pp. x–xi). And Babad (1998) argued that "teacher expectancies have not been demonstrated empirically beyond a doubt to have systematic and lasting effects on student achievement independent of any other causal factor" (p. 204).

These interpretations rest on averaged effects over short periods, not on a consideration of where, when, how, and for whom expectancy effects are magnified or diminished. Is it true, as many scholars suggest, that most teacher expectations are accurate, most of the differential treatment of students is appropriate, and most of the effects of this differential treatment simply maintain rather than widen preexisting differences among children?

In questioning these conclusions, I take a fresh look—using another and wider lens that includes the institutional and historical context that gives rise to and reinforces such practices and policies, as well as interactions between the characteristics of individuals and environments across grades, levels of the educational system, home and school, and multiple players.

Gaps in the Knowledge Base

FOR WHOM? Most expectancy studies explore the treatment and outcomes of high- and low-expectancy students within classrooms and pay little attention to demographic group membership and special characteristics of the children. Further, the majority of research focuses on the transmission of interpersonal expectancies to individual students and ignores evidence for even stronger effects for ability-based groups within classrooms, for ability-tracked classrooms, and for schools and districts. Charting what happens to particular populations of children—ethnic minorities, poor, disabled, gifted, immigrant and linguistically different, and girls and boys—proves critical to understanding for whom expectancy effects are accentuated.

WHERE? As noted earlier, the majority of studies report averaged effects across teachers, students, and schools. A closer look depicts variation within these groupings in the strength of effects. Further, schools differ markedly in the populations of children and teachers that make up its membership—an ecological reality that may shape the degree of susceptibility to negative expectations and expectancy effects. Most expectancy research has also ignored subject-matter differences and the implications for generalization across subjects—missing, for example, the insidious effects of high school tracking, which links classes across disciplines. We have also neglected to investigate expectations for teachers and principals that run parallel to student experience, for example what Merrilee Finley (1984) has described as teacher tracking. And we have been blind to the expectations that characterize each successive level of schooling, continuing beyond K–12 to college and university (where teachers are trained). Moving beyond average effects to evidence of contextual differences will enable a clearer understanding of where expectancy effects are heightened. Although for simplicity we discuss each effect as if it acted in isolation, in reality, these effects are interactive—that is, they are compounded or cancelled out across levels of experience.

WHEN?   Brief periods of time and cross-sectional studies rather than longitudinal investigations have been emphasized. Thus, the findings underestimate the cumulative effects of expectancy processes. Children spend long days and twelve years in one classroom after another, forging a school career rather than engaging in a set of disparate and disconnected experiences. Children carry images of themselves as learners from subject to subject and from classroom to classroom. Differential exposure to the curriculum and instruction carries critical implications for opportunities farther along the educational pipeline. Emphasizing longitudinal processes across school careers will allow carryover and cumulative effects to be seen and the *when* of expectancy effects to be understood.

IN WHAT WAYS?   Differential curricular exposure may be among the strongest mediators of expectancy effects, yet few studies chart the interactive and cumulative effects of these direct as well as indirect influences on student achievement. And as Thomas Good and Elisa Thompson (1998) underscore, conclusions about the power of expectancy effects are drawn without evidence that expectations have indeed been communicated. Further, measurements of differential teacher treatment made by the usual adult, trained observers can be misleading. As our research has shown (Weinstein 1989), children notice subtle aspects of teacher-child interaction that are not reflected in coding systems. Single critical incidents count and are remembered, contributing to the creation of a classroom culture. Yet the work on children's perceptions of teacher expectations has been given short shrift in many models of expectancy effects. It has been argued that "students exaggerate the strength and consistency of these differences" in treatment (Brophy 1983, p. 656). Questioning this failure to take student perspectives seriously, Babad (1990) underscores that students' perceptions of teachers' expectancy-related behavior are a critical link in the mediation of expectancies. Exploration of these understudied issues from the perspectives of both participants and researchers, and across a range of both affective as well as cognitive outcomes, will broaden what we learn about the ways in which expectancies shape children's experiences in school.

AGAINST WHAT STANDARD?   Finally, we must ask against what standard we deem expectations accurate and treatment appropriate. Although some hold these as objective truths, both are in fact judgments that rest heavily on imperfect criteria. We often forget that the standards against which teachers' beliefs are judged accurate or inaccurate—that is, IQ or achievement scores—are themselves flawed because they are sensitive to educational exposure, language usage, preparedness, anxiety, and error (Neisser et al. 1996). Expectations based on a single narrow criterion of current performance on a standardized achievement test cannot possibly capture the potential to learn or the full range of competencies. Differential treatment that stigmatizes children or places a ceiling on learning can never be appropriate. Even if expectations are judged accurate, they can still sustain a current reality, whereas some would argue that the larger purpose of schooling is not to predict performance but to improve it.

HOW TO CHANGE?   While the call is out to "raise" expectations in schooling, remarkably little empirical work in the educational context has addressed how negative self-fulfilling prophecies might be prevented (Weinstein et al. 1991; Babad 1993). The best known effort is TESA (Teacher Expectations and Student Achievement), a classroom-level intervention that trains teachers to equalize their interactions with students, for example, in the allocation of praise and criticism (Kerman 1979). Despite its ready adoption in virtually every staff development program across the country, the little evaluative data available has not been favorable (Gottfredson et al. 1995). Further, this behaviorally based effort addresses only a small part of the problem. Other intervention efforts include giving recommendations to teachers (Brophy 1983), experimental studies that explore the efficacy of giving feedback to teachers about differential interaction patterns (Good and

Brophy 1974; Babad 1990), system interventions (Proctor 1984; Weinstein et al. 1991), and interventions directly with children (Rappaport and Rappaport 1975; Cohen and Lotan 1997). As Babad (1993) suggests, we need the application of findings about expectancy effects to keep pace with progress made in research.

Toward an Ecological Paradigm

Because it addresses the interrelationships between individuals and environments, an ecological theory better describes the realities of self-fulfilling processes and better addresses the identified gaps in our knowledge. Despite Kurt Lewin's (1935) classic observation that behavior is a function of both person and environment, the historical focus of psychology has been largely on enriching our understanding of persons and of interactions among people, with relatively little empirical work done on environments and the interrelations among persons and environments. The work of Roger Barker and his colleagues, which began in the 1950s, is a striking early exception (Barker 1968; Barker et al. 1978; Schoggen 1989).

There has been growing interest within psychology in the opportunities afforded by the ecological perspective. Borrowing from biology and building on Barker's work, researchers have adapted the principles of ecological theory to study problems in community psychology (Kelly 1968; Kelly et al. 2000; Moos 1973; Trickett and Birman 1989; Vincent and Trickett 1983), environmental psychology (Holahan 1986), human development (Bronfenbrenner 1979; Bronfenbrenner and Morris 1998), social perception (Zebrowitz McArthur and Baron 1983), and health psychology (Stokols 1992). This perspective has broadened the examination of biological processes within the physical environment to include a greater focus on the social, institutional, and cultural contexts of person-environment relationships (Stokols 1992). The following are critical theoretical assumptions that make up the ecological paradigm.

Environments as Nested Settings

The ecological environment is complex and multilevel. It can be thought of as a "set of nested structures, each inside the next, like a set of Russian dolls" in which the interconnections between the immediate settings of individuals and the contexts in which such settings are embedded are critical for development (Bronfenbrenner 1979, p. 3). Urie Bronfenbrenner labels these contexts the microsystem (the roles, activities, and interpersonal relations within the immediate environment), the mesosystem (relationships between two settings in which the individual participates, such as home and school), the exosystem (a setting beyond immediate experience that affects or is influenced by the individual, such as the school or school system), and the macrosystem (consistencies between systems that reflect institutional and cultural beliefs).

Individual Differences

The individuals within their environments are complex as well. They differ in myriad ways related to their genetic, physiological, psychological, social, and behavioral attributes. Engagement with environments also occurs in a diversity of forms, ranging from solitary individuals to aggregates of individuals in dyads, groups, and populations of various sizes (Stokols 1992). As Rudy Moos (1973) noted, the diversity in attributes as well as in environmental participation defines the "milieu" of inhabitants, one important feature of environmental context.

The Perceived Environment

What individuals perceive and understand about their environments constitutes an essential source of information for ecological theory. Bronfenbrenner (1979) argues that "what matters for behavior and development is the environment as it is perceived rather than as it may exist in 'objective reality'" (p. 4).

Ecological Transitions

Shifts in setting, or in an individual's role in that setting, promote development as well as serve as a product of development (Bronfenbrenner 1979, p. 6). These alterations in the ecological environment include such normal transitions as school entry and such uncommon transitions as early parental death. As Bronfenbrenner describes it, "roles have magiclike power to alter how a person is treated, how she acts, what she does, and thereby even what she thinks and feels" (p. 6).

Interactions between Person and Environment

Human development occurs as a result of the "dynamic interplay" between the qualities of a person and his or her environment (Stokols 1992, p. 7). This suggests a process of mutual accommodation in which the cause-and-effect relationship between person and environment is reciprocal rather than linear (Bronfenbrenner 1979). It follows that the source of problems lies not solely in individuals but rather in the fit between individuals and their environments (Cowan 1970). Further, the relationships between individuals and their environments are best described in complex systems terms (Stokols 1992). James Kelly (1968) uses the principles of adaptation, cycling of resources, interdependence, and succession to describe these natural cycles of mutual influence.

ADAPTATION.   All behavior serves an adaptive function—that is, it is responsive to the demands or adaptive requirements of the system. One task, then, is to identify what opportunities an environment invites or limits (environmental affordances) and how individuals pick up on such cues (Zebrowitz McArthur and Baron 1983). Intriguing work on the characteristics and consequences of underpeopled settings suggest that environments with more roles to play than individuals to enact them cultivate wider participation from individuals and broader competency development (Barker and Gump 1964; Schoggen 1989).

RESOURCE CYCLING.   Resource cycling in field biology "refers to the ways in which biological communities develop, distribute, and use nutrients and energy" (Trickett and Birman 1989, p. 364). Resources can be conceptualized in a variety of ways as material goods, people, settings, or events and activities. As Edison Trickett and Dina Birman (1989) argue, a resource perspective highlights the strengths and competencies inherent in systems that allow systems to adapt, evolve, and sustain themselves. They note as well that most systems use only a small part of the resources available to them. Examining human behavior in the context of resource definition and allocation is critical.

INTERDEPENDENCE.   Interdependence describes the interactive nature of a system's parts. This principle suggests that changes in one part of a system have both intended and unintended consequences for the other parts (Kelly 1968). Thus, in order to understand any phenomenon, we must first explain the many multilevel interactions both within and across the systems that individuals must negotiate (Trickett and Birman 1989).

SUCCESSION. Succession refers to the pattern of changes over time as systems evolve in response to internal and external forces. Interestingly, many system theories point to the concept of homeostasis, in which systems are viewed as existing in a steady state and are likely, following a disturbance, to return to their original equilibrium (Kelly 1968). The biologist Seth Reice (1994) attributes this view to Charles Elton, who in 1927 proposed that interspecies interactions, particularly competition and predation, contribute to the stability of species in natural environments. Newer nonequilibrium theories (such as disturbance theory, patch dynamics, and supply-side ecology) suggest that natural ecosystems are rarely in such a steady state. Instead, in biological communities, physical disturbances such as flood and fire are frequent. Reice argues that "disturbance is the re-initializing step in the successional development of a community" (p. 428). Although such disturbances may result in species loss, they also open up niche space to new and more diverse species through migration of adjacent species and recruitment of species from outside the context. Reice suggests that this theory "deemphasizes competition and predation as determinants of community structure by focusing on the nonequilibrium nature of the environment" (p. 434). This is what provides opportunities for biodiversity. The concept of succession alerts us to natural disturbances within systems (planned reforms or experiments) and their consequences for changes in the diversity of participant involvement and behavior.

The ecological metaphor focuses our attention on individuals as well as on population groups within natural settings and it requires that processes be examined longitudinally (Kelly 1968, 1969). With such an approach, the potential match or mismatch between a person and the environment becomes central, and the research goals clear: an understanding not only of reciprocal interactions rather than linear cause and effect relationships, but also of adaptation, perceived experience, and the interdependence of effects within and between systems.

Four ecological principles guide the presentation of evidence in this book:

1. Any understanding of how teacher and institutional expectations affect children must be informed by the perceived and lived experience of participants in the process.
2. The effects of such expectations are nested in interdependent environmental contexts, within and across systems—a nesting that has implications for both the nature of and the links between beliefs about ability, interventions made to nurture ability, and the development of multiple competencies and children's perceptions of self and others.
3. Interactions between individuals and environments and variation (both natural and planned) in these nested environmental contexts create expectancy processes that are aligned or nonaligned, thereby increasing or reducing the susceptibility of all players to the effects.
4. Attention to time (including history, longitudinal unfolding of academic careers, cognitive-developmental shifts in children's understanding and readiness, and grade-level transitions) adds to our understanding of expectancy effects and their carryover and cumulative consequences.

These principles are useful for broadening as well as synthesizing the research evidence concerning the unfolding of expectancy processes. They also can inform the design of preventive interventions. Addressing in this way the gaps in our knowledge requires alternative theoretical frames, an examination of other research literatures for evidence, a creative integration of quantitative and qualitative findings, and a new agenda for research and educational reform. In addressing the gaps, it is important not to resort to superficial dichotomies. It is my hope that, by adopting an ecological model, researchers can integrate disparate findings across a wider band of research literatures and examine both the coherence and contradictions of the larger story of expectancy processes in schooling. Moreover, prevailing theories have prematurely narrowed the scope of the evidence and determined that teachers' expectations of a child have only a small effect on the academic outcome for that child. I question that conclusion.

CHAPTER 3

Revisiting Educational
Self-Fulfilling Prophecies

> If a child scores low on an intelligence test and then is not taught to
> read because he has a low score, then such a child is being impris-
> oned in an iron circle and becomes the victim of an educational self-
> fulfilling prophecy.
>
> —Kenneth Clark, 1963

This is a critical time to revisit the role of negative self-fulfilling prophecies in
schooling. Such a revisiting is crucial not only because of prevailing (and I
will argue, erroneous) skepticism about the magnitude of the problem, but
also because of changes in the conditions of children and families who come
to school and in schools themselves. We have embarked on a trajectory of
educational reform that has been slow to recognize the disparities that lie
beneath the average performance of students. This trajectory of reform also
fails to dismantle the differential and inferior pathways built into the very
fabric of schooling and to link the raising of expectations with the implementation of effective educational interventions for all children and schools.
These conditions exacerbate the growing problem of differential expectations and negative self-fulfilling prophecies—at a time when we as a nation
can least afford it. These conditions will also undercut any success we might
have with current efforts to raise educational standards for all children.

It is hardly a new assertion that we must address expectations about ability as we seek to explain the unequal patterns of school achievement we see
in this country. Such assertions arose in the aftermath of desegregation efforts (*Brown v. Board of Education,* 1954), when it was clear that simply placing children of different races under one roof could not solve the problem of
educational disadvantage and racial discrimination (Clark 1963; Patterson
2001; Schofield 1995; Wineburg 1987). Rosenthal and Jacobson (1968) argued then: "As teacher-training institutions begin to teach the possibility

that teachers' expectations of their pupils' performance may serve as self-fulfilling prophecies, there may be a new expectancy created. The new expectancy may be that children can learn more than had been believed possible . . . The new expectancy, at the very least, will make it more difficult when they encounter the educationally disadvantaged for teachers to think, 'Well, after all, what can you expect?'" (pp. 181–182).

Samuel Wineburg (1987) named this early excitement about such findings "the self-fulfillment of the self-fulfilling prophecy." Despite this excitement, broad claims by the media, and staff development programs implemented in virtually every school district, skepticism by researchers regarding the causal role of such beliefs in the black-white achievement gap persisted, with one recent exception (Ferguson 1998). Wineburg argued: "Training programs and courses in teacher education programs notwithstanding, the painful gap in school performance between children of different colors and social classes remains. This is not to dismiss the contributions made by research on the educational self-fulfilling prophecy. But *writ large,* the attempt to solve the ills of American schools by changing the expectations of teachers diverts attention from basic social inequities by claiming that the central, if not entire, cause of school failure rests in the minds of teachers" (1987, p. 35).

While the cause of school failure cannot simply rest in the minds of teachers, the prevailing view we hold about the workings of self-fulfilling prophecies is incomplete. Paying attention simply to perceptions or to teachers alone leads to an exceedingly narrow perspective on the phenomenon—a legacy of psychological theory. Expectations and their workings are institutional and societal as well as intra- and interpersonal. They are reinforced at multiple levels of schooling and linked with powerful and differential educational interventions. And they occur over time, influenced by previous history and creating new and cumulative histories. In broadening our explanation, we need to understand that those who judge children's performance and capability are embedded in complex and changing organizational, cultural, and historic contexts that extend beyond the teacher-student relationship.

A broadened perspective must also address the varied meanings of academic expectations across constituencies, history, and cultures. While research on teacher expectancy effects has focused largely on beliefs about the intellectual capability of children (whether they are smart or dull, capable or not), the current "high standards" reforms frame the curricular objectives that we expect students to master for each content area and at each grade. Whether about general capability, cognitive skills, or factual knowledge, expectations can range from the global to specific and can apply across domains (a smart student) or within domains, such as in reading or mathematics. Closely tied to the content of expectations but less often examined are our beliefs about the ages at which children are expected to master certain skills and the time periods within which children must demonstrate their knowledge (for example, on timed tests). Our expectations may remain fixed over time or fluid, shift upward or downward, and become positive, negative, or simply different, over time or in the face of new information.

The question of common versus differentiated expectations—that is, which populations of children will and will not be provided with what kind of opportunities to learn—has been a subject of heated philosophical debate throughout most of human history (Cremin 1976; Richardson 1994). A broadened and ecological theory of expectancy effects should address unequal social realities, not divert attention away from this important issue. Change has not been dramatic because we have yet to address the deeply institutionalized roots of expectancy processes in schooling and we have failed to equip teachers and principals with the knowledge, resources, and support to teach all children in ways that help them reach their full potential.

The Changing Profiles of Children and Schools

Sweeping changes in the demography of our society, in family and community conditions among the children who come to school, and in the institutional nature of schooling itself have transformed the real-world context in which academic performance is judged and nurtured. These changes—increases in immigration, the diminished safety net of family support for children, the growing bureaucracy and segregation of school programs, and decreases in the proportion of children in the population overall—create a more difficult task for education. The increasingly diverse backgrounds of children coming into schools foretells increasingly troubled times because the policies and practices currently in place poorly serve children with varied learning needs. Given these demographic shifts, there is an even greater sense of urgency than before about not wasting a single drop of academic talent.

Increasingly Diverse Backgrounds of Schoolchildren

The races, cultures, languages, and special needs of children in public schools are more varied now than at any time in U.S. history (see Pallas, Natriello, and McDill 1995). Immigration is at its highest level since 1900–1910, more immigrants and refugees are accepted into the United States than into all other countries in the world combined, and more than a third of the growth in U.S. population is due to immigration (Stewart 1993). Contemporary immigrants are more heterogeneous in terms of country of origin and socioeconomic means than in earlier eras, with the fastest growing groups being Hispanics and Asians. There are also enormous differences in the resources of different immigrant groups; for example, more than 60 percent of foreign-born immigrants from India report college degrees versus 5 percent of those from El Salvador and Mexico (Zhou 2001).

In 2000, 61 percent of U.S. children were white, non-Hispanic as compared to 74 percent in 1980; 15 percent were black, non-Hispanic; 17 percent were Hispanic; 3 percent were Asian / Pacific Islander; 1 percent were American Indian / Alaska Native; and 3 percent were more than one race (Kids Count Data Book 2001). Most importantly, this ethnic diversity is distributed differently by states, regions, and cities, and therefore in school settings; in California schools, for example, white youth are now a minority at 35 percent and urban schools nationwide draw the largest numbers of poor, ethnic, and linguistic minority youth (Rury and Mirel 1997). It is estimated that by the year 2020, more than two-thirds of the nation's school population will be ethnic minorities, with Hispanic youth representing 20 percent of the total (Meece and Kurtz-Costes 2001). The rise in diversity of the school population is also due to the inclusion of children with disabilities. Prior to the passage of Public Law 94–142 in 1975 (which was later renamed the Individuals with Disabilities Education Act, or IDEA), at least one million students were prevented from enrolling in school (Terman et al. 1996).

There is also growing concern that the plight of children has worsened as compared to previous generations—in exposure to poverty and inadequate access to healthy family and neighborhood environments. In urging a national and sustained policy for children and families, the National Commission on Children (1991) warned that "America's future is forecast in the lives of children and the ability of their families to raise them" (p. 2). Despite the economic boom of the 1990s, almost 19 percent of all children and 22 percent of children under age six live in poverty (Federal Interagency Forum 1999). Income disparities among families with children have also increased since 1980, with families at the upper income levels getting richer, and middle- and low-income families remaining at the same level or becoming poorer. The disparity by race is even more striking (Federal Interagency Forum 1999). While most children in poverty are white, non-Hispanic, the proportion of black and Hispanic children living in poverty outnumbers whites (37 percent and 36 percent as compared to 11 percent, respectively). This racial factor in the distribution of poverty is matched by other negative consequences for blacks and Hispanics: greater exposure to health risks, more single-parent families, and diminished access to early childhood education and afterschool care during infancy and childhood, all conditions that contribute to poorer school achievement (Federal Interagency Forum 1999; McLoyd and Lozoff 2001). When social supports are undermined at critical periods of growth, schooling increasingly brings together children who because of extreme deprivation are less ready to learn. In the face of these unmet needs, schools are being called on to do substantively more to address increasing differences among learners at the start.

Failing and Stratified Educational Programs

An unintended side effect of legislative victories that gained more equitable access to and resources for education (such as the desegregation of schools, Title I funding for economically disadvantaged children, and Public Law 94-142 for handicapped children) was intensification of the bureaucracy of schools and the funneling of funds away from regular education to administrative costs and to specially targeted programs for children. Indeed, there is growing evidence that the multiple ways in which we differentiate the instruction of children through the use of ability-based grouping (reading groups and academic tracking), special education, bilingual education, grade retention, and school expulsion are all failing us, and in remarkably similar ways.

Research has shown that once children have been placed in differentiated learning groups, they seldom move, they experience striking differences in curricular exposure and academic expectations, they are labeled according to their placement, and, in the case of those in the lowest groups, their sense of connection to and identification with school begins to erode. There is a compelling literature on differential opportunity to learn—that is, the curriculum gap—that results from elementary school ability-based grouping (Barr and Dreeban 1983; Gamoran et al. 1995; McGill-Franzen and Allington 1991) and secondary-school tracking (Oakes 1985; Page 1991; Wang 1998).

Further, grade retention, by and large, has been found to be ineffective (Pagani et al. 2001; Reynolds and Wolfe 1999; Shepard and Smith 1989). Disciplinary practices such as expulsion from school can start a cycle in which students continually lose ground academically (Bear 1998; Galloway et al. 1982; Skiba et al. 2000). Bilingual and special education programs are also under increasing attack for their failure to move children into more challenging educational opportunities (August and Hakuta 1997; Finn, Rotherham, and Hokanson 2001; Porter 1990; Terman et al. 1996). For example, an increasing proportion of children has been found eligible for special education (one in ten children on average), and costs have reached 25–40 percent of the total budgets in some districts (Terman et al. 1996). Special education programs have been found to suffer from "mission creep" in that the ever-growing lists of referred problems are described as "ambiguous in origin, subjective in identification, and uncertain as to solution" (Finn, Rotherham, and Hokanson 2001, p. 359). Research points to the importance of enriched learning for all children that takes place among a community of learners (Brown 1997; Levin 1987). Research evidence also demonstrates the beneficial effect of an inclusive education, where learners with diverse needs are integrated into regular classrooms but most importantly only with major changes in the nature of classroom instruction and the fluid use of appropriate educational supports (Baker, Wang, and Walberg 1994).

It is also clear that children are even more segregated by ethnicity and social class in schooling today than they were at the time of the desegregation or mainstreaming legislation (Orfield and Yun 1999). African American and Latino students have been found to be overrepresented in lower reading groups, lower academic tracks, and in special education, as well as to be more likely to be retained a grade and suspended from school (Meier, Stewart, and England 1989; Miller 1995). Further, with regard to gender differences, in the early grades, boys are more likely to be diagnosed as learning disabled or as having attention deficit hyperactivity disorder, to be held back a grade, and to be placed in special education, whereas in the later grades, girls are less likely to take advanced math and science courses beyond middle school and are severely underrepresented in these fields in college and later careers (Entwisle, Alexander, and Olson 1997; Graue 1993; Sadker and Sadker 1994).

This increasingly separate and specialized nature of schooling occurs in the context of severe fragmentation of support services to children and families in general—a phenomenon apparent throughout the history of the development of children's services (Knitzer 2000; Namir and Weinstein 1982). The categorical funding structure, the entrenched and warring specialty groups, and the enormous distance between the classroom teacher and these distinct bureaucracies make it exceedingly difficult to plan creatively, flexibly, and sensitively for the whole child and for all children. It is not surprising in such a segregated climate that beliefs about the potential of all to learn prove hard to sustain and that the solving of the problems of children, families, and the classroom becomes increasingly more difficult.

A Declining Proportion of Children versus Adults

Another important demographic change concerns the declining proportion of children in the U.S. population as older people live significantly longer and families have fewer offspring. Children constituted more than one-third of the population in 1970 versus one-quarter of the population in 1990. During the 1990s, while the rate of growth in the number of children increased, it did not increase as rapidly as during the baby boom years from 1946 to 1964, so the child population stayed at a steady 24 percent (Federal Interagency Forum 1999). This means that in the future fewer youth will bear a greater share of responsibility for supporting an aging and longer-living population. As the National Commission on Children (1991) notes, "Given this trend, the nation can ill afford to waste the talents and future productivity of even a single child" (p. 6). Educational failure proves costly not only in human capital but also in increased social services (Carnegie Council on Adolescent Development 1989). James Catterall (1987) estimated the lost income and taxes over a lifetime at $260 billion for each class of dropouts each year. This changing proportion of future earners to retirees occurs at a time when the world of work has drastically changed. Work for the undereducated has largely disappeared, and the gap in earning power between the haves and have-nots has become increasingly large (Wilson 1996; Wolff 1995).

In the face of this growing diversity (in race, culture, language, economic advantage, and special needs) of children who come to school, and given schools' struggle to do more in increasingly more segregated educational programs, our perceptions about and interventions in response to differences among children will determine how well we will educate these children. Yet the social context for including such children equally in our educational vision has been far from welcoming. We have had a historically negative view of the intellectual capacity of non-English-speaking persons, and we seriously devalue the learning and use of multiple languages in schools (Garcia 1993). This less-than-welcoming view is also true with regard to disability (Ingstad and White 1995; Safford and Safford 1996; Trent 1994). The challenge for schooling is to not repeat our mistakes in underestimating the ability of those who are different in their ways and in their needs but instead to see talent in all and to provide both challenges and supports (fluid and nonstigmatizing) that nurture the development of a diverse population of learners.

Reframing Educational Achievement

Beneath the Averages

The 1983 report *A Nation at Risk* by the National Commission for Excellence in Education unleashed a feverish and long-lasting era of educational reform. The major thrust has been on international comparisons—how we as a country compare with other industrialized nations (Schmidt et al. 1997). In the face of what has been described as the United States's dismal record, the blame has been directed toward children (American children are lazy), parents and our society (we are ambivalent about academic excellence), and schools (we lack national standards and high-stakes accountability for performance). Based on this analysis, our nation embraced the goal to become first in the world in mathematics and science achievement by the year 2000, a goal that was not met. The latest results, based on the performance of eighth graders in 1999, place the United States in the middle of the distribution of thirty-eight countries (TIMSS 1999, 2001).

As David Tyack and Larry Cuban (1995) caution, there is no simple or politically uncontested answer to where we are with regard to educational outcomes: one needs to "ask how people have judged progress, from what viewpoints, over what spans of time" (p. 14). While the lion's share of attention has been focused on the *average* achievement of our nation's children in comparison to other countries, beneath the averages lie striking disparities in academic attainment between groups of children—disparities that until recently have escaped the national spotlight (Fischer et al. 1996; Jencks and Phillips 1998). The research evidence points to startling and differential educational outcomes between these groups, not only in test scores and grades, but also in course taking, high school graduation rates, college enrollments and completions, and ultimately choice of careers (Meece and Kurtz-Costes 2001; Ferguson 2001).

To describe the problem in bold strokes, children living in poverty, children with limited English, children who are African American, Latino, and Native American, boys in the early grades, girls with regard to math and science in the later grades, and children with special needs are more likely to have poorer outcomes on a variety of achievement indices. Interestingly, this includes children with different learning styles, such as the spatially gifted, when they are taught in a way that focuses primarily on linguistic-mathematical skills (Gohm, Humphreys, and Yao 1998). While Asian students have been viewed as the model minority as a result of their high academic achievement, there are differences in performance among subgroups of this population and there are ceilings on achievement because language differences shape career choices toward math and the sciences (see Nakanishi and Nishida 1995).

Many of these achievement gaps are dramatic. While the high school dropout rate for whites is 8.6 percent, the rate is 12.1 percent for black, non-Hispanics and 30 percent for Hispanics. Similarly, while the high school dropout rate is 12 percent on average, the rate is 23.2 percent for children from low-income families versus 2.9 percent for children from high-income families, and 30 percent for children with disabilities (National Center for Education Statistics 1995; Terman et al. 1996). While estimates of the prevalence of school failure begin as low as 15 percent, such rates become compounded in populations that include high concentrations of poor families, immigrants, and ethnic minorities; some schools experience up to 60 percent school failure rates among their students. Gary Natriello and his colleagues (1990) highlight five closely related indicators (racial / ethnic minority group, poverty status, single-parent family composition, mother's low education, and non-English language background) that predict poor school achievement on average for an estimated 40 percent of all schoolchildren.

With regard to black-white differences, as seen in the Baltimore School Study, there is evidence that while such differences are small at the start of schooling, they grow larger each year (Entwisle, Alexander, and Olsen 1997). The analysis of Meredith Phillips and colleagues (1998) points to achievement gaps at school entry that widen in elementary school but remain relatively stable in the high school years. They argue that approximately half the gap in scores is attributable to preschool differences and the other half to as yet unidentified variables in school, although not to school differences nor to socioeconomic status as measured in their studies; instead, "Black students who start elementary school with the same test scores as the average white student learn less than the average white student between the first and the twelfth grade" (p. 257). They suggest that attention to the factors that cause this learning gap in schools could erase half the identified test score gap.

Much less visible are systematic gaps in achievement outcomes that appear regardless of individual and status characteristics and are associated simply with *relative* distinctions within a subset of the school population, such as one's grade level or place in the classroom's achievement hierarchy. These distinctions, the subpopulations they define (such as the first grader or the average student), and the differential patterns of accomplishment are also important to consider. A *Time* magazine article described the so-called average children as "lost in the middle" (Ratnesar 1998).

As noted earlier, these achievement gaps occur in the context of large disparities in educational conditions—in fiscal, testing, curricular, instructional, grade retention, and disciplinary practices that create different pathways through schooling. Many groups of children are found to be disproportionately represented in less challenging and more stigmatizing educational environments not only within schools but also between schools (O'Day and Smith 1993). Schools with large concentrations of poor, ethnic-minority, and immigrant children have been found to have fewer resources and less-qualified teachers (Rury and Mirel 1997). As Jonathon Kozol (1992) has so vividly described, there exist schools in this country where the expenditure per child is half of that spent at suburban schools—where there are no books, paper, and computers, and where instruction takes place in leaking, peeling classrooms.

What Kinds of Achievement?

There has yet to be a serious debate by policy makers about the kinds of achievement we should strive for. The national goals are about being ready, about the speed with which students learn and perform relatively simple, routine skills, about performance in discrete and noncontextualized conditions, about competency solely within a subject-matter framework, and about individual rather than collaborative accomplishment (National Educational Goals Panel 1991). Who is asking about the creativity and adaptability of the critical thinkers we are producing, about the quality of the lifelong motivation to learn we are stimulating, and about the kind of citizens we are encouraging? The intensity of this race blinds us to the important question of whether a first-place standing on standardized achievement tests is a worthy goal for us as a nation and at this time.

A look at the dramatic advances in our increasingly technological society underscores the continually changing demands of the modern world, calling for higher levels of critical thinking and greater adaptability of individuals in schooling, in the work force, and throughout a longer life span (Committee on the Changing Nature of Work 1993). What we covet as facts, our knowledge base, changes every day. Disciplinary definitions and the boundaries between them are continually shifting. To cope successfully within such a changing world, one must *want* to learn and know *how* to learn. What is required is adaptive problem-solving—across disciplinary borders, in real-world contexts, and with interpersonal collaboration across a diverse workforce—as well as a continued motivation to learn. Speed is less likely to be the cutting issue, but flexibility, self-regulation, persistence, and cooperation will likely decide the day. Many have questioned the competitive ethic that drives schooling, focusing student attention on the evaluative question "how am I doing relative to everyone else?" rather than on the demands and the intrinsic rewards of the task itself (Aronson 1978; Covington 1992; Kohn 1993; Nicholls 1989). The development of social-emotional competencies and a prosocial community has been shown to provide a critical foundation for learning in school (Caprara et al. 2000; Elias et al. 1997; Goleman 1995; Solomon et al. 1988). The civic development of children and youth in an increasingly diverse and global world is also essential to the foundation of our democratic society (Flanagan and Faison 2001).

Misguided and Incomplete Educational Reforms

Two major reform initiatives are under way: first, the development of more challenging curricular standards by which to guide instruction (higher standards), and second, the intensified monitoring of achievement scores on standardized tests to hold children and schools accountable for meeting higher expectations (testing with the high-stakes outcomes of retention and failure to graduate for students and of fiscal incentives for teachers and schools). While these reforms importantly emphasize higher expectations (in this case, standards about what students should know about a subject), this national effort fails to dismantle an enduring school culture that overlooks the capabilities of far too many children and continues to fall back on the sorting of children for different (and often inferior) educational trajectories. Further, we have intensified the equation of children's worth with their one-time performance on standardized achievement tests.

These qualities of educational reform have alarmed many social analysts concerned about the unjust and further penalization of poor, ethnic minority, immigrant, and special needs children (Natriello and Pallas 1999). Suffice it to say that until unbiased instruction is provided to children—resulting in equal exposure to challenging material, equal opportunity to respond and demonstrate knowledge, equally nurturing relationships, and the absence of discriminatory labels and barriers to accomplishment—one cannot fully rule out environmental explanations for the achievement gaps that are documented. The way teachers and schools respond to student differences— through assignment to ability-based academic tracks and reading groups, special-education classes and bilingual classes, as well as through practices such as holding back, suspending, and expelling students—proves to be not maximally effective, indeed of dubious quality, for students in the lower ranks. Indeed, these accommodations to individual differences in characteristics, need, or behavior may in fact widen preexisting differences between students, so that children fall farther behind in their exposure to academic content, are stigmatized by the label, and lose interest in learning. Most schools present academic content in a rigid, sequential way, and there is evidence that, once students are placed, mobility to higher levels is predicated on what is achieved—what is not taught cannot be learned. As John Goodlad (1990) argues, "We must rid ourselves of the dangerous notion that individual differences such as interests and rate of learning call for significantly differentiated curricula" (p. 11).

A story in the *San Francisco Chronicle* (Olszewski 1999, p. A1) provides a telling example of how low expectations and unchallenging educational pathways can persist—even in the face of higher standards and heightened accountability. In a local school district, fully one-third of the student population began mandatory summer school and faced grade retention in the fall—a threat that was not acted upon. This case was heralded as "a troubling forecast of what other districts across California may soon face because of new laws ending the widespread 'social promotion' of failing students." Of special interest, in this summer program children would "not be taking enrichment courses, but would be struggling to grasp the basics." The school board president was quoted as saying, "Clearly, we didn't do a good job teaching them during the traditional school year. But unless the students and their parents bring a different attitude to school, we will be throwing money down the drain. Parents have to take responsibility for their children."

Blaming students and parents, repeating a basic curriculum, cutting out enrichment opportunities, and holding students back—these are the very ways that stifle motivation to learn and that block successful mastery, especially for children whose different ways and needs, be they cultural or related to language, learning style, exposure, or prior failure are not being addressed by prevailing modes of instruction. Our attention must shift to the qualities of school culture that turn perceptions of ability toward children's potential, that provide challenge as well as support mastery, and that ultimately foster a climate of continued learning for all participants. As Mihaly Csikszentmihalyi and his colleagues (1993) suggest, based upon their study of talented teenagers, talent must be *developed* with opportunities both to learn and to use the skills that have been so carefully polished.

If indeed we are interested in the development of all children, we must link higher standards to effective teaching strategies for diverse learners. Our assessments of achievement must inform the next steps of instruction, rather than simply hold children accountable for what they may not have been taught. Our evaluations must monitor the degree to which diverse populations of children meet educational goals, rather than track achievement gains on average—because assessments based on averages focus energy on raising the performance of those already high achievers while ignoring those who fail to get it right on the first round. Further, if we are interested in broader indices of achievement, should not our national report card highlight evidence that children are becoming independent and sustained readers of challenging material, that they demonstrate a continuing motivation to learn, and so on? Should not our report card also reflect whether the opportunity to learn has indeed been provided?

Academic Expectations in Historical Context

Elitism and Ambivalence

Historically, Americans have demonstrated an enormous ambivalence about the idea that *all* children can learn. Despite the call by Thomas Jefferson for an educated citizenry in America, universal schooling is a relatively recent phenomenon, emerging only in the late eighteenth and early nineteenth centuries (Gutek 1991). The historian Lawrence Cremin (1976) said it well: "For most of human history, men and women have believed that only an elite is worthy and capable of education and that the great mass of people should be trained as hewers of wood and drawers of water, if they are to be trained at all" (p. 85). As responsibility for education shifted away from parents toward the state, changes in access, fiscal support, and educational practices have always been tempered by the need to provide for a differentiated labor force. And as access to schooling was extended to more and different groups of children, and as compulsory schooling was lengthened beyond elementary education, the increasing differences among children proved to be problematic. Cremin (1976) further wrote, "Now, in the twentieth century, we have turned to the more difficult task, the education of those at the margins—those who suffer from physical, mental, and emotional handicaps, those who have long been held at a distance by political or social means, and those who for a variety of other reasons are less ready for what the school has to offer and hence more difficult to teach" (p. 86).

Unfortunately, we begin the twenty-first century with continuing concerns about those at the margins and even greater challenges from the increasing diversity of learners that attend our schools. Differences among children have been handled largely through segregated and exclusionary means—from outright exclusion from schooling to warehousing, separate and unequal schools, and separate and unequal curricula within elementary and secondary schools (Entwisle, Alexander, and Olson 1997).

Fueled by the victory of African Americans in the 1954 *Brown v. Board of Education* decision, which led to desegregation, federal legislation and court decisions have expanded the access of excluded groups to educational opportunities. These include the passage of Title I of the Elementary and Secondary Education Act in 1965 (for the economically disadvantaged), Title IX of the Educational Amendments Act in 1972 (for gender equity), *Lau v.*

Nichols in 1974 (for linguistic minorities), and Education for All Handicapped Children, Public Law 94–142 in 1975 (for mainstreaming children with special needs). Each of these changes has altered the social environment of schooling (Garcia 1990; Patterson 2001; Sarason and Klaber 1985; Stromquist 1993). Each have raised questions of whom to teach (all or some), how to teach (in integrated or segregated settings and in what language), and what to teach (core or differentiated, academic versus vocational). But research has shown that increased access to schooling has not always been accompanied by increased access to knowledge and greater opportunities to learn (Darling-Hammond 1996; Goodlad 1990). The evidence is overwhelming that children live different lives within our system of universal schooling. Universal access to schooling and equal opportunity to learn have proven to be far from the same phenomenon.

Two very different views of appropriate and equitable academic expectations have vied for attention. The pendulum swings back and forth: equal access to the highest level of educational experience, viewed as a common set of expectations and a common curriculum, versus equal access to an educational experience that best meets student needs, a differentiated education based on abilities, special needs, and vocational goals. Legislative reforms and legal victories have secured both types of equity in educational expectations: equal access to the same schools (for example, for blacks), as well as accommodation to special needs in order to ensure equity of access (for example, for the disabled). The equity question has also come to encompass the pursuit of common outcomes such as reducing the performance gap between groups of children unjustly differentiated by race, class, gender, language, and disability and bringing up the achievement of all children to meet national grade-level standards, or differentiated outcomes, according to special need. The concepts are slippery ones indeed and often the distinction between means and ends is a spurious one; for example, is access to college a means issue (an opportunity to learn) or the outcome of high-school achievement?

Which Perceiver and What Theory?

Most importantly for our interest in self-fulfilling prophecies, perception and judgment about children's capabilities undergird both aspects of the dilemma, in quite different ways. In the setting of common as well as differentiated expectations, the potential and the needs of children must be defined. By which key players, by what criteria or standards, with what floor or ceiling effects, and over what developmental period are capability and aspiration in students to be determined and student needs to be addressed? That they are determined underscores that capability and need are constructs created and judged by the educational system and not a property of individual children.

Supporting the observed exclusionary practices were underlying beliefs about capability—that nonwhite races, non-English-speaking people, and females were inferior in intelligence, that poor people were poor because of their poor intellectual endowment, that physical and mental handicaps carried with them limited intellectual capacity, that failure to meet age-level norms meant lessened intellectual ability, and that educational interventions would not enhance intelligence. While theories about the heritability and immutability of intelligence at the turn of the century provided the rationale for differentiation of educational opportunities, the development of intelligence tests offered the so-called scientific, objective basis for such selection as well as the tools for measurement (Gould 1981).

In his book *The Mismeasure of Man,* Stephen Jay Gould (1981) writes, "Biological determinism is, in its essence, a theory of limits. It takes the current status of groups as a measure of where they should and must be" (p. 28). To illustrate the point, Gould quotes the words of psychologist Lewis Terman who in 1916 described his assessment of a child with an IQ of 75: "Strange to say, the mother is encouraged and hopeful because she sees her boy is learning to read. She does not seem to realize that at his age he ought to be within three years of entering high school. The forty-minute test has told more about the mental ability of this boy than the intelligent mother has been able to learn in eleven years of daily and hourly observation. For X is feebleminded; he will never complete grammar school; he will never be an efficient worker or a responsible citizen" (Gould 1981, p. 179).

This historic ambivalence about the capacity of all children to learn can also be seen in the *A Nation at Risk* report (National Commission for Excellence in Education 1983), where it is argued that "a solid high school education is within the reach of virtually all" and that "there remains a common expectation" (pp. 69–70). Yet underlying this common goal is an acknowledgment of necessary differentiation, that chances be given to youth "to learn and live according to their aspirations and abilities . . . and to work to the limits of their capabilities" (p. 16). But who is to determine the limits of a student's capability (and how)? We would hope not solely the policy makers. In the recent debate in Congress about the reauthorization of the 1965 Elementary and Secondary Education Act (ESEA), policy makers appeared willing to mandate high-stakes achievement testing with regard to tracking, promotion, and graduation—without looking beneath the averages, without mandating testing in children's native language, without accommodating special needs, without determining whether opportunity to learn has been provided, and without considering other indicators and other competencies beyond single standardized test scores.

Such proposed practices led Senator Paul Wellstone of Minnesota to initiate several amendments to the bill, for which the American Psychological Association successfully lobbied, to "ensure that the tests comply with the newly recognized professional and technical standards for such assessments and that the assessments are of adequate technical quality for each purpose for which they are to be used" (*APA Monitor,* Oct. 2001, p. 25). Wellstone commented on his own experience with the misuse of these tests, but most importantly here for our purposes, on how these tests were used to predict what a student would—and would not—accomplish: "I was one of those students who received consistently low scores on standardized tests . . . Because of a learning disability, I was told repeatedly . . . that because of my test scores, I would fail academically. I am convinced that I would have never received my doctorate if I had listened to those who put so much credence in what they measured." (*USA Today,* Jan. 13, 2000, p. A17).

Although it is too early to fully comprehend the 1,200 pages of the reauthorized ESEA bill (the "No Child Left Behind Act," P.L. 107–110) signed into law in January 2002 by President Bush, many provisions appear to have improved upon its earlier intent. These include requirements to disaggregate achievement data (that is, look beneath the averages), bring all children up to standards of proficiency, mandate more than one performance indicator in high-stakes decisions about schools, meet test standards as well as diagnostic goals, provide school report cards on teacher qualifications, place in schools improved, research-validated instruction in early reading, and offer those low-income students who do not improve the opportunity to transfer schools and to receive tutoring. The overwhelming emphasis, and likely fiscal spending, however, remains on accountability for narrow results—in the annual standardized testing in reading and math of children in grades three to eight to meet subject-matter standards.

From Underestimates to "Overestimates" of Potential

Attention to this historical context suggests that we have seriously underestimated the ability of both individual and groups of children. By taking a historical approach, we have seen both fundamental and superficial changes in which educational expectations and opportunities are considered appropriate for whom. Some examples include shifts in expectations differentiated by gender (Tyack and Hansot 1990), age and grade (Zimiles 1986), special needs such as Down's syndrome, learning disabilities, deafness, and blindness (Safford and Safford 1996), and immigrant group (Stewart 1993). We also have learned that when "opportunity" has been provided, students have risen to the challenge. Examples include the GI Bill, which offered financial assistance and lowered admission requirements for returning war veterans to enable them to attend college—a door opener that many used to successful advantage (Ravitch 1983).

Looking to the cross-cultural studies of Harold Stevenson and James Stigler (1992), American children are likely capable of more than is expected of them. Stevenson and Stigler argue that our educational system "allocates resources to create a thin layer of the population that is extraordinarily well educated and highly skilled" but that the majority of children are not well prepared by schooling (p. 205). In their research on elementary education in China, Japan, and the United States, despite equal cognitive functioning, American children performed worse in math and reading, with the gaps beginning as early as kindergarten and growing worse by fifth grade. Fewer American children met grade level in reading and they were disproportionately represented among both the best and the worst readers. In mathematics, American children were disproportionately represented among the worst performers only. Given that cognitive differences could not explain these cross-national disparities, Stevenson and Stigler suggest that a broad array of cultural differences were at play, reflecting differences in the importance placed on effort and hard work rather than on ability, in the time allocated to instruction, in the depth of coverage within the curriculum, and in the use of whole-class versus ability-based grouping strategies. The Asian countries cultivated the achievement of more children in the early grades by providing a common and a deeper curriculum to all students through whole-class rather than ability-based instruction, and by focusing on student effort as a key to mastering the material.

The disparities we observe in performance by grade and by achievement level are in part likely constructed by us. An early study by Nicholas Anastasiow (1964) documented how teachers assigned reading material to their elementary school classes: grade level material went to students in the middle, above grade level to the top group, and below grade level to the lowest group, irrespective of the average achievement level in the classroom. Judith Singer and her colleagues (1989) demonstrated that "where you live affected what you are labeled" in the special education system (p. 261). They found that those school districts that were diagnosing more cases of mental retardation were actually serving less impaired students. When teaching is guided by relative standards and offers few higher-order or accommodative learning opportunities, differences between students can widen. Thus, underlying the "dire" average performance of American children are large disparities in achievement that are associated with race, social class, language, gender, disability, learning style, age, and relative position in the achievement hierarchy. Although some resort to genetic explanations for these disparities, claiming to control for social class but to be unable to control for exposure to prejudicial and inferior treatment (for example, Richard Herrnstein and Charles Murray in their 1994 book *The Bell Curve*), there are far too many similarities in the experiences of these different population groups (including simply membership in the average and below average two-thirds of the achievement hierarchy) to suggest other than systematic social construction or enhancement of these differences. Thus, far too many children are at special risk for low expectations and less-than-rigorous teaching even in the face of higher standards.

Finally, while historical forces have shaped the prevailing belief that intelligence is inborn and immutable, our views about the necessity for environmental intervention and therefore our beliefs about the malleability of intelligence also appear to vary widely depending on which group of children is being discussed. In our review of the early literature on educational treatments for different child populations, my then graduate student assistant Jennifer Alvidrez pointed out that for the gifted, we appeared more likely to bemoan the lack of challenging classroom environments that might better develop their talents, whereas for children at the bottom of the achievement hierarchy, we more likely concluded that educational intervention would not make a difference. Attention to the historical context in which academic expectations are framed should shake our faith in the "accuracy" of our beliefs about children's potential to learn and the "appropriateness" of treatment driven by the achievement differences that we perceive among children.

*   *   *

To understand the achievement problem, we must look beneath the averages. Disparities in both performance and, importantly, opportunity between groups of children are of concern; herein lies the potential for the low expectations and self-fulfilling prophecies. We must also look across different child populations, a rare perspective indeed (Grant and Sleeter 1986). All of us have one or more of the distinctive qualities discussed here: the systematic achievement gaps and disparities in opportunities affect all children, not merely some. Further, all of us belong to multiple groups—each reflecting only a part of ourselves, our gender, race, learning style, age, and so on. Overlapping membership in these groups can compound the effects on children of teacher expectations and self-fulfilling prophecies.

Significantly, the characteristics that place us in one subgroup or another are often fluid, arbitrary, and subject to social and historical conditions, making such categorizations incomplete and often not meaningful. For example, the immigration policies of different historic eras have inadvertently boosted the educational and social-class standing of some groups over others—for example, of Asian immigrants over Mexican immigrants (Stewart 1993). The highly restrictive immigration policies of the nineteenth and early twentieth century reduced the flow of Asians to only the most educated, whereas the passage of the 1965 Immigration Act facilitated the entry of Mexican immigrants with more limited educational attainment specifically for agricultural and lower-skill jobs. The arbitrary nature of these distinctions can also result from practices such as delaying boys' entry into kindergarten until they are ready and more skilled, linking the diagnosis of disabilities to the mix of children in the district and available funding, and valuing linguistic ability more than spatial ability in schools (Gohm, Humphreys, and Yao 1998; Singer et al. 1989).

The psychological research literature on expectancy effects has paid scant attention to the increasing diversity of children, how groups of children are distributed in classrooms and schools, and our historical propensity to treat differentness with lowered expectations and differentiated instruction. Thus, those studies that claim that the effects of teachers' expectations are small—all of which are based on averaged findings—are suspect indeed. The full power of these expectations are instead best seen through ecological lenses that can open our eyes to where, how, and for whom such processes unfold, interact, and change in multiple contexts such as classrooms, schools, families, and society. If we thereby discover that low and narrowly construed expectations linked with inferior educational practices are at the very root of our achievement problem, if research provides evidence that different beliefs about ability and its nurturance improve and expand desired outcomes for all children, then such expectancy processes must be targeted for intervention. It is time to revisit the urgent issue of negative self-fulfilling prophecies in schooling and to examine what fosters the promotion of positive prophecies for all of our children.

PART II

Expectations in Classrooms: Through the Eyes of Students

CHAPTER 4

Children Talk about Expectations for Achievement

Like half the class is pretty smart and . . . the other half isn't. And these people . . . that's not smart, she'll just let 'em go, she won't really care what they do. 'Cause she knows they don't care. And the rest of the people, she'll just push and push, and says, We gotta have some survive, you know.

—A fourth grader

The teachers they work with them [high achievers], like, um, they don't even need help. And they work with them, like, "Ah, you could do that easily." They just show them and they expect, um, they can do it.

—A fourth grader

The images are still vivid, culled from my rounds of classrooms to learn from children about their teachers' expectations for them and their peers. I have visited many first- through fifth-grade classrooms in inner-city schools from numerous cities. I have entered some classrooms where I see children with their heads on their desks, eyes closed, sleeping or daydreaming to escape the drone of instruction. I hear much teacher talk but little student talk. And when students are called upon, there is silence. "Dunno," a student might mutter. The teacher turns to me to apologize. "Not very bright students, are they?" the teacher comments, well within earshot of the children.

I take the students out of class, one by one, to a small room with a table, two chairs, and my tape recorder. I ask if they are willing to talk to me about their lives in school. Most are surprised to be asked, some are flattered, and some are tongue-tied over the responsibility. The beginnings are often slow. I promise confidentiality about what they tell me, and I explain how research findings are summarized, with no individual teacher or student ever identified. I tell them that there are no right and wrong answers, and that I am interested in their opinions, what *they* think, about life in their classroom. And I begin the interview with a concrete task for the children to complete. I give them a sheet of paper with thirty circles on it, the circles representing the students in their classroom, with "Top of the class" written at the top of the page and "Bottom of the class" across the bottom. I ask them to place an *X* in the circle that best describes their position and how well they will do in school this year as compared to their classmates. In this task adapted from an instrument developed by John Nicholls (1976), they reveal their academic expectations. Some students puzzle over their decision, others act quickly to place their mark. I then say: "You have just guessed at how well you think you will do in school this year. How did you figure that out? How did you learn whether or not you are smart in school? What things happened that gave you that idea?"

So begins my questioning about how they have defined themselves, as one kind of achiever or another, in their classroom setting. And most of them talk—eagerly, shyly, painfully, happily—telling me about their lives in school. A major reward at the end of our half hour together is rewinding the tape and having them listen to their own voices speak with newfound authority. On the way back to their classrooms, many of the children have taken my hand and asked me if I would come back to see them again. I am touched by these gestures and by the trust that they have placed in me by sharing their stories. I realize also that the special nature of our time together means that they are rarely, if ever, asked for their opinions.

At the end of each study, when I provide feedback to participating teachers, I often read aloud from student interviews, without identifying student or teacher, to illustrate major points. Teachers are surprised by the sophisticated, thoughtful analyses provided by the students. They are often embarrassed to learn of the children's awareness of subtle behaviors that the teachers thought had gone undetected, and amazed to learn that some of the perceptive comments they heard were the words of so-called low achievers. These realizations are often followed by expressions of envy that I had the opportunity to sit down and talk with their students one by one, which is something that classroom teaching as currently conceptualized rarely allows. Until life in the classroom enables one-to-one as well as whole-class conversations in which each and every student's contribution is demanded, counted on, and valued, we will not see the wisdom that I glimpsed daily in my talks with children of all sizes, colors, learning styles, and economic means.

Elementary school children are aware of different lives being lived within the same classroom as a function of how smart children are perceived to be by their teachers. Their nuanced descriptions of differential treatment by teachers toward high- and low-achieving students tell us about the implicit demands of their classroom environment to which they are asked to adapt. Children rely on these clues to develop their ideas about what smartness is and to make inferences about their own place within the classroom achievement hierarchy. Children's reports illustrate, in broad strokes, a complex and subtle classroom culture that communicates the expectations of teachers to students.

The Ignored Voices of Children

In research efforts to understand the factors that shape children's learning in school and that shape policy initiatives to improve schooling, children's views of their educational experiences are virtually absent. The voices of the primary consumers of education are largely unheard. This lack of interest in, as well as lack of respect for, the perspectives of children is not surprising when examined in historical context.

Until relatively recently, children's rights were extremely limited; children were seen as the property of their parents and parents were free to do with them as they wished (Hart 1991). Given that children could neither vote nor lobby, attempts to improve their conditions, such as through the provision of social services, had to be undertaken by adult advocates (Namir and Weinstein 1982). It was this unmet need for advocacy that led Marian Wright Edelman to found the Children's Defense Fund, which issues regular reports on the conditions of children and asks at every juncture, "Who is for children?" (Edelman 1981). During the twentieth century, governments increasingly interceded over the rights of parents to ensure better treatment for children—for example, in the prevention of child abuse and neglect. More recently, however, as noted by Stuart Hart (1991), the 1989 United Nations Convention on the Rights of the Child ("the best available formal expression of international opinion on the rights of children") has shifted the pendulum from protection to personhood status for children—toward greater "participation and autonomy or self-determination rights, in balance with protection and nuturance rights" (p. 55). As always, the evolving capacities and maturity of children are at issue in determining the "progressive development of the self-determination capacities of children" (p. 56) and hence, the progression of choices offered to children. Despite the controversy over the relative balance of protection and choice, Gary Melton (1987) has levied an important criticism at our routine ways of studying children's needs without including their perspective. A growing children's rights movement also seeks to invite the participation of children.

The absence of children's voices in our research also reflects the dominance of a positivist experimental paradigm, in which the perspective of the "objective" observer has always been valued over the perceptions of the participants themselves. Further, although the classic work of Jean Piaget (see Cowan 1978) fueled interest in how children make sense of the world, knowledge of these cognitive developmental changes proved to be a double-edged sword. To the extent that children's thinking was found to be qualitatively different from that of adults—reflecting distinct developmental stages in understanding concepts of object, self, and other—children's understanding was considered somewhat inferior to adults'.

It is important to understand, however, that much of this research on developmental social cognition has been conducted without an investigation of the environments in which children learn. A study by Deborah Stipek and Denise Daniels (1988) highlights that even children as young as kindergarten age are capable *far earlier* of understanding and making use of social comparison information (in self-ratings of both competence and future attainment) in those classrooms where teachers make the comparative evaluation of ability more salient. With similar findings that the organizational features of classrooms frame children's perceptions of ability, Susan Rosenholtz and Carl Simpson (1984) raised the discomforting question of whether conceptions of ability reflect a "developmental trend or social construction" (p. 31).

In this context, it is not surprising that researchers are skeptical about what young children can understand about their life in classrooms. For example, in their studies of the effect of ability-based reading groups on children, Aaron Pallas and his colleagues (1994) have argued: "It is probably unreasonable to expect young children to have internalized a functional ideology as fully as have adults, who have been more extensively involved in schooling and have had a wider exposure to social norms and expectations. The fact that tracking and grouping are socially legitimated structures can thus be plausibly expected to affect parents and teachers, but is less likely to influence the perceptions of individual children and their peers, at least in the early grades" (p. 31). Yet children spend much of their day, five days a week, and ultimately thirteen years as captive participants in the life of classrooms. What children see and understand, even in these earliest years, creates the social context in which they develop a sense of mastery about learning and a framework for assessing and valuing their accomplishments. The extent to which children's views match the views of observers and adults is simply beside the point. As ecological theorists would argue, children's perspectives are important in their own right, both in framing the course of their development and in driving their actions and self-perceptions (Bronfenbrenner 1979; Moos 1973).

Assessing Children's Knowledge

When we first began our research on children's perceptions and their understanding of patterns in teachers' interactions with different students in the classroom, the territory was as yet uncharted. While classroom observers had captured differential treatment by teachers toward children for whom they held high or low expectations, no studies had explored children's perceptions of such differences in teacher treatment. Despite a growing research literature on children's perceptions of the classroom environment, these studies aggregated perceptions of the instructional climate across children to reflect the environment for the class as a whole (see Fraser 1998; Levine and Wang 1983; Schunk and Meece 1992; Weinstein 1983). Our interest lay in exploring the differential experiences of children in the same classroom whose teacher held varying academic expectations of them. New instruments and new methodology needed to be developed.

The Teacher Treatment Inventory

We created a questionnaire that we named the Teacher Treatment Inventory (TTI). The instrument provides standardized and quantifiable information about elementary school children's perceptions of how often the teacher interacts with different students. This allows us to pursue comparative questions across classrooms and across types of children as well as predictive questions—that is, questions that explore relationships between what children reported and how they developed in school. The TTI also offers a way to measure the degree of change in children's reports of differential treatment after a planned intervention. The TTI consists of thirty statements, chosen to capture a range of interactions between teachers and students that observers in previous studies and children in our pilot work had identified as expressive of academic expectations (Weinstein and Middlestadt 1979; Weinstein et al. 1987).

Items are read aloud and children are asked to rate on a four-point scale the frequency of their teacher's behavior toward an imaginary high- or low-achiever in their classroom. These two forms of the questionnaire are given in counterbalanced order. The imaginary students are described as follows:

> This boy/girl is someone who does really well in school. In fact, he/she always gets the best grades in the class. Everyone thinks he/she is very smart.

> This boy/girl is someone who does not do very well in school. In fact, he/she always gets the lowest grades in the class. Everyone thinks he/she is not very smart.

Perceived differential treatment is measured indirectly, rather than directly, by taking a difference score between the high and low achiever form to reflect the degree of differentiation. This method of independent reporting was chosen to free children from the moral dilemma of sharing what may be viewed as undesirable behaviors on the part of teachers. While this instrument is a measure of student perceptions of others—imaginary others who can be identified as male or female or in nongendered ways—the instructions and items can be modified to capture children's perceptions of their own treatment by the teacher on these same items. The 30 items are organized into three subscales: negative feedback and teacher direction; work and rule orientation; and high expectations, opportunity, and choice. A short version of eight highly differentiating items was also created.

The "Learning about Smartness" Child Interview

While the Teacher Treatment Inventory provided information about the frequency of predetermined differential behaviors by teachers, our interviews with children enabled a deeper and unconstrained examination of what children observed, how they interpreted what they saw, and how they felt about their observations. The TTI results could not tell us if these were the only behaviors or the most salient behaviors that children noticed. Nor could it tell us about whether and how children used teacher cues to develop notions about their relative smartness in the classroom setting. The semistructured interviews allowed us to move beyond the awareness question to the interpretive question—capturing in children's own words the nature of these differential climates within classrooms and the inferences children drew about ability differences between students. Here, in addition to asking children about teacher treatment toward peers, we asked them to think about their own treatment by the teacher in the classroom—how they learned about their own smartness relative to that of their peers.

As indicated earlier, we began the interview with an adaption of the Nicholls (1976) expectation measure. Children's expectations were assessed by asking them to rank themselves against their peers in order of expected achievement at year's end in reading, math, and overall schoolwork. The questions then probed for how they knew how well they were doing in school. The questions examined how children learn about their own level of smartness in the classroom, how children perceive the consequences of "smartness" (teacher and peer treatment and the meaning of smartness to teachers, peers, and self), and how children understand smartness (its causes, perceived stability, and underlying differentiating characteristics of smart and not-so-smart students). The interviews were tape-recorded, transcribed, and coded with excellent interrater agreement (Weinstein et al. 1980).

Children Report Differential Treatment

Using the Teacher Treatment Inventory, we have found that in children's eyes, high and low achievers are treated quite differently in the classroom by their teachers. These findings are drawn from five separate studies, sampling first graders to fifth graders in urban elementary schools that reflect ethnically and socioeconomically diverse populations (Brattesani, Weinstein, and Marshall 1984; Kuklinski and Weinstein 2000; Kuklinski and Weinstein 2001; Weinstein and Middlestadt 1979; Weinstein et al. 1982; Weinstein et al. 1987). Across these studies, children report on average that high achievers are favored in their interactions with teachers. They are accorded higher expectations, as measured by children's more frequent endorsement of statements such as these for highs ("The teacher trusts him"; "The teacher is interested in him"; and "The teacher makes him feel good about how hard he tries"). High achievers are also afforded more opportunity ("The teacher asks him to lead activities") and more choice ("The teacher lets him make up his own projects") in the classroom than low achievers. In contrast, in the eyes of children, low achievers are likely to receive more frequent negative feedback ("The teacher scolds him for not listening" and "The teacher makes him feel bad when he does not have the right answer") and more teacher-directed treatment ("When he is working on a project, the teacher tells him what to do") than high achievers.

Interestingly, gender differences in teacher treatment were not reported by children in these studies—perhaps because the gender of the target child was measured across, not within, classrooms or perhaps because of the age groups studied and the particular teacher behaviors captured in the questionnaire. Other studies have shown that gender differences in treatment emerge by the middle school years, particularly favoring boys over girls in the areas of math and science (Sadker and Sadker 1994). Across these studies utilizing the Teacher Treatment Inventory, we demonstrate remarkable consensus of perceptions within classrooms and across age groups. High as well as low achievers, boys and girls, and even children as young as first graders perceive these differences in teacher treatment toward high and low achievers. Individual differences in perception were minimal except for the finding that low achievers were more likely than high achievers to report higher frequencies of negative teacher feedback regardless of which student was being rated. This perhaps highlights a greater sensitivity on the part of low achievers to such feedback. These findings highlight, on average across classrooms, elementary school children's awareness that regardless of gender, more is expected of high achievers and more opportunities come their way, whereas greater negativity and more structure is accorded low achievers.

How Children Learn about Ability Differences

The TTI provided evidence that elementary children are aware that high achievers are favored in myriad ways in the classroom. But what do children observe and understand about these as well as other kinds of teacher-student interactions? What do children infer from patterns of differential treatment and how do they apply this knowledge to themselves? Here, I draw upon the interviews we conducted with fourth-grade children—a stratified sample of 133 children chosen to represent both male and female, and high- and low-expectancy students (as rated by teachers) from each of sixteen inner-city classrooms—and expand upon findings we reported (Weinstein 1986; 1989; 1993). These interviews reveal children's surprisingly complex interpretation of teacher behavior.

The Teacher as Informant

EYES ON THE TEACHER.   Our opening question asked children how they learned about their own smartness, with prompts such as "How did you figure that out?" "How did you learn this?" and "What things happened to let you know?" that left the door open for a broad array of answers. The results suggest that children learn about their relative smartness largely from the teacher—not from the appraisals of peers and parents nor from their own self-evaluations. Almost two-thirds of the identified cues (66 percent) concerned information derived from what teachers told them, what teachers did or did not do, and from the structure and content of learning activities. For example, one child emphasized "My teacher doesn't need to help me" and that means the child is smart. Another child located where, exactly, he stood in the classroom achievement hierarchy from what the teacher had told him: "I'd never be the top one in this class—well, there's two other people. I'm right—well . . . I'm the third one . . . the teacher really tells you how you're doing . . . And so I find out *how good* I am." Interactions with peers ("'Cause the other kids ask me to help them") and with parents ("My mom checks over my papers and tells me") were infrequently mentioned as the source for learning about ability, each accounting for less than 5 percent of children's answers.

Remarkably, only one quarter of the children's comments identified processes where children gleaned information about ability from monitoring themselves—that is, how well they mastered classroom tasks. Examples of such self-evaluation can be seen in this child's conclusion that he is smart because, as he said, "I'm good at figuring things out." What children tell us is that they are socialized primarily to look to the teacher as the defining agent of ability, not to themselves or to their peers and family.

PATTERNS IN THE CLUES ABOUT SMARTNESS.   When we looked at the clues described by children as informative about their smartness, the most frequently mentioned one was feedback from the teacher. This feedback was most commonly in the form of marks and test scores, and accounted for more than three-quarters (78 percent) of children's answers. The remaining clues were derived from curricular and instructional practices (21 percent) such as the structuring of learning activities, and from classroom climate (1 percent), which includes the quality of relationships between teachers and students. But when children were asked to identify more specifically what events told them about good or poor performance, the patterns of their responses shifted. Children were more likely to refer to teacher praise and rewards or to teacher criticism and punishments, rather than to marks and to test results. Significantly, twice as many children (40 percent) now cited the structure of learning activities, in particular the assignment of remedial work and the amount of help given, as informative of poor performance.

An examination of children's reports of the qualities of teacher feedback is also revealing about what children learn from these messages about performance. Most commonly (in 58 percent of responses), the evaluations reported by children stress absolute judgments, such as "They (the teachers) tell me very good." Yet a substantial proportion of the feedback messages (39 percent) refers to a comparative evaluation, such as a child's description of the teacher's question, "Who knows who my best readers are in the top group?" Remarkably few of the teacher comments (3 percent) focused on an evaluation of individual progress, like that in one child's description of his teacher's message, "You can do better [than a past performance]." Further, relatively little of the reported feedback from teachers contained specific information about the quality of the schoolwork (36 percent), such as about correctness or rate of completion, or causal explanations for good (15 percent) or poor (35 percent) performance. Tellingly, most of the reported causal explanations for successful or unsuccessful performance (75 percent and 79 percent, respectively) referred to task-conformance behaviors such as paying attention or following directions.

As with the Teacher Treatment Inventory, boys and girls as well as high and low achievers largely described their learning about achievement differences in highly similar ways. There was, however, one important exception. High achievers were more likely than low achievers to describe more general rather than specific performance information from teachers, to explain poor performance as a function of lack of effort rather than failure at task-conformance behaviors, and to perceive more comparative than absolute judgments from teachers. The patterns of teacher behavior identified in these interviews with children mirror as well as deepen what children reported on the TTI.

THE PUBLIC NATURE OF CLUES ABOUT ABILITY.   The classroom setting in which children are captive members, year after year, is an environment where efforts at mastery are evaluated largely within public view unless teachers take specific actions to do otherwise. When asked "What do teachers do to make you feel you are doing well or not doing well?" a majority of the children describe the information as being widely shared. For 67 percent of the children, at least one public incident made up the context in which they learned about poor performance, and for 59 percent of the children, with regard to good performance. Thus, in the words of the children, the teacher might "point out the good and bad students" or there might be "a chart that shows how we are doing." One fourth-grader's depiction of learning about poor performance is especially poignant: "She [the teacher] reads all the papers and see if you get a U or anything . . . and the class you know start laughing at you and it makes you feel bad."

CHILDREN AS SOPHISTICATED OBSERVERS. Most striking is the sensitivity with which children interpret the implicit meaning underlying teacher behavior. Children respond to subtle and complex nuances in teachers' actions, often alluding to nonverbal clues. The importance of tone of voice and facial expression, both during single interactions as well as comparatively across different interactions, is seen in these two striking examples. One child shared, "They ask you questions if you're not even raising your hand, for if you know or not. And they um, they just really put down on you hard (knocks on table). 'No, that's not it' and they kinda scream at you. But when it's someone who, who's better experienced in the class, they say 'No.'" Another child described the following look from his teacher: "She has another funny way of looking at you. Not only that she is not smiling though. She's looking mad, unhappy, disappointed. She gets that look and says 'I am very disappointed in you.' I hate that feeling. I hate it. I hate when she does that . . . She makes me feel like I've just started school today. It makes me feel like I'm stupid. Just dumb, crazy, stupid, dumb."

Still other examples demonstrate the powerful message of single incidents that remain etched in a child's mind. A fourth grader recalled: "Well, one person, her pulse is bad, she just jumps up and hollers too much and skips around. She [the teacher] says 'Sit down, dumb Diana,' my teacher says that and everyone starts laughing." These single, remembered incidents, although sometimes unique to a particular child, often reveal a common underlying theme when examined across children within the same classrooms. In this particular classroom, one child seized upon the teacher practice of inviting only some children to her home. Another child focused on name calling and labeling of children by the teacher. Yet another child described a threat about failure from the teacher: "Like she say you're gonna flunk: sometimes she mean it, sometimes she don't." Another child picked up on the same theme and stated: "She [the teacher] told [a student] that when he came to school, she was going to flunk him." While these cues about smartness reflected different kinds of teacher behavior, they all depicted public communication about academic standing. Despite their uniqueness and sometimes infrequent or single-time occurrence, collectively such behaviors create a culture of differentiation for the students. Further, the subtle distinctions that children report underscore the limitations of relying on behavioral categories alone to communicate expectations about ability. And children's reports of single critical incidents suggest that the frequency of differentiating behaviors is only one kind of observation that children use to place themselves within the classroom achievement hierarchy.

Inferences That Children Make

INFERRING ONE'S PLACE IN THE ACHIEVEMENT HIERARCHY. Facilitated by the predominantly public nature of classroom performance information, children engage in a social comparative process—contrasting teachers' interactions with and among peers and with themselves. And it is in this comparative analysis of differential treatment that children learn about relative differences in ability. The sophistication of children's reasoning can be seen in this child's response, a very typical one: "Sometimes she [the teacher] says, 'Oh, that's very poor reading' to someone else and she says 'pretty good' to me . . . I kind of marked myself in the middle on reading because . . . to other people she says 'excellent reading.'" At other times, the meaning of teacher behavior is derived from subtle comparisons made both between students and across time yet focused on the same teacher behavior. In one example, children distinguished between a variety of ways of "calling on students": The teacher "calls on the smart kids for the right answer . . . she expects you to know more and won't tell answers." With regard to low achievers, the teacher calls on them sometimes "to give them a chance" or because they "goof off." The teacher also often "doesn't call on them because she knows they don't know the answer."

And sometimes it is the teacher, rather than the student, who makes the explicit comparison between students. One student's loss can become another student's gain, as seen in this child's description: "He, when my teacher um complains he's too um gets mad at some people who don't do their own work he say—why can't you learn like . . . like me or someboy like that . . . That's what makes me feel good. I don't know about other people but I guess that's what makes me feel good." Comparisons like these provide the information needed for deriving one's relative position in the classroom achievement hierarchy.

EMERGENT THINKING ABOUT SMARTNESS. While children might know where they stand relative to others in ability, what conceptions do they develop about the nature of ability as seen across classrooms? Given how children have described the content of teacher performance feedback, it is not surprising that when asked about how one gets to be a smart student, their most frequent responses (52 percent) referred to task-conformance behaviors like sitting still or listening attentively rather than effort (26 percent), native ability (13 percent), or external factors such as the quality of teacher or parent (9 percent). For these fourth graders, smartness meant behaving well in school. One child described it this way: "Smart is um you pay attention or being obedient and doing your math like, doing your math right or taking homework and bringing it back the next day. Without the teacher having to remind you to bring it back." Smartness to these children is also about finishing the work fast and without struggle and about producing right answers. As one child suggested, "You know how to do it [your work] in a one-day training." Another child reasoned in the following way: "I don't think I'm a very wise student . . . I think I'm a little slowful, cause I am not quite . . . And in reading, it takes quite awhile to finish the book, and um, while in arts, it doesn't take me very much . . . When I finish more faster, I know that I'm getting a bit more smarter." Another child emphasized, "School's easier for smart kids cause they don't have to struggle all through classes—through math and spelling and reading—but they just do it real fast. They can go all the way through their work. Instead of putting in the wrong answers, they're putting in the right answers." This understanding of smartness stresses conforming behaviors from students and the importance of a speedy and smooth performance, without struggle or errors.

HOW CHILDREN FEEL. In talking to children, it becomes resoundingly clear that they feel strong emotions in response to messages from teachers about their ability. In learning about poor performance, children speak of actual physical discomfort at the news. As one child noted, "When I get a bad grade, I don't feel that well." Another child commented: "Mr. J like rolls his eyes when he's correcting—like he goes 'Ooooh.' He calls on another person. It always used to make me feel—Uuuuuuh." Another child described his hurt feelings with these words: "The teacher would tell you personally, you know, but I'd rather have it down by writing or something . . . Because you know one time when I was in first grade—the teacher told me personally and it really hurt my feelings."

Still others report an erosion of their motivation or their liking for the subject matter, with implications for their future performance: "Like if the teacher always yells at you whenever you do something wrong—if you don't understand something and she yells at you and says 'you should already know'—then you might not do as well. You might say well, I don't like that part." There are also examples of children who try to ward off or ignore the negative messages from either teachers or peers. One child described a rather stoic response to negative feedback: "Well they say something like 'poor reading.' I get that about once a month. But um, and usually she doesn't really make me feel bad. I try and take it." Another child described a successful attempt to disregard negative messages from peers and parents in the context of expressed support from the teacher: "Between that time I moved up in groups. (The teacher) she says that you could do more better if you try, and I think that I just didn't try because other people was just sayin—well, you can't do that. So that one of the reasons why I moved up. I say—well, forget them, I'm gonna try at least and so I did."

In learning about good performance, children also emphasize the pride that can come from success and positive feedback from the teacher: "Well, for me they ask me questions and I answered 'em right and they tell me very good, you're doing very well. And you know, I feel proud of myself when I do, I really, ah, like it." But children also talk about a downside to high performance. Children describe pressure that can emanate from successful performance and the need to maintain one's position: "[Smart kids] they're so strict, they do all their work—they just work. Like they have to do their work because it's *our* work and we have to do this. I mean I have to do this because I won't be an A—I have to have this A." There is the expressed fear of slipping in performance, which generates worry for some children: "Like sometimes I get nervous . . . in studying like that . . . and I really know I'm doing my work. When it's hard I think about 'did I get the right answer?'" Another child expresses his worry in this way: "Well [school] it's happy for them cause they know how to do good work and they get real high in the groups. So they don't have to worry. But sometimes you do have to worry about goin' down in groups because sometimes you could forget what you're doing. An' you know just go straight down. All the way to the lowest group." This worry is evident in the possibility, children tell us, that you will be pushed beyond what you can achieve: "You can only do your best and she tried to push you much farther than your best."

An Emerging Model of Expectancy Communication

As children have shown us, clues about ability can be found not only in interactions between teachers and students but also in the structural organization, or microsystem, of classroom life, in which such interactions are embedded and in which opportunities to learn are both allocated and evaluated. Looking beyond the discrete teacher behaviors that have been identified, children's descriptions alerted Hermine Marshall and me to the elements of an underlying classroom culture that drives some teaching practices over others (Marshall and Weinstein 1984). Clearly evident in children's descriptions is their knowledge that multiple and complex features of classroom instructional life provide them with information about ability, their own and that of their peers. These include:

1. The ways in which students are grouped for instruction,
2. The materials and activities through which the curriculum is taught,
3. The evaluation system that teachers use to assess student learning,
4. The motivational system that teachers use to engage student learning,
5. The responsibility that students have in directing and evaluating their learning, and
6. The climate of relationships within the class, with parents, and with the school.

These features of the classroom microsystem frame the instructional environment for students in three important yet distinct ways. First, the instructional choices made in these six domains may result in the differential allocation of educational experiences to different groups of children. Second, these choices may accentuate or minimize the available information about ability differences between students. And third, these choices may expand or constrain learning and performance opportunities for all children. These are the demand characteristics of classrooms, "environmental affordances" to which children adapt in order to survive as learners.

How Children Are Grouped

In children's eyes, how students are grouped for instruction within their classroom provides clues about their relative smartness. As one child explained: "And so you know they're smart cause they're in the highest group." When asked what it told a child when the teacher moved that child to a higher reading group, another student replied: "It told me I was a smart person." Children readily report that membership in ability-based instructional groups informs them about ability differences between students simply by group name, book, or book color used. One child reasoned: "I know my level, I know what I'm doing, and I know the level in my book . . . usually the teacher might tell you, or your book has a certain color, and colors mean which is high and low." Another child noted: "Our teacher wouldn't say, you know—like the lowest group in our class is the Blue Bee and that's a math-group book and they're the lowest in our class. But she would say Blue Bee and we all know that's the lowest in the class."

Sometimes children can discern with remarkable precision their individual achievement level within the context of ability-group membership. This fourth grader views himself as number thirteen in the classroom achievement hierarchy: "Because I know there are ten All-stars and there are two people in my group that read and do math better than me . . . All-stars are the highest group and I'm in the Blazers, the second highest group." Another fourth grader notes that "the best reader in this group is so and so." In some classes, student ability is reported by children to be low across the board. One child commented: "I wouldn't know what she thinks is smart because she says nobody's smart. I don't think she acts like any of us are smart in class." This capacity to differentiate between classes, groups, and among students enables a precise accounting of the degree of smartness in subject matter or in general. With rare exceptions, higher is better and as this child expresses it, "I wanted [the teacher] to put me in the smarter group."

The Curriculum Provided

The nature and difficulty of curricular tasks that children are assigned and the ways in which they are paced and monitored by teachers provide information about relative ability differences among students. Children become aware of these ability differences through the sequencing of curricular materials. For example, a child notes that "he is the only one in the highest book in the class." Another child describes the exchange that took place in his classroom when the teacher asked, "'Who isn't past Unit 12 stand up' . . . and she [the teacher] says, 'All you people are way behind.'" Children also know that smarter kids are given more challenging work ("They give 'em harder things than the other people"), extra work ("Mr. J usually gives them extra work to do"), and special tasks that are not offered to other children ("The teacher gives them special work for just them [smart kids] to do . . . some work that other people don't get to do.") Further, the "not so smart" children often miss events that are fun in order to finish or improve their academic work: "When people do bad, they don't get to go out certain places like to PE or recess and you do . . . They announce your name—say that you're doing very poor."

Congruent with reports on the TTI, children also perceive the monitoring and structuring of work to be greater for lows than for highs. In fact, highs are reported to be left alone by the teacher—as one child described it, "The teacher doesn't actually work with the smart kids because they know how to do their stuff." Another explains these differences in this way: "They put 'em [smart kids] each in the corners and give them their work and they all, like one person tells the answer, and the other person tells her and then everyone gets a turn . . . And then the other kids that are not smart, they have to sit . . . in the groups . . . what need more help. And they have to work with the teacher." In many cases, the teacher's extra monitoring is paved with good intentions that the children appear to acknowledge: "She doesn't work with them as much as she works with the kids that's not as smart. Because the kids that are not as smart—she wants to teach them more."

The Evaluation System

Children also acknowledge differences in the performance opportunities offered students and in the feedback received from teachers—elements of the classroom evaluation system. Children allude to the fact that high achievers often are given more chances to demonstrate their knowledge. One child described the favoritism as follows: "I was put in a reading book, and I found out pretty soon that only our group was called, and then my teacher changed me to the medium group, and we hardly don't get called." Another child underscored this perception of bias: "Well sometimes some people they think they're really smart because the teacher calls on you really a lot. And that's what she does to me."

As noted earlier, differences in feedback from teachers loom largest in children's minds. Even grades can require interpretation from the teacher: "So that's how you know you get good grades or not, because she'll put a smiley face or a bad face on it." Earlier, we were sensitized to children's reports of the public nature of performance information, whether these messages were positive ("When you're reading, she says 'Very, very good reading'") or negative ("'Now here's one thing that is wrong with your paper' . . . She announced it to the class"). Children also allude to the shame that poor performance can bring, as evident in this child's sharing of name-calling by the teacher ("She [the teacher] calls them [the not-so-smart students] lulus"). Even well-intentioned attempts by teachers to soften the blow of negative feedback by raising hope for the future can backfire in children's eyes. One child, for example, explained: "Well, they tell you like for a report, they'd probably say 'I know you'll do better on your next report.' And that kinda give you a hint that you didn't do that well."

The Motivational System

Children express awareness of the use of extrinsic rewards for good performance and how good such rewards feel for those who get them. One child told us: "She [the teacher] gives us treats and she gives us a gift." Another child comments on the pleasure these rewards give the recipients: "Like today, the teacher gave me award saying I was the second top in the class. And the first top—she had a big grin on her face." Many of the children's descriptions link ability to performance, right and wrong answers, and membership in higher reading groups—that is, on "how I am doing" issues rather than on the challenges of the task they are completing. As this child describes his reasoning, "When it's hard [the work], I think about did I get the right answer?"

There are some examples that children shared, however, about the importance of effort in improving academic performance and the possibility of reaching for membership in that higher group. As one child suggests: "You can get smart by really studying hard and by trying to understand everything that you're doing and maybe you can ask for help—extra help from the teacher if you really want to get better—do better at the things you are doing." And examples emerged of teachers who give hope that effort can make a difference: "They [the teachers] gave me courage. Let's say my teacher was giving me a math problem and I think I said I couldn't do it and she said 'Just try and you could.' So I tried and I did it." This child offered advice to those students who are not doing well: "Other kids, like the not smart [kids] really doesn't like school. [They] say well, I'm not gonna try because I'm already down low. But if they do try, they'll get up *high,* because I tried. I said—well, I want to be in Kaleidoscopes and I'm gonna try it."

There are some students, particularly the low achievers, who are perceived as not liking schoolwork and, as noted above, as unmotivated to do better perhaps because they are "already down low." A fourth grader described the difference in motivation this way: "Some people don't care in our class, some people do." Another child points to the lack of motivation of the "not-so-smart" kids: "They [the not-so-smart kids] don't like school and they give the teacher a rough time. And the kid don't like doing his work that the teacher give him. He only likes to draw and do other work." Another child underscores that the work the low achievers are assigned is often boring. "They [the low achievers] say I don't like my teacher because she is always giving us boring assignments. She always yells at me when I'm not doing well."

Student Agency

According to children, most of the interactions that occur are directed and controlled by teachers. While remarkably little student agency is described, children do note that there are different opportunities for high and low achievers to make choices and to hold responsibility in the classroom. High achievers are "let on their own more." Children suggest that "the teacher doesn't actually work with [the smart kids] because they know how to do their stuff." In letting high achievers work on their own, the teacher is described as providing them with more independent opportunities: "Sometimes, she has 'em [the smart kids] find out for themselves. She may sorta answer their question and have them figure out the answer, or she may just not and say 'Figure it out.'" Another child described this greater independence in these words: "She'll like give them a special assignment and she'll want it due the next day or so. And most of the time when smarter kids do that, it's like they feel more responsible." Often, these extra opportunities are linked to the different rates at which the children complete classroom tasks: "Well, the teacher asks me to help people every once and awhile. And they ask me to do errands for them cause I finished my work."

The Climate of Relationships

CLASS RELATIONSHIPS.   Students seem to believe that the quality of relationships that teachers have with the class as a whole and with each student indicates differences in their academic abilities. Children describe differences in the expression of warmth, trust, humor, and concern to high and low achievers. They speak to the differential trust that teachers show concerning individual student capability, a trust that carries with it more sustained interaction. One child described this trust: "So if you got that problem wrong she would naturally get after you cause she *knows you know that.*" A look by a teacher and certain kinds of teasing also suggest ability differences as well as evoke good feelings: "When they look at you when you answer a question or something. Makes you feel good." Another child shared, "Teachers sometimes they tease me a lot and everything. That makes me feel like I do well." Teachers are also described as feeling special pride in as well as responsibility for students who do well in school: "[Being smart] means a lot to my teacher because she'll be *proud* of you. She'll say, Well, hey—like in the future, she'll say "Well, hey, that's my student—she was in my grade."

The relationships that classmates have with each other often mirror the tone that the teacher sets with the class. Pride in a student's accomplishment, regardless of his or her achievement status, is shared by classmates in this example of a supportive classroom: "Well, sometimes she tells the class, she says this person is really doing well and I just wanted to say that he or she is doing really well, maybe you can give them a hand . . . And everyone feels kind of happy when somebody else is doing well if they were really having a hard time." In other examples, children speak of the high achievers as the popular students who are granted a leadership role by their peers: "[Smart people], well, they're usually the top people and everyone votes for 'em to become—like to do stuff, to be table monitors and other stuff. And they're just very popular." Children also comment on divisiveness between the students who do well and those who do not—a tension to which both highs and lows appear to contribute, although there appear to be individual differences in such responses. This child described the struggle for the lows: "When they [the lows] see they have a sad face on their paper, they say I'm not smart. They be mad then they start kicking the college kids." Another child describes the divisive role of the highs in these words: "They [the highs] tease them too. They say 'Oh, you can't be as good as me' and 'You're nothing big an' you'll never be smart.' And that just humiliates them and then they think that they can't do it." This child differentiates between highs who help and those who don't in this description: "Well, sometimes when you ask them [the smart kids] a question since they're a little smarter than you, they'd say 'You don't even know that?' But some of the smart ones, they'll help you with that."

PARENT-CLASS RELATIONSHIPS. Children say remarkably little in these interviews about their parents and the educational process, perhaps because of the questions asked. What is expressed is that parental support is critical for their achievement and is present for some students and lacking for others. One child describes such support: "If there's a tough question, you could ask your mother and then she helps you figure it out." Another child shares that "I just practice my reading when my mother an' father is home—that's how I get my reading up to third [place]." This child points to her parents' pride: "Well, it makes [my parents] proud of me too because they can say, 'Well, here's my girl. See she does her work in class and I really like that and I can be proud of her when she gets a good job and stuff.'"

Children express gratitude for their parents' concern. One child puts it this way: "And you're glad that you have the kind of parents that teaches you and the teacher that teaches you." Most poignantly, this child's story paints an unhappy picture about the behavior of low achievers and suggests that not all parents are concerned about their children's school achievement in helpful ways. In these comments, parents are described as responsible for the poor behavior of the "not so smart" kids: "They won't act like . . . they have house manners or anything . . . They mother and father don't teach 'em anything at the home and then they come to school, act the same way they do at home. Stick their feet all on the table . . . Kicking the door. And they don't care. And then when they get sent down to the office, they care a lot. But the mother and father won't never do nothin'. They just let 'em go right on by and then they say, 'The next time you do that, I'll whip you for that.' But then the next time they do it, same thing."

SCHOOL-CLASS RELATIONSHIPS. Children report that opportunities to get outside of the classroom and gain school-level recognition are most often accorded to high rather than low achievers. Allocation of school-level opportunities becomes one way that children know a student is considered smart by teachers. As one fourth grader put it, "The way you know a person is smart, [the teacher] always picks on them to go to different places . . . Well they get to do more stuff . . . I don't really think it's fair because they *always* get to do stuff—like they get to go to the *office* and color posters—do *everything*—every single thing but the other kids don't get to do anything." Often, these opportunities arise because work is completed fast or work is rewarded by teachers. This same child recounts, "And they [the teachers] ask me to do errands for them 'cause I finished my work." Another child elaborates: "She [the teacher] let 'em [the smart kids] go on field trips with other classes—go on field trips . . . for camping overnight. They let them go like they get good rewards on their spelling and reading and math. And they don't give the teacher a hard time."

Lessons Drawn: Learning from Children

Children Know

As we have seen, elementary school children, even young ones, know that teachers, on average, treat high and low achievers differently within the same classroom. High expectations, trust, and opportunity from teachers are linked with doing well in school, whereas scolding, monitoring, and lots of help are associated with poor performance. Regardless of whether these teacher behaviors are helpful in their own right, in children's eyes, they spell out one's placement in the classroom achievement hierarchy.

Children of different ages, abilities, and genders are remarkably consistent in their capacity to identify differential teacher treatment on a brief questionnaire. Consequently, we have been able to use the Teacher Treatment Inventory as a quantifiable assessment tool to characterize the qualities of classrooms as they exist or as they might change in response to planned intervention. That different treatment is reported within classrooms raises questions about the meaningfulness of studying teacher effectiveness and classroom climate by looking at teaching behaviors averaged across all the children in a classroom. These averaged measures may wash out shared and systematic differences in the perceived experiences of children within the classrooms. Rather than one climate, it seems that for children many climates may coexist.

In listening to children, we can also see limitations in our sole reliance on counting the frequency of discrete teacher behaviors to measure the communication of expectations to students. We need to make room for the single but critical incident and for the meaningfulness, in children's eyes, of certain teacher behaviors that are understood solely in context. Only multiple passes through the data, both qualitative as well as quantitatively directed, will more fully portray the classroom culture—a place where meanings are forged from sensitivity to the interaction between verbal, nonverbal, and institutional messages as well as from long-term participation.

A number of other studies confirm our questionnaire and interview findings. Using direct comparative ratings by students of teacher behavior (more often, the same, less often than classmates), Harris Cooper and Thomas Good (1983) documented that fourth through six graders perceived differential treatment on four of the nine teacher behavior items. Using frequency ratings with third graders about their own treatment, Alexis Mitman and Andrea Lash (1988) found perceived differential treatment of high and low achievers for six of the thirteen teacher behaviors studied. In several studies by Elisha Babad and his colleagues, children's awareness of differential teacher treatment has also been documented (e.g., Babad 1993). In an experimental study of teacher behavior as displayed in brief context-minimized videotaped clips, Babad, Bernieri, and Rosenthal (1991) showed that ten-year-olds could detect the academic standing and likability of the "unseen" student from these brief clips of teacher behavior but could not rate these same behaviors for differential treatment (for example, on ratings of warmth) as did the adult observers. We, as well as Babad (1990), have had greater success, consistently across types of children at different ages, in identifying differential treatment through indirect methods where children independently rate teacher behavior toward a hypothetical high- and low-expectancy student. When children report on their own treatment or when they are asked to make comparative judgments relative to the treatment of others, more complex and individualized social information processing comes into play and we see more variability in children's responses, which perhaps accounts for differences in findings between studies.

The Mitman and Lash study (1988) found that student and observer consensus about the treatment of students grouped by expected achievement was greater in classrooms where ability cues were accentuated and thus perhaps more obvious to all. In this study, student and observer consensus was greater for interactive than for feedback behaviors, perhaps because feedback behaviors are more difficult for students or observers to interpret. Cooper and Good (1983) also documented consensus between student and teacher ratings for a number of teacher behaviors. Like in the Mitman and Lash study, disagreement was greatest for teacher praise, with students reporting high achievers as the most frequent recipients and teachers claiming the same for low achievers. Observer reports were more likely to match teacher rather than student reports. Also similarly, while Babad (1990) documented agreement between teachers and students about the more frequent learning support and less pressure directed toward low rather than high achievers, controversy existed over the provision of emotional support. Here, akin to the lack of consensus in the more sensitive areas of feedback and praise, students viewed high achievers as receiving more emotional support while teachers reported low achievers as the more frequent recipients of such support. Babad explains this discrepancy by the fact that the communication of expectancy occurs in different and sometime conflicting ways. In many cases, while the teachers are consciously offering low-expectancy students more learning support, they are also communicating in nonverbal ways a negative meaning (Babad, Bernieri, and Rosenthal 1989a).

It seems clear, then, that elementary school children are aware of differential teacher treatment in the classroom. Such awareness is more consistent and heightened in classrooms where ability cues are more salient. Consensus between student and teacher perceptions is also greater in ability-salient classes and greater for some behaviors and less for others. As noted earlier, however, the match of perceptions between student, teacher, and observer is not the most critical question. That children's interpretations of teacher behavior reflect subtle, cross-channel and cross-student observations highlight that it is the perspective of the student, the one who is most strongly affected by teacher expectations, that needs to be most vigorously studied.

The Microsystem of Teacher Practices

Whether one is smart or not smart in school is largely learned from the actions of teachers, communicated in often comparative ways in full view of classmates. But underlying discrete teacher behaviors are the institutional structures that deliver the curriculum, group students, evaluate and motivate learning, promote student agency, and create a climate of relationships in the classroom. These institutional arrangements play an important role in differentiating instruction, highlighting ability differences, and constraining educational opportunities. They also help children make sense of differential interactions with the teacher. Any theory that addresses this issue must consider the two dimensions of learning support and emotional support (Babad 1998) within larger instructional and classroom management practices.

Conforming to the academic task, being in the highest group, and getting the work done quickly, quietly, obediently, and without struggle is what smartness primarily means to elementary school students, as seen here and consistent with the findings of Phyllis Blumenfeld and her colleagues (1982). The classrooms described here are, to children, places where teachers largely drive the action; little emphasis is placed on processes of self-regulation and self-evaluation. The interviews with children underscore the powerful role of the teacher in defining "what is smartness" and "who has it" for children and (as we have already seen in Chapter 1) for their families. Further, the power and credibility of the expectation source—here, the teacher—increase the potential that children will confirm such expectations in their behavior and thus enact self-fulfilling prophecies.

As we have seen, children rarely look to themselves or to the qualities of the task in which they are engaged for information about how they are doing—a fact that emphasizes in spades the dependent role in which we place students in classroom settings. That we do not foster self-monitoring of their work and their accomplishments as a primary source of feedback about capability is perhaps our downfall, given the growing evidence about the important role of self-efficacy in human development (Bandura 2001). As I will discuss later, our research findings also show that children who engage in such self-monitoring are more likely to resist the effects of teacher expectations than are children who look to the teacher as their primary source of such monitoring and feedback (Madison 1993). Further, in a rapidly changing world where new challenges demand an adaptive responsiveness, an independence of judgment might well be the best life strategy to cultivate in students.

Children's awareness of the subtleties of their teacher's differential treatment is impressive, sophisticated, and even embarrassing for those who believed that one could deceive and control children without their knowledge. As members of a classroom culture, children are privy to patterns of events, to single critical incidents, and to the communication of disparate and conflicting messages—observations that depict a reality to which prevailing theories and research instruments cannot do full justice. Children, even young children, are useful sources of information, and we can and must learn from them about the communication of expectations in schooling.

CHAPTER 5

Differences among Classroom Achievement Cultures

If the brains aren't there, the brains aren't there . . . I don't want the children in the top group to get bored just adding and subtracting fractions . . . Your lower student needs to be regurgitating day after day after day the same thing for it to set in.

—Mrs. Iver

It's not how much brains you've got, it's how you use them . . . I try to run spelling more as a whole group because I feel that the more they can see, say, and hear it, the better they are going to be. And I used to worry more about the faster kids in spelling, . . . because I thought that's so repetitive . . . and they said no, they don't always know the meanings, so they said it was OK.

—Mrs. Kay

In *Ways with Words* (1983), Shirley Brice Heath writes movingly about Mrs. Gardner and her class of nineteen African American first-grade students from the rural South, "all of whom had been designated as 'potential failures' on the basis of reading readiness tests" (p. 284). Heath describes the ways in which this teacher changed her teaching methods to meet better the needs of youngsters whose cultural patterns of language use differed greatly from what was expected at the start of schooling. In Mrs. Gardner's own words: "I was angry when I learned these children were designated 'no chance of success' before entering school. I decided to try methods I had pulled together that had worked with individual children over the years. My three guidelines are: have them read a story that's fun, that can build suspense; have them talk about how what they have read helps them know what will happen; then have them take apart all the pieces of what they've had to use to read for fun" (p. 286).

In implementing these guidelines, she used a diverse array of reading

114

methods (phonetic and whole-language approaches) in varied action contexts (the classroom, the playground, the auditorium, and the neighborhood). She assigned children the old primary-level textbooks that had been in storage for years, but she also drew examples from children's own environments and helped them to produce their own books and advertisements. Not surprisingly, Mrs. Gardener noted that "students learned to use the environment about them to recognize letters, to hear different kinds of questions and answers, and to talk about stories. In short, they came to see themselves as readers" (p. 287).

By the end of the year, all but one of the nineteen students had reached grade level in their reading skills and many had moved beyond (with eight at the third-grade level and six at the second-grade level). Key to Mrs. Gardner's success was the diversity of methods used that both respected and capitalized upon children's own "ways with words." Yet it should not be overlooked that underlying the implementation of these instructional strategies were a belief that each and every one of these youngsters had the capacity to learn, as well as a relentless determination to help make such learning happen. Despite the external prophecy of potential failure, this was a classroom in which all children were expected to become achievers, were helped to reach these goals, and did.

As we saw in Chapter 4, elementary school children draw inferences about their ability and that of peers from patterns they discern in teacher behaviors and in the organization of classroom life. Just as children describe high achievers as receiving more opportunities to learn and more positive responses to their efforts than do low achievers within the same classroom, they also report differences in the degree to which teachers differentiate their treatment of high and low achievers. In some classrooms, children report large differences in the trust and opportunity, negative feedback, and structure given high versus low achievers. In other classrooms, little favoritism is noted. These differences between classrooms are particularly evident with regard to both the perceived treatment of low achievers and the amount of public display of poor performance.

Despite the obvious fact that classrooms are indeed different, and despite substantial evidence documenting the nature of these differences, most research on expectancy effects in schooling considers teachers in general. As noted earlier, this aggregation across classrooms can wash out differences in the strength of expectancy effects from classroom to classroom. Even more importantly, such aggregation obscures the work of teachers who create alternative cultures that support the more equitable treatment of students. If such teachers are identified, their work will be better understood and perhaps can be emulated.

This chapter uses children's perceptions of differential treatment, as documented on the Teacher Treatment Inventory (TTI), to distinguish between classrooms with great or little reported differentiation. In expanding on previously published work (Marshall and Weinstein 1984, 1986, 1988), I draw more extensively from interviews and observations in two such exemplar classrooms in order to capture in teachers' own words and own ways the interactive features of their thinking and practice that, in children's eyes, work to create a culture of differentiation or equity.

Two Classrooms, Two Cultures

Two fifth-grade teachers (their names pseudonyms) are highlighted here. These exemplars were drawn from an intensive study of twelve classrooms (four each from grades one, three, and five), which were part of a still larger sample of thirty first-, third-, and fifth-grade classrooms from two urban and ethnically mixed school districts. All thirty classrooms were ranked within grade level on the extent to which children reported differential teacher treatment on the TTI. The two highest and two lowest scoring classrooms within each grade were selected for observations of, and interviews with, the teachers. The interview and observation transcripts of these teachers reveal subtle but systematic differences in their philosophies about student capability and teacher responsibility, as well as in teaching practices that are derived from such conceptions. While these differences are sharply contrasted here, they appear in some form, in high- versus low-scoring classrooms at the first-, third-, and fifth-grade levels.

The two exemplar classrooms were comparable in many important ways. Both teachers were female, both had roughly the same number of years of teaching experience, and both classes were of comparable size and of comparable ethnic and socioeconomic composition. Mrs. Iver's class (in which children reported a great deal of differential treatment) enrolled twenty-seven students, with an ethnic makeup of 37 percent white, 37 percent black, and 22 percent Asian (4 percent of unknown ethnicity) and with 84 percent of the children eligible for free lunch. Mrs. Kay's classroom (in which children reported little differential treatment) enrolled thirty-two students, with an ethnic composition of 38 percent white, 40 percent black, and 12 percent Asian, and with 88 percent of the children eligible for free lunch.

Assessing Teacher Beliefs and Practices

TEACHER INTERVIEWS.   Just as we had assessed children's academic expectations, we asked teachers to sort students in their classroom with regard to expected achievement at the end of the school year. Teachers were given two piles of cards, one for reading and one for math, in which each child's name was listed on a separate index card. They were asked to rank the students in each pile from top to bottom in order of expected achievement in the identified subject matter area. This sorting task and our classroom observations provided the context for our interviews with the teachers. After the teachers had rated the expected achievement of their students, we began our interview with these words: "When we observe in your classroom, we only see what you are doing at one point in time and from a limited perspective. We'd like to have your help in understanding what happens over the year. It will help clarify some of the things that we have been observing."

Our questions probed teachers' beliefs about students and about the instructional accommodations that they, the teachers, made to address perceived differences in achievement among students. Guided by the model that had emerged from our interviews with children, we asked questions about grouping practices as one example. We offered this introduction: "When you have visitors in your classroom (or an observer), they can see you working with children, but they can't tell how you decide on whom you will work with. Can you describe briefly how you group for instruction?" This was followed by questions about the basis for such groupings, mobility, regrouping, and curricular assignments related to grouping. We also explored curricular sequencing, evaluation practices, the assignment of responsibilities to students, perceptions of students they had placed at the top and bottom of their ranked piles, and effective strategies for high and low achievers. These interviews were taped and transcribed.

CLASSROOM OBSERVATIONS.   In addition to the teacher interviews we collected narrative records of classroom interactions with the Classroom Dimensions Observation System (Marshall and Weinstein 1982). Trained observers who were blind to the differential treatment score of each classroom created a running written record of classroom events by following the teacher and capturing her interactions with students as a class, as a smaller group, or as individuals. All teacher statements were recorded as close to verbatim as possible. A minimum of twelve hours of observation per classroom was conducted over a two- to four-week period, capturing at least three lessons each in reading and math, and some whole-class instruction that did not involve ability grouping. The narrative records were typed and then subjected to a theme analysis. Teacher statements about student ability, classroom management, and teaching strategies were identified in each classroom, and a summary was made of recurrent themes. The transcripts were reread to search for additional confirming or disconfirming evidence of these themes and of the factors identified in the model. These themes were checked with the material gathered in the teacher interviews, and corroborated by triangulating multiple perspectives.

Grouping Practices

Eyes on the Top Group: Mrs. Iver

Mrs. Iver used ability grouping in three subject-matter areas: reading, math, and spelling. Classroom observers noted that the seating was also arranged according to group membership, and consequently was primarily by race, with ethnic-minority children more likely to be in the lower groups. In reading, children were often called together by the name of the reader they were currently using. In other instances, the label "top group" was frequently used. Mrs. Iver based her grouping decisions both on ability ("good brain and all that") and relative skill level ("worst handwriting in town"). Her grouping assignments for reading and spelling turned out to be very similar. She noted: "So if you look at my spelling list, you'll see the group of children who have the most difficulty in expressing themselves in comprehensive reading sentences are going to be usually my group that has trouble with spelling as well."

Based on a variety of tests given at the start of the year and "my thinking of what a fifth-grader should know," Mrs. Iver made assignments into four or five groups and retested the students after two or three months. She expressed concern that the pressure to keep up with the group might be too much for some children. Her grouping decisions, as well as her grouping changes (up or down) reflected that assessment: "In my top group in reading, I have to consider the child's ability to keep up in both areas. Though he may be able to read and orally comprehend, can he carry on the summary writing, the expected written assignments? If he can't carry that on, then I can't put him under pressure, or her under pressure. That child may fall into the second group." With regard to group changes, Mrs. Iver comments, "If the child has outgrown the group in the meantime, he just moves up. Or down. It depends on what he has been able to keep up with."

Although Mrs. Iver described movement between groups as the norm, such movement could only happen at certain times. Movement also appeared to be dependent upon student, rather than teacher, actions. She provided several examples of how she thinks about changes in group assignment. These examples depict the prestige and motivational pull of placement in a higher group, as well as the pressure felt once there. Mrs. Iver said about Sheila: "I've had to take her out of the top group because she wasn't able to keep up. She herself felt under too much pressure. So she said to me, 'I think I'd better go back into the other group.'" Similarly, with regard to Kenny, a student who "has moved up, in reading and math," Mrs. Iver noted, "He was just moving along average, very confused, and very unsure of his own ability, and now he feels he can hack it. Yesterday, when I gave him the reader, I said, 'Now look, if it gets too much, I want you to say something. I don't want you to start dancing a jig around here and getting nervous, because there's no big deal. You can still move into the Galaxies, because I'll open up the Galaxies Group when this middle group gets out' . . . which will give him sixth grade reader. But that won't be until maybe the end of March."

These examples also suggest that the burden of keeping up lies largely with the students. With few exceptions, as seen in her comment that "I'll do that [test] just to see if they need more drill rather than move them out of the group," these and other responses in the interview do not reveal strategies to ensure that children "keep up" and have a more successful experience in the assigned group. Mrs. Iver appeared willing to move children into higher group placements "as long as he [the student] can get help and support at home, and as long as he is happy, then I'm going to let him go." The potential for upward mobility was indeed communicated to the children. Mrs. Iver delivered the following message to students in her lowest reading group: "Use your books as tools. When you guys learn to answer these kinds of questions [defining words through context], then you will move on fast. When you can use your book as a tool, you will move on rapidly." But in this classroom, the threat of downward movement is ever present as well: "Come on, work on your math. You haven't worked on math for three days and I'm aware of it. You going to drop out of the group? No free loaders."

Students are also threatened about being removed from the "top group" if they do not "stop fussing." To one student who is not paying attention, Mrs. Iver remarks, "You are either in or out of the top group."

"Your Family Will Help You": Mrs. Kay

Mrs. Kay described using a variety of grouping strategies. She noted that although she often has to group by ability when she teaches, she also uses a "mixture of academic and social" information to place children into "families": "I mix them because they can learn from each other and help each other." Observers documented heterogeneously grouped families for seating and study periods. Desks were arranged into groups of four double desks, with eight students forming families named 49'ers, Golden Unicorns, Garfield Gang, and Artesians. Family membership was reshuffled after a period of time so that all the children had an opportunity to work with each other. As Mrs. Kay told her students, "I'll give out the family awards later. I told you that after a couple of weeks, we would change families. New families may get inspired to do super jobs."

Mrs. Kay's instructional groups were flexibly implemented, and group assignments reflected much cross-checking of test results, prior records, and her own perceptions, which she admitted may be wrong or may evaluate different dimensions. She noted, "At the beginning of the year I give my own tests. Sometimes it's written; sometimes it's oral, depending upon what the subject is. I work it out after I get to know them a little bit, and then I check out the records. Then I want to see if my perceptions fall in line at all with where they supposedly were last year. So if there is any real discrepancy, then I want to see where I went wrong, or if maybe we were evaluating in a different way. So after I check the records and then see how it kind of jives, and then I group." Mrs. Kay reports that changes in group assignment are commonplace and that she informs students about that reality: "I make changes and I tell them that the groups are certainly not put into concrete and we make changes as we go. We're always making changes."

Mrs. Kay uses ability-based grouping for reading and math but not for spelling. She describes the differences between these subject areas that make grouping simple, more complex, or not necessary:

> Grouping with regard to math is a lot simpler. I just go through the tests and I just kind of see how they fall. Every year it is different. This year I had three groups.

Reading—there's so many areas! You talk about decoding or you talk about character analysis or story development. You know, there's so many different facets of that, that I find it a lot more difficult.

And then there's spelling. We have those district mandated lists. So I try to do that whole group because we are using the See, Say, Hear, Write method . . . I try to run that more as a whole group because I feel that, the more they can see, say and hear it, the better they are going to be. And I used to worry more about the faster kids in spelling, or the good spellers, naturally good spellers, more than I did the lower spellers because I thought that's so repetitive . . . , but I found that the kids who were good spellers said no, and they don't always know the meanings, the morphographs, so they said it was OK. And one kid actually told me last year, "This is the one time in the day I don't have to worry."

In these descriptions, Mrs. Kay conveys sensitivity—to student cohort differences that might change the size of her groups each year, to the different demands of different subject matter, and to gaps in the knowledge of high achievers as well as low achievers. She describes that she cannot work with more than three groups, and given individual differences among students, she works around them. In contrast to Mrs. Iver, who placed responsibility on students for keeping up with the group or dropping down, Mrs. Kay described using strategies ("Either meet with them individually, or maybe try to pick up the pace of the group") that showed she took responsibility for moving students along. She frequently used whole-class lessons, relied on family groups in instruction, and made no reference to ability differences between instructional groups. Children were called to reading groups by reader and to math groups by name. Math groups were reshuffled during our periods of observation.

Curriculum

A Highly Differentiated Curriculum: Mrs. Iver

Despite a multidimensional view of children's abilities as depicting both strengths and weaknesses (in her words, "Just because a child . . . is reading at top level doesn't mean that I have to automatically think that the top level knows all its skills"), Mrs. Iver implemented a sharply differentiated curriculum in reading, math, and spelling that was tied to group membership. She shared that the top group in reading was given daily written assignments, whereas the other groups were required to prepare bimonthly book reports. With regard to grammar skills, Mrs. Iver noted: "I'll do a brief review while I'm teaching the whole class the lesson and then I'll . . . split off and give these children [the top group] a harder set of skills combined with the skill that I've taught the whole class." In math, Mrs. Iver expressed concern about keeping the interest of the members of the top group: "I don't want the children in the top group to get bored just adding or subtracting fractions, so I'm covering from page 77 to 88 and I'm taking a row here and a row there of different skills related to what they've already learned. And a couple of division problems. So they don't get bored doing one thing, because they're a better student and they will get bored." In sharp contrast, she described the instructional needs of her lower ability groups in reading and math: "Your slower student needs to be regurgitating day after day after day the same thing for it to set in . . . You see their work habits are so underdeveloped—I don't like to say 'poor'—I guess poor in the sense that they are not pushing themselves. But they'll be lucky to get through the basic series."

Mrs. Iver did acknowledge the large gap in content coverage (the top group was working at a seventh-grade reading level and the low group was working at grade level, which was fifth grade)—a gap that she tried to reduce. She described her efforts to prepare her lower group for more challenging material: "As it is, I bypass the fourth-grade series for them, because I feel that if you stay at baby vocabulary, that's all you're going to develop. So I put them in fifth-grade vocabulary books mostly to develop a better vocabulary. And a deeper comprehension question that's not so babyish and that they have to sort of push themselves a little bit to think of how to answer." The classroom observations also underscored the differentiated and sequenced nature of the curriculum (of which children were made aware), the predominance of convergent rather than divergent tasks, and the emphasis on tasks as "work to be done"—task choices that all focus attention on the evaluation of comparative ability. Classroom observers noted that Mrs. Iver labeled the difficulty level of the material for students, as in the following example in which she told a group of students not to use the reader Galaxies because "it is a lower reader."

The activities assigned to students involved primarily convergent rather than divergent tasks, as was evident even in an art lesson in which students were taught a representational style of drawing a face. Although children were advised by the teacher, "Don't worry about it not looking right the first time," the message was that there was only one right way to do the task:

"What I am seeing is people dissatisfied. People are not following directions. . . . Never do the nose like this. You shade. . . . One thing I will not do with class is let you think art is play time. If you do that, we will put art away and not have it for two weeks." The tasks were also described as work that needed to be done. Students were urged to finish their work so that they could "go out to recess" or "get out of that book" rather than enjoy the process of thinking and learning. In a social studies class, even when engaged in a divergent task, the teacher-led discussion focused on the procedures and compliance, rather than on the ideas.

Mrs. Iver: Last time, I gave you an assignment. I asked you to write a paper on living in the northeastern, middle or southern colonies. You were supposed to choose the colony you would like to live in and tell why. Just keep quiet now. A number of you did the assignment and a number did not.

Alex: What if they did it [the assignment]?

Mrs. Iver: Quiet. I'm not going to discuss that now. Tomorrow I will bring the list. Fifty percent of you did, fifty percent didn't. End of the world won't come. It won't hurt me if you didn't do it. I am asking you to put your ideas together . . . When you don't do an assignment, you're hurting only yourself.

Thinking and Quality for All: Mrs. Kay

Mrs. Kay described herself as using "more supplementary material than basic things." Her curricular assignments were similar for the whole class in spelling and language arts (whereas Mrs. Iver used ability-based instruction), science, and social studies. In these subjects, Mrs. Kay tried to promote collaboration—for example, "In science, I try to get those who are really interested paired up with those who are not." Where she differentiated the curriculum, in contrast to Mrs. Iver, she did so in fluid ways—for example, in math, she explained, "One group definitely needed to start with reviewing subtraction. One group needed to start with multiplication and one group could add, subtract, multiply, and we started with division." Mrs. Kay thus began with three groups in math, but then noted that the "last time when I tested, they clearly broke into two groups." She responded to these changes by shifting her instruction: "So the one group I kind of pushed a little bit. I helped the group that was ahead just a little, with review and some other things, while I could catch the few kids up. And then the other ones really needed to review . . . so I had them go with the other group. . . . So if they needed it [to go in the lower group], I'd say, 'You know, you can always work your way up again. Don't worry about it. But I would really like to have you listen again to the instructions.'"

Mrs. Kay described one way that she differentiated the instructional practices she used with highs and lows. When asked about effective strategies for high achievers, she responded that they need both direction (her teaching) and freedom:

> They seem to thrive on taking responsibility for assignments, whether it's the contracts or projects. They can really use the skills that they have in their own way, or something that they feel is not just "here's the ditto, answer the question," but to use that in a directed sense, to be creative . . . They need direction but they need freedom. You can't just say "Here's the book, go to it and see me if you have problems." I don't believe in that. Because otherwise, I told them, "Why don't you just do correspondence courses, because you are bright but I think I have something to offer to you." I feel that they need directions, but they need to feel that they make choices and they have time to decide for themselves.

With regard to the low achievers, Mrs. Kay noted,

> Unless we're talking about students like the learning disability students (that's something beyond their control kind of thing), the lower achievers, I think a lot of their problems, just from what I've found, many of them have ability, but what's holding them back is really a lack of self-direction or self-control: "I'll do it because you make me" or "if you make me." I find that I have to be more directive, "This assignment is due tomorrow" because they will do it if you tell them. But if you give them a choice, they will choose not to. And what I would like, *hope to do*, would be to get them motivated enough that they *want to*.

Mrs. Kay suggests that her goal is to help low achievers become more motivated and hence self-directed, like the high achievers. These comments also show that she feels it is her responsibility to help the low achievers achieve.

A number of strategies were observed in Mrs. Kay's classroom that diminished comparisons of ability among the students. Any sequencing of material was not made evident to observers, except in the use of the titles of the basal readers—and even in this case, no comments were made publically or privately about the levels of the readers or of the instructional groups. References to family-group names were more frequent than to ability-based groups. Mrs. Kay frequently assigned tasks that required divergent processes, such as creative writing, "decision-making lessons," and even math lessons in which students could arrive at the correct answer in different ways. These strategies widened the opportunities for student participation, student responsiveness to each other, and student success. In math, for example, Mrs. Kay asked students, "When do you estimate?" thus encouraging them to share their reasoning. In her attention to the methods that students used to solve math problems, she asked, "What is one way of doing it?" and then "What is a better way?" A student spontaneously shared what he noticed about the book, and Mrs. Kay responded: "Oh, very good. Good! Joe noticed something in the book. He noticed a good way to check it [which she went on to describe]. Great. I like to see that kind of stuff." To another student, who was working on the addition of decimals: "David, I'm proud of you. You heard moans and went on and did your own thinking. I thought I was gonna get you." In another lesson, Mrs. Kay asks, "Does someone else have a different opinion? Can you convince Melanie?"

Finally, Mrs. Kay conveyed to students that the purpose of the work is to learn, and that learning is both challenging and fun. She frequently begins lessons with "I have a fantastic thing for you to do" or "I have a challenge for you." She encouraged the children to think: "Thinking, that's what's important. Everyone be thinking. Gonna get you next." Her expectations of the students were that they would do work of high quality, not simply that they would get the work done: "You can whip through it and say 'I'm done.' [But] I want quality, creativity. And I wouldn't mind decent spelling."

Judging and Evaluating Ability

A Ceiling on Student Ability: Mrs. Iver

What beliefs did Mrs. Iver hold about the capability of her students, beliefs that guided her strategies for nurturing and assessing student performance? On the one hand, in an interview, Mrs. Iver acknowledged that ability is what you see: "It is in the eye of the beholder, the teacher that has been working with him [the student]. The teacher [last year's] said they were such geniuses . . . And Thomas, he had no writing skills." She also expressed the belief that teaching practices can influence what you "get" with regard to achievement—that is, that ability is partially malleable. She noted, "When kids had better work habits . . . I did [individualizing] in spelling, reading, and math and found no problems with it at all. And found that test scores at the end of the year were totally different from test scores where kids were kept in groups . . . You had a bigger spread."

Yet on the other hand, Mrs. Iver saw limits in the malleability of achievement, particularly for low performers. She went on to say, "When you did a semi-individualized reading program or math or all three, what you got was . . . a really spread-out distribution from the middle up. You still had some low children. If the brains aren't there, they aren't there. But you didn't have these knotted groups." Here she emphasized that ability is inborn and fixed at birth, thereby providing limits on capability. The malleability she perceived applied primarily to children in the middle group and beyond. Similarly, by saying "I'm not going to stick [a certain student] . . . in the top group when he is a retention," she reaffirmed the fixed nature of ability. A student who has been retained is not likely, in her view, to become a high achiever. Mrs. Iver's vision of the distribution of ability in her classroom suggested a normal curve, however, with relatively few distinctions made among the lows and many more distinctions made among the middles and the highs.

Given Mrs. Iver's perceptions of the limited malleability of intelligence, particularly at the lower end of the distribution, she was not likely to describe herself as someone who takes responsibility for improving student performance. This was evident earlier when she emphasized that the burden lay on the student to keep pace with the instructional groups. This was also evident in her description of a low achiever with a serious reading problem. She notes, "He [Donald] is a child that has been held back, retained. He should be in sixth-grade. He doesn't say much but probably resents it . . . He's really a very nice child. When you talk to him, he's extremely polite; he has an exceptionally good vocabulary. His oral vocabulary is fine. He can't write it . . . A really pleasant child but just sort of spinning his wheels. But he does have the reading disability that is serious." And what of his future prognosis? Mrs. Iver responded, "I think he'll survive . . . He just feels very low about himself, and I think that's unfortunate. But I think when he gets into the more adult world and finds his niche, finds really something that's interesting, he may find redoing cars, or mechanical drawing, or something of interest. Once he finds that, I think you will see a difference in Donald." Although deeply concerned about this child, Mrs. Iver viewed his problem as a result of fixed attributes that she could not affect much. Improvements fell largely on the shoulders of students, on programs such as "a special learning problem class," and on the future world of work, where she hoped this student would find his "niche."

Classroom observations revealed frequent public revelation of students' errors and poor performance as well as great differences in expectations. In a math lesson, Mrs. Iver routinely and publically announced how individual children performed. To one student, she said: "You did very well. Practice two rows." To another student, she noted: "You did all right. You did better but you made some mistakes." On another occasion, in the oral correction of math problems while answers were being read aloud, Mrs. Iver asked, "How many people made mistakes? Be honest with yourself and me." The children did not raise their hands, but Mrs. Iver added, "I've got one here who got the whole row wrong." With students from the lower groups, Mrs. Iver was likely to note publically, "You are behind." She also differentiated among both high-performing and low-performing students in her comments to the observer. She noted: "This is what I mean by top students who don't read directions," and at the close of one session with the lowest reading group she remarked aloud, "Now do you see why this is the lowest group?"

High expectations were primarily expressed for students in the higher-level groups who were told to read "semi-adult books" and advised that poor behavior and performance were not expected from them. Mrs. Iver said, "I don't expect you people in the top group to get low grades in spelling" and "I don't expect that [inattention] out of you guys." When Mrs. Iver corrected children for their failure to respond successfully, she sometimes focused on their ability—urging them to use it *if* they had it. For example, Mrs. Iver commented, "Some people have the brains to do it without being told. I don't think you are without brain power." On other occasions her attributions for poor performance targeted what she perceived as malleable factors such as work habits and drive (which she described low achievers as lacking), as well as immaturity. She urged students from her mid-level reading group to "work faster so you can get out of that book. You are in it because you have good work habits." She also said to this group: "Do you realize how immature you are acting now? You people are hard to work with because you get babyish. You have been in fifth grade the past six months now. Not one of you sitting here who doesn't have the brain power to be in the other [top] group. You act as if this is play school."

Student Ability as Malleable: Mrs. Kay

In contrast, Mrs. Kay stated her belief that many of the low achievers are indeed very capable: "They really have ability, and they're just putting a lamp shade over it . . . because I know it's there and they'll do it *sometimes,* but not consistent[ly] enough that they're finding the joy because they have enough skills." As noted earlier, she said that her role is "to get them motivated enough that they *want* to achieve." Mrs. Kay appeared to hold an incremental theory of intelligence—that is, that intelligence can be augmented with experience. She argued that children's achievement is subject to improvement with direction, feedback, and help from the teacher and peers. She suggests, "If they could get over that hump . . . The lower achievers who I feel maybe don't have as much potential as some of the others—I mean they are working, but they have a lot of difficulty, it really is just direction. I've got to teach and I've got to say 'It's due today. Let's go over it' and be much more controlled." The "we" in her next comment includes high and low achievers: "I also feel that you don't improve if you're never given suggestions . . . It just means that we can always improve." Nowhere in the interviews did Mrs. Kay describe ability as distributed along a normal curve in her classroom, although she did make distinctions among low achievers "who have potential," low achievers "who don't have as much potential," and high achievers who "don't act smart." Mrs. Kay held very differentiated beliefs about children's strengths and weaknesses, reflective of a multidimensional rather than unidimensional view of ability. Both high and low achievers were described in terms of capability, work habits, and personality. With regard to one low achiever, she talked about his strengths, saying, "He is working a lot harder, [he] questions more . . . He is really an approachable student."

Classroom observations revealed few public evaluations of students, and especially few mentions of poor performance. Mrs. Kay conveyed a positive view of errors as informative for learning and remediable with help. She communicated very positive expectations for all children with a focus on "capability," and attributed student success to effort and student failure to the difficulty of the task, such as a tough book or a tricky test. Mrs. Kay also gave students choices about how much public board work they wanted or felt they needed in math: "Raise your hand if you want one done on the board." Students were given cards to hold up their answers in math (for the teachers' eyes only) and were asked to "put up a zero if you are lost." Mrs. Kay frequently probed student responses until a student successfully arrived at the answer. After probing the responses of one student, Mrs. Kay said, "Very good, if you are unsure, we'll go over it after." In these ways, she both increased the chances that children would respond with the right answer, and, if they had difficulty, gave the children some control over how public their responses would be.

Mrs. Kay also used a lot of positive feedback directed to the class, groups, families, and individuals. She commented, for example, that "All of you did really well on that last homework, we'll be doing more." To one student, she said, "This is right. This is good. This part is right, but not the addition and multiplication. Danny, you did the hard part—the important part right." She held individual conferences with children regarding contract work and she gave feedback privately. Much of the feedback given by Mrs. Kay focused on effort; for example, she said, "I want to compliment you [on how you worked] during spelling." The word "ability" rarely came up in this classroom except in our discussion about "smartness." Mrs. Kay explained that different people have different opinions about who is the smartest in the class and about what smartness means. She gave an example of a person with good grades who "doesn't act smart." In reading the classroom narrative records, it is impossible to distinguish between high and low groups or between high and low achievers on the basis of teacher expectations or feedback. Also of interest is that there were virtually no interruptions from other students during group work.

Mrs. Kay did make some public revelations of individual performance, however: there were times when she announced the good scores in math and spelling. This reflected her use of a point system for families, based on how many children within families passed the tests: if every member passed one test, the family was awarded twenty-five points; if they passed two tests, fifty points, and so on. In addition to noting family success, she also high-lighted individual accomplishment, as in these three examples:

Correcting papers [math] at lunch was a pleasure. As you can see [on the wall], there are many names added to the [pass] list.

Compliments to these individuals [naming them]. Superstars. Lots of you were close. I think you know the answers. Some in your family passed all four. So your family has someone to be a teacher and helper . . . Let's give them a big hand [a T-shirt with "math champ" to the students who passed all four tests].

[To the Golden Unicorns:] Got lots of points. Compliments on your spelling scores. A lot better. One family has fifteen points, none with twenty-five. Bookmark awards for those [individuals] who had 100 percent on the spelling. Lots of people got awards. You may want to hold your applause for the end. Then you can clap for your family . . . I'd like to conference with a few of you. For some, spelling is the hardest subject. Your families are going to help you.

Perhaps any negative effects of these public displays were compensated for by Mrs. Kay's focus on potential ("lots of you were close"), on improvement from last time, on respect for individual differences in children ("for some, spelling is the hardest subject"), and on help available from families. Mrs. Kay cautioned children "not to put someone down because they didn't pass the test but say 'Let me help.'"

Mrs. Kay also reframed the meaning of errors for her students. She noted that errors can inform us about what went wrong in the thinking process, that everyone makes errors, including the book and the teacher, that we must make note of errors so that we know where to study extra hard, and that help can make a difference. Such reframing of errors is seen in these responses by Mrs. Kay during a math lesson:

If you make a mistake, it's OK. Don't change it. 'Cause we can figure out what went wrong. You'll catch me some day.

Wait, I'm doing heavy thinking [Mrs. Kay is working on the problem]. I'm in trouble. Any one else, like I am, with a problem you can't solve?

If you made a mistake, write it correctly so you know which ones to study.

If you make mistakes, don't worry. This is the first day. Book goes fast. Faster than the book before. So we have to work extra hard. And use the time wisely.

This ditto is more of what we just did [in math]. Just put in the signs. First work by yourself. If you think it's right but you're not sure, put a question mark. Get someone in your family to go over it later with you.

As noted earlier, Mrs. Kay used a lot of divergent tasks in which there was no possibility of errors, and she asked divergent-style questions about problem solving in tasks with right and wrong answers: "No one else can help you. Cause there's no right or wrong answer. Don't answer [what you would do] now. Just think. What will happen? What else might you do and what will happen? There're lots of choices. No one else can tell you what to do. Don't worry about spelling. You'll be graded for ideas. I'm interested in what you say."

Motivational Strategies

Learning for Status: Mrs. Iver

Mrs. Iver's description of effective teaching strategies for high achievers underscores the performance aspect of learning in her classroom rather than learning for learning's sake. Mrs. Iver said: "I think all high achievers want to be challenged. And . . . even though they know they're capable of reading, say at the seventh-grade level, they're proud of that, and they're proud of doing the harder math program, and all sorts of things. It all boils down to wanting to feel that they're known for being a high achiever. They want status. And when they get the status in a way that's . . . [genuine]. You don't lie to them. You don't say, 'You're wonderful' when they know they haven't reached that status of wonderfulness." When asked about low achievers and the kinds of motivational strategies that are effective for them, Mrs. Iver replied: "Oh, I think the same. They don't want it any different than anyone else. They want their lump of sugar and they want their pat on the back." In this focus on performance and the status it brings, Mrs. Iver also communicated the belief that we learn because other teachers will require it later on, not for its own sake: "In junior high, you will be expected to draw faces and bodies, so you may as well break into it now."

Mrs. Iver also used extrinsic rewards to motivate the students. Classroom observers noted frequent references to points gained or lost and to awards given. Two students, for example, received certificates for Outstanding Student of the Month. When the observer asked one of these students what the awards were for, she said she thought they were for improving in something but that she was not sure what she had improved in. Neither competition nor cooperation were particularly highlighted in the classroom interactions observed. But the pressure to keep up with group placement, the value placed on the highest groups, and the threats of demotion created a competitive atmosphere.

Learning for Process and Challenge: Mrs. Kay

As noted earlier, Mrs. Kay focused on the processes of learning (such as find-ing ways to solve problems or making note of errors that tell about unsuc-cessful strategies of thinking) and of the challenge inherent in learning. She prefaced many lessons with this question: "Ready for a challenge before we go on?" Thus, Mrs. Kay encouraged motivational goals related to task mas-tery, rather than performance goals focused on how students are doing rela-tive to others. By appealing to children's interests in being paired for science projects, she also encouraged intrinsic motivation.

Mrs. Kay used extrinsic motivators to engage her students with points and awards. In contrast to Mrs. Iver, however, she introduced cooperative goals into her point system—that is, the entire "family" was to take responsibility for the learning of its members. These heterogeneously grouped families, which must help each member succeed, compete against each other or against the teacher: "Let's see which family can clear off desks and get out math homework." Students hurried to clear off desks and were given beads as points. Mrs. Kay described changing the composition of these families from time to time ("to inspire good work") and also changing table place-ment—at which point, she wiped the family point slate clean. With the change of family table placement, she remarked: "Clear off your points [from the board] and start fresh. You want a fresh start, now that we're changing." These strategies enabled the mixing of children within the class-room and the potential to start over and improve. Mrs. Kay's focus on the process of learning and the importance of help make that potential to im-prove a real—not imagined—possibility. The competition between groups, too, pits groups of equal status against each other and against a tricky teacher or challenging book: "Now what if I did this [in an apostrophe les-son]? To see if I could trick you. You know how sneaky I am." This teaching strategy fosters fairer competition and encourages help-giving as well as help-seeking.

The Development of Student Agency

Teacher as Director: Mrs. Iver

In her interview, Mrs. Iver said that she let students choose, in part, the proj-ects they worked on and the students with whom they collaborated. Class-room observers noted that students were indeed given such choices. When the teacher was working with one instructional group on a given subject, other students could choose which assignment they might work on.

Yet despite this element of choice, classroom interaction was heavily teacher-directed. All eyes were on the teacher for correction of work and for help when needed. Teacher responsibility, rather than student responsibility, was evident in the teacher's tendency to respond for students by reading their answers aloud, completing a problem, or drawing a face. Mrs. Iver was continually interrupted during small-group instruction by other students who needed her to correct their work and answer questions. Indeed, Mrs. Iver invited such interruptions. She told her students, "When you get stuck in math, stop, and I will help you" and "Hand me your math papers. I'll correct them as far as you've gone." This pattern of turning to the teacher was also evident in interactions with members of the top math group. When Lyn said that she didn't have the paper she had been given earlier, Mrs. Iver replied, "You should have come up and gotten another paper from me." Lyn said: "I didn't know I could get another one," and Mrs. Iver responded, "You are either in or out of the top group." Thus, although choice was given to students, tight control was maintained by the teacher, and the students were dependent upon her judgment and help regardless of whether they were high or low achievers.

Teacher as Facilitator: Mrs. Kay

In Mrs. Kay's classroom, children were seen as resources for themselves and for each other. They were given substantial responsibility in the classroom for learning, for evaluating their own work and the work of others, for giving help to other students, and for carrying out a variety of tasks to make the classroom a community. In assigning students to work with partners in a math strategy game (a cooperative task), Mrs. Kay asked the children to decide on the rules. She responded with delight to their ideas: "That would be a variation. You can make up your own games." Or she invited students to create their own math problems: "If you want to make up your own problems [for homework], OK. I'll help you." Mrs. Kay noted that her students ask for a study hall period: "That's the chance for kids to do back work if they were absent or didn't understand—they can see me. If the kids were caught up, that's the time they can do games or their own projects . . . Like I'll take an hour and a half to teach, then they have an hour and a half to do the assignments in whatever order they feel they want to."

When families were rearranged and placed at different tables, Mrs. Kay encouraged students to make decisions together: "It's your choice where you sit and how you arrange yourselves. Your family has to decide the best way to arrange it. I'll give you 'til nine o'clock to arrange yourselves. The captains don't pick where members sit. It's up to the family. They're not bosses, just helpers." Mrs. Kay told the observer that she is surprised students don't necessarily sit with their buddies.

Mrs. Kay also encouraged students to take a role in evaluating their own work, not only for its correctness but also for goals reached. In going over math homework, Mrs. Kay asked students, "If I say X, are you gonna know whether it's right or wrong?" She also said: "This way, to do the answer. Do you agree? Do some disagree? Know what the book is trying to do. Trick you too?" When assigning contracts to students, Mrs. Kay said, "I give a cover sheet where I do my grading and I ask them to grade themselves first. And I put each part, the vocabulary, the character analysis, or whatever part is included in the contract. I have three boxes that say 'Very Good,' 'OK' (or 'Satisfactory'), and 'Needs Improvement.' I also include handwriting, organization, neatness, and so forth. And then I have them check themselves because I like to see how they see it."

Mrs. Kay cautioned that in self-evaluation there is the potential for disagreement between the teacher and the student. She acknowledged, "A lot of times we agree, and there are times we don't . . . When they grade themselves higher, then I try to watch the way I comment, like 'It's really good, but you might work on . . . ,' so if a student says it was superior or excellent and I feel it's satisfactory, I don't want to crush them and I don't want the joy to go out. But I won't change my grade, because I think I have to be honest . . . I understand that it is a part of them, but I also feel that you don't improve if you're never given suggestions. And it doesn't mean that it's bad or awful. It just means that we can always improve. So I really feel that it's important that I put in my two cents. I feel like that's why I'm here." When a student informed Mrs. Kay that a peer (Barbara) had just changed her answer in math, she replied: "That's fine. If you have a correcting pencil, I want you to correct it. I hope you are doing it in a way you know you're correcting it. Make notes to yourself."

By giving these responsibilities to students, Mrs. Kay tried to motivate them to take pride in their work: "I know you have beautiful handwriting when you want. Let me ask you, are you proud of it? I want you to be proud of it. Don't turn it in unless you're proud of it in the first place." In assigning classroom responsibilities, Mrs. Kay described trying different strategies. She might ask for volunteers and for ideas from the students: "What things do you think need to be done in this room? Because it's our room. You know we all live here." At other times, she assigned responsibilities to families: "This family will take this part of the room." Classroom observers noted two students emptying the wastepaper basket, one student erasing one board, and another erasing another board. Students were also dismissed to lunch by the students in charge of each family.

Classroom Climate

Labels and Threats: Mrs. Iver

The relationships in Mrs. Iver's classroom were characterized by the frequent use of labeling and threats—much like we saw earlier with regard to named instructional group assignment, where there were demands to keep up with the group and threats regarding the possibility of downward mobility. This atmosphere of threats is illustrated in this comment by Mrs. Iver to a student: "Either you are going to read or you won't be in the group." To another student who shows a visible red-faced reaction, Mrs. Iver says, "Ilan, I'm not going to argue with you. I will take you out of the top group. You are not my baby in here. You stop fussing. There comes a time when even my patience wears thin." Mrs. Iver often labeled students babies: "I've got the biggest bunch of babies in here I've ever seen." And sometimes children were described as social misfits, as in this exchange: "Kobie, get to your own seat please. If you can't sit with society, leave . . . We have people who don't know how to get along socially in this room."

In another example, Mrs. Iver complained to the observer about a student being hyperactive. This time, a student joined in the labeling and replied that "We could call him 'hyper.'" On another occasion, fellow students mirrored Mrs. Iver's negative tone when a student, Kevin, who was working at the board on a math lesson, was unable to solve a math problem. Mrs. Iver asked: "How many parts if half? That's where you have trouble." One child snickered when Kevin could not answer, and Mrs. Iver replied, "I'm not putting you on the spot to laugh at you." Nothing was said to the students, however, about the inappropriateness of laughing at someone's failure.

Many such negative exchanges occurred in public and they involved putdowns of a student who was performing poorly or misbehaving. Although

Mrs. Iver frequently called students "sweetie," her tone, the content of what she said, and her actions were at times demeaning. To a student who had said "shut up" to another child, Mrs. Iver responded: "What is your problem? Somebody has to grow up in this room. Are you going to stay the baby?" To a student who failed to understand the instructions, she responded: "Do you understand English when it is spoken to you? What did I say?"

Parents (particularly mothers) were mentioned as threatening authorities who could be called to take students home: "Melissa, don't talk to Rachel. I've already talked to your mother, and I will again, but I don't want to be a tattletale." Similarly, to another student, Mrs. Iver said: "If I see you doing anything else but math, I will call your mother at ten o'clock and she can come get you." This negative tone was also illustrated by Mrs. Iver's refusal to hold a Valentine's Day party for the students. When a student asked, "Are we having a Valentine party?" Mrs. Iver replied, "No. When I have to spend forty-five minutes cleaning up after the Christmas party, I don't have a party."

Individuality and Community: Mrs. Kay

In contrast, the relationship between Mrs. Kay and her students was filled with trust, respect, dignity, and humor. In the following quotation, she described a student with a learning disability who learned to face his areas of weakness. She referred to the implicit trust between them:

> His key to success is attitude, because he was going through a period of not wanting to admit that he was having difficulties, especially when there were other students around. So he wouldn't question. He would cover up through "Oh, this is easy," when you know it isn't. But he didn't ever want to ask a question that showed any weakness. He went overboard to show that he didn't need help. Although he's gotten over that . . . When he's doing his thing [admitting avoiding his areas of weakness] and you call him up and say "Seth." He says "I know." [Laughter.] Which is really neat, you know. If you can't have that going, you don't have much going, you know.

Mrs. Kay frequently peppered her requests and responses with appreciation, options, and humor. She said: "Raise your hands if you think you'll be ready in three minutes. How many need longer? Thank you for waiting patiently." On another occasion, she stressed, "I appreciate how some are so quiet and waiting for others to finish." Mrs. Kay's demands for student attention were laced with humor and explanation, as she noted: "I know I'm beautiful, but your eyes belong on the book, not on me" and "More than one person is talking. I'm not talented enough to listen to more than one at once." Even when angry, she was respectful, humorous, and upbeat, as seen in this comment to the class: "Wait folks. I'm going to start again. What is the best way to get the answer? Close your mouth and keep up. I'll start again." Humorously, she commented, "Better watch out or I may strangle Noah. Get your book. Open your book. Do numbers 11, 12. Get your brain started. Don't moan and talk. You're going to think."

There was also evidence of positive parent involvement in the class. As one example, a parent came to the class to explain the Chinese calendar and Chinese animal symbols for years, and to bring a snack to share with the students. Mrs. Kay followed this lesson with a related assignment involving a chart of animal year signs. By chance, a student whose dog had followed her to school that day asked if, just for one day, the dog could stay. Mrs. Kay replied: "I'm not encouraging you to have pets here. We don't need fifteen pets. But the dog seems quiet. So we'll just get along." She then used the dog and its owner in the lesson, exploring the characteristics of this dog that could help the students think about the Year of the Dog. Mrs. Kay also complimented the visiting parent's presentation of the Chinese calendar with these words, "It is fun the way your mom told us." She called on students to turn to Rebecca as a resource by noting that "Any trouble over here, you have Rebecca to help you—her mom gave the lesson." In this example, Mrs. Kay validated two students and helped build a sense of community around learning about the Chinese New Year.

There was also talk about the class interacting with other classes, participating in school-wide-events, and taking field trips. Students were planning for a schoolwide assembly—a "jogathon" to raise money for charity—and they were collaborating with another class in this effort. Mrs. Kay announced, "Two weeks to get ready. Help! Help! I'll talk to these helpers and to Alice's father [who is helping us]." The boundaries of this classroom and the opportunities for relationships were thus able to expand to include parents, other classes, and the outside world.

Lessons Learned

Implicit Theories Matter

The differences in the classroom achievement culture created by these two fifth-grade teachers are consistent with the perceptions reported by elementary school children. Further, this look at what teachers believe and what observers see inside classrooms extends our understanding of the complex and interactive relationship between the implicit theories of teachers (and the educational system) and the practices that flow from these conceptions. Were we simply seeing more or less differential treatment by teachers? Clearly, these classrooms did differ in the frequency of differential treatment of high and low achievers and in the use of practices that heightened ability comparisons among students. But deeper still, very different educational theories gave rise to radically different achievement cultures in each classroom. While these particular classrooms reflect the extremes of this variation, the profiles nonetheless make clear that there are choices to be made about how we educate children with varying levels of "achieved" performance, however defined—and that these choices have interactive effects, thereby creating a classroom culture.

There are many ways to conceptualize the tasks of classroom teaching. As Philip Jackson (1968) noted, "The complexity of the teacher's work extends beyond the fact that he is concerned with a complex organism, working toward complex goals, in a complex setting. He is also, in most instances, working with a group of students" (p. 161). It is this work with what Jackson calls a "crowd" of children, each with distinct attributes and needs—work performed in the context of intense societal expectations and accountability—that makes classroom teaching uniquely challenging. Formally, children must master a wide array of academic material, and informally, children must learn how to interact appropriately as students with peers and with an authority figure: the teacher. To make this learning possible, teachers must create a classroom culture that engages students in their academic work, that evaluates the products of their work, and that provides resources to aid the completion of their work, all while managing behavior (Doyle 1983).

It is important to underscore that both teachers highlighted here worked hard to do the best for their students. Their practices, however, were guided by different implicit theories (see Sternberg 2000) about intelligence, motivation, subject-matter knowledge, assessment, and classroom management. In broad strokes, there have been two major traditions with regard to our thinking about educational growth and its measurement. As Larry Nucci and Herbert Walberg (1981) point out, these traditions were "anticipated" by the differing views of Plato ("teacher as the 'midwife of ideas'") and Aristotle ("learning as the association of discrete ideas")—and they reflect "the structuring, integration, and stage-wise transformation of knowledge [versus] the accumulation of discrete elements . . . the steady amassing of knowledge" (p. 202). Philip Jackson (1986) calls these differing views the transformative and mimetic traditions of instruction. Transformative approaches engage students in co-constructing knowledge through inquiry and participation, whereas mimetic approaches transmit knowledge and skills from teachers to students. Embedded within these traditions are different views of curriculum, motivation, and so on. But these layers of theories are not always aligned. As Mary McCaslin and Thomas Good (1992) have persuasively argued, in many classrooms a social-constructivist academic curriculum coexists with a behavioral classroom management approach, a condition that calls for "compliant cognition" from the students. Of these differing traditions, McCaslin and Good (1996a) go on to suggest that "teachers likely do both; the issue is one of proportion, and within that, quality" (p. 627).

A Selection-Driven Achievement Culture

Mrs. Iver's overall teaching philosophy leaned toward a mimetic approach; instruction was largely teacher-directed and focused on transmitting knowledge. Her concerns about the futility of overreaching children's readiness levels suggested a sequential subject-matter theory whereby higher-order learning was seen to rest upon the mastery of lower-order skills (Stodolsky 1995). She espoused a behavioral theory of classroom management based on teacher-directed rewards and punishments (McCaslin and Good 1992). She also characterized children's ability (particularly for the low performers) as a fixed and inherited attribute that was not changeable with experience; she was an "entity" theorist (Dweck 2000).

In addition, Mrs. Iver perceived intelligence as a global factor (a G [general factor] theory that includes verbal and spatial abilities) and as distributed within a population along a normal curve of above-average, average, and below-average performance (Vernon 1971). The motivational goals that Mrs. Iver adopted for her students have been described as performance goals that focus attention on how the student is doing rather than on what the student is doing (Ames 1992). Performance goals evoke the ego, elevate the role of social comparisons, and have greater potential to threaten self-worth, whereas learning goals fuel a sense of challenge and sustained immersion in an activity (Covington 1992; Csikszentmihalyi 1990; Nicholls 1989).

Given these theories, Mrs. Iver's teaching practices reflected greater curricular differentiation and ability grouping, narrowly defined performance opportunities, and performance-oriented and competitive motivational goals. She did, however, use several strategies to minimize the salience of ability differences among students. These included potential and actual movement between instructional groups, student choice of tasks, and task variety within a teaching period. Yet on balance, there were many more practices that heightened ability differences. In particular, she used labeling and differential expectations, a stratified curriculum with group-based instructional strategies, movement among groups limited to certain time periods (opportunities arose only every three months), pressure to keep up with the group without teacher assistance, and the public display of errors and poor performance. The relationships among the teacher, students, peers, and parents appeared primarily negative both for high and for low achievers, involving threats and put-downs, and pressure was particularly great for high achievers to keep their status.

These views about the nature of teaching and learning, which prevail in the United States today, shape low, narrow, differential, and largely fixed expectations for children's academic performance. The focus is on differentiating among high, middle, and low achievers and between age-grade groups. Differentiation is aided by the belief that errors reflect the failure of individuals rather than provide diagnostic information about how children learn, that the time taken to solve a problem or learn a skill indicates ability rather than different developmental trajectories, and that failures in learning illustrate the limits of the student's cognitive ability rather than the teacher's failure to instruct. When academic expectations are focused on differentiation, attention is directed toward practices that select rather than develop talent. Teaching practices and policies focus on identifying and distinguishing among students and on setting expectations about types of students rather than creating common expectations for all. In addition, developmental expectations lead to the setting of ceilings, above which children should not reach, and lock-step subject-matter expectations restrict exposure to the curriculum. In particular, children are not offered (1) interpretive questions until they have mastered decoding skills, (2) mathematical problem-solving strategies until they have successfully learned math facts, and (3) creative writing assignments until they have mastered grammar. In this worldview, remediation becomes the repetitive teaching of lower-order skills rather than the introduction of more varied and alternative methods for moving students ahead to the study of higher-order skills.

A Development-Driven Achievement Culture

In contrast, Mrs. Kay viewed intelligence as malleable through instruction; she held an "incremental" theory of ability (Dweck 2000). She also believed that intelligence was multidimensional rather than global in nature. This was reflected in her emphasis on interpersonal relationships, problem-solving, and creativity such as in her art lesson. While school tasks largely focus on linguistic and logical or mathematical abilities (note the characteristics of both learning activities and assessment tools), more recent theories of intelligence critique the narrowness of this view, which leaves out many critical and unrecognized abilities such as the analytic, creative, and practical intelligences emphasized by Robert Sternberg (1999), and the musical, spatial, kinesthetic, and intra- and interpersonal intelligences described by Howard Gardner (1983). Mrs. Kay also focused more attention on absolute—that is, criterion-referenced—standards rather than normative comparisons, so that success was possible for all (Goodlad and Keating 1994). She emphasized native curiosity and the interests of each child in stimulating motivation and improving performance (Covington 1999; Csikszentmihalyi, Rathunde, and Whalen 1993).

Mrs. Kay highlighted task-mastery goals, targeting challenge and the strategies used to solve problems, and cooperative rather than competitive approaches to problem-solving (Ames 1992; Aronson 1978; Slavin 1983). Her beliefs and strategies recognized the limitations of rigid developmental-stage theories about learning: she believed that more learning is possible given support and additional time when needed (Bloom 1976). Her approach to teaching was largely transformative. She believed that knowledge was socially constructed in complex interactions between the teacher, the student, and the material. Her task was not only to meet children where they were, but also to extend their cognitive reach by providing the essential scaffolding to help them learn (Brown 1997; Vygotsky 1978). Her theory of subject-matter learning emphasized the teaching of higher-order skills (such as critical analysis of quality literature, mathematical problem solving, and writing) concurrently with instruction of decoding skills, math facts, and grammar. Mrs. Kay also worked hard to develop child agency, self-reflection, and self-regulation as the critical components of a classroom management program and as the means to overcoming obstacles encountered in learning (Corno 1993; Corno and Rohrkemper 1986).

Mrs. Kay focused on the challenges and processes of learning, rather than on performance. She targeted the importance of help and feedback in shaping improvement. Her teaching strategies reflected high curricular demands for all students, flexible and interest-based grouping, varied methods and multidimensional performance opportunities, and student agency. The cooperative and inclusive climate she created in the classroom, in schoolwide activities, and with parents featured trust, humor, responsiveness to individuality, and the nurturing of community. Although she used ability-based instructional grouping in reading and in math, some differentiation of curriculum and teaching strategies, classroom competition, and public display of good performance—all practices that heighten comparisons among children—she counteracted potential negative effects with her grouping and instructional strategies. Mrs. Kay introduced flexibility in her grouping by grouping later in the year, by regrouping (moving children up and down), and by changing the number of groups. These groups were not identifiable by labels or by differential expectations and further, the effects of ability grouping were counteracted by children's membership in heterogeneously grouped seating and work-group families that were occasionally regrouped to provide more opportunities for mixing among students. This worldview raises and broadens academic expectations, moving away from differentiated instruction that places ceilings on learning and labels on the learners, toward greater variety of teaching strategies but common expectations for all. In contrast to the emphasis on appraising ability and sorting children, here the *development* of student ability is taken seriously—and most importantly, the teacher takes responsibility for helping children keep up and move up.

Teacher Accountability

These differing beliefs about students' capacity to learn have enormous implications for how teachers perceive and handle individual differences among students and for the role that teachers are likely to take in educating children. Will they hold themselves accountable for student outcomes? Will they develop a sense of efficacy that the efforts they make will bring about the desired outcomes (Ashton and Webb 1986; Bandura 2001)?

For Mrs. Iver, there were vast differences in what she expected from high achievers ("I don't expect you people in the top group to get low grades in spelling") and low achievers ("They'll be lucky to get through the basic series"). Further, low achievers were not viewed as likely to show much academic growth, and a child who had been retained was not expected to make it to the top group. She saw little that she could do to teach one of her students who had a learning disability: as we learned earlier, Mrs. Iver believed he needed to find his niche in the adult world, perhaps in redoing cars or in mechanical drawing. Given these beliefs about limits, she avoided holding children accountable for higher-level skills ("If a child can't keep up, I can't put him under pressure"). Her practices appeared to reify student differences; she reinforced ability differences in classroom seating patterns (which were tied to racial or ethnic membership) and neglected to teach children not to laugh at others' behavior. Mrs. Iver believed that she could help those who were already motivated and had good work habits, but that the onus lay with the child, not with the teacher. At the conclusion of the interview, when asked about her wishes for the future, she illustrated her belief that there is little she herself can do to change the achievement of students. Mrs. Iver's plea was for parents to be more involved: "Parents are so busy working nowadays, and I don't think it's anything the parents intend to do. Parents are really so involved in working. They've really lost, between television and work, they've lost a lot of them [children]. When you have a child that's really succeeding, you have a parent that's really interested."

For Mrs. Kay, high and low achievers were not perceived as very different from each other, and both were expected to improve. She provided whole-class spelling lessons because both highs and lows could benefit from it. She described individualizing the lessons by meeting with children one-on-one and picking up the pace so she could "catch the few kids up." She believed that low achievers had the necessary ability—her goal was to help them become more motivated and self-directed. She described herself as holding a child with a learning disability accountable when he avoided working on his areas of weakness, but in the context of a trusting relationship. The narrative records also documented that Mrs. Kay taught her class not to put down other children and that she mixed up the "family" groups because she believed that her charges could all learn from and help each other.

Mrs. Kay truly believed that she could make a difference in the learning of both low and high achievers. Feedback, suggestions, and efforts to individualize instruction could move students along and improve their performance—regardless of their starting point. Her concluding wish was illustrative of her high sense of personal accountability. Mrs. Kay wished for greater sharing among teachers as an opportunity for her own development: "That's what I think is really lacking in this school, a real chance to share, and to observe, and to see, because I betcha there's a teacher in this school right now doing something that would really help me out, but I never get to see it. Once you get in your little box you just struggle along all by yourself. That's really true for most teachers. Teaching is a very private thing."

What is it like for children to live as students in these two very different types of classroom achievement cultures? The next chapter examines their experiences.

CHAPTER 6

Children's Lives in Contrasting Classrooms

Not much they [the low achievers] can do.

—A fourth-grader

They [the low achievers] can go up an' up!

—A fourth-grader

That children are aware of patterns of differential treatment favoring high over low achievers and that children report variation among classrooms in such differentiation have helped us identify markedly different classroom achievement cultures. At one extreme, a classroom culture will emphasize the sorting of children for different educational pathways; at the other, the talents of all children will be guided toward a common educational pathway. Yet most classroom cultures fall along a continuum between these two extremes—a continuum where all teachers will recognize some of the instructional choices they have made. These differences in classroom culture are shaped, in part, by the kinds of beliefs that teachers hold about intellectual ability and about how best to nurture it, and by the policies and practices that teachers choose to instruct as well as manage their students. Indeed, as we shall see later, the beliefs, practices, and policies of a Mrs. Iver are more likely to be reinforced by schools as they are currently constituted and by the values and policies of our broader society. But what is it like for children to learn and live in such disparate achievement cultures, not only over the course of a school year but ultimately for an entire school career?

In this chapter, I turn to an examination of quantitative as well as qualitative data about the perceptions and the behaviors of children who live in these two disparate classroom cultures—with a particular interest in children who find themselves at the top or bottom of the classroom achievement hierarchy. From our interview study with a stratified sample of 133 fourth graders from sixteen urban classrooms, I look in-depth at the reasoning of four typical students. These children come from classrooms that all students ranked as high or low in degree of differential treatment on the Teacher Treatment Inventory. They also had been ranked by their teachers as in the top or bottom of the class with regard to their expected achievement at the end of the school year. Coming as they do from classrooms that vary in the emphasis placed on ability differences among students and representing both the highest and the lowest achievers (as perceived), how do these children differ in their understanding about smartness in school, and in their educational hopes and dreams?

Kiaisha and Kevin are students in a classroom very much like that run by Mrs. Iver, and Robert and Thurmond come from a classroom like that of Mrs. Kay (all of these names are pseudonyms). Although these fourth graders belong to different classrooms than the ones we visited in the previous chapter, they were chosen on the basis of the same student-identified criteria and speak to comparable processes of accentuated or minimized differentiation among students. All four students are African American—members of an ethnic-minority group in this country that research has suggested is at greater risk for lower academic expectations and is more often placed in lower-ability instructional groups and tracks. But highlighted here is the effect of relative placement within the classroom achievement hierarchy, regardless of the level of achievement. It is this relative distinction among those who are more able and those who are less able—as perceived—that may shape school experiences within the classroom achievement culture.

In a Classroom Culture with Differentiated Treatment

Kiaisha: Ranked High

Kiaisha is a fourth-grade student for whom her teacher holds high academic expectations. As Kiaisha describes it, in her classroom, the smart kids find school easy, know their stuff, and are rewarded with special privileges. The "not-so-smart" kids need extra help, behave poorly, and do not try hard enough. Consider, for example, this discussion about a recent field trip that was restricted to the best students:

Interviewer: What do teachers do to make you feel you're doing well?
Kiaisha: Um, tell me to do, um, they take me around on a field trip.

Int: What do you mean they take you on a field trip? They take just the students who are doing well?

Kiaisha: No, um, like we—the teacher had to see, um, who was the best student and write it down and then give it to the office and they went on a camping trip.

Kiaisha also reported that she learns about who the "not-so-smart" kids are by her teacher's responses to them.

Int: What do teachers do that lets students know that they're not doing so well?

Kiaisha: Yell at 'em . . . Um, go sit in the corner (Yeah, they do that) and put your nose to the wall. Oh yeah, and make you write a thousand times.

Int: What do they have to write a thousand times?

Kiaisha: Ummm, like I'll be quiet for the rest of the hour. And I will not disturb the teacher.

For Kiaisha, some kids are just smart and some kids are not, and these differences will likely persist.

Int: If a student is smart in school this year, will that student be smart next year?

Kiaisha: Probably.

Int: Probably, why is that?

Kiaisha: Hmm, because they learned a lot of things this year.

Int: What does it mean to be smart in school? When you call somebody smart, what do you mean by that?

Kiaisha: They know how to do most of their work and sometimes all of it, when it's real hard and um, and when the teacher gives them special work for just them to do.

Int: What kind of special work?

Kiaisha: Some work that the other people don't get to do.

Yet Kiaisha suggests that it is possible to become smart by listening and improving one's behavior.

Int: How does a person get to be smart?

Kiaisha: Listen to the teacher and what she's trying to teach you. And don't make noise when she's talking because it could be something important.

Kiaisha also perceives marked differences in what school is like for smart and "not-so-smart" children and in how they behave in class, noting that smart kids express their superiority. When asked about gender differences in ability and behavior, she replied that smart girls and smart boys "all learn the same thing." She views life in school, and the schoolwork, as easy for the smart kids.

Int: What is school like for students who are smart in school?
Kiaisha: It just makes 'em feel easy.
Int: Makes them feel easy?
Kiaisha: Makes the work look easy because they know it and how to do it and they have the teacher teaching somebody else how to do it and they already know how to do it.
Int: How do smart kids act? What are they like?
Kiaisha: They act like they the smartest person in the classroom . . . They think the other people are dumb because they don't know how to do the problems.

Further, the not-so-smart kids are blamed for their own situation.

Int: What is school like for students that are not so smart in school?
Kiaisha: They get boring [bored].
Int: Tell me a little more about that. What do you mean by that?
Kiaisha: 'Cause, um, they try not to learn anything, then they can't learn so they keep on talking to somebody. And so they wouldn't know how to do it. Do anything but, um, ah, to learn.
Int: And what are not-so-smart kids like?
Kiaisha: Um, they walk around asking and not doing their work—they just keep on talking to other people. Then when it comes time to answer a question they don't know how to do it.

Most tellingly, although Kiaisha expresses the belief that improvement is possible, she sees little that a teacher could do to improve the performance of children who are not doing well in school. When she is asked, "If you were the teacher of the class, what would you do to help students learn?" Kiaisha is far from hopeful that intervention would make a difference in their learning.

Kiaisha: Hmm, to help 'em?
Int: Yeah, to help them learn.
Kiaisha: Hmm, I don't know. I don't know. Cause it seems like there's nothing much they can do.

Int: Nothing much they can do?

Kiaisha: 'Cause they don't listen and it's just their fault.

Int: It's just their fault?

Kiaisha: 'Cause they won't try to listen.

Kevin: Ranked Low

Kevin is a fourth-grade student from the same classroom who is ranked low by his teacher with regard to expected year-end achievement. He shares with Kiaisha a similar view of the different worlds of the smart and the "not-so-smart" students in their classroom. Like Kiaisha, he appears resigned to the fixed nature of low achievement. But he expresses much more emotion about it, perhaps due to his perspective from the bottom of the academic hierarchy. He is neither optimistic nor hopeful about the future of others in his position, and perhaps his own future in school. In terse but poignant language, he describes learning about smartness in his classroom in these ways:

Int: How did you figure that out, how well you'll do in school?

Kevin: The teacher tells you.

Int: The teacher tells you? OK. How else do you know how well you do?

Kevin: The way you act.

Int: The way you act, how's that?

Kevin: By not finishing your contracts.

Int: You mean if you don't finish your contract that lets you know how well you're doing, huh? OK.

Kevin: When the teacher gives you grades.

Int: OK. When the teacher gives you grades. Any other way you know how well you're doing?

Kevin: Hmm . . . by the way she look at you.

Int: How does she look at you?

Kevin: Smiles or she mad at you and kind of grim.

Although Kevin indicates he has been told that a student will be smart if certain steps are followed—that is, if he or she studies more, takes contracts home, and concentrates better—his later comments belie such easy advancement. For one can easily distinguish the smart students from the not-so-smart students (and like Kiaisha, Kevin believes that smart boys and smart girls "got the same brains"), and the distinguishing characteristics are not likely to disappear quickly. The not-so-smart students not only misbe-have; they also talk poorly and ask the wrong questions:

Int: Could you tell the difference between a student who's smart in school and a student who is not so smart? How could you do that?
Kevin: By behavior.
Int: By behavior? How do they behave?
Kevin: Yell a lot in the class, never do their work.
Int: Who's that? Who does that?
Kevin: This boy in my class.
Int: OK. And so you can tell by looking at how they behave in class. Could you tell if they were not in your class? And were just out on the play-ground?
Kevin: Yeah.
Int: How could you tell then?
Kevin: By . . . they cuss a lot and don't say the right words.
Int: The kids who are not so smart?
Kevin: Um hm. And they always get in fights.
Int: Always get in fights? What do you mean they don't say the right words?
Kevin: By not putting their words in correct sentences. Using not too intelli-gent words.
Int: Oh yeah, what do you mean by intelligent words?
Kevin: Like asking words, asking questions that everybody should know.
Int: How do you know that a student is intelligent then? How do you know a student is smart?
Kevin: By his reading, math, English and the way he talk.

It is interesting that when Kevin is asked to define intelligence, he moves beyond his previous answers into the realm of creative activity. In his an-swers, he shares a remarkable sophistication about scholarly discovery.

Int: Intelligent, how do you mean that?
Kevin: Intelligent is like when you know plenty. It's like a professional, like a professor—they call them intelligent . . . Professors that discover things, they call them intelligent.
Int: Why is that? Why do they say they're intelligent?
Kevin: Because they're always finding things that nobody else can ever think of.

In sharp contrast to the activities of inquiry and discovery, for Kevin, smartness in school means finishing one's work fast and getting it right. Implied in his responses is a plea for just a little more time, a little more patience from both his teacher and his parents. But in this classroom culture, the acknowledgment of the need for such help defines that one is not smart.

Int: What does smart mean to your parents, do you think?

Kevin: Smart?

Int: Yes, to be smart. What would they say that means?

Kevin: You have to do your work. You know how to do it in a one-day training.

Int: In one-day training? Why? What does that mean?

Kevin: Like, ah, . . . they say to do math and that they'll be helpin' it and then, ever since then, you never asked them again. And they be correcting the work and it's right. That's it. And then they say "you're very smart."

Kevin directly shared one personal experience with the interviewer, saying, "I was accused of cheating the other day. In my math." He poignantly described this difficult situation when his right answers were not trusted: "It's like . . . man. You're accused of something and you haven't done it—not whether it's right—but you haven't done it. And they accuse you of cheating because you got it all right but you haven't [cheated]."

Kevin saw another, perhaps related, predicament for the smart kids—one in which the trust goes too far—the teacher fails to appreciate that such a student might experience difficulty with learning. He goes on to explain: "Like you say you got a problem and you put it up there and she [the teacher] would think you're just putting on."

Kevin's vision of himself in the role of teacher conveys the importance of help-giving and of caring, and of trying not to hurt the feelings of students.

Int: Imagine right now, pretend that you were the teacher of your class. How would you help students learn in school?

Kevin: By on your own time, helping 'em.

Int: On your own time? Yeah.

Kevin: And after-school. And tell their parents to do a little bit more studying with 'em.

Int: Yeah, you tell their parents that, huh? What else?

Kevin: And . . . help 'em with all their work. And tell 'em how good they're doing. But never try to hurt their feelings.

Kevin notes (as did Kiaisha) that the smart kids make life unpleasant for the not-so-smart kids. The two groups of students experience very different worlds while at school, and the not-so-smart kids seem destined for failure.

Int: How do other kids act with not-so-smart kids?
Kevin: They tease 'em.
Int: Yeah, what do they say?
Kevin: Well, they call 'em dumb. Stupid. Not too bright. Just in general.
Int: They say that?
Kevin: Yeah, and they brag.
Int: What is school like for kids that are smart in school?
Kevin: You really want me to say it?
Int: Yes, sure. I'm really interested in your ideas.
Kevin: Sorta like heaven.
Int: What is school like for students who are "not-so-smart"? What is that like?
Kevin: Boy! [sigh] Not so smart? They feel that they can do better. They don't know how.
Int: They can do what better?
Kevin: Their work and stuff. They don't know how.
Int: But they don't know how. So what is school like for them?
Kevin: Well, actually one of my friends in school is just a bump. Kinda like a bump, like they all like to drop out because they don't know too much. They feel like they don't belong in school. That they don't know.

In a Classroom Culture with Equitable Treatment

Robert: Ranked High

Robert has been ranked by his fourth-grade teacher as likely to perform at the top of his class at the end of the school year. From his description of life in his classroom, the climate appears ripe with the possibility for growth. Students are divided by ability into instructional groups for certain subjects, but Robert describes the group boundaries in this class as fluid. Robert expresses the belief that with effort everyone can move up into "higher quality" groups. Furthermore, even for those students like Robert who are in the advanced group, the teacher expects improvement and provides materials to encourage and challenge them.

Consider, for example, what Robert thinks most helps him figure out how well he's doing in school. He reports group placement as the critical indicator of how well a student is doing, "the group you in, comes first, then the, um, paper; 'cause you know after you get done doing it in your group, then you put it on the desk, teacher corrects it, puts your grade on the paper, an' then it goes to your, uh, report card." The questioning continues.

Int: What do teachers do to make you feel you're doing well?
Robert: Well, they'll just say "You're doin' good . . ." or you know . . . or um . . . or they'll um . . . um [clears throat] or else they'll put you in a higher group an' that makes you feel good when you up in a higher group.
Int: What do teachers do to make you feel you aren't doing well?
Robert: They either holler or scream at you or put you . . . prob'ly in the, put you in the lower group. Or else give you some, uh, uh, lower papers and then by the . . . and by the quality of the work you was in, at first then you could see . . . 'Cause she put you with some lower papers.

According to Robert, the teacher also emphasizes effort and high quality work as informative about performance, beyond the information contained in group placement.

Int: Okay. So you can see that . . . that you're doing not so well because she gives you what? Easier work?
Robert: Hm hm.
Int: That's what you mean by lower papers.
Robert: Like she . . . well see . . . my teacher she says, she don't care what good I do and what group you in, just long as you be doin' something and whatever you do that's good work. Whatever . . . low, high, medium, whatever group you in. That's good work, whatever you doin'.

Underlying Robert's responses are certain beliefs about the malleable and multidimensional nature of smartness. Instead of seeing intelligence as fixed, Robert believes it can change from year to year, depending on student memory and behavior. In addition, ability is measured by things other than performance in classroom activities.

Int: If a student is smart in school this year, will that same student be smart in school next year?

Robert: Well that doesn't have to really be a possibility of that because, um, um, just because he's smart in one grade that don't mean he has to be smart in a different grade. See, if . . . he be in highest group in this grade, he could . . . when he gets to another grade he can be in the lowest group in the class.

Int: Oh yeah? How . . . could that happen?

Robert: Well, uh, just like he can forget, 'cause, see, I was in third grade, and I was doin' . . . I was in the highest group . . . You see now I got up here, I coulda been in the highest group in the class, but see, I forgot about my times tables and I'm in the second highest.

Int: How do you get to be a smart student?

Robert: Well, you just bring up all your homework. Just . . . study it—do it and try your best to do it—all of it. And, um, learn it good an', um, listen to your teacher in school. When she knew she explainin' it to ya, an' then you know, know how to do it.

Smartness, according to Robert, has numerous dimensions, and may vary among different contexts. For example, he distinguishes between school smarts and street smarts:

Int: What does it mean to be smart in school? What does that mean to you?

Robert: Well, means to me, to, uh, be able to do high-quality work. Um, but um, to other people sometimes I'd mean that you just smart in class. But see, sometimes, you can be smart in class but when you get out on the street or somethin' you . . . you dumb.

Int: Yeah? How's that? How could that happen?

Robert: Well you . . . you know what you be doin' in class an' stuff but when you get out on the street, you don't know what to say, um . . . You just don't know what to do when they, um, messin' with you or something.

As Robert depicts it, for his teacher, smartness ("high" work) appears to be a possibility for all children.

Int: What do you think that means to your teacher? Being smart.

Robert: It means that you proud, see, 'cause some your kids'll be able to be in high work. And, um, just movin' up in work. And just gettin' up and up 'til you get into the highest, uh, uh, work.

Since all students in the class have the potential to be smart, smart children are difficult to distinguish on the playground unless they are asked about their grades. There appears to be little connection between smartness and any behavioral characteristic. Indeed, Robert describes children with positive and negative traits among both the smart and the not-so-smart students.

Int: If you met kids in your neighborhood or out on another playground somewhere, can you tell the difference between the kids who do well . . .

Robert: Well you can . . . like you know you can make friends an' say "Well what grade did you get on your report card?" [he laughs] and they'll tell you sometimes.

Int: And then you could tell. Then you could tell how smart they were. Otherwise you couldn't, though, if you didn't know their grades?

Robert: Nope.

Int: You couldn't tell at all?

Robert: Nope.

Int: What are smart kids like?

Robert: Well, they uh . . . some . . . some of 'em have a nice personality. But some of 'em, they very mean. But they got . . . they got high IQ's but they're mean. Some of 'em are mean.

Int: How do [the not-so-smart kids] act?

Robert: Some of 'em act very bad. And some of 'em . . . most of 'em act nice.

Int: Yeah? OK. What . . . can you tell me more about what they're like? Not-so-smart kids are like?

Robert: Yeah, they like to, um, play. Then, . . . you know they like to do it [their work] real fast so they can get another paper and do that one an' do it an' do it. So they can get up there to a high group.

The desire to be in high-level groups and the possibility of both upward and downward mobility inspire the not-so-smart children to work harder, but they also make the smart kids somewhat anxious about dropping to a lower group. In this class, the drive to be smart and the possibility of becoming smart are not without costs.

Int: What is school like for students who are smart in school?

Robert: Well it's happy for them 'cause they know how to do good work and they get real high in the groups. So they don't have to worry. But sometimes you do have to worry about goin' down in group because sometimes you could forget your work what you're doing. An' you know, just go straight down. All the way down to the lowest group.

Int: What is school like for students who are not so smart in school?

Robert: Well, sometimes it can be miserable. But sometimes it can be very fun, too, 'cause you get to do smarter work. But most of the time you just be happy 'bout what you got . . . doin' right now.

Int: Yeah?

Robert: Uh huh.

Int: Most of the kids . . . most of the not-so-smart kids are happy about what they can do?

Robert: Some of 'em are. But see most of 'em wanna get up in to higher groups.

As Robert sees it, there is room for everyone to excel. Consequently, students do not compete for success; rather, they help each other find answers to problems. The teacher's job is to help each student go "up and up."

Int: How do other kids act with, uh, not-so-smart kids?

Robert: Well, they'll help 'em out but like if they doin' somethin' and they don't know how to . . . they'll help 'em out.

Int: Uh huh. That's how they . . . that's how they mainly act with them?

Robert: Uh, huh.

Int: Anything else? Any other way?

Robert: Yeah, they . . . They like to help each other out. Like if there's one who's not-so-smart and one *is* smart, the one that's not-so-smart like to have a friend that's real smart so then . . . if they get in a real tight situation, they can call on they, uh, smart friend to help them out.

When asked what he would do if he were the teacher, Robert's vision was to continue the strategies of his own teacher.

Int: If you were the teacher in your class, what would you do to help students learn?

Robert: Well I'd, um, help 'em out, you know . . . I'd just y'know give 'em . . . see just test 'em out on different papers . . . I'd help 'em in, um, uh, with higher grades. I'd help 'em, um, encourage 'em to, uh, try to do they best . . . they best quality in work.

Int: Would you say something to them?

Robert: I'd say, "Now, here's a paper." Um, an' "I want you to try ta do this paper, and then, if you can do this one, I'll get you a higher paper than this, so you can just do that one too." And then I'd just keep sayin' that, so they can go up an' up.

Thurmond: Ranked Low

The potential for improvement that characterized Robert's description of his classroom is also evident in Thurmond's interview, even though Thurmond is characterized by his teacher as falling at the low end of expected achievement relative to his peers. As we learned from interviewing both Robert and Thurmond, students in this classroom judge their success by the groups in which they work. Since they report movement between groups, the potential for improvement is emphasized. The teacher encourages students to work hard so they can move to higher groups. If students' work slips, they may be put into lower groups. Such emphasis on the level of group placement appears to be stressful for the students, but success is open to all and help is available for those who slip and need review.

Int: You just guessed at how well you think you'll do in school this year. How did you figure that out?
Thurmond: 'Cause the way the teacher taught me. The way she taught me. That's how I know.
Int: The way she taught you? How is this?
Thurmond: Um, she taught me and den, she make me review it over so I won't forget. Then she make me go in another level.
Int: What else does she do to make you feel that you're doing well?
Thurmond: They move me up into a higher group and I had to review it and then she be happy if I get 'em all right. And when I go into another group, she be happy.

To Thurmond, the possibility of "being smart" will likely continue from year to year. But this stability in smartness stems from students' willingness to learn instead of from some innate intelligence.

Int: If a student is smart in school this year, Thurmond, will that same student be smart in school next year?
Thurmond: Yep.
Int: Yeah, why is that?
Thurmond: 'Cause he be learnin'.
Int: Be learning what? Can you tell me more about that?

Thurmond: Be learnin' about math problems, spelling, language, how to read well. How to learn, how to study, how to listen, how to act.

Int: When? When do they learn that?

Thurmond: Um, every Friday, they do math. I mean, every Friday, we do handwriting and she'll, how you improvin' in the handwriting, see if they writing good.

Int: Well, . . . why does that mean that, um, a person will still be smart next year, if they're smart now?

Thurmond: Well, they be knowin' how to do it.

Int: Well, how do you get to be a smart student?

Thurmond: By learnin', listenin', don't act stupid in the class. Don't get up and go to da water an' don't get up and go to da bathroom every five minutes.

Ability-based grouping for instruction causes some tensions in this classroom. Thurmond appears more aware than Robert of the occasional animosity between smart and not-so-smart kids. Nevertheless, poor behavior does not appear to type students as not-so-smart; both groups seem to have their share of misbehaving.

Int: What are smart kids like?

Thurmond: They nice. Some of 'em nice and some, some of 'em mean. Some like to fight and tease people on the low grades they in. Some people teasin' about how they do this better than you and all that.

Int: How do other kids act with not-so-smart kids?

Thurmond: They try to learn sometimes. They wanna learn and all that. They wanna get up inta a higher group. They wanna tease people, who are, who are a lower grouping than them. They wanna fight a lot and fuss a lot.

Thurmond sees the teacher working the same way with smart and not-so-smart kids. The teacher challenges all children in her class and gives them opportunities to move into higher groups. The smart/not-so-smart distinction seems reinforced by the children more than by the teacher.

Int: Ah, how does the teacher work with [the smart kids]?

Thurmond: She help 'em learn more what they learned in the ah third, fourth grade and help 'em learn how to carry an' borrow and if they don't know how to do that, they review it over and over and over, until they get through they brain and mind. Then they get in a other group.

Int: Until they get it through the brain, what? And?

Thurmond: Mind. Den they go on to the other group. Den dey can do der work. If they cain't do dat work, they go back down. They gonna be in the same group, they hafta do it *all* over again.

Int: How does the teacher work with . . . these kids who are not-so-smart?

Thurmond: She—she work wid 'em almost every day. Give 'em practice copy sheets, den they come and they do it over and they get the hand [hang] of it. They move up to a higher group.

Ultimately, all students can be smart; each can make the teacher proud.

Int: What do you think it means to your teacher to be smart in school?

Thurmond: It mean her to be happy about what she doin', be proud of herself.

Int: Oh, you mean for her students to be smart. It means that she can be proud of herself?

Thurmond: And she can be proud of *us.*

Implications for Children's Development

The interviews with these four fourth graders illustrate how differently children from disparate classroom achievement cultures think about students' potential to learn in school. Within each classroom culture, the detailed reports are largely consonant with each other regardless of how the children are ranked by the teacher. This within-classroom congruence of children's perceptions is supported by our studies using the Teacher Treatment Inventory. And looking across these two classrooms, children's reports also parallel many aspects of what we had observed to be critical differences in teachers' beliefs and practices between these achievement cultures.

With regard to their feelings, the two children from the classroom that was ranked high in differential treatment appeared devoid of hope for low achievers—those who cannot seem to learn, whom teachers cannot seem to help, and whose effort has eroded. In this classroom, both students report vast differences in the characteristics and behaviors of high and low achievers that keep them apart and stand in the way of the learning of low achievers. In contrast, both the high and low achiever in the classroom that ranked high in equitable treatment speak more optimistically about the potential for all to learn and the important role of effort. They perceive high and low achievers more realistically as individuals with good and bad traits, as more similar to each other, and as part of an inclusive community. In this class-room, and for the interviewed high achiever, the pressure for improvement carries with it some anxiety, a fear that he may "go straight down"—a fear perhaps fueled by his group demotion between third and fourth grade for, in his words, "forgetting his times tables." Here we see the carryover in chil-dren's minds of past school experiences into the present classroom con-text—a theme I will consider in the next chapter. But overall, in these chil-dren's eyes, this classroom is one in which all students, even low achievers, can improve. To what extent is the thinking shown by these four children in their interviews supported by empirical findings from studies that link stu-dent outcomes to membership in these different classroom achievement cultures?

A Widening of the Achievement Gap

What have we learned about the predictive relationship between the expec-tations of teachers and growth in academic achievement, most importantly as a function of the type of classroom environment in which children are placed? In a study of 234 fourth through sixth graders from sixteen class-rooms (Brattesani, Weinstein, and Marshall 1984), we showed that in class-rooms where children reported greater differential treatment, teachers' expectations for children's reading performance in the fall were more pre-dictive of their year-end reading achievement than students' initial achieve-ment differences would suggest: in such high-differential-treatment class-rooms, teachers' expectations explained 9 percent to 18 percent of the variance in student achievement as opposed to 1 percent to 5 percent in classrooms ranked low in differential treatment. These findings highlight a widening gap in actual performance between high- and low-expectancy stu-dents over the course of a school year in classrooms where, according to children, ability differences among students are made more salient.

What mechanisms might explain this widening of the achievement gap? One is differential exposure to the curriculum and to learning opportunities. Indeed, as the interviews illustrate, children report that students are being given different texts and tasks. Another mechanism is children's knowledge of differential treatment—children learn what their teacher expects of them and they come to see themselves and their peers differently. Three of our studies are particularly relevant here. First, in a study of 101 third through fifth graders from seven classrooms (Brattesani, Weinstein, and Marshall

1984), we demonstrated that in classrooms with more differential than equitable treatment, students were more likely to perceive their own treatment from the teacher as congruent with the expectation that their teacher held for them. That is, children for whom the teacher held lower expectations reported more negative treatment from their teachers in classrooms where ability differences among students were made more salient. Thus, not only are children aware of differences in the teacher treatment of peers, but children also report differences in their own treatment by the teachers— treatment differences that reflect actual teacher expectations and that are heightened in certain classroom environments.

Second, given evidence that young children identify differences in their own treatment from the teacher, does this information shape their own academic expectations? In a study of 234 fourth through sixth graders from sixteen classrooms (Brattesani, Weinstein, and Marshall 1984), after controlling for any preexisting achievement differences, children's expectations of themselves matched teachers' expectations more closely in classrooms in which children reported a great deal of differential treatment by the teachers than in classrooms in which teachers were judged to treat students equitably. In those classrooms in which ability differences were made more salient, children from whom the teacher expected less, expected less from themselves.

Finally, supporting what we heard from Kiaisha, Kevin, Robert, and Thurmond, our quantitative analyses of the interviews for all 133 fourth graders showed that children in more differentiated classrooms perceived significantly greater differences in the academic behaviors between high and low achievers. In such classrooms, children described high achievers as displaying more positive academic behaviors than low achievers, as well as a better attitude toward themselves and school. As one child from such a classroom described smart students: "Well, after they do their work, they just sit down and read a book. They don't walk around the room, go up to people and bug 'em. They'll go up to the teacher and ask 'em all these questions and . . . They take care of their self and not other people." By contrast, this same child describes the not-so-smart students as unmotivated to learn: "Well, they just sit around. They don't do nothing. And they talk and they jabber all the time an' they never get anything done. And that's why that they—they say 'I can't do this' and that means that they just don't want to do it and you tell yourself you can't. So you just give up on it and you can't do it."

In contrast, in more equitable classrooms, fewer differences emerged in the task behaviors of high versus low achievers. As Thurmond told us, both highs and lows listen, learn, and thus can move up in group membership. These findings suggest that in classrooms where ability differences among students are heightened, the gap is wider between highs and lows in children's own expectations and in their academic behavior, at least as perceived by their peers. Thus, adding to the effect of having different opportunities to learn in such classrooms may be an erosion of motivation and a tendency not to engage in task-appropriate behaviors that would facilitate learning.

Spillover to Social-Emotional Competencies

Our findings also suggest that not only academic mastery is at stake for children. Three of our studies provide evidence for spillover of expectancy effects to nonacademic outcomes, that is, to the development of social and emotional competencies. Given the greater gap in how high- and low-expectancy students are perceived to do their academic work in differentiated as compared to equitable classroom environments, we wondered whether such differences spilled over to children's willingness to choose low achievers as a work partner or playmate at school. In a sample of ninety-two fourth-grade students from seven classrooms, Meryl Botkin (1985) examined the relationship between the classroom-level reports of differential treatment and children's perceived as well as actual social competence. She found that in classrooms in which children reported greater differential treatment, children who were the target of low teacher expectations saw themselves as less socially competent and were, in fact, chosen less often as a work partner or playmate by their peers than were children for whom teachers held high expectations. By contrast, in classrooms where children reported more equitable treatment, no such differences in the social domain were documented. Thus, in elementary school classrooms where achievement levels are made highly salient, how a child performs academically has implications for social relationships with peers, thus narrowing the opportunities for the perceived low achievers to develop competencies in other domains.

As part of, and in addition to, developing social competencies, children learn at school to regulate their emotional reactions so as to better monitor and adjust their behavior. Our interviews with children have made clear that learning about one's relative smartness in school elicits emotional responses from children. Botkin's doctoral dissertation (1990) explored, using a projective method, the unconscious strategies that children use to ward off their anxiety about this issue. Children were asked to report their thoughts, feelings, and behaviors in response to pictures of two difficult school scenes, one that depicted a student's public failure to answer correctly and the other, rejection by peers at the lunch hour.

In a sample of third through fifth graders from fourteen classrooms, Botkin found that after controlling for achievement differences, children demonstrated more defensive responses in classrooms where the achievement differentiation was more salient than in classrooms with more equitable treatment. These responses included greater use of distancing defenses to ward off feelings of worthlessness and powerlessness. Such defenses included devaluation (negative statements about the self), omnipotence (unrealistic claim to special powers), denial (retreat to fantasy), and regression (reverting to earlier means of managing feelings). This tendency held true for children who were the target of high as well as low expectations, suggesting that both types of students in such classrooms experienced great anxiety. In classrooms where teachers provide clear messages about who is a "high" and who is a "low," children who are the targets of low expectations may use defensive distancing to maintain self-esteem, and children who are the targets of high expectations may feel that their performance carries with it a constant threat of losing face and status.

Which Children Are Most Vulnerable?

While children can readily identify differential treatment by teachers, it is becoming clearer that not all children are equally vulnerable to teacher expectancy effects.

TARGETS OF LOW ACADEMIC EXPECTATIONS. The case study of Adam suggested that children with learning difficulties are placed at special risk for lowered academic expectations—a risk that is heightened in certain educational environments. Similarly, we have evidence that this risk holds for African American students and, similarly, is exacerbated in certain classroom achievement cultures. With regard to the formation of teachers' expectations, in a study by Lauren Jones (1989), using the thirty first-, third-, and fifth-grade classrooms described earlier (Weinstein et al. 1987), teachers were found to have lower academic expectations for African American students than Caucasian students, even after controlling for achievement differences among students. These findings were documented in third and fifth grade, but not in first grade. Most importantly, however, this tendency to underestimate the ability of African American students relative to measured achievement was more common in classrooms where children reported more, rather than less, differential treatment by teachers. This evidence strongly suggests that despite equal achievement, African American students are more likely to be the targets of less positive expectations from teachers, particularly from teachers whom students judge as highly differentiating in their treatment of high and low achievers.

AGE AND EXPECTANCY CONFIRMATION.   Our research has explored the extent to which cognitive-developmental capacities, demographic characteristics, and individual differences of children play a role in how vulnerable children are to confirming teacher expectancy effects. In a number of studies, we have found developmental or grade-level effects in children's responses to teacher expectations. Younger children were more likely to adopt a teacher's opinion of their abilities in classrooms that children had identified as having high differential treatment. By fifth grade, however, children were less likely to be influenced by the perceived classroom climate in framing their own expectations (Weinstein et al. 1987). Older students for whom teachers held lower expectations had more negative perceptions of their abilities in both high- and low-differential-treatment classrooms. This finding may mean that as children age, their self-view becomes more stable and enduring, and less responsive on average to information from the teacher.

In the case of achievement, we found a complex relationship between environment, development, and individual differences in predicting children's responses to teacher expectations. In the same sample of first-, third-, and fifth-grade urban elementary school children noted above, Charles Soulé (1993) classified children who were the target of inaccurate expectations by teachers (relative to entering achievement score) and charted their pattern of achievement gain across a school year, either toward or away from teacher expectations. The findings confirmed those of our earlier study (Brattesani, Weinstein, and Marshall 1984): The greater the salience of ability differences in classrooms, the more evidence that children confirmed teacher expectations in their achievement gains or losses. (Individual child characteristics predicted the rest of the response to inaccurate teacher expectations.) In first grade, classroom environment was the most salient predictor of susceptibility to teacher expectations, whereas in third and fifth grades individual differences among children were the most prominent predictors. Our most recent study of elementary students confirms that both classroom environment and developmental differences moderate the strength of teacher expectancy effects on achievement and on children's expectations (Kuklinski and Weinstein 2001). In general, we found that differences in achievement may become magnified in earlier grades but sustained in later grades, in part as a result of internalized expectations and self-perceptions.

Finally, children differ by age in how they defend against low teacher expectations. First graders who ended up confirming low teacher expectations with decreased achievement generally evaluated themselves highly and misperceived teacher expectations as positive. Consistent with Botkin's study (1990), this suggests that young children in this predicament may defend against the anxiety of low expectations, and preserve self-esteem, by endorsing extremely positive self-views and by unrealistically and defensively misappraising low teacher expectations. For third and fifth graders, the most salient predictors of susceptibility to low teacher expectations included extreme teacher expectations, the child's vigilance to specific qualities of differential teacher treatment, and congruent self- and teacher expectations. Thus, in contrast to the younger susceptible children, older susceptible children were more accurate in their appraisals, and less protected by positively skewed views of teacher behavior.

Most importantly, Soulé's study underscores that both younger and older children can show susceptibility to teacher expectations.

ETHNICITY, GENDER, AND EXPECTANCY CONFIRMATION. In this same sample of thirty classrooms, we contrasted the responses of African American and Caucasian students, as well as the responses of male and female students, to teacher expectations over the course of the school year (McKown and Weinstein 2002). We were interested in how being a member of a group about which others hold achievement stereotypes would affect children's responsiveness to teacher expectations. In a sample of high-risk children who were the targets of extreme teacher over- and underestimates of ability (as measured by the relationship between early teacher expectations and entering achievement), both the ethnicity and the gender of the students moderated their response, as shown by achievement changes in the direction of teacher expectations during the year. In third and fifth grades (but not in first grade), African American children were more likely than Caucasian children to confirm teacher underestimates of reading ability but less likely to confirm teacher overestimates—a tendency that may exacerbate the achievement gap between these groups over time. Similarly, with regard to gender, in fifth grade but not in first and third grades, girls were more likely than boys to confirm teacher underestimates of math ability but less likely to confirm teacher overestimates of math ability. (This finding was specific to math achievement.) In contrast to previous research, which suggests that expectancy effects are stronger in the early grades (Raudenbush 1984; Rosenthal and Rubin 1978), it may be that, overall, teacher expectancy effects become smaller throughout the elementary grades but that moderator effects, such as individual characteristics of the student, become more exaggerated with age.

SELF-EVALUATION AND EXPECTANCY CONFIRMATION. We have also explored relationships between the ways in which children think about themselves and the potential for teachers' expectations to influence children's achievement outcomes. In this same sample of thirty classrooms (Weinstein et al. 1987), focusing on the subgroup of 285 third and fifth graders from twenty of these classrooms, Karen Brattesani (1984) found that children with average (neither high nor low) self-concepts of ability were most susceptible to teacher expectations. It appears that children who have more extreme self-evaluations were less likely to show achievement changes over the course of the year in the direction of teacher expectations, perhaps because they are more sure of their own self-evaluations and thus rely less on information from teachers in forming their self-image. In contrast, children who view themselves as average in ability may be less sure of themselves and may look to authority figures, such as teachers, for validation.

Also documented with two different measures of self-evaluation (cognitive competence and self-expectations) is the finding that children whose self-views were only moderately different from perceived teacher expectations were more likely to confirm those expectations (Brattesani 1984; Madison 1993). When teacher expectations are not far removed from children's self-perceptions, children may find the message more plausible than when expectations depart more radically from self-evaluations. Sybil Madison's masters' thesis also demonstrated that those children who confirmed teacher expectations with gains or losses in achievement were more likely to share perceived teachers' views of their ability and to rely on comparative and external information to support their own appraisals ("'cause most of the kids, they're not doing better and I'm doing a lot better"). In contrast, those children able to resist teacher expectations had self-views largely discrepant with perceived teacher views. Further, they were more likely than more susceptible children to rely on their own self-evaluations (for example, "If I study a lot, I will be real good") rather than referring to the teacher's judgment or to comparative standards to support their appraisals. Unfortunately, however, the children we interviewed rarely said such "I" statements or otherwise showed a capacity for self-evaluation.

Interpreting the Patterns

In giving voice to elementary school children, these findings identify children's awareness of teachers' expectations, students' capacity to distinguish between classroom environments with more or less differential treatment by teachers, a marked correspondence between what children report and observers document (particularly when cultural rather than behavioral observations are made central), and predictable, differential outcomes that are associated with contrasting classroom cultures. When it comes to defining one's smartness in school and, most importantly, developing that smartness, it matters greatly to which classroom a child is assigned, particularly if that child is a low-performing student.

The findings highlight the predictive validity of these classroom distinctions, observed by children as young as six years old. Importantly, children's reports of greater differential treatment were associated with a gap between "high" and "low"-achieving students (as defined by teachers) across a wide variety of outcomes, not only in academic expectations and achievement but also in social and emotional competence. In the case of achievement outcomes, the evidence also points to a widening gap between high and low expectation students beyond any initial achievement differences. It is also significant that classroom environmental differences could not explain all: both developmental and individual differences in children played a complex role in moderating children's responses to teachers' expectations. Given the increasing stability of self-perceptions as children age, the early years of schooling may be especially critical for framing children's self-views, motivation, and achievement in positive ways. By fifth grade, children's perceptions of their ability become perhaps less changeable, regardless of the classroom culture.

This set of findings comes from correlational studies conducted in naturalistic classroom settings. Such research does not permit inferences about causal connections between instructional practices and children's outcomes. Yet there are important strengths in the evidence. These include the ecological validity of the data (real classrooms and naturally occurring expectations), the controls for prior achievement differences between students, the use of longitudinal designs over a school year that allow the temporal ordering of early teacher expectations that precede later student outcomes, and theoretically consistent findings. There is a coherence in the findings that depicts a student role in expectancy effects in classrooms and that presents an integrative model of contrasting classroom cultures that may accentuate or minimize expectancy effects in schooling. Given such classroom and student differences, it would be simplistic and misleading to continue to examine expectancy effects on average.

There are a number of disturbing features about these findings: the early age and sophistication with which children read teacher cues about ability; the expressed hopelessness about the potential for low achievers to improve associated with highly differentiated classroom cultures; and the wider and widening gap between high and low achievers in differentiated versus equitable classroom environments. All of these features show up both as *perceived* differences in how children describe the behaviors of others and as *actual* differences in schooling outcomes. How might the beliefs and practices of teachers widen the achievement gap between students? And is it appropriate for teachers to treat students differently from each other and have different expectations for them?

The Opportunity Structure

Early on, Jere Brophy and Thomas Good (1974) made a distinction between direct and indirect effects that is critical here. Teachers' expectations as expressed through differential treatment can have direct effects on student achievement, for example, through differential exposure to curricula. But indirect effects on achievement could also result if student awareness of teacher beliefs leads to an erosion of motivation and effort.

The evidence presented here, obtained from teachers, observers, and students, paints a picture of very different opportunities to learn, to demonstrate that learning, and to overcome obstacles in learning for high and low achievers in these contrasting classroom cultures. I remind readers of Adam, whose curricular exposure was vastly reduced by remedial math assignments and low reading-group placement, with the gap growing daily in coverage between him and his twin brother. In another school with a different educational philosophy, he was exposed to more challenging material and offered a broader range of performance opportunities where he could excel, all while working hard to overcome learning problems. Remember as well the differences in the approaches of Mrs. Iver and Mrs Kay. Mrs. Iver restricted curricular coverage through ability-based grouping over a wider range of subjects, with assignment for a set period of time and talk of (and perhaps practice of) much demotion. Mrs. Kay, however, used more flexible ability grouping with greater movement between groups and offered more whole-class teaching, which demanded the same from both lows and highs. Her focus on the process of learning widened performance opportunities, and in contrast to Mrs. Iver, she took responsibility for moving children along with more individualized approaches.

There is converging evidence about the importance of curricular exposure to gains in children's learning. A consistent body of findings highlights large differences in content coverage in both elementary school (in assignment to special classes and grade retention, and between ability-based groups in reading and math) and high school (in the availability of honors and advanced placement classes, and between academic tracks)—coverage that predicts student performance beyond preexisting achievement differences (see reviews by Entwisle, Alexander, and Olsen 1997; Shepard and Smith 1989; Wang 1998). Further, these differential assignments are not isolated events but in reality are combined. Doris Entwisle, Karl Alexander, and Linda Olson (1997) show that "more than half the children in low reading groups in first grade were receiving special education in sixth grade, compared to only 6 percent of children in the high group in first grade" (p. 87). Studies have also demonstrated that placing students higher enhances their learning. For example, in a field experiment, eighth-grade students were assigned to pre-algebra rather than lower-level mathematics classes despite not having the scores for such placements (Mason et al. 1992). The students placed higher, did better academically, and took more advanced courses than similar students from previous years who were enrolled in general math, with no detriment to the other students' performance.

Finally, differences in opportunities to learn reside not only with curricular exposure but also with exposure to self-regulation skills (such as choice, leadership, and self-monitoring) and to varied instructional and assessment modalities that tap the full range of human abilities and learning styles. Greater opportunities to self-regulate learning and to learn in more varied ways predict higher performance. As one example of an experimental study (Sternberg, Torff, and Grigorenko 1998), third- and eighth-grade students were taught lessons constructed to highlight either memory-based (traditional), critical-thinking (analytic), or triarchic instruction (which uses a combination of analytic, creative, and practical teaching strategies). Teaching triarchically (that is, tapping these multiple abilities in instruction) led to superior performance, even on memory-based multiple-choice tests.

The Belief System

The evidence presented here also captures differences in teachers' and children's beliefs about ability and learning across these two classroom cultures. A growing research literature suggests that the beliefs and practices that Mrs. Kay demonstrated and children described have been associated with greater teacher effort to persist at instruction, greater student willingness to engage in schooling, and better student academic performance. Mary Lee Smith and Lorrie Shepard (1988), for example, found that kindergarten teachers who believed that readiness to learn results from a biologically based unfolding of abilities (nativist beliefs) were more likely to recommend grade retention than teachers who believed readiness to result from an interaction between the child and the instructional environment.

Classroom motivational climates that stress intrinsic motivation, learning rather than performance goals, and cooperative rather than competitive rewards have been found to be associated with greater effort by children, more persistence on challenging tasks, and more positive social relationships among peers and across racial lines (Ames 1992; Aronson 1978; Slavin 1983). Children's beliefs that intelligence is malleable are also associated with children's willingness to try hard and in the face of failure not to exhibit learned helplessness (Dweck and Leggett 1988; Dweck 2000). Children's beliefs that intelligence is fixed, not only hold across subject-matter domains, but also predict more superficial strategies and lower performance (Stipek and Gralinski 1996).

Increasing student choice and responsibility for learning uncovers new talent and increases intrinsic motivation (Corno 1993). Significantly, when a teacher was highly involved, allowed for student autonomy, and provided optimal structure, the students were more motivated throughout the school year—and the relationship proved reciprocal, in that students who were more engaged at the beginning of the year received more of all three teacher behaviors (Skinner and Belmont 1993). Classrooms with more activities that demand student participation (what has been described as "under-peopled" settings) increase competence building (Schoggen 1989). Further, classrooms and schools that successfully implement a caring community (through student collaboration) show student gains in motivation and engagement, social competence, prosocial behavior, and in some cases, achievement (Solomon et al. 1988, 2000).

Also relevant to varying emphases on performance versus learning goals is a growing body of experimental studies, conducted primarily with college students, that suggests certain test situations can evoke societal stereotypes about achievement. Claude Steele and Joshua Aronson (1995) showed that both African American and female college students who had been randomly assigned to one of two testing situations performed more poorly than Caucasian students on achievement tests when they were told the tests were diagnostic of ability, in contrast to test situations in which ability was not mentioned. The researchers argued that students respond with anxiety in the face of what they perceive to be stereotypes about the lower achievement of ethnic minorities in general and women with regard to mathematics. Clark McKown and I (under review) examined the development and consequences of young children's stereotype consciousness and found, similarly, that "stereotype threat" conditions (such as tests that are announced to be diagnostic of ability) affected performance only for stigmatized minority children who reported awareness of stereotypes in the world. This is compelling evidence that awareness of such societal stereotypes (and priming for that awareness in testing situations) leads to decreased achievement.

Fallacies of Differentiation and Accommodation

There are a number of fallacies underlying our appraisals of student ability differences that raise questions about the meaningfulness of such appraisals for instructional accommodation. At every step of K–12 schooling, both inside and outside classrooms, children are appraised regarding perceived ability differences or special needs so that accommodations can be made through different educational pathways. These include decisions about readiness for kindergarten, the placing of children in grades by age, retention, ability-based instructional groups for reading and math in elementary classrooms, and ability-based tracks in middle and high school. Compensatory instruction, special education, bilingual teaching, gifted programs, and disciplinary practices further differentiate school experiences. But as we saw here, the accommodations also include aspects of the relationship between teacher and student: different patterns of interaction, expectations expressed, and trust and warmth exhibited. Not surprisingly, then, these appraisals rest heavily on difficult-to-measure and easily biased social processes.

Supporting this concern about appraisals of student ability differences are several recent findings. First, research highlights the large margin of error in test scores and the limited predictability of tests for adult accomplishments, yet decisions are made for or against placements and about the ability of children on the basis of single-point differences (Neisser et al. 1996). Second, judgments about student ability are often relative: they assume a normal curve distribution but are applied within a captive population. Thus, regardless of objective scores, a student can be identified as a high or low achiever dependent upon his or her position in a particular classroom's achievement hierarchy (Pallas et al. 1994). Third, differences in rates of children's development, although unrelated to future performance, can become predictive when early labeling locks children into certain pathways. Fourth, appraisals about ability have been found to reflect race, class, language, and gender groupings, even when differences in ability have been controlled (Entwisle, Alexander, and Olson 1997; Meier, Stewart, and England 1989; Sadker and Sadker 1994). Thus, poor children, certain ethnic minority children, children who speak another language, and girls with regard to math and science are often the recipients of low expectations.

Finally, the perceived scarcity of coveted positions—for example, in high reading groups or great books programs—exists by design. That is, differences in the opportunity structure are created through current funding mechanisms and program conceptualization. The point is that these patterns of differentiation catch some kinds of children more than others (with unfortunate social consequences), and they also reflect a process of skimming off the top, where those identified as high get more while those identified as average and below average receive less favorable instructional conditions. Given these underlying processes, all children face this risk in a stratified schooling, not just the demographic and social groups that have been identified most commonly as recipients of low expectations.

Given the lack of meaningfulness of these distinctions made among children and given that the lower-level pathways and treatments (repetition, less curricular exposure, less trust) are often not effective in raising the achievement of those who encounter obstacles in learning, we need to challenge differentiation at this early stage and in these ways. Instead, the more individualized approaches used by Adam's learning disabilities teacher and by Mrs. Kay as she intervened to move students along, coupled with an overall program that is broader in its conceptualization of all student abilities, would likely be more productive for children's learning.

That children's friendships and social competence as well as academic outcomes are implicated, that children's increased sensitivity to differential treatment by teachers may carry into other school years, and that children differ in their susceptibility to teacher expectancy effects all point to the importance of longitudinal research across longer periods of time and encompassing multiple aspects of (and players in) children's worlds. When faced with low expectations, some children may find themselves locked into a cycle of low achievement out of which they cannot escape. Others may experience supports along the way that buffer the effects of limiting expectations. Chapter 7 explores these questions by considering the achievement histories of children.

If Children Were Teachers

In this chapter, we examined children's thoughts and feelings as members of different classroom achievement cultures that emphasized either differentiation or equity among children. What would children do if they found themselves in the role of the teacher? Some children were struck silent by the question, unable to put themselves in the place of their teacher. Other children answered in the voices of their teacher, mirroring the beliefs and practices that their teacher implemented in the classroom. And still other children suggested strategies that differed starkly from the approaches chosen by their teachers.

One cannot help but be moved by children's pleas for greater understanding, kindness, and most importantly support—in particular for the low-performing student. They argued for the importance of implementing conditions that develop the abilities of all students. As one child said so poignantly: "If I were the teacher, I would have it so like everyone wins. It's just that I mean—nobody will lose." Another child cautions about the effect of labeling by the teacher: "I wouldn't call them [the not-so-smart kids] the lowest group." In creating a world in which nobody loses, everyone wins. Further, no one is labeled the lowest, the appraisal of ability and sorting of children is minimized, and attention is focused on development. Children also wanted a more positive, respectful, and trusting climate: "Easy on the kids, wouldn't criticize. Let them say their side of the story, not just believe the smart kids." Another child suggested, "If I were the teacher, first I'd work with each of them *before* I put them in their groups. Miss H. just said, 'What books were you working in before?' I told her and she said, 'You should be in Group B.'"

Children also spoke to the need for a broader curriculum and a more motivating and less coercive working climate. One child commented: "I'd try and be nice and teach them not just school work but art and music and things." Another child proposed, "Well, I'd probably given them, like board assignments . . . or that you should watch something on TV, you don't have to but you should . . . Like an interesting book on science and a history of something. But they wouldn't have to, I mean, it wouldn't be a 'do-or-get-in-trouble'—if you like or want to find out about something, read it."

Some children would engage parents as helpers in the tasks of guiding children to learn, holding children accountable, rewarding their efforts, and communicating pride about their accomplishments. One child urged, "Tell their parents to do a little bit more studying with 'em." A different child suggested, "I would set homework for them every night so they can take it home and do it for their mother to sign. And if they didn't bring back their homework, I would call their parents and ask what happened to the homework. And if they do all their homework right . . . I would give them a paper . . . I would say, 'Dear parents, your kid has brought back all his homework and been good and helped me.'" And most of all, let us remember Kevin's words of wisdom: "Help 'em with all their work. And tell 'em how good they're doing . . . But never try to hurt their feelings."

CHAPTER 7

Achievement Histories of Vulnerability and Resilience

Too often, small failures live longer in the mind than larger successes, and their power echoes correspondingly. Such experiences can be seared into one's mind and take on almost mythical proportions.

　　—A graduate student

The main key here was something very basic, yet something with great power . . . they believed in me.

　　—An undergraduate student

The charting of an achievement history is relatively unexplored territory. While we are familiar with the details of medical or psychological histories, we are less accustomed to thinking about what Cremin (1976) calls an educational life history, beyond the typical listing of schools attended, and degrees and grades attained. So much of the research about schooling is cross-sectional and examined at one point in time; if longitudinal, research typically covers somewhat short time periods and provides limited information about the nested environments, classrooms and otherwise, in which children learn and live. Not surprisingly, then, the issue of carryover of the effects of academic expectations from one grade to another has also been largely understudied in research on self-fulfilling prophecies. By carryover, I mean the ways in which curricular exposure, accomplishments, labels, and expectations from one school year can have implications both for the next year's placement and achievement and for the expectations of teachers and parents. By carryover, I refer also to the internalization of beliefs and feelings, and the learned behaviors by children that can shape how they themselves construe and experience their subsequent schooling. These effects can be maintained, accumulate (that is, intensify), or dissipate over time (Smith, Jussim, and Eccles 1999).

Within the literature on self-fulfilling prophecies, investigations of carry-over of expectancy effects across grades are few, narrowly framed, and far from conclusive (see Crano and Mellon 1978; O'Connell, Dusek, and Wheeler 1974; West and Anderson 1976). For example, in the *Pygmalion in the Classroom* study conducted by Rosenthal and Jacobson (1968), although the fifth-grade students who had been identified as "late bloomers" showed no expectancy advantage in test scores during the experimental year, they did show such advantage during a subsequent year, with teachers who had not received the positively biasing information. This is perhaps suggestive of carryover, although there was no effect at the prior grade level and no evidence for mediating mechanisms. The 1970 study by Ray Rist, however, while it did not collect information about achievement, documented a potential mediating factor in the relatively fixed nature of reading-group assignments—and hence, curricular exposure and labeled ability—that persisted from kindergarten through second grade.

A recent study by Alison Smith, Lee Jussim, and Jacquelynne Eccles (1999) tested the question of carryover of self-fulfilling prophecies by examining whether the correlation between earlier teacher perceptions and later student grades and standardized scores in math increased, decreased, or stayed the same from sixth through twelfth grades. Their results showed both stability of these predictions during successive years and some decrease in correlations. They concluded, "Our results, however, did not provide evidence of accumulation . . . Thus, it is no longer necessary to speculate on what may happen if self-fulfilling prophecies accumulate. At least in the classroom, they do not" (p. 564). They did find, however, that "students who were the targets of higher expectations in seventh grade took a greater number of nonremedial high school math courses than students who were the targets of lower expectations," which they argue raises "the possibility that perceivers' expectations influence target behavior long after contact between perceiver and target has ceased" (pp. 558–559). That teachers' perceptions of student ability in seventh grade were linked to the students' taking (or not taking) challenging math courses throughout high school (akin to the Rist finding regarding the persistence of reading-group placement) is indeed evidence of the carryover of expectations—which ultimately may shape children's achievement trajectories.

As noted earlier, studies of decontextualized and average effects can underestimate carryover. The Beginning School study, conducted by sociologist Doris Entwisle and her colleagues, provides more contextualized and multilayered evidence about how both the economic resources of parents and the social organization of schools affect the development of children between the ages of six and twelve, in ways that may reflect the workings of self-fulfilling prophecies. Among many findings, first-grade teacher ratings on interest-participation and attention-span restlessness scales were correlated with student achievement test scores at the end of that year and over the next three years (Alexander, Entwisle, and Dauber 1993). African American students not only received lower marks in first grade than did Caucasian students (despite equivalent test scores and family resources), but these lower marks were also more likely to remain stable throughout their school years, thus resulting in a widening gap between groups (Entwisle and Alexander 1988). With regard to socioeconomic status, research showed that while poorer children entered first grade with lower scores, they made similar educational progress at the start (Entwisle, Alexander, and Olson 1997). They were perceived and treated differently by teachers, however, as shown by their lower marks, placement in lower reading groups, more frequent retention, and greater inclusion in special education classes. As Aaron Pallas and his colleagues (1994) also demonstrated, children's reading-group rank independently predicted test score gains beyond teacher marks through fourth grade, suggesting that differential opportunity to learn or labeling effects may have been a potential mediating factor.

This relative neglect of a longitudinal perspective in expectancy research creates a critical gap in our knowledge, particularly about how diverse populations of children in varied environmental contexts negotiate the ups and downs of their schooling experiences—with some perhaps getting caught in cycles of negative self-fulfilling prophecies and others finding ways to overcome the obstacles in their path. Without such a perspective, we also learn little about how teachers, parents, children, and siblings collectively, either in synchrony or conflict—shape educational expectations, a will to learn, a strong sense of ability, and realized intellectual competencies.

Carryover of Expectancy Effects

To the Next School Year

In the last chapter, I showed that children's own expectations were more likely to mirror their teachers' expectations for them in classrooms where differential treatment toward high and low achievers was greatest. This heightened mirroring was true as well for children's achievement—with evidence that the gap between highs and lows in achievement grew over the course of the school year. In this study, we asked whether such effects carried over into a second school year. In a sample of 103 first and second graders (a younger cohort) and seventy-five third and fourth graders (an older cohort), Margaret Kuklinski (1992), a former doctoral student of mine, examined the carryover effects over two school years of membership in classrooms that children had identified as having high or low differential treatment by teachers.

First, for both the younger and older age groups, she found that children who were the target of either high or low teacher expectations perceived more differential treatment in the next school year if they had come from a classroom with a lot of differential treatment (as compared to children who came from classrooms with less differential treatment). This finding held true even after controlling for differences in student achievement and for the qualities of the classroom environment during the second year. Thus, for both younger and older children, membership in classrooms where achievement differences are heightened is associated with increased vigilance about differentiation in teacher treatment during the next school year.

Second, for the older children only, membership in such a classroom during Year 1 also predicted greater congruence between teacher perceptions and children's perceptions of academic competence in Year 2 (again controlling for differences in the achievement level of students and for the qualities of the subsequent classroom environment). These findings suggest that for these older elementary school children, increased vigilance about differential treatment and greater sensitivity to teacher expectations are carried into the next school year regardless of the qualities of the next year's classroom environment. These findings of carryover could explain the anxiety of "Robert" about group demotion, even in a classroom where equity of treatment was emphasized (see Chapter 6). Ironically, such hypervigilance to ability differences does not benefit students; students are better off concentrating on mastering the task at hand rather than focusing on social comparisons (Ames 1992).

Over Fourteen School Years

While the above study focused on children's perceptions of teacher treatment and academic competence, this study examined children's achievement outcomes over fourteen years. We used a longitudinal data archive on the ego development of children (Block and Block 1980). With this sample of 110 children, Jennifer Alvidrez and I (1999) charted the fourteen-year predictive relationship between teacher perceptions of the intelligence of children at age four and high school grade-point averages (GPA) of the same children at age eighteen. We created a measure that we called teacher over-estimation and underestimation of student intelligence—relative to measured IQ score. And we found this measure to be significantly related both to the child's socioeconomic level and perceived attributes. That is, teachers appeared to overestimate the intelligence of children from higher socioeconomic classes and underestimate the intelligence of children from lower socioeconomic classes, relative to their measured IQ scores at age four. Once social class was controlled, the race of the child did not predict the degree of teacher over- and underestimation of intelligence. (These findings are similar to those of other studies that have found certain groups of children at risk for lower expectations, despite equal achievement.) Further, children whose intelligence was underestimated by teachers were also perceived by teachers to be more immature and insecure, again after controlling for IQ and social class differences.

Most importantly, even after controlling for IQ, social class, and the perceived behavioral attributes of children, preschool teachers' over- and underestimates of child ability significantly predicted both grade point average and SAT test-taking in high school fourteen years later. The relationship was strongest for the underestimated children. That is, on average, children who at age four were perceived by teachers as less intelligent than their IQ scores suggested indeed earned lower GPAs and were less likely to take SAT exams in preparation for applying to college. Equally important to this predictive relationship, however, were qualities of the home environment as rated by trained observers. The ability of teachers to predict how students would likely perform was weaker when children came from home environments rated more orderly and predictable (and perhaps more conducive to achievement), and in which mothers were more career and community oriented (and perhaps more achievement oriented).

What do we make of these findings? Naturalistic studies of children's achievement trajectories are by definition correlational rather than experimental: one cannot distinguish between the prediction of an unfolding reality and the influence of a self-fulfilling prophecy. There may be other as yet unmeasured factors that influence children's growth in achievement. It is possible that the teachers were more sensitive than IQ scores in predicting children's achievement trajectories fourteen years later, perhaps because they could identify child behaviors that might stand in the way of achievement. But it is also possible that teachers' underpredictions of children's ability reflected biased perceptions, which caused them to expect less of poorer children, even after IQ differences had been controlled for—and that their perceptions may have carried over in a way that may have influenced subsequent achievement through labeling and curricular exposure. That mothers' more positive beliefs and / or actions may have buffered the effects of lowered expectations underscores the variability in, and hence malleability of, achievement among the "underestimated" children. That is, not all children whose abilities were underestimated subsequently underperformed. Such evidence speaks to the critical interrelationships between home and school in the unfolding of children's academic mastery.

Exploring "Critical Incidents"

What are the processes that may underlie the carryover or dissipation of expectancy effects? The analysis of Adam's twenty-two-year school history illustrated that limiting expectations about ability can quickly become reinforced schoolwide with implications for curricular exposure and labeling in subsequent school years. Adam's achievement history also described how he overcame these limiting expectations through educational interventions— by parents, teachers, and alternative school environments, and Adam himself. The examination of a child's schooling history and of critical incidents within this history enables us to learn more about the *holding* power in children's eyes of the messages they receive from teachers about their ability and helps us learn if, when, and how negative messages and less favorable educational pathways can be overcome.

In order to examine how others (beyond Adam) both remembered and negotiated messages about ability, I asked students in my undergraduate and graduate classes at the University of California, Berkeley, about the incidents that had shaped their self-definitions of ability. I have long used the exercise of reporting "critical incidents" during one's achievement history as a way to actively engage individuals in remembering their own experiences in schools—with the express purpose of reawakening identification with the young student role and making the communication of academic expectations more vivid. What I ask these young adults to recall in a brief essay is very similar to the questions we asked of young elementary school students: "Briefly describe in not more than one or two pages one *incident* during your schooling experiences from preschool through now that helped define your self-concept of ability. In your description, identify the key characters in the incident, your age at the time, the context of the experience, what happened, and what inferences you drew from the experiences." A critical incident methodology enables the participant rather than the researcher to define events and outcomes on their own terms (Vispoel and Austin 1995).

I collected essays from a series of classes with undergraduates and graduate students. This yielded a sample of 161 incidents (all submitted anonymously), which I coded and counted, noting the time period in which they occurred, the positive or negative nature of the message, and the positive or negative nature of the eventual outcomes, as described by the students. A qualitative analysis of the themes underlying these incidents was also conducted and was framed by questions such as these. How similar were these retrospective accounts of critical incidents to the clues that young children today report as informing them about ability differences in the classroom? If very similar, this would suggest that incidents like those reported by the elementary school students in our studies were, indeed, remembered long past the year in which they occurred. I was curious about whether and how these critical incidents were resolved and with what implications for defining an academic self. I wondered also about the existence and nature of positive buffering effects. That is, did experiences with significant adults and did actions taken by the self alter, in students' eyes, the interpretations and perceived effects of negative messages about ability?

It must be emphasized that the retrospective accounts I collected reflect a sample of schooling successes. By gaining admission to a highly competitive public research university as an undergraduate or graduate student, no matter how bumpy the ride, these students have already reached high levels of academic accomplishment, in contrast to the samples of urban, inner-city elementary school students discussed earlier. Nonetheless, there is much to be learned from these students' retrospective musings.

Similarities among Critical Incidents

Critical incidents were vividly recalled by this sample of young adults. Indeed, simply completing the task unearthed powerful memories from the participants. Just from an epidemiologic perspective, it is interesting to note that these remembered incidents represented events from elementary school (47 percent of the incidents), junior-high and high school (38 percent), and even college (15 percent). These painful, uplifting, or simply informative incidents were remarkably similar to the events described by our elementary school student samples. Looking across the narratives, the range of critical incidents remembered by this university sample of students could be categorized as reflective of: (1) public incidents in front of classmates that carried shame, ridicule, or praise, (2) cases of assignment, or failed assignment, to a reading group, a class, a track, or a program for the gifted or being given a special test that communicated information about ability, (3) interactions with teachers, primarily about providing feedback and help, and (4) relationships with teachers that conveyed, or failed to convey, high expectations, trust, and enthusiasm.

Much like the elementary school children we interviewed, one of the college students remembered a time in her first-grade classroom when she forged her sense of academic ability:

My most vivid memory of this class is of our math assignments. The teacher would hand out math dittos and exercise sheets that were of varying degrees of difficulty. I sat in the rear of the room along with four or five other kids who everyone knew were smart. We all used to compete to see who could finish their math problems first; the first one finished would whisper "done" so that the others around this end of the table would know. I remember being able to keep up with this self-imposed pace and soon I was being given the hard math too. This was my initiation into the "smart group." I remember feeling like I had attained some insurmountable amount of social status. I don't know if the children whom I looked up to really thought of themselves that way. Or, if they were aware that their friendship and recognition was so important to our class of first graders as well as the other first grade classroom at school. You see, we knew who in their class was smart too. I am not sure whether it was the notion of performing better than the other kids or that I was accepted into the status group, but I remember my first grade as a time when I formulated much of my academic confidence.

Another student described public failure in a fifth-grade spelling bee. She wrote, "It no longer mattered how many correct words I spelled in the game for my last try told me that I, too, was a bad speller." Another student recalled that she felt like one of the smartest people in her third-grade class when she was one of only two children chosen to attend a special class labeled "More Capable Learners." Another student described the following interactions with her third-grade teacher, which she interpreted as prejudiced against Hispanic children: "The teacher aided other students when they erred and allowed them to continue, but at my first mistake, I was stopped from continuing. Throughout the year, there were many similar instances, little injustices that children are aware of." Another student wrote of the special relationship he had developed with a junior-high-school teacher: "The bond with this literature teacher gave me the self-confidence many of the other students could not get from any teacher. It allowed me to confront all the other difficulties, because I felt strong and anchored."

Perceived Effects That Endured

To the students, these incidents had enduring consequences for academic self-image, educational aspirations, the motivation to learn and work hard, and actual achievements. Importantly, they also noted how such incidents guided their interest toward or away from different subjects. In some cases, their feelings and interests generalized from one domain of learning to multiple domains. And although most of the identified incidents were positive, even in this sample of students who by all measures had achieved school success, 42 percent of the recalled incidents were negative in their messages about academic ability.

Positive Effects

The positive messages and support received from teachers have encouraged and inspired these students—many to this day. In reading the narratives, one can see the powerful effects of formative educational experiences and the pivotal role that teachers can play in children's lives. One student described his remarkable world history teacher in high school, Mr. L., "who obviously liked teaching, and it showed":

> His self-ease and relaxed manner were catching to all of the students . . . He was . . . the teaching master who transmitted a love and a curiosity of learning to students. He had the ability to make history come alive with his stories and to make you feel good by just being around him. One always felt included in some special intimate circle of his . . . He transformed us kids

from our usual half-frenzied state of anxiety-ridden "I'd rather be any-where else" raving maniacs into a group of sensitive, attentive students who were happy to be there. Mr. L. provided me with a down-to-earth role model that I admired and respected . . . at a time when I especially needed a male model that I could identify with.

Another student recalled the recognition that she received in a writing class when the teacher asked her to read her story aloud to the class. She proved too afraid and so he, the teacher, read the story aloud for her: "This teacher's encouragement rings in my ears to this day whenever I doubt my ability. My dream to write still persists in due part[ly] to this experience, as well as the ease and pleasure with which I wrote the story." Another student wrote about her high school French teacher, whose philosophy emphasized self-directed learning: "Her belief in our capabilities and respect for us as fellow human beings bolstered my self-image, in addition to helping me perceive myself more as a potential college student than 'just' a high school student, with no particular academic future." Another student related how a compassionate chemistry teacher helped her put her difficulty with chemistry into perspective: "Her words were a literal turning point in my career. From then on, I was motivated to make academic and career goals that recognized my strengths and helped me accept my weaknesses."

The first-grade teacher of an African American student fought hard by threatening to quit if the student was not allowed to take an IQ test to see if she would qualify for placement in a program for gifted students: "I really felt as if I could do anything I wanted to do. Ever since that day I have always felt that way. I know that because of that test I had more advantages than other children throughout my days at school." Another student had been moved by a fifth-grade teacher's simple words of praise for her artwork: "I guess for an immigrant child there isn't one single event of discouragement in the academic world; the whole beginning seems discouraging. So when a voice of encouragement comes it stands out . . . For me, who was having such a terrible time with my English and math to find something I could do in the classroom *that couldn't be corrected* was a thrill of accomplishment." She wrote of the positive effects of such praise on her: "I did go on winning art awards into my high school years; I then found other subjects just as rewarding as art."

These inspiring moments carry their weight, as yet another student acknowledged, in part because of the power and credibility of teachers in children's lives: "To this day, I see myself as a 'writer' and I have my fifth grade teacher to thank for recognizing my ability . . . I believed my teacher unquestioningly and looked up to her and trusted her completely." Emphasized in these student narratives is that the enthusiasm for learning goes hand in hand with feeling good about oneself, with acceptance and recognition, and with being valued.

Negative Effects

Evident as well in these narratives are painful memories of failures in school, which as one student described in the opening quotation of this chapter, seem to have lives of their own. Most of these incidents involved public shaming of students. Students who had been publicly shamed reported opting out of class participation, feeling stupid and insecure about their abilities, and fearing and losing interest in the particular subject matter. For example, one student's second-grade teacher "ridiculed me, called me stupid, and generally reduced me to tears" for having difficulty with the concepts *right* and *left*. While the incident left her feeling shy and fearful about participating in class ("From then on, I always tried to hide in classes so my teachers wouldn't pick on me"), she also remembered the support of her first-grade teacher. She wrote, "I still think of my first grade teacher. Sometimes I think if she hadn't made me think I was special, this second grade teacher would have been able to do a lot more damage than just making me shy." She emphasized that, as a second grader, "I never even thought that what she did was wrong; I honestly thought I was an idiot, even though I continued to get good grades."

Another student wrote about the public ridicule she received from her fourth-grade teacher when, after many tries, she was unable to match his note in singing. She had been singled out and brought to the front of the class to sing solo, while all of the students laughed at her failure: "Prefaced with the word 'stupid,' he informed me that if I could not succeed in singing I would not succeed in anything else . . . In fact from that time on I would never volunteer an answer in classroom, or show that I could achieve in any way for fear of being ridiculed. This fear has persisted throughout my academic life. When faced with unfamiliar situations or when called upon to speak before a group, the old fear of ridicule and the thought that everyone is better qualified than I, continues to recur."

When another student talked about Frederick Douglass as a famous person, her first-grade teacher told her that slaves could not be famous people. She wrote that she felt stupid that she had not known *not* to mention Douglass's name: "It made me question the value of black contributions, and my own worth as a black child. It stifled intellectual growth, because it was communicated that there are certain things I shouldn't know about and that I shouldn't pretend to know what I really didn't . . . It encouraged passivity, since participation led to humiliation." For some students, such public incidents were associated with long-term fears about the subject matter: for example, in math ("this incident in fifth grade is the earliest one that I can recall in which I felt incapable in learning math") and in French ("the fears from that first French class are still with me").

Even other, seemingly more benign incidents of differentiation carried perceived long-term consequences and emphasized the power of the teacher's judgment. One student wrote about a traumatic change of schools in second grade, where the new teacher asked her if she had used any of the books the groups were using in reading. She wrote:

> I pointed to a familiar text and that was enough for the teacher to put me in a "low level" reading group. Although these groups were not distinguished by any signifying names, but instead by the names of animals, the students, myself included, seemed to know who were the "smart" ones and who were the "dumb" ones. Because the teacher didn't test me, I felt she knew right off that I belonged in the lower-level reading group, that I was obviously dumb if she didn't even have to test me. While I cannot say that this single incident caused my self concept of intelligence to be a poor one, I find myself doubting my intelligence/ability because authoritative figures conveyed the idea that my ability is of a lower caliber.

As a member of a family that opposed the Vietnam war, another student was singled out in third grade to illustrate the meaning of the word "hypocrisy." As he described his feelings of stupidity and his futile attempts at formulating a response, he stressed the final authority of the teacher: "All attempts at self-defense, however, were powerless in light of the teacher's better rhetoric and authority. I remained a hypocrite by decree."

Overcoming Negative Messages about Ability

Of the recalled negative incidents, 44 percent (that is, almost half) were reframed or buffered so that they were perceived as ultimately having posi-

tive consequences. In considering these percentages, both of negative instances and of reported reframing, it is important to remember that these
findings were obtained in a sample of schooling successes. The percentages
may well differ in the reports of students who have not completed high
school or have not done well academically. Interestingly, only three of the
eighty-five positive incidents were reported to have been reframed in negative ways. Thus, the reported long-term outcomes were mediated by individuals' perception of the incident, its continuity or lack of continuity with
previous life events, and actions by the student or significant others (such as
parents, other teachers, siblings, or peers) to change the meaning or consequences of the event—most frequently, to turn negatives into positives. Yet
even in the negative incidents that are reframed and overcome, one can see
evidence in some of residual effects.

The Role of the Student

SELF-EVALUATION AND CONSTRUCTIVE ACTION.   In some of these
reframed negative incidents, students described themselves as taking an independent point of view regarding the academic failure. This involved self-
evaluation and analysis, efforts to try again, a search for alternative strategies and greater challenges, and a focus on self-improvement rather than on
comparisons with others.

Such students appeared able to strike out on their own and craft their own
judgment, as this female student described in telling about an incident in
kindergarten. She wrote that she and another student had been called out of
class to play games with a man who clearly was engaged in assessing their
ability. She shared: "I sensed that she [the teacher] felt something was
wrong with us, so when we were taken aside together, I knew that there
was to be some kind of test which we either had to pass or to fail and prove
the teacher right. This experience was the first in a few in which I felt my
abilities were not challenged but questioned. It was also an experience in
which I felt fully confident in my ability to succeed. This incident . . . did allow me to be confident even in the context of feeling underestimated."

Other students described turning failures into successes through their
own hard efforts to improve their performance. One student recalled: "I
will never forget my feeling of accomplishment (in fourth grade) at having
started by knowing none of the sevens (multiplication tables) to knowing
them all so well. This incident more than many others helped to build my

self-confidence, as an apt person, a person who could do anything if she set her mind to it." Another student described moving into a new school halfway through first grade and noting that unlike the other children in the class, he had not begun to learn to read. Despite "feeling inferior to and envious of his classmates," he worked furiously to catch up, engaging his older brothers and sisters in helping him. He wrote: "Perhaps the most rewarding aspect of this incident was that I went from relative illiteracy to a heightened sense of scholastic ability. The ability to read was magical to me, and I associated that magic with school."

Other examples reflected students' pushing themselves into higher tracks in junior high and high school (even though teachers had not recommended them), trying more challenging classes in college, trying again for sought-after positions (a place in the school orchestra or band), and eventually succeeding. Obvious from their self-reflections is the belief that effort makes a difference ("I could do anything if I was willing to put out the effort"), that grades are not everything ("despite the poor mark, I learned a lot and enjoyed the class"), and that challenging opportunities, wherever they could be found, were valuable in and of themselves ("It didn't matter to me whether it was a band or orchestra; all I cared about was making good music with good players").

This emerging philosophy focused attention on the self, not on self-other comparisons, as emphasized by this college student who described her current attitude at her university: "I learned not to measure my ability based on what others do. Others may do better than me . . . but if I feel confident in myself, I will be happy with my own accomplishments. I know that if I put forward my best efforts, then I will have my own self satisfaction." For another student, however, the stiff competition at college has modified an insight that he had gained in high school: "I still believe that I can do anything, but I no longer believe that I can do anything just as well as anyone else. Aptitude is nearly as important as effort and *time* is the ultimate limiting factor . . . But there I go again, setting limits."

THE "I'LL SHOW THEM" MOTIVATION.   Still other students expressed an oppositional motivation that came from a desire to disprove a prophecy about their capabilities. An immigrant student from the Philippines, for example, recalled a critical event in his senior year of high school when one of his teachers said in front of the class that he was not university material and even if he did get accepted, he would not make it. The student wrote: "After he said that, I was more determined than ever to go to college and do well. I was determined to excel in college and to prove to my high school teacher that I could make it. This particular teacher, then, has been one of the most influential people in shaping my college career. Even though I still dislike him, he made me feel determined and self-confident . . . Moreover, whenever I feel like I want to give up, I think of his words which help me to go on through college."

It was not only teacher predictions but also parental predictions that students sought to overcome. Another student described herself as "so heavily dependent upon approval from my parents that the following incident really helped define my concept of ability." She recounted her own obsession with gymnastics in the face of her parents' belief that she lacked talent, and her eventual success in an event that her parents did not attend. She wrote: "The desire to disprove their statements drove me ever more to master the sport . . . Not having my parents' support did not matter. I suddenly became aware that *I* set limits for myself and the abilities and skills which I wished to acquire were mine to have, if I want to work for them." For some students, the costs of this "I'll prove them wrong" motivational stance were high indeed. One female student recalled that a cynical high-school chemistry teacher told her she would fail in college, feeding into her own worst fears:

> My reaction to Mr. S. was twofold. Part of me was bound and determined to prove him wrong while another part, which was fearful in the first place, became just a little bit more scared. In one sense, wanting to prove him wrong gave me a motivation not to give up (his predictions did tap a large sense of spite in me). I hung on (during a difficult freshman year) in part to prove him wrong, but I did not feel good about myself in the process and as a result went through a lot of emotional turmoil. Now as a senior, . . . his words don't have too much of an effect on me anymore, but at one point in time they were quite devastating to a pretty emotionally vulnerable high school senior.

Another student wrote about the horror of the first three months of first grade in which her teacher "believed that all the students were stupid unless they could prove otherwise, and I was no exception." She recalled multiple incidents of public humiliation, including being called "academically retarded" in front of her peers, and she wrote, "I can still feel the shame which flooded through me at that moment when everyone was looking at me." Despite the fact that her parents soon pulled her out of that school, many bad feelings remained, particularly with regard to the need to prove herself: "Throughout my school years, I have always felt it necessary to try as hard as I can at whatever I do. It is almost as if I am protecting myself against judgments like 'you are not capable of learning' . . . I have had to work through the fear that maybe my teacher was right and I am 'stupid.' It never mattered that I was always the top student in every class after the first grade, I still felt uneasy about my ability."

Beliefs and Actions of Significant Others

Other students credited the beliefs and actions of teachers, parents, siblings, and peers with helping to turn failed events into successes and thereby providing an alternative perspective. When one student began to have trouble with reading comprehension in third grade, her teacher stepped in with the right advice to slow her reading pace, with lasting positive effects on her enjoyment of reading. She wrote: "I see its significance very clearly . . . I may have put up a mental block against reading for the rest of my life. . . . my teacher, by taking me aside and showing me my problem, helped me to correct it and improve not only my reading skills, but my self-concept as well."

Another student wrote movingly of Mr. M., his communications teacher in high school shortly after he had moved from Mexico to the United States. The student had been extremely shy about speaking English in public, and Mr. M. had tried all sorts of ways to encourage him. The critical event was an invitation to teach a lesson to the class in Spanish, which went exceptionally well. When he saw his fellow classmates struggle with the Spanish language yet still continue, he "felt very good about myself, and from then on I was even more eager to improve my English, and as this was happening, my self-confidence was growing and still is, thanks to Mr. M."

So, too, do parents play a critical role in advocating for their children and in helping to buffer the negative effects from these remembered incidents. In the college-student sample, such actions included parental tutoring and interventions for placement in higher track placements in high school. Others described the important role of siblings in tutoring and mentoring, in one case teaching a child to find value and uniqueness in his own qualities.

Finally, there were examples of parents helping their children to recognize the signs of discrimination and advocate for change. One student wrote that on the first day of high school, in a college-preparatory English class, when asked her name she pronounced it with her native Spanish intonation. Her teacher asked her to say it in English. When the student refused, she was told to see the counselor so she could be assigned to remedial reading. The student responded that she belonged in the college-preparatory class—and was sent to the principal. Her mother fought back:

> She demanded that the teacher, the principal, myself, and she have a meeting immediately . . . My mother explained to the teacher that because I was a Chicana and chose to pronounce my name with a Spanish intonation did not mean that I belonged in a remedial class, and that in fact, because we were in America, that gave me the right to pronounce my name the way that I felt was appropriate. My mother then told the teacher that if she ever tried to change my culture, language, or beliefs, she would make it a point to have her position reviewed by the board. She then told the teacher that to be successful does not necessarily mean that one has to give up one's culture or values.

An African American student wrote about a traumatic shift from a predominantly black school in the South to a predominantly white school in the West, which led her from being on the honor roll to being suspended when she "had trouble understanding many of the phrases that the teacher and the other kids used, and I felt like I was left out of everything except trouble." It was when the school recommended institutionalization for "a mental problem" that "her parents drew the line." When they realized that I wasn't the problem, "this was a turning point or awakening for me. I realized that reaching my goals wasn't going to be easy. I would have to deal with many disguised incidents of prejudice. This incident also made me want to prove myself to others. I wanted to prove that I could be as good as anyone else. I look back and see how I could have lost my chance to go to college and to become a dentist because of a group of people who denied my capabilities and my potential. To this day, recognition of this event enables me to go on and to be persistent in reaching my goal."

Implications:
Enduring and Changing Effects

These retrospective accounts of critical incidents in schooling highlight the similarity between what young elementary school children have told us and what college students remembered many years later. What we see here are highly comparable events that both groups perceived as pivotal in shaping the will to learn, the belief in academic capability, and an interest in the subject matter. The narratives highlight memories of positive critical incidents in the classroom that are cherished and endure for their inspirational power to motivate and support these young adults. These positive incidents mirror what Eigil Pedersen and his colleagues (1978) described in their study of a long-remembered first-grade teacher, who reportedly fostered supportive, motivating, and helpful relationships with her students from a disadvantaged community. They found that with background differences in the socioeconomic means and educational level of families controlled, the educational attainment achieved by her students as adults was significantly higher than that achieved by the students of the other first-grade teachers in the school.

Also remembered are incidents of shaming that were perceived to create a stigma and erode the students' confidence. These narratives suggest enduring effects, even in this sample of high achievers. The costs were to self-esteem and to a loss of interest in (and loss of confidence about) subject areas for which expectations were harsh and limited. The research of Robert Pianta (1999) points to the importance of the student-teacher relationship for children's adjustment to school. More positive relationships were found to be associated with better adjustment and reduced referral for special education and grade retention. In addition, upward and downward deflections in student adjustment were associated with changes in the quality of relationships with teachers. Further, Pianta (1994) has demonstrated that teachers vary widely in the percentage of negative student relationships in their classrooms.

In this sample, we also have evidence that almost half of the reported negative events were reframed, reinterpreted, and reworked in ways that ultimately, in the eyes of these students, lessened the negative effects but did not always completely eliminate them. The narratives tell how negative incidents were overcome through the beliefs and actions of the students themselves, including self-regulative strategies—strategies that are not well fostered in education. Further, supportive and instructive relationships with significant others helped children overcome these difficulties by reframing negative incidents. This reframing conveyed not only a belief in the student ("they believed in me"), but most importantly was accompanied with effective and nonstigmatizing interventions.

Such incidents that communicate limits in ability are risky for children and are more frequently encountered in classroom achievement cultures that differentiate the treatment of high and low achievers. These narratives and our studies highlight the risk for formation of low and negative expectations in the face of student differences—in language, race and culture, learning disability, socioeconomic means, or even prior curricular exposure (such as when a child changes schools). There is also a growing body of research on the resilience of some children in demonstrating positive outcomes in the face of equal exposure to risk, an evolving research paradigm that can very usefully be applied to the study of expectancy effects (see Luthar, Cicchetti, and Becker 2000).

Other research, on self-efficacy beliefs, lends support to our findings about factors that can buffer children from the negative consequences of lowered academic expectations. In a recent prospective study of sixth and seventh graders (Bandura et al. 2001), it was found that socioeconomic status was associated with higher parental aspirations. In addition, the more parents believed that they could help their children in school, the higher their educational aspirations for their children. Further, the effect of parental aspirations on their children's career choice was mediated by children's own efficacy beliefs. That is, Albert Bandura and his colleagues note that "aspiring parents act in ways that build their children's academic, social and self-regulatory efficacy, raise their aspirations, and promote their scholastic achievements" (p. 198). Finally, children's perceived academic self-efficacy was more predictive of career choice than was actual academic achievement.

That motivation is critical can also be seen in the oppositional or "I'll show them" response—a stance that proved energizing in overcoming low expectations. Mavis Sanders (1997) described an achievement ethos that "allows African American students to respond to racial discrimination in ways that are conducive rather than detrimental to academic success" (p. 85). In her sample of eighth graders, she found a subgroup of children who had a high awareness of racism and perceived it as a challenge. As one student put it: "All my life, I have hated to hear anyone say, 'You can't do this.' If someone tells me that I can't, I just find a way to do it. It makes me want to do it more" (p. 90).

There is also a growing body of research that builds on the life course perspective of Glen Elder (1974) in *Children of the Great Depression* and follows diverse populations of children during their entire school careers to uncover important influences. Existing studies paint a picture of largely stable achievement trajectories. It is well documented that the children who perform poorly early in school continue to perform poorly over time (Dauber, Alexander, and Entwisle 1996). But the potential for malleability in these trajectories is also apparent. In a longitudinal study of disadvantaged first graders followed to grade six and then again to age sixteen, Shane Jimerson, Byron Egeland, and Adrian Teo (1999) found a widening gap: those children with the lowest economic means performed worse than would be expected from their early achievement and children with higher economic means performed better than could be expected.

Unfortunately, little is known about the incidence of deflected trajectories and thus, success stories. Using the National Educational Longitudinal Study (NELS) of 1988, a longitudinal database that followed a nationally representative sample of adolescents from eighth grade to the end of high school, Elise Cappella and I (2001) found that only 15 percent of students who entered high school with the lowest reading proficiency were able to turn around their reading achievement by the end of twelfth grade. This low rate of turnaround emphasizes first, the importance of getting it right early in a school career, and second, the need to increase the availability of buffering influences so that, in the face of risk, we can help children of all backgrounds succeed.

Our knowledge is increasing about the kinds of influences both inside and outside schools that may help create, maintain, or turn around a failing achievement trajectory. Indeed, the overall stability of achievement trajectories is a function of how we test and teach within a highly selection-driven educational system; that is, one cannot demonstrate what one has not been taught (Entwisle, Alexander, and Olson 1997; Sternberg, Grigorenko, and Bundy 2001).

Jeremy Finn and Donald Rock (1997), in their longitudinal study of students from grades eight through twelve, showed that higher levels of self-esteem, a greater sense of control, and more engagement in school distinguished an at-risk group of poor minority students who succeeded in school from a comparable group of students who dropped out. Finn and Rock (1997) emphasized that "unlike socioeconomic status (SES) and race, engagement may be manipulable: that is, educators may be able to encourage engagement behaviors to increase a student's chances of completing school successfully" (p. 221). The study by Jimerson, Egeland, and Teo (1999) of disadvantaged students documented that the quality of the home environment (stimulation, parent support, and organization), parent involvement in school, and fewer years in special education were all associated with positive changes in achievement trajectories from first grade to age sixteen. Similarly, the Cappella and Weinstein (2001) study of changes in achievement trajectories from eighth through twelfth grade showed that academic resilience could be improved when students have a sense of control and take more challenging classes in high school.

Indeed, these narratives provide vivid examples of how, despite obstacles, teachers and parents foster and support children's engagement in learning. Indeed, teachers have the power to inspire student growth in ways that students remember and draw support from well into their young adult years. Influential teachers and schools are critical socializing forces in our society that enable children and youth to develop fully. What the positive transformative incidents seem to share is another person's empathy for the student point of view and provision of resources and strategies—all while recognizing the pain, fear, and uncertainty of failure. One student wrote about the remarkable teaching assistant for her undergraduate calculus class. By inviting her to use him as a resource, by never making her feel stupid, and by patiently trying different learning strategies, he helped her to turn F's into eventual A's in ever higher-level math courses. She wrote: "It made me see that education could be a lot more effective if teachers took the time to take the students' point of view, and remember what it is like to not understand something, and adjust their teaching procedures accordingly. Often, teachers forget this, and I think this makes communication and teaching more difficult."

The essays also brought to light the importance of identifying and appreciating the individuality of each student. One student wrote about a fortuitous "mistake" made in a painting class at age five when she spilled some red paint under the eye of a face she had been working on. Her action, to incorporate those drops as tears, and the comments of her teacher to her mother that she had "spontaneously changed the whole context of the drawing by converting some meaningless drops of paint into running tears," became, in her eyes, a metaphor for a flexible creativity that she possessed—an awareness that she has carried with her to this day. What moves one in this narrative is the student's comment that "My teacher was carefully watching me all the time that I drew, and he *saw* what was going on." A teacher who watches carefully can come to know the uniqueness of children, and in doing so, can give a tremendous gift to children by leading them to appreciate their own special qualities.

If we have at hand evidence that the academic expectations we set for children and the educational interventions we implement can, under certain conditions, promote negative self-fulfilling prophecies that place children at risk for school failure, it is time to turn to preventive intervention—to intervene earlier to prevent the negative effects of low expectations and self-fulfilling prophecies in schooling and to put in place conditions that promote positive prophecies for all children.

Promoting positive prophecies on this scale for all children may seem to be nearly impossible. Note this exchange taken from a published interview by researcher Ursula Casanova with Sharon Robinson, then assistant secretary of education for the Office of Educational Research and Improvement (Casanova 1994, p. 28). Researcher Ursula Casanova asked:

> Suppose an ambitious, energetic, and clever graduate student came to you wanting ideas about what she might study for her dissertation . . . what would you say to her?

Assistant Secretary Sharon Robinson responded:

> The question I guess that I have is, "Can we really tolerate having all students learning?" . . . Is the principle that all students can learn and live productive and fulfilled lives so threatening to some basic aspects of our identity and fears as individuals and as a society that we just can't accept it? Because I am wondering what's keeping us from getting there? . . . And I would want to know, "How do we work with prospective and practicing teachers to develop an orientation to all students, which has them see in each and every one a precious potential that has to be developed in spite of everything? . . . I'm not sure a graduate student wouldn't look at me and say, "I'm trying to get out of school, not into heaven."

Chuckle as we might about the plight of the graduate student who would dare take on such a challenge, what is keeping us from "getting there" is a question we can no longer afford to ignore.

The current zeitgeist of educational reform is to set higher, national standards for expected educational outcomes. It comes with sharp teeth: the assessment and monitoring of progress and high-stakes accountability. It also comes with a mandate for districts to use research-validated models of whole-school educational reform in schools that serve disadvantaged children and to work toward scaling up successful innovative programs in order to promote positive changes throughout schools, districts, and nationwide. Unfortunately, the research on expectancy effects in schooling is not informing these efforts beyond the call for "high expectations for all." Not only have the national goals regarding educational standards been narrowly framed, but these reforms also miss the mark by failing to revamp the educational system in which such expectations are embedded and differentially nurtured. Asking for accountability without systemic change is foolhardy; and as the research demonstrates, expecting or willing change without addressing the supportive interventions is simply half of the expectancy equation—belief without action (Weinstein 1996).

Yet how we implement programs in schools and in teacher preparation classes that can develop and support these positive qualities and practices of teachers is a relatively understudied question. Can helpful ways of interacting with a diversity of students be learned and nurtured? Can we maximize the opportunities for children to participate in such caring and instructive interactions with teachers and in schools? Chapter 8 considers how we might intervene to shift from highly stratified climates in schools and classrooms (with high expectations for some, and low expectations for others) toward more inclusive but equally rigorous climates of high expectations for all—in particular, for the forgotten students at the bottom of the achievement hierarchy.

PART III

Expectations in Systems:
Through the Eyes of Educators

Changing a Stratified School Culture

We have had to learn to guard against lowering our expectations for these students, just because they have been labeled low-ability . . . We have fallen into the trap of believing that the "noise" which is generated in an honors class is productive, while the "noise" which happens in a low ability class can only be nonproductive and distracting to learning . . . Thanks to our meetings which relentlessly, yet gently, reprimand us whenever we fall into the trap of dealing with our students in this manner, we have found that indeed we can expect our students to do the same tasks which we expect of our higher ability students. Sometimes it takes a few extra steps to achieve the desired product but we often achieve it. In fact, our students become more interested and are more willing to perform when higher demands are placed on them.

—A high school teacher

How can we change limiting and differentiating beliefs and practices so that high expectations for all students are nurtured through the inevitable yet diverse obstacles to learning? How can we transform schools so that principals and teachers are supported in their efforts to engage diverse student populations in a challenging education? Limiting perceptions of students, colleagues, and the system are reinforced by a web of institutional policies that affect teachers and students alike. Once formed, perceptions and practices are rarely reexamined or changed, particularly in the isolated teaching conditions of most schools. These are precisely the conditions that can breed self-fulfilling prophecies about student achievement. The reframing of belief, action, and policy is far less likely when teachers work apart from each other, when administrators remove themselves from the instructional life of schools, when the work of schools is disconnected from research advances in the field, and when school staff members do not know how every one of their students is progressing. Thus as we seek to raise expectations, we need to consider the interrelationships between the culture of schools and the culture of classrooms.

There are examples of school systems that have equitable or differentiated environments. Such school systems can reinforce or undermine the culture created by individual teachers, whether they are expressed within classrooms or across classrooms and departments, such as in tracks, special education, and gifted classes. While expectations are often manifested in interpersonal interactions between teachers and students, their long-term consequences are ultimately driven and reinforced by an array of institutional arrangements at a school level. These institutional arrangements vary in elementary, secondary, and postsecondary levels of education and have implications for both those who teach, and who are themselves continual learners, and those who learn. Such arrangements can turn fleeting judgments into lasting beliefs and can determine what labels, which educational opportunities, and what kind of supports are offered to whom.

This chapter examines the efforts of an urban high school to shift a highly stratified culture of academic expectations toward an enabling culture of high expectations and appropriate instructional supports for all students. What structural arrangements and processes are necessary to enable this reform? I draw upon the data and findings from a collaborative intervention study to raise expectations for incoming ninth-grade students at risk for failure through systemic changes in classroom practices and school policies (see Collins 1988; Cone 1988; Mehlhorn 1988; Simontacchi 1988; Weinstein et al. 1991; Weinstein, Madison, and Kuklinski 1995; Weinstein 1998).

An examination of expectancy change is especially critical in light of the feverish national agenda to implement higher educational standards for all children and to improve upon the scaling-up of reform from individual classrooms to whole schools, districts, and states. As currently conceptualized and implemented, these efforts lack a coherent understanding of the deeply institutionalized dynamics of expectancy effects and will likely go the way of previous reforms. As Seymour Sarason (1971, 1996) has long lamented, schooling has been largely impervious to waves of educational reform, whether implemented using bottom-up or top-down strategies. Most educational improvement has been found in isolated settings like single classrooms, almost never in whole systems—a regularity that Richard Elmore (1996) calls the fundamental pathology of the education system. And despite repeated cycles of reform, changes rarely make it past the classroom door (Cuban 1990). These reforms fail and fail again, as Sarason argues, because they never change the underlying culture of schooling. Although we are knee-deep in raising educational standards and holding schools accountable, remarkably little is known about how to effectively and enduringly implement and support equitable expectations in schools that have for so long differentiated sharply among students in providing educational opportunities.

Research on Expectancy Change

In Schools

The experimental studies of expectancy effects are, in fact, expectancy "change" efforts that implant falsely positive expectations on unsuspecting teachers. As discussed previously, such manipulations have improved student achievement or intelligence scores under certain conditions, particularly when they are conducted early in the school year when teachers have little prior knowledge of students (Raudenbush 1984). Relatively few studies have directly manipulated the expectations of students, what Margaret Rappaport and Herbert Rappaport (1975) have called targeting "Pygmalion, the other half of the expectancy equation" (p. 531). Using a sample of five- to six-year-olds in a randomized experiment implemented over twelve weeks, these researchers found that inducing positive expectations in young disadvantaged students (through praise and positive predictions for future performance) was more successful (resulted in greater achievement gains for the students) than doing so with the teacher and was as successful as the condition in which both teachers and students received the feedback. Further, Elizabeth Cohen and her colleagues (see Cohen 1986; Cohen and Lotan 1997) have developed a series of interventions to produce equal-status interactions in the classroom and thereby change children's perceptions of their own and peers' ability. In this instructional strategy for heterogeneous classrooms, teachers are trained to talk about multiple abilities (that none of us has all these abilities; that each one of us has some of these abilities) and to assign competence to low-status children. Cohen and Lotan (1997) have documented that when teachers use the status treatments, low-status or low-achieving students participate more in the classroom.

There are also a small number of intervention studies that seek to increase teacher awareness of their differential expectations for and treatment of students as a first step in changing these expectations. The results have not been uniformly strong. Using observational data (Good and Brophy 1974) or feedback concerning the gap between teacher and student perceptions of teacher treatment (Babad 1990), the interventions help teachers become aware of their differential expectations for students and teach them to equalize their patterns of interacting with students so that, for example, praise and criticism are given more evenly. Babad (1990) found that half of his treatment teachers resisted the intervention feedback and further, that student reports did not match teacher reports of change. Good and Brophy (1974) noted changes in teacher participation and interaction with target children, but no change in negative behaviors toward these children.

This empirical work has been scaled up to schoolwide inservice programs, such as in the work of Patrick Proctor (1984) or the widely known TESA (Teacher Expectations and Student Achievement), which has been a regular fixture in staff development nationwide since the mid-seventies (Kerman 1979). In TESA, teachers are taught about fifteen classroom behaviors (concerned with response opportunities, positive feedback, and personal regard) that research has demonstrated are used more often with perceived high achievers than with perceived low achievers. Teachers are trained to increase their use of these behaviors with low achievers. Evaluations of this widely adopted program have been sparse. A recent evaluation by Denise Gottfredson and her colleagues (1995) did not find positive effects. These researchers concluded that "well-implemented TESA training delivered according to the specifications of the developers in the context of a high-level district support for the program model did not produce changes in teacher practices among the teachers participating in the study" (p. 162). Further, the predicted changes in student achievement were not documented.

The passage of legislation has provided another avenue of addressing unequal expectations and learning supports for certain groups of children. By extending the right to education to girls, blacks, and Latinos; desegregating schools; mainstreaming handicapped children into regular classes; and implementing educational standards and high-stakes accountability, these legislative interventions have sought to improve the educational opportunities of those for whom lower expectations were held. Today, too, there is considerable debate about legislatively dismantling tracking systems in high school as a means of equalizing opportunity and raising expectations for students assigned to the lower tracks. While the effects of these legislative mandates are complex to evaluate either in the short-term or long-term (in part because any conclusion depends on the outcomes considered [Wells and Crain 1994]), evidence suggests insidious processes of resegregation that can take place. For example, although children of different ethnic groups were brought together by law into the same schools, they were then resegregated within schools into separate programs, separate classes, and within-class subgroups, with blacks and Latinos still overrepresented in the less challenging programs (Epstein 1985). Without addressing the underlying processes that give rise to and sustain differential beliefs about the potential to learn and differential allocation of educational programs, such segregation will likely recur in these and other forms.

In Work Organizations

In a similar vein, there exists an experimental literature on the implanting of falsely positive expectations or the reframing of test results in work organizations. This literature was recently summarized in a meta-analysis by Brian McNatt (2000). Studies targeted managers or their subordinates in a variety of work settings and included actual performance as a dependent variable. For example, Sasson Oz and Dov Eden (1994) documented raised productivity of subordinates when leaders were led to reinterpret low test results not as evidence of inability but rather as the result of test unreliability or a lack of effort and motivation at the time of testing. In targeting subordinates, Dov Eden and Yaakov Zuk (1995) demonstrated that those naval cadets who were trained to believe that given certain test results they would overcome seasickness in rough seas did perform better at their tasks than did a control sample of cadets. In McNatt's (2000) meta-analysis of seventeen such management studies, the results were strongly supportive of expectancy effects overall, with the effects strongest and most consistent in military organizations where authority is more centralized, with men, and with individuals for whom low expectations were initially held.

Of import to expectancy change in schools, only two of these seventeen studies examined leader-subordinate relationships involving previous contact. The existence of preestablished relationships and the use of deception greatly limit the effectiveness of Pygmalion principles (Eden et al. 2000; McNatt 2000). In the words of McNatt, "Interpersonal expectancy-raising may be a weak long-term, stand-alone intervention and could benefit from being embedded with a credible program that can serve as a focus for raising expectations" (p. 320).

In the Research Laboratory

Like the research on expectancies in industry, which has intervened at the point of first contact, much of the empirical evidence on behavioral confirmation and disconfirmation has been conducted in "laboratory analogs of first encounters with strangers" (Snyder and Stukas 1999, p. 293). Researchers have demonstrated behavioral as well as perceptual confirmation in a variety of settings and with different expectancies (Snyder 1992; Claire and Fiske 1998). Despite the limitations of this work, the research on stereotype change points to social contextual features under which negative perceptions are successfully challenged. These include conditions where disconfirming information is systematically made available, analyzed, and generalized (Bar-Tal 1989; Olson and Zanna 1993; Rothbart and John 1985; Rothbart and Park 1986), where motivational goals stress accuracy and accountability (Neuberg 1989), and where interactions are cooperative, coequal, successful, and lacking in conflict (Desforges et al. 1991). Research has also shown that certain attributes of the person targeted with bias can limit behavioral confirmation, including awareness of the stereotype (Hilton and Darley 1985) and certainty about one's own self-concept (Swann 1987). Self-fulfilling prophecies require *powerful* perceivers and *powerless* targets of others' perceptions and actions (Copeland 1994).

A More Comprehensive Expectancy-Change Model

Previous reform efforts have made clear that neither deception, nor insight, nor policy mandate are sufficient to alter an established school culture of stratified expectations: the relationships and instructional practices have too many embedded and interdependent components. To address more than the overt symptoms of the problem and to institutionalize the changes made, our intervention model needed to address both the vision (all the parts of a positive expectancy culture) and the change process (the working conditions) for teachers and administrators who have long-term relationships with each other and with students. To promote an enduring psychological as well as systemwide change that will get inside the classroom door, school staff needed regularized and continuing opportunities, tools, and resources to reexamine underlying beliefs, to observe and monitor what is actually in place, and to adapt, design, implement, and evaluate more effective practices and policies derived from the research findings.

The Vision

We targeted changes in the six features of the instructional environment identified earlier as critical in creating a differentiated and selection-driven achievement culture. With the goal of working more effectively with heterogeneous learners, we focused on changes in (1) ability-based grouping and tracking practices, (2) curricular challenge and differentiation, (3) ability beliefs and evaluation systems based on inborn, global, and normal-curve notions about ability, (4) motivational systems that promoted performance goals, extrinsic reinforcement, and competition, (5) opportunities for student agency in learning, and (6) the climate of relationships in the classroom, in the school, and with parents.

In practice, this meant increasing the use of heterogeneous, flexible, and interest-based grouping practices with more challenging curricula, which would widen exposure and invite more students to meet academic challenges. This included fostering the intrinsic motivation of students by encouraging work that speaks to children's own interests instead of being linked to external rewards, by supporting learning goals that focus on the demands of the task rather than on performance, and by nurturing cooperative rather than competitive ways of working. These motivational strategies deepen student involvement and willingness to expend effort in the face of hard challenges. Further, they increase student choice and responsibility for learning, through the use of self-regulation strategies and leadership opportunities. This increased student agency would also encourage intrinsic motivation, enable new talent to be uncovered and appreciated, and help students to become less dependent on teachers in organizing and evaluating their work.

If teachers are fully persuaded that children have multiple abilities, that ability is malleable, and that all can meet a specified standard, they will feel encouraged to broaden their teaching strategies and offer a wider range of performance opportunities that would measure competencies. Such a change in attitude would also shift the responsibility for failure from students to teachers and underscore absolute rather than relative criteria for judging accomplishment, focusing critical attention toward making sure that all of the students improve to the point of reaching grade-level standards. Finally, classrooms and schools that insist on a challenging curriculum while offering diverse and unlimited opportunities for participation in the classroom and schoolwide, foster warmer, more concerned relationships among teachers, students, and parents—and thus a more inclusive community.

These changes, when coordinated, focus attention on the development rather than the selection of talent in students.

The Change Process

Informed by laboratory research on stereotype change and expectancy disconfirmation as well as research on school reform, our change process drew heavily upon collaborative rather than prescriptive approaches. Organizational change theory, and in particular, findings from follow-up studies of school reforms that persisted over the long-term, emphasize the importance of involved key players. Given such participation, innovations can be reshaped to fit local conditions, to create coherent changes at multiple levels, and to weather continuing threats to implementation and institutionalization (Maehr and Midgley 1991, 1996; McLaughlin 1990). Research findings on school-university collaborative partnerships and on the norms of workplace settings suggest that collaborative approaches extend resources and provide support to sustain the difficult challenge of systemic change (Gifford 1986; Lieberman 1992; Little 1993; McLaughlin 1990; Rosenholtz 1989). Our change process included these critical components: (1) a school-university collaborative partnership, (2) a membership of key players that included teachers, administrators, and university researchers, (3) a regular two-hour weekly meeting, with additional planning time, (4) a long-term perspective, (5) shared responsibility for students, (6) an opportunity to read research findings and translate them into practice and policy, and (7) the monitoring of conditions and outcomes at multiple levels. The hands-on access to research findings, the built-in monitoring and evaluation of school practices, and the diversity of input to the process both expanded and challenged sources of information and analysis—which was also critical to promoting expectancy disconfirmation. In addition, it is important to highlight that the collaborative ways in which teachers, administrators, and researchers were asked to work together mirrored the features of a classroom culture that they were encouraged to create for their students.

The Case of Los Robles High School

The Invitation

Our collaboration began in a graduate seminar on school reform designed to field test this expectancy-enhancement intervention. By design, it included diverse membership, the reading of original research, classroom and school observations of the instructional features that shaped differentiated or equitable achievement cultures, and a final project culminating in demonstrations and evaluations of innovative lessons and policies. In order to stimulate exchange across research and practice communities, the course was opened to principals and teachers in addition to graduate students from the psychology department and the school of education at the University of California, Berkeley. For the community participants, course or district credit was arranged through university extension. The seminar's activities were crafted to make vivid the communication of expectations and to empower participants to change their own and others' practice to promote more positive educational prophecies for children.

A participating high school teacher wrote this about the seminar experience: "I found myself changing as a result of the research I was reading and applying in my classroom. For a long time, I had seen myself as an effective teacher of 'at risk' students—mostly because I was 'sympathetic' to them—I cringe at that word now . . . At the end of this class, I was certain of two things: I knew that my way of teaching 'at risk' students had dramatically changed and I knew that the teachers at my school needed to be exposed to what I had learned." She challenged us to help her apply this expectancy-change model to her high school—a challenge I accepted with some trepidation, given the more complicated departmentalized structure of high schools and the wider and more entrenched achievement gap between students at that level.

The School

The mid-sized urban high school was described by staff as "aging, graffiti-marred, and badly in need of repair." Its district was suffering greatly from reduced per-pupil funding for education. Los Robles (a pseudonym) was one of six comprehensive high schools in the district with approximately 1,500 students and a certificated staff of approximately eighty, almost equally divided between men and women. Drawing students from both wealthier hill areas and poorer industrial flatlands, the school served an ethnically and socioeconomically diverse student body with an ethnic composition of 47.7 percent black, 5.0 percent Hispanic, 16.3 percent Asian, 30.1 percent Caucasian, and 1.9 percent unknown, and with 13 percent of students on AFDC (Aid for Dependent Children). Ethnic minorities made up 68 percent of the student population and 20 percent of the certificated staff. Almost half of the school staff had masters degrees and 88 percent were age thirty-six or older. The teacher-student ratio was 21.2 to 1, the student-counselor ratio was approximately 388 to 1, and teachers were assigned five of seven teaching periods per day. With some classes as large as forty students, teachers worked with 125–200 students each day. Like in most high schools, these were exceptionally challenging working conditions for teachers as well as administrative staff.

Student achievement scores at Los Robles placed the high school just below the state median level, yet the school was known to rank high in the number of graduates it sent to the University of California system. Four levels of instructional tracking were in place: remedial, general, honors, and advanced placement. A look at course enrollment patterns as described in accreditation reports revealed the familiar bimodal distribution found in many high schools: proportionately higher enrollments of whites and Asian Americans than blacks (there were few Hispanics in this school) in certain subjects as well as in higher-challenge classes. For example, while 64.5 percent of white students took chemistry, only 24 percent of black students did. This mix of students and the racially and socioeconomically linked curricular differentiation was reported to create underlying tensions in the school.

First Contacts

The principal and vice-principal as well as the superintendent responded enthusiastically to the project and to its collaborative nature. Tellingly for the future and in line with the curricular differentiation in place, the administrators pledged their own participation but they proposed first, a voluntary model of participation for the teachers and second, a focus on more effective teaching of low-stanine classes, especially for teachers who taught these classes. Thus, we were confronted early on with where the school stood— bound to individual participation rather than a whole-school commitment, and bound, too, to highly differentiated academic expectations. Especially discomforting to us, we later discovered that students assigned to low-stanine classes at ninth grade (on the basis of previous achievement scores and grades) were enrolled in courses that did not meet the requirements for entry into the California State University (which admitted graduates in the upper third of the class) or the University of California (which admitted the top 12 percent of the class) systems. Even if they were eventually moved out of these classes, students could not earn the required four years of college preparatory English necessary for four-year college or university admittance. This was a reality that many students and parents did not know: indeed, while the student handbook indicated forty credits of college preparatory English was required, at that time there was no mention that "some English classes do not meet this requirement, so ask your counselor"—a caveat that was added after our project began. The disproportionate membership of certain ethnic minorities in these classes was fueled as well by white flight, as we later observed. In the first weeks of class, numerous Caucasian students transferred out, perhaps at parental urging—leaving these classes with an even higher representation of African American students than planned, and than existed in the school as a whole (68.3 percent compared to 47.7 percent). Thus, we began with what was already in place at the school, just as teaching begins with where the students are.

The Introductory Meetings

The project was introduced at an inservice meeting, which at the school's request was entitled "Working with Low-Stanine Classes" and to which all staff were invited. In three ninety-minute afterschool sessions designed to mirror the expectancy-change process, we asked teachers and administrators to read brief research articles about each of the components of the expectancy communication model (we provided packets of assigned materials), to observe themselves or each other, to write about and share what they learned about these practices (we required written field notes), and finally, to brainstorm about changes in practices and policies that would offer high expectations and instructional support to all students. These inservice workshops were attended by the principal, vice-principal, and twelve teachers from the departments of English, history, science, and math.

Teachers wrote honestly about the complexity of what we were trying to do in such a short span of time, amid hectic working conditions: "I found it impossible to complete the assignments within the time limits. As do most teachers, I was in the middle of a unit and could not devise an ideal lesson in just one day . . . so I tried to use the principles as I understood to revise a lesson already in progress to meet the requirements." Implementing these new ideas successfully was, of course, not easy and required modifications. The opportunity to reflect upon and share what elements worked, what elements did not work, and the small successes helped teachers to move forward with improved efforts. Another teacher wrote that "her organizing of the [cooperative] groups was poorly done: students resisted, and absences prevented a balance." But she added, "Here, the task was mine—they [the students] didn't do such a bad job. Interest and involvement for the rest of the assignment was substantial. I was free of fighting for their attention and could see how they worked together. Students stopped to share what they were doing in their groups as they left class."

In three weeks, we had engaged administrators and teachers in the shared tasks of reading research findings and applying new thinking to their classes with low-stanine students. And we had evidence that despite the feeling of "too much for too little time," new learning did take place. An administrator wrote, "I discovered and re-discovered several important things for my teachers, that is, the value of using small groups for noisy ninth graders." The workshops "created a marvelous atmosphere for tired teachers at the end of their day . . . and reached a few people who were floundering." A teacher also commented, "The opportunity to discuss with other teachers was most meaningful."

The Culture of Expectations for Teachers

Yet the working climate we had created in the inservice sessions stood in stark contrast to the ways in which the teachers routinely worked. When we asked "How much do you exchange ideas?" One teacher's response was particularly revealing: "It is not consistent. On the average, there seems to be an atmosphere of competition—the inference is . . . Well, I've done that. You mean you haven't done it?" Typical of many schools, we saw remarkable similarities between the teachers' work culture and the differentiated achievement culture that children had reported and we had observed.

The teachers described their curricular work as creative and satisfying with the brighter students but tough and often boring with the less bright students. While they often decried the monotony of many of their routine tasks, they reported feeling overwhelmed by the challenging tasks of the inservice—the reading of research, classroom observations, and written assignments. The feelings they expressed were much like those they later reported for their lower-track students, in the face of increasingly difficult curricular assignments. The teachers also described themselves as "tracked" just like their students, a phenomenon Merrilee Finley (1984) has noted. Their interactional groupings largely reflected the ability level of the students they were teaching as well as their departmental affiliation. There existed remarkably little interaction across disciplinary lines. It was also commonly acknowledged that the newest and perceived weakest teachers were assigned to the lowest-track classrooms, whereas honors and advanced placement assignments were seen as rewards given out by the administration. Many teachers who expressed a special interest in teaching the lower-track students saw costs to their involvement: "They were taking on the most difficult groups in the school, ones that other teachers wouldn't work with." A major risk of this project, voiced by many, was that the involvement of some teachers would signal to others that they did not need to take responsibility for these students. This risk was on our minds as well, because such a result would militate against whole-school reforms.

Not surprisingly, the sharing of classroom observations in front of administrators and other teachers proved scary. A competitive atmosphere prevailed that emphasized performance and comparison, rather than learning and individual improvement. Teachers described an implicit achievement hierarchy that distinguished among the good and the not so good, the fledgling and the more experienced, the more flexible and the more rigid teachers. The opinion that "some dogs can't learn new tricks" was expressed numerous times. Akin to teachers' beliefs about students, teachers' beliefs about colleagues' capacities for change reflected largely fixed rather than malleable notions about ability to learn. Further, agency among all teachers was not actively being developed. In contrast to many staff development activities, the structure of our inservice sessions demanded participation from all, through the sharing of required assignments. Yet some resisted this approach. As one teacher put it: "I understand that you set up a program to help me discover things for myself but I guess I wanted to be fed information." Finally, the climate of relationships with fellow teachers and administrators was described as lacking in trust and as failing to create a larger, inclusive community. Teachers decried that they could not "choose their colleagues" and that relationships with administrators were "filled with misunderstandings and differing perspectives."

In short, the climate in which teachers worked mirrored the differentiated culture described in classrooms like that of Mrs. Iver. These working conditions likely kept differential expectations for students in place, both within and across classrooms. Why did this unhealthy work environment persist? First, this way of interacting was what teachers knew best: indeed, it was reinforced on a daily basis and not surprisingly, modeled in classrooms. Second, without the regular opportunity to review research that would improve instruction for students with diverse needs, to examine school data about how different groups of students were actually doing, to challenge each others' perceptions, and to provide support to improve practice and policy, educational prophecies that were positive for some and negative for others remained largely in place, subject to individual differences between teachers. We theorized that if school staff members changed their beliefs about themselves, their colleagues, and the system, as well as refined different kinds of educational interventions with the support of their peers, they would be better able to make such changes for students.

Adapting the Expectancy-Change Model

The inservice workshops elicited commitments from twelve staff members, eight teachers from a variety of departments (English, history, science, computer science, and special education), and four administrators (the principal, vice-principal, one counselor, and one dean) who joined the collaborative team for the first year of the project. We negotiated the details of our shared vision in a two-day planning meeting held during the August following the April inservice workshops. Using the principles of the model outlined earlier, we targeted all incoming ninth-graders assigned to the lowest track of English classes. Students were assigned to one or more of the classes of participating teachers, who shared a common group of students as well as a common preparation period each day, scheduled around the lunch hour. This created, in effect, a school within a school to test the expectancy-enhancement intervention.

This model of expectancy change was implemented and evaluated over a two-year period, although the project continued well beyond my involvement. Our evaluation, also collaboratively negotiated, captured the course of the intervention over time as well as evidence of change at the multiple levels of student, teacher, and school policy. Our data were narrative records of meetings, pre- and post-ratings of practices by teachers, and pre- and post-data collected from student records, examining the target students as compared to students from previous years. We followed a sample of 158 students (the first-year cohort) over the two-year project, a group whose progress we contrasted with an archival sample of 154 comparable students from the two previous years' classes.

Challenging Entrenched Beliefs, Practices, and Policies

This vision reflected the ideal, of course. In reality, even getting around the same table at the same time proved problematic. The teachers and administrators who joined in this effort were passionate and experienced educators already committed to these students, open to trying anything that worked and open to working with each other. Yet at the start of the project, even well-intentioned teachers and administrators reported negative perceptions—of the project, colleagues, administrators, and students. Indeed, the thorny problem in disconfirming negative expectations and developing more positive expectations is that there exists ample evidence for the negative perspective. To the extent that expectations are perceived to have been confirmed, each fresh interaction provides additional support for prevailing beliefs. There exists a rich knowledge base about optimal conditions for fostering motivation and learning as well as substantial and underutilized resources within schools that if harnessed can engage students and support teachers. Yet sadly, teachers are often not working in conditions that expose them to a wealth of alternative strategies—so instead they foreclose too early, before optimal opportunities to learn have been provided to students. And administrators, buffeted by multiple and conflicting demands, fail to engage their teachers in problem definition and resolution—before the opportunity to succeed with diverse learners has been provided teachers.

The cornerstone of our intervention was to promote a change in "working conditions" that could challenge or undermine these negative perceptions and support alternative pedagogical interventions that would ultimately, after considerable trial and error, bring about more positive results. Our work to reframe expectations (cognitive change), refashion instruction (behavioral and programmatic change), and change the school climate and policy (institutional change), was interwoven seamlessly to promote an interdependence of influences, as an ecological theory would suggest.

Reframing Expectations

The initial setback in securing a common conference period meant a short lunch hour for shared work, with two subgroup meetings at the beginning and end. This difficult starting point fueled teachers' already low expectations about obtaining administrative support. As one of the teachers explained, "Teachers gave up on joint projects because of the amount of overwork, combined with the lack of administrative support and follow-through." Adding to this understandable frustration was the teachers' desire to be credited for our weekly meetings. One teacher spoke for all when she said, "I feel I should get units for this," but an administrator countered that the district would not award credit for planning, only for teacher develop-ment and teacher education.

Teachers also admitted misgivings about the project that they had not shared at the inservice. There were concerns about "a confused start with little prior notification" and about "having expected higher-achieving stu-dents." Some teachers felt that "they had been assigned to the project, rather than choosing it" and that "the amount of time asked for was too much, the lunchtime was a crazy, pressured time to meet, the program of readings was burdensome, the readings while wonderful did not apply to their school," and so on. Not surprisingly in the context of tough conditions, teachers felt "overwhelmed—exhausted by teaching, extracurricular, and career-development obligations."

There were also doubts about their colleagues. Teachers, including them-selves, were viewed as unlikely "to make the time commitment," unlikely "to use period substitute teachers in order to observe each others' teaching," and unlikely "to profit from the intervention." Indeed, teachers felt unable to meet the demands of a leadership role. As one teacher pointed out, there was "no way teachers could run these meetings, they didn't have [the] au-thority." Teachers and administrators argued over what could be required of teachers and parents. For example, administrators noted that they "would like to require that teachers attend [school] rallies but can't due to union contracts." Teachers complained that despite their best efforts to arrange parent conferences, "these parents did not show up."

Finally, many reservations were shared about the students' capabilities to benefit from the project. It was felt that this "lower group of students needed behavioral improvement before we can really make a difference aca-demically." Student disruptiveness, such as taunting, was seen as "a large part of the adverse conditions under which teachers operated." It was agreed that these students "couldn't follow directions, remain on-task for ten minutes, and would rapidly take advantage of lapses in discipline." It was emphasized that "these kids want to be force-fed information and resist tasks that require independent thinking or higher-level operations." It was also noted that so few of these students "participated in any extracurricular activities . . . they lack particular talents and skills." One teacher explained: "The reading level of our students ranges from third grade to seventh grade. Their writing skills are extremely deficient. They bring with them very little background knowledge from which they can draw to enhance learning. Many of the students hate to read, have trouble listening, do not study, and in fact, know very little about studying."

Thus, we began with our backs up against these multiple perceived constraints. Our task, as researchers from outside this system, was to identify and confront the constraints systematically and to avoid being stopped in our tracks. We were aware that we were seeing student behavior in the context of membership in so-called low-ability classrooms, where all the students had suffered prior failures, the models for school success were limited, and the curriculum provided was remedial rather than challenging. But for the school staff, attention was initially focused on the limitations of these students, not on the limitations of the context of instruction. This is not to deny that the observed deficiencies of the students were indeed enormous. As we were told by participating teachers, "some negative attitudes were justified, both about teachers and students." Another teacher countered that "teachers might need to accept students' limits." But at what point do we accept "limits" in a student's capability to learn?

Our question, increasingly shared, was how to understand these observed "deficiencies" (what they were and under which contexts they were perceived) and how to intervene pedagogically from this point onward. By providing directed assignments, focusing our inquiry through agenda-setting, identifying potential resources, redefining the problem, and affirming positive expectations as well as examples of individuals' strengths, the spirited discussions in our weekly meetings began to shake up perceptions, albeit slowly.

This exchange illustrates the reexamination of underlying assumptions—in this case, the capacity of low-performing students to engage in more challenging material and the kind of teaching support that is required. A teacher reported that one of the writing exercises ("What's It Like to Be a Ninth Grader?") had originally been assigned only to her advanced classes but based on the advice of the last meeting, she had given it to her project class as well. She shared samples of student writing that pointed to an overall sad tone and to the students' feeling as if they were of second-class status in the school. Several teachers commented that the purpose of giving different assignments was to better target or address the particular needs of students. But another teacher countered with a description of the positive results of assigning her project class a reading task from a ninth-grade-level text. She said, "They could see that it wasn't babyish, and they liked that . . . They really tried to work with it." She did describe the difficulty they had with the text, however, due to their limited vocabulary. Another teacher recalled that when she first taught, she had a reputation for "teaching anybody anything," but over the years, she'd slipped away from being "so democratic." I interjected that the school could maintain the same high expectations for all students using similar tasks but also create resources and strategies to help lesser skilled students move forward to meet the same goals. The "disillusioned" teacher responded that most of the group wanted to do exactly that, but did not know how: "I guess I'm not a very creative person because I find it hard to come up with those." Another teacher quickly replied that "it was hard for everyone; teachers needed to support each other in learning how."

By the next meeting, although concerned about the time it took, our "disillusioned" teacher reported on a lesson that she had tried in advanced, average, and project history classes. Prior to showing the film *A Tale of Two Cities,* she had spent three days preparing the project classes with "silent reading of the story synopsis, class discussion of reading, important points, relation to class content, and vocabulary" in order to avoid failure. In the past, her "low students got nothing from the film and just snickered that it was too funky," but this time, with the preparation, the students themselves told her how "good" they had been in responding to the film. Another teacher summarized our learning by pointing out that while "student behavior continued to be of importance, higher-order changes, as in the curriculum, led to changes in student behavior."

Not only were perceptions of student capability shifting, but as the challenging demands of the project became more familiar, it was perceived by many of the teachers (but not all) as less onerous and more rewarding. As one teacher described it, "Our meetings were planned and focused so that we had a sense of progress and accomplishment; we were committed to attending regularly and preparing by reading research or attempting new practices in our classrooms." She went on: "Occasionally after teaching three classes Thursday morning, I was disheartened or exhausted and longed for an hour of quiet solitude, but my commitment to my colleagues always won out and the support and stimulation of the meeting was always energizing and refreshing." Another teacher described a shift from fear of sharing to a real colleagueship: "From the years of isolation where some teachers were afraid to ask for help or suggestions for fear of admitting they had a problem, we came to see each other as colleagues and collaborators, people with strengths that could support us and ideas that could help us be better teachers." And indeed, despite their initial disbelief, teachers began to take leadership roles in these meetings: "We continued to read one or two papers a week with each of us volunteering in turn to lead the discussion the following week. Reading the research and discussing its application was one of the most interesting aspects of the project to me."

Refashioning Instruction

We worked hard to address what "teachers did not know how to do" and what teachers found "scary to implement"—namely, teaching challenging material but with varied supports that helped students from diverse backgrounds to respond successfully to that challenge. Systematically, we experimented with all the features of the instructional climate that students had told us were critical to the development and support of high expectations for diverse learners.

This experimentation was not easy work. Successful implementation of changes in each area required embracing new attitudes, gaining access to resources for problem-solving through research and other faculty, and persisting through multiple trials. For example, in applying cooperative learning techniques, one teacher described the ups and downs of our efforts:

> Although cooperative learning activities have a definite structure, students are responsible for much of the instruction and direction of activities. This shift in responsibility from teacher to student is sometimes difficult. It can be uncomfortable for a teacher to allow students to control and direct classroom activities, especially in low stanine classes, where teachers feel a need to establish and maintain control. Our first attempts at cooperative learning were not completely successful. Some students refused to participate in activities and some found it difficult to work in groups that were organized for activities.

Happily, we began to experience some positive results, which proved reinforcing and even changed some beliefs, as this teacher described:

> One of our history teachers divided students into groups. Each group was given a part of the industrial revolution to research. Within each group, each student was responsible for researching a particular set of facts con-

cerning her group's topic and then explaining her findings to the group. The group in turn had to teach their area of the revolution to the rest of the class. Student work was compiled into booklets covering the entire revolution. Each student was given a booklet to keep. Although the teacher did encounter some difficulties with the activity, the results were well worth his efforts. Students proudly showed their work to their peers and other teachers.

The multidisciplinary membership of the project also enabled joint efforts across departments. As one teacher illustrated, for example, common expectations became possible: "Just being in an environment that reinforces the same behavioral demands as students move from class to class seems to provide students with a confidence about what is expected of them . . . They aren't confused by trying to meet the varying expectations of different teachers." Entire integrated lessons, developed jointly across departments, also became feasible. One such lesson across English and history focused on fostering students' personal relationship to history, engaging their families in student work, and providing more challenging texts. A teacher described these efforts:

> We agreed that we want to give students a strong sense of history and its relevance to their lives. We began by asking them to write about their names: how their parents chose them, what they meant, and how students felt about their names. They wrote first drafts in class, went home, and interviewed their parents, and then revised their papers, adding what they learned about their family history and how that history sometimes determined the name chosen for them. From this point on, it has been easier to draw parallels about how they are influenced by history. We have also selected reading materials that coincide with the ninth grade world history curriculum. For example, we asked our students to read *Animal Farm* to enhance their understanding of the Russian Revolution, while simultaneously providing them with a demanding book that is also read in ninth grade honors classes.

As we moved forward with higher-challenge materials, we experimented with ways to improve the poor reading skills of the students who were sorely tested by the more complex texts. We developed a tutoring program for students, as well as a study-skills curriculum that was utilized in English and world history, integrating skills important to both these subjects. We incorporated reading aloud, shared reading, brainstorming before and after reading, techniques to enhance listening skills, lunch-hour tutoring, and so on, but most importantly we worked toward developing or rekindling an interest in reading—in becoming a reader, a writer, a historian. Awakening interest in the students and providing teaching support to help them succeed nourished many students' willingness to work hard on addressing gaps in their basic skills. Many of our innovations were focused on the development of student agency and their capacity for self-reflection. We asked students "to write about the classes they are doing best and worst in." Students "talked about the reasons why they think they are succeeding or failing and how they think they might improve their performance." As one teacher noted, "This type of reflection presents students with an opportunity to evaluate their performance and hopefully, make the necessary changes for improvement."

A large part of our efforts targeted the building of a sense of community—in the classroom by showcasing successes with meaningful products that the students could share, in the school community with participation in schoolwide events, through extracurricular activities, and through outreach efforts to parents. As one example, student writings were published in each classroom; this allowed students to read each others' work as well as take home a record of their accomplishments. A teacher described the project's work in fostering school engagement: "No longer willing to have our students settle into the portrait of the at-risk student who plays on no team, joins no clubs, attends no school events . . . we wanted them to have a taste of the larger life at our school because we believed that this involvement helps students enter into the academic life as well." As she also noted, "Unlike other students who had found a niche easily, our students had neither confidence nor experience with extra-curricular activities . . . they had not had years of music lessons, participation in little league soccer and baseball, and roles in community drama productions . . . ; they merely went to class (if they did) and went home again."

One strategy used was to draw together a group of active seniors who were involved in a variety of extracurricular activities and invite them to talk to each of the project classes early on in the school year. A teacher pointed out, "There were two particularly nice aspects to these presentations: the ninth graders got to meet some 'famous' students—captains of the league-winning volleyball, wrestling, and basketball teams, stars in the school musical and jazz ensemble, student body and class officers—and they got acquainted with the procedures for joining activities so that taking the first step—signing up—would not seem an impossible barrier. As teachers, we got to see another side of our students: the side that aspires to be an actor, a third baseman, a sprinter." Seeing this "other side" of students was precisely what we were after—changed instructional conditions that enabled us to see qualities of students that had not been expressed in the classroom before. With a graduate student intern supported by the University of California, Berkeley, the project also developed a community service program for students to volunteer in elementary schools and day care centers, medical and veterinary hospitals, recreation centers, and nursing homes. Of the twenty-five students placed, fifteen (65 percent) participated successfully; further, a number of students were offered part-time jobs at the end of their service and others developed new career interests.

Fostering parental involvement proved to be most difficult, for these were parents who "rarely came to school except to deal with problems of poor grades and misbehavior." Project teachers began regular phone calls home, introducing themselves and acknowledging something positive about each student. Not surprisingly, many parents were hard to find, numerous phones were disconnected, and families had moved. Conferences about individual students, newsletters, and special meetings with dinner provided were some of the activities tried, but the results were disheartening, with parental interest growing slowly, almost family by family. The most successful outreach effort grew out of disappointment and reflected what the teachers considered as their last-ditch attempt:

> Instead of writing letters to the whole group, we began to write letters to parents on an individual class basis. My first letter of the new year included a newspaper article I had discussed with my class which dealt with a Northern California family who had just heard that their third home-educated son had been accepted at Harvard. In the letter, I described an independent reading unit I was beginning and asked parents to assist me in getting their children "hooked on books." The response was wonderful. Parents wrote that they would take their children to the library and check out books with them, they would encourage them to read the daily newspaper, they would cut down on their children's TV time. Because they had taken the time to answer so enthusiastically, I wrote back to them immediately, including direct quotations from their letters. Before sending that letter, I read it to the class. Students were delighted to see their parents' names and ideas in

print—some students even circled their parents' paragraphs . . . Now every time we include quotations or ideas from parents . . . and every time we get more and more response.

This teacher emphasized the underlying principle central to this success: "It has taught us a valuable lesson, a lesson we used constantly in our classrooms and had forgotten in our dealings with parents; that is, personal attention and acknowledgment bring positive results."

We worked hard to put in place more challenging instruction, with more varied supports for the different skill levels and different learning styles of students, and to integrate all the components of a more positive expectancy climate into classroom practices. While we saw some evidence of success, we also saw obvious limits to efforts made solely within classrooms. So began our examination of obstacles at the interface of classrooms, schools, and districts.

Reconstructing the Institutional Climate and Policy

From the very start of the project, contradictions surfaced between what teachers were attempting to do in the classroom and the prevailing norms of the school. The failure in the first year to obtain a common conference period for all participants and the denial of staff development credit from the district for these planning meetings were just two such examples. When school staff are not given sufficient time or credit to collaborate, they cannot nurture or sustain collaborative work as effectively. Further, interventions had to be individualized for those students whom we failed to reach and there was as yet no institutional mechanism to track student performance across classes. As one teacher put it, "Despite our attempts at instructional and curricular innovation, we have lost some students along the way . . . Some students disappeared for long periods of time, only to pop back in again for short intervals." More targeted interventions required information about how students were doing across classes and over time (including about absences, grades, and detentions), as well as problem-solving with deans, counselors, and parents.

Further, teachers began to see that instructional innovations could only go so far within the bottom rung of tracked classes:

As we read the research . . . and applied it in our classrooms, we came to know that we could no longer tolerate our department's rigid tracking system and its damaging consequences on teachers as well as students. What we did not know is how to dismantle that system or how to teach untracked classrooms . . . We had begun with ninth grade "low" students. We struggled to unlearn beliefs years of teaching remedial classes had made gospel, forced ourselves to identify limiting assumptions about students, pushed each other to stay optimistic when students ignored homework assignments, turned group work into chaos, came to class with no materials and little intention of learning. By the end of the first year, we were frustrated: high expectations, . . . shared responsibility, calls to parents were not enough. Classes limited to low achieving students did not work: our students needed student models of scholarship and good behavior.

Ultimately, the project could not rest on some teachers and not others. Responsibility had to be shared with all teachers and across all departments—a common vision of high expectations for all students needed to be forged.

Thus, the project teachers moved forward with systemic goals, by monitoring the performance and behavior of these students so as to better individualize interventions, by detracking the project students out of limited opportunity classes, and by improving the working conditions and the spread of the project. That the counselors, deans, vice-principal, and principal attended meetings only sporadically during the first year, and that there was turnover in the second year (a new dean, counselor, and vice-principal), made working through these contradictions all the more challenging. These intermittent administrative appearances kept alive the feeling that "nobody cares what we do as long as the kids don't jump out of the window." Teachers felt isolated and unsupported by counselors. Deans, too, were seen as undermining teachers' intent when dealing with disciplinary referrals. Most could not believe that everyone would "come around to appreciating or striving for project kids . . . who were not going to Cal anyway." One teacher described his frustration over the lack of administrative support to acquire computers that eventually became available through our school-university partnership: "A project like this should have greater priority and administrative support."

Differences between the culture that was developing within the collaborative team meetings and the culture in the school became more and more evident. One teacher described our early attempts to engage the administration:

We came to the meeting with the administrators looking for an exchange of ideas. They wanted us to have an answer and take responsibility for the solution. When we proposed different possibilities, we were met with "See, you don't really know what you want" . . . We learned that we had to come to a meeting with a strict agenda, express no public reservations among ourselves, leave the meeting with a statement of agreement, and follow up with a written note spelling out exactly what we had understood had been agreed to.

With hard work as well as administrative turnover, this teacher acknowledged that "our task was much easier (and more collaborative) with our next administrators who saw us as visionaries, shared our vision, and did their best to support us in any way possible."

The project pushed on, generating strategies to build more effective communication among the teachers, administrative staff, counselors, and deans. Our weekly meetings provided a regular opportunity to bring school staff together around new and joint missions. In these ways, we inched forward with our agenda.

In order to address concerns about individual students who were not responding to changed instructional conditions, we clearly needed more, and more timely, information. Although early on there was much talk about "the students who skipped late period classes" and "the students with multiple detentions, many of them not served," our question became "how can we systematically follow students' attendance and discipline patterns?" We suggested meetings with project teachers and the two deans. Despite the perceived problems that "arranging a time when both deans are available would be impossible since it is a zoo in there," and despite the tension that "time spent on one problematic student is taken from someone else," we forged ahead with the deans, and then, with the counselors.

Bringing this wing of the high school staff more fully into the collaboration enabled both the classroom teachers and the deans and counselors to learn from each other. One of the counselors argued for "reducing the number of times students were sent out, suggesting that a trip to the dean was not . . . preventive of future problems." Hard work on this collaboration resulted in regular progress reports about students in all of their classes, which enabled the project to monitor student attendance, grades, and detentions. With this information, we were able to access teachers who did well with certain students and learn from them, to meet with parents informed by a student's entire record, and take a close look at how our own work was affecting student engagement and success in school. We regularly held case conferences about particular students in our weekly meetings and held joint conferences with students and their families, which included several teachers as well as a dean or counselor.

Step by step, we also worked to detrack the instruction of the project students. That these students, because they would lack the needed credits, would never qualify for admittance to a four-year college, even with more demanding instruction, became unacceptable to the project. The first policy change, hard won, was described by one teacher: "It was instigated through collaboration between the teachers and administrators, allowed college-preparatory designation, and facilitated moving capable, motivated students out of non-college-bound classes." This retroactive credit for students who met certain standards proved difficult to implement because district computers printed out designations only for entire classes. Thus, this policy had to be implemented by counselors on student transcripts: importantly, extensive follow-up was needed since a number of the recommended students had "not received intended credit due to resistance from counselors."

Moving beyond individual cases, the next policy change targeted the dead-end, bottom-rung English classes. Despite lingering concerns of some (as one teacher explained: "I have real issues with heterogeneous grouping because we are getting these kids after nine years of tight tracking"), we gained approval at the end of the first year to dismantle non-college-bound English classes and to broaden the inclusion of students in the higher-level ones. This initiative depended on "the help of our administrators who painstakingly programmed our classes to achieve a balance of achieving and non-achieving students." As one teacher emphasized, "We pushed ourselves to use our accelerated (honors) class lesson plans in our college prep classes, to hold college prep students to the same kind of expectations about deadlines and final drafts and homework assignments that we had for accelerated students, to bring into our college prep classes the kind of freedom, opportunities for shared locus of responsibility, and long-term activities generally given only to high achieving students . . . so that in signing up for college preparatory English, our students were signing up for less quantity, not less quality." Our third policy change opened up Advanced Placement English classes to student choice and contractual agreement to do the work assigned. As this teacher remarked, "For the first time, AP was open to students who had been in ESL [English as a Second Language] and remedial English classes as freshman, students with combined SAT's of less than 800, students with less than a 3.0 grade point average."

Finally, we worked on improving the conditions for the project and widening its reach throughout the school, the district, and nationally. Teacher workshops were designed and held within and outside the school, and we continually invited others to our weekly meetings. The project struggled to keep all of its participating teachers, to include new teachers, and to influence all departments. Each meeting began with a brief update and introduction of new members so that teachers felt free to visit and try out the collaborative process. The special challenges of the different disciplines were examined: The consensus was that suggestions to math and science teachers must be handled differently given the "perceived" lockstep aspects of the curriculum. Grants were applied for and won, awards were received, and collaborative papers about the project were presented at national meetings and published. In all of this work, the thrust was to monitor, and with feedback, to redesign our efforts; to develop performance incentives that reinforced positive changes; and to shift more of the shared leadership to the school and away from the university.

Results of the Intervention

We followed the first cohort of project students through two academic years—the first year when they were tracked into the bottom rung, and the second year as they were integrated into average college preparatory classes taught by nonproject teachers. Had expectations changed for these low-performing students, were they being guided by more positive and challenging teaching practices and policies, and had their school performance changed?

The narrative records of meetings documented that, over time, the project teachers shared more complex, differentiated, and positive views of student abilities. Early talk was focused on the deficits that these students brought to the classroom: low motivation, negative self-image, lack of skills, and poor behavior. Later discussion shifted to the capabilities of students and to what teachers could do to enrich the curriculum, enhance their instruction, and solve the problems they experienced with students. Teachers became more active agents for change—in their own school, as mentors to other teachers in the district, and at a national level in writing about their work. Indeed, the school gained state and national recognition for this effort. Teacher ratings showed an increase in the use of positive expectancy practices. Further, project participants gained a common period in which to meet, district credit was granted, and grants brought new resources to the school, such as xerox machines, teaching materials, and computers. New school policies had been implemented to detrack these low-achieving students more generally and to broaden the curricular challenge offered.

But there were also failures. As we struggled to widen support for the project, the district agenda for magnet schools, which led to financial ruin, worked at cross-purposes with our expectancy-change effort. A changing administrative staff and the absence of consistent administrative leadership militated against the project taking hold in the entire school. There was also some teacher attrition after the first year. One teacher left due to "time de-mands and press of other responsibilities." Another left in anger over failed "high" expectations for the project; this teacher was disappointed in an ad-ministration that dumped low-stanine students on project teachers and failed to give teachers incentives for their hard work: "No one should have such a tough combination." The teachers varied in their comfort with the collaborative rather than the prescriptive approach; one teacher wanted to be given the "nuts and bolts" of what to do. The teachers who signed on for a second year wrote that "we have discovered that teachers who are unwill-ing to read the research, rethink their perceptions of students, and examine pedagogy do not change their negative attitudes." Instead, despite efforts to work with all departments, the project remained very much a single depart-ment effort during this second year.

Some change in students was documented. Beyond prior achievement differences, project students in contrast to comparison students earned higher GPAs and received fewer disciplinary referrals. But we were not able to affect the absence rate after one year in the program. The narrative re-cords underscored the more positive presence of these students in the school: there were reports of students arriving at school early to use the computers for their writing assignments, student applause for each others' work, students' sharing their accomplishments with other project teachers, and students' expressed excitement about the honors-level materials. Also for the first time in the school's history, two of the freshman class officers elected to the student council came from project classes. At a one year follow-up, by the end of tenth grade, only half as many of the project as op-posed to the comparison students (19 percent vs. 38 percent) had trans-ferred out of the school. This greater holding or motivational power of the school was a behavioral confirmation that the intervention was positive for students. While it was not accompanied by significantly higher grades, there were changes in the predicted direction. The unevenness of these follow-up findings (greater holding power, but not significantly higher performance), can be explained by two possible confounding factors. The lower attrition rate of project students might have meant that more low achievers were staying among the continuing project students and pulling grade averages down (at least temporarily), as contrasted with the continuing comparison students. In addition, these continuing project students, but not comparison students, had been placed in college-bound classes for the first time, and were being graded in contrast with higher performing students. Both these factors could potentially mask the higher actual achievement of the project students at the end of tenth grade.

Without a control school, one can only suggest that the changes documented in teacher thinking, classroom practices, and school policies derived from the intervention itself. The evidence for student change is stronger, however, given the availability of a comparison sample of students from previous years. The more positive perceptions of teachers and the greater holding power of the school at a one year follow-up are important confirmations that the intervention had some positive effect. It is possible that given the evolving implementation, the model was evaluated too early and not yet at its fullest strength. It can also be argued that given the high-risk group of students targeted (and a high absence rate that we could not change), one year of a positive expectancy climate, at this late date in these students' school careers, was not a strong enough intervention. Nonetheless, because of the consistency of improvements across the school, improvements that matched those predicted by expectancy theory, the evidence is promising for this approach to expectancy change.

The influence of this project extended well beyond its partnership with the university. For example, one of the teachers became a teacher-researcher who now writes extensively about detracking reforms. And under the leadership of project teachers, more changes were made in the detracking of students for instruction. In subsequent years, heterogeneous classes for English and history were expanded beyond ninth grade to tenth, eleventh, and twelfth grades, and honors and advanced placement classes in English were opened to student choice (except in the ninth grade). This exception for ninth graders was an effort to keep parents of high-achieving students from defecting from the district. After a teacher-initiated student survey indicated that students could not make the choice about an honors curriculum without exposure, the English teachers voted unanimously to program all ninth graders into carefully balanced heterogeneously grouped classes of twenty students. During the fourth year of this program, outside evaluators underscored the positive atmosphere in mixed ability classes, noting that it was "inspirational to see the mix in classes of African-, Asian- and European-Americans." The students interviewed were "unanimously enthusiastic about their English teachers" at Los Robles High School and described their teachers as individuals who "made sure you do your work." It should be noted, however, that a later evaluation by a university researcher found unevenness in effectiveness across the heterogeneous classes. And some parents of the highest-achieving students mounted heavy protests.

While the detracking effort spread very far in this high school, it continued to face enormous obstacles and lack of administrative support, not unlike what other schools have experienced in the implementation of detracking reforms. As Jeannie Oakes and her colleagues (1997) have noted, "Detracking reform confronts fundamental issues of power, control, and legitimacy that are played out in ideological struggles over the meaning of knowledge, intelligence, ability, and merit" (p. 482). They go on to argue that "these prevailing conceptions of and responses to intelligence are grounded in ideologies that maintain race and class privilege through the structure as well as the content of schooling" (p. 484).

These are the thorny challenges at the heart of what Robert K. Merton (1948) described as the "specious validity" of self-fulfilling prophecies—where perceptions of limited ability lead to teaching strategies and labels about relative smartness that ultimately confirm the original judgment, either in fact or in perception. Thus, the prophecy and its confirmation contribute to an unending cycle of events that proves difficult to break. Such challenges exist because these processes are embedded in complex social and political settings and unfold over long periods of time. When we enter into the self-fulfilling prophecy midstream, we must grapple with a reality that has already been confirmed. The pressure from all sides is to accept that reality as accurate and as unalterable.

While there is compelling evidence that implanting falsely positive expectations can under certain conditions produce more positive outcomes, this is very difficult to do in real-world settings such as schools, where there are achievement records on students, tracked educational opportunities, and diverse student populations with varied educational needs, all operating within a larger political context. The induction of positive beliefs is neither long-lasting nor sufficient. On the perceiver side, we need to change how schools and teachers interpret the capabilities of students, provide opportunities to learn, and ultimately reappraise student performance. On the target side, we need to increase the agency of children and families, lessen their vulnerability to limiting judgments and limited learning opportunities, and open their eyes to untapped capacity. Interventions that deceive parents, students, or teachers, that prescribe specific teacher behaviors, or that legislate school policies in isolation will likely fall short of the mark. Such interventions fail to address the interaction between individuals, systems, and policy.

Changing the culture of academic expectations is not only about the detracking of instructional groups and classes, and not only about higher standards and more challenging curricula. Such a culture change must address, link, and apply our newest theories of learning to the development of effective pedagogy and a set of policies that support it in every classroom. Only when we change the learning as well as the assessment conditions (see Shepard 2000) will we see this as-yet untapped potential of all students.

There is an emerging knowledge base about such effective pedagogy for a diversity of children (see Bransford, Brown, and Cocking 2000; Cohen and Lotan 1997; Pressley et al. 2001; Tharp and Gallimore 1988; Wheelock 1992). There is also growing knowledge about how to create new educational communities based on alternative theories of learning and school organization (see Comer et al. 1996; Chasin and Levin 1995; Mehan et al. 1996; Oakes and Quartz 1995; Peterson, McCarthey, and Elmore 1996; Slavin et al. 1996). Most critically for expectancy change, teachers and administrators need to work collaboratively as practitioner-researchers, within and beyond the borders of their schools. They need to conduct their own assessments of local conditions; adapt and align effective teaching practices and policies; and evaluate their results for each and every student under their care. And they need to link up with other school sites and laboratories in which effective pedagogy is being refined.

Such a context for learning is lacking in most schools. Sarah Warshauer Freedman and her colleagues (1999) point to how such a collaborative network of teacher-researchers can enhance teachers' knowledge about effective literacy teaching in multicultural classrooms. And Kenneth Wilson and Bennett Daviss (1994) argue for systems of schools that "can function as a laboratory, uniting skilled and willing teachers, able researchers and designers, students of diverse backgrounds and abilities, and classroom innovations, all working together to improve each other" (p. 199).

Our intervention goals clashed with changing mandates of the principal and district. Rapid turnover of administrative leadership made it difficult to forge alliances with administrators who could encourage participation of all the teachers, across all departments. Until such support was secured, not all teachers were held accountable for diverse learners or offered help to teach them more effectively. Finally, equity in expectations for learning carried enormous political consequences, as seen by the increasing dissent of parents of the "high achievers" when the context for enriched classes was broadened to include all students. If a commitment to expectancy change is to endure, all participants, including parents, must learn to see and nurture ability differently.

In the end, a dedication to lifting expectations for "low achievers" is a commitment to continued improvement in teaching. As one of the teachers wrote: "Our classrooms are changed places, we are changed teachers because of the project. It allowed us—invited us—to share our frailties, our loss of faith, our failures with each other and to create a vision of the possibilities for public education when teachers work together . . . it has been about our achievement as much as our students. When we started this project it was about the kids, now we know it is about us."

CHAPTER 9

A School Culture for the Fullest Development

> Talent is best viewed as a developmental rather than as an all-or-nothing phenomenon. It is a process that unfolds over many years rather than a trait that one inherits and then keeps unchanged for the rest of life. Children are talented only in the sense of future potential; to fulfill that potential, they will have to learn to perform to state-of-the-art standards and will have to find opportunities for using their talent after their skills are developed.
>
> —Mihaly Csikszentmihalyi, Kevin Rathunde, and Samuel Whalen, 1993

In this chapter, I look inside an elementary school where positive expectations (both in vision and in practice) are already in place, and where one can clearly see the interwoven elements of a development-focused achievement culture. What structural arrangements and what acts of principal leadership enable schools—not only classroom by classroom but also in the aggregate—to believe in and develop the capability of all students to learn? Together, these two case studies at different levels of schooling (high school and elementary school), framed by the different perspectives of teacher and principal, capture what it means, from particular viewpoints and overall, to harness positive prophecies in education.

This case study began in the same university seminar on school reform described earlier, which was attended by the former principal of Landmark School (a pseudonym). Barbara Butterworth (the principal) and I (a parent and school-board member) reflected on our shared participation in a unique private school known for its rich learning opportunities. The material for this case study was drawn from archival records, such as the handbook and newsletters, as well as from retrospective essays written by the principal about representative events and interactions across a school week. This chapter also builds upon the analysis in a previously published paper (But-

233

terworth and Weinstein 1996). In our view, the unique character of this school was achieved with a relatively heterogeneous student body and as a result of conceptual innovation rather than from its small size or private-school status, thus its example would be relevant to public schools.

How does the organization of schools enhance the development of talent in all children? As a parent, I watched this school ritual from afar, having raced to get my twin sons to school on time as they chanted, "Not to miss opening! I can't miss opening." At "opening," the school's daily welcoming assembly, there were announcements to make and announcements to hear. This was the lifeline of their elementary school: an important opportunity on a daily basis to connect to and feel part of a larger school community, and the students felt pride in as well as responsibility for this special morning welcome. Their principal described the school's morning routine in this way:

I am usually in the kitchen when a fifth grader checks his digital watch and purposefully rings the bell to officially start our day. Conversations with parents or teachers are finished as we head for our morning gathering swept up in the surge of students congregating in the appointed meeting place . . . *Opening* is led by a triumvirate of students—two members of the student council who in turn select a younger child to hold the flag . . . The mayor calls for announcements . . . The school historians come forward to inform us of special events associated with this day . . . A kindergarten or first grader never fails to remind us about birthdays. Birthday students and teachers come to the front to be serenaded with "Happy Birthday" and applauded on their special day . . . Tuesday is talent day. The kindergarten teacher introduces budding young piano players and lifts them to the bench to perform. A student might recite a poem or a group of older students might be persuaded to give a break dance demonstration . . . A group of fifth graders troops to the platform. To promote the (school) store, they hold up newly arrived items that will be on sale that Friday afternoon . . . The third grade teacher announces that she still wants to hire someone for a job in her room filing Project Write . . . I announce a . . . lunchtime field trip to listen to a lecture on wildlife rescue at the nearby Conservation Center . . . "Let's close with the school song" is the final familiar direction issued by one of the three students still standing before us. The song was written several years ago by a parent and third grade teacher; it reflects the sentiments we all share, "Our school is a special place to be, I'll tell you just what it means to me," although the pace has been known to drag and it has proven to be totally unsingable in Spanish. Each class has a verse which they sing in

turn, changing with the seasons, the classroom activities, or daily as with
the sixth grade who enjoys teasing us with contrived and dreadful rhymes
. . . "The 14th's the day for the fourth grade's little play." "And that's what it
means to me" chimes in everyone to bring the meeting to a close.

This morning routine linked members of the school community around
common purposes. But which common purposes? Here, children were not
sifted by "ability" to determine how to allot a scarcity of enriched opportunities. Rather, a diversity of challenging opportunities demanded student engagement, provided necessary supports, and developed the talents of many.
This ceremony reflects not a culture of competition and winner takes all, but
one of individuality, interdependence, and mutual appreciation. In celebrat-
ing the individuality of students, teachers, and parents, in full view of all, the
daily ritual conferred a shared sense of wonder at the range of accomplishments of this community.

The institutional arrangements of this school culture did not treat individual differences among children with differentiated expectations and stratified educational opportunities—conditions that promote the creation of
negative self-fulfilling prophecies. Instead, this culture held common and
high expectations for which all were held accountable. Most importantly, it
called for the development of a broad range of abilities and also provided
multiple and diverse pathways to meet the challenges—pathways that are
respectful of individual difference and need. Such a development-focused
culture works both inside and outside of classrooms and nurtures teachers
and parents as it supports children. In this kind of culture, successful teaching is understood to be a process of continuous learning both individually
and organizationally—a process that is enriched by human relationships
and unbounded by the walls of classroom or school. As Csikszentmihalyi,
Rathunde, and Whalen (1993) suggest, based upon their study of talented
teenagers, such conditions of enhancement require developmental and unfolding processes, with opportunities to learn as well as to use the skills that
have been so carefully polished.

Promoting Positive Prophecies: Landmark School

Established in 1973, Landmark, an independent elementary school, is located in a suburban community in California. At the time of our case study,
in addition to a full-time principal, there were seven full-time teachers (one

for each grade from kindergarten through sixth grade), five part-time specialist teachers (in science, art, Spanish, physical education, and music), a learning-disabilities consultant, and a director of the afterschool and summer-school program. The average class size was sixteen to eighteen students (reflecting the school philosophy as well as the physical limitations of the classrooms), yielding a total student population of approximately 112. Landmark was guided by an active board composed of parents, church members (where the school rented space), community members, and a teacher representative. Financial support came from tuition, which was among the lowest in the area, foundation support for a scholarship program, and fund-raising activities. Although it was a private school, Landmark's admission and financial aid policies and its afterschool program made it more diverse ethnically (with 30 percent ethnic-minority children) and socioeconomically than the local school district.

As described in the school handbook, Landmark's philosophy was charted by its founder, a respected teacher who "recognized the need for a school environment that offered a strong academic program with a warm, nurturing atmosphere." In her five-year tenure as principal, Butterworth continued her predecessor's focus on a "family" school, while working to improve the school's fiscal health and its articulation of policies, achieve accreditation, extend the use of specialist teachers, and expand the wealth of programs. The teaching of Spanish, the implementation of a school economy with banks, businesses, and jobs, and the expansion of environmental education were among the innovations introduced.

The Climate of Expectations

While common and high expectations were an important feature of the Landmark culture, the school held such standards not only for academic learning but also for a broad range of competencies. As described in the handbook, Landmark School sought "to provide a community in which children develop academic proficiency, individual creativity, and social responsibility." Further, the handbook spelled out a vision that involved students as active agents in creating knowledge and developing proficiency: "An atmosphere which encourages academic proficiency permits children to raise questions and stimulates them to pursue answers. A creative environment is one in which children explore, discover and develop their individual gifts . . . which exist in all children . . . in a variety of ways. To be socially responsible is to accept the obligations of community membership, . . . to assume leadership roles, to acknowledge and respect the rights of others, and to give of self for the common good."

Clearly articulated here were goals beyond a narrowly conceived set of academic skills—goals that honor student rights and place student inquiry, action, and responsibility at the very heart of learning. The school handbook contained a Student Bill of Rights, written by the fifth-grade class of 1983, which outlined children's rights to have a safe school environment, to learn, to be heard, to be treated equally regardless of race, religion, and sex, to pursue responsibility, to pursue their talents, to express their ideas freely as long as the expression was in good taste, and to have their possessions inviolate.

Alongside the articulated rights came responsibilities to the school community, which included self-regulation of behavior with regard to conduct, timely attendance, academic work and homework, as well as participation in the running and improvement of the community. For example, Landmark's economic system enabled students to hold regular and often interesting jobs around the school, such as classroom aide, office aide, or specialist aide, for which they were paid a weekly salary in the local scrip, known as landmarks. Students could save landmarks in the school bank, spend them at the school store or bookstore, and/or use them for field trips or special equipment like computers.

Also communicated in the handbook was the belief that talent exists in all children and in diverse ways. This belief was reinforced by the student admissions policy, which mirrored that of a public rather than a private school in its commitment to educate a diversity of children. Critically important, Landmark adopted an academically nonselective admissions policy. Admission to the school was largely on a first-come, first-served basis, except to ensure sibling priority, family participation, and ethnic minority and socioeconomic representation. Serious outreach efforts and a strong scholarship program resulted in ethnic minority representation in each class at a higher level than the surrounding public school district. An afterschool program also drew single-parent and two-worker families from a variety of socioeconomic positions, and the school's belief that "all children have individual gifts" led to the inclusion of a large proportion of children who had been identified as learning disabled.

Given Landmark's philosophy that ability is malleable and that it increases with opportunities to learn (and with age), learning opportunities of increasing competency and of increasing responsibility were in place. Curricular goals that guided instruction were articulated for each subject matter area and integrated across the grades: these were shared with parents and children. All children were also expected to participate in the school-level programs, with developmental milestones of increasing responsibility built into the system. During the time of our study, for example, although all children held jobs, job opportunities were advertised as appropriate for younger or older children. Further, children in the higher grades were assigned specific and increasingly complex responsibilities: the bookstore and literary magazine were run by the fourth grade, the school store by the fifth grade, the bank by the sixth grade, and the newspaper and yearbook by the fifth and sixth grades. The fifth-grade students and their parents cooked for and hosted the graduation dinner, and all sixth-graders were required to prepare and deliver graduation speeches. The outdoor education program involved younger children in two-day camping trips and coordinated fourth through sixth graders in a five-day trip to a sea, desert, or mountain region.

Talent Developed and Celebrated

All children at Landmark received an enriched and diverse program not only in core academic subjects but also in science, art, physical education, music, and a required second language (Spanish). In addition, a variety of school-level programs were integrated with and designed to enhance daily classroom activities. These included student government, a school economy, publishing, theatrical and musical performances, art exhibitions, an outdoor education program, community experiences, a before- and afterschool program, and special celebrations. One alumna described these opportunities as boundless when she wrote for the school newsletter, "I am deeply indebted to Landmark. Even though it was such a small school—if you can call boundless opportunities small—the teachers encouraged me to grow in any way I could." Importantly, all competencies were equally valued by the school community.

Thus, while curricular expectations were common for all, the pathways to reach them were highly differentiated. The myriad of classroom and schoolwide learning opportunities capitalized on and valued individual differences, drawing upon the artistic, political, mathematical, literary, and scientific interests of students. These diverse opportunities enabled the reinforcement and extension of prior academic exposure in a variety of ways, capitalizing on different learning styles and on different supports for learning, including the modeling of peers. The administration of the school bank made real the lessons of math and economics, as older students explained to younger students how a bank actually works. The student government provided opportunities to link students' own experiences with current and historical political processes, both national and local. Performances of Shakespeare, for example, both enhanced the reading of such texts in class and were in turn illuminated by the study of the pertinent historical period in social studies. A five-day camping trip to an area of ecological interest enhanced data-gathering techniques learned in environmental sciences. Moreover, student success in these outside endeavors renewed confidence and interest in classroom activities.

At Landmark, diverse and meaningful performance opportunities for all showed off the emerging talents of the school community. For example, Landmark's publishing activities included a monthly student newspaper staffed by students from all grades, a literary magazine published twice a year by the fourth grade, and a yearbook, with photographs, prepared by the fifth and sixth grades. Each of these publications included artwork and writing by all of the students. Celebrations during the school year involved everyone and included daily opening, Halloween parade, Thanksgiving luncheon, Martin Luther King's birthday, Inventions Unlimited Day, Grandparents' Day, school work days, and graduation dinner. These traditions showcased the diverse talents of many and warmly involved the family and broader community. Most importantly, as articulated in the handbook, they were opportunities to show appreciation: "Landmark believes in celebration of the value of each student's contribution, celebration of events that tie us to cultural and historical traditions, and celebration of our creative instincts and talents." These celebrations also richly contributed to the neighborhood community. For example, the school invited local seniors to join in the Thanksgiving festivities, including a Thanksgiving dinner for which each class prepared a dish.

Enrichment and Accommodation through Resource Development

THE CREATION OF "UNDERPEOPLED" OPPORTUNITIES.   The multiple and diverse school-level activities were created not only to challenge and support a variety of talents but also to develop new talent. By design, all children were required to be involved, with some activities class-run and others individually chosen, and with many more roles to play than individuals available—a key ecological principle. Research has shown that in settings where (either by size or conceptualization) there are more roles than people, there is pressure for greater involvement of more diverse individuals, with concomitantly greater development of talent (Schoggen 1989). Thus, while interest first drove student involvement, socially constructed need also recruited a more varied group of students.

Landmark's system of student government, for example, held twice yearly elections for mayor, vice-mayor, secretary, treasurer, and social coordinator. Those running for office were required to appoint a campaign manager who, along with the candidate, prepared a speech. Representatives from each class completed the membership of the governing body. All of these features broadened participation in student governance. Participation in the two schoolwide performances held each year (a musical for the holiday season and a dramatic or musical comedy at the end of the year) was maximized by modifying scripts and by using different casts for each act so that every student in the school performed in the play. In addition, each grade produced a play for the school and parents to see.

REFRAMING TIME. By design, Fridays were special, with mornings devoted to class projects and afternoons to involvement in schoolwide activities. The Friday schedule freed teachers and students to more fully engage in classwork, in varied activities beyond the classroom, and with a broader segment of the school community. Fridays also were used for class visits to the theater, concerts, and museums; student performances to local homes for the aged; and bringing community resources into the school, such as when two architects helped fifth-grade students design a model community for their social-studies assignment. The performance opportunities scheduled throughout the year not only directed activities, but also importantly provided the school community sufficient time to engage in high-quality work and sustained effort.

EXPANDING RESOURCES TO INCLUDE CHILDREN. Much of the energy for the school's enriched activities was provided by the children. Capitalizing on children's energy and ideas meant giving them actual responsibility and training them to be good classroom aides, store and stage managers, newspaper editors, or school guides for new and prospective students and parents. While the upfront costs for teachers are high in the initial training and set-up of such programs at a schoolwide level, they become self-sustaining beyond the first year as each student cohort trains the students who follow. And teachers gain the opportunity to share center stage, to be a facilitator rather than an instructor, and to bring more of themselves into the classroom and school. Giving responsibility to students enables them to broaden and nurture the talents they have discovered within the school environment, as well as increase opportunities for giving instruction (and asking for it) in a personal way.

INCLUDING PARENTS AND THE WIDER COMMUNITY.   When the individual talents of parents are needed by the school community and highly valued; when school events are held on evenings and on weekends so that working parents can come; and when such events involve their own children in meaningful ways, parents attend, work hard, and contribute enormous energy to the system. When school events reflect cultural knowledge, involve celebrations and rituals (such as the Landmark's graduation dinner hosted by fifth graders and families), respond to the needs of the community (such as its twice-yearly clothing exchange and afterschool program), and rest upon the energy of parents working with their children, the resource pool grows. Because of Landmark's school economy and publishing activities, local businesses and newspapers exchanged visits and materials with the students. Senior citizens were partners in a gardening program, and a local university provided tutors (undergraduates interested in exploring careers in education). The local community also offered additional audiences for the student activities; for example, the children performed plays and gave choir concerts in homes for the aged. Rummage sales, sales of the school business product (chutney), school performances, and the Halloween parade also invited community participation.

Tapping this energy, motivating people to put forth time and effort, is a function of the value and the appropriateness of the opportunities provided and the degree to which the system is hospitable and supportive. All parents were expected to participate, but importantly, their commitments could be met in a variety of ways, with no one way valued over another. Annual financial giving to the school was expected, but the focus was on 100 percent participation of families rather than on the dollar amount, with one-dollar contributions possible and indeed made. The skills of parents were critical to ensuring the wide range of school activities and celebrations. At the start of each year, a detailed inventory was sent home to ascertain the vocations, special skills, and interests of members of each child's extended family. Family members were recruited in advance for short-term and long-term commitments that drew upon a wide variety of talents, from cooking to carpentry to computer skills. Twice a year, the entire school community turned out on a Saturday for projects to improve the school building or grounds, with students, teachers, and families working alongside each other and sharing a lunch prepared by one working team. Such efforts brought out the parents because all of the children participated, because their efforts were visible and appreciated (for example, by thanks in the principal's *Wednesday Letter* or with plaques placed on walls), and because members and friends of each child's extended family were invited.

INVESTING IN TEACHERS AND STAFF DEVELOPMENT.   An underlying principle of Landmark School was a commitment to "overpopulate the setting with adults." The adults—specialist teachers, a teaching principal, and parent volunteers—not only helped to create diverse learning opportunities for the children, but also, most importantly provided "slack" time for teachers to reflect, plan, and participate in staff development events. As the principal described it, "Slack time is time where there is space to breathe, to think, to interact with other teachers, to get ideas going, to generate new activities. All too often, schools have no slack time. You are running from one thing to another, you have five hundred things on your desk, and you just can't get around to talking to your neighbor about a fun project you might do with your classes together." The teachers had regular preparation periods throughout the week where they were free to plan class projects and meet with colleagues to organize interclass and schoolwide events.

The school also invested in its teachers by addressing their individual needs and maximizing their rewards. Teachers were encouraged to visit other schools and programs. Flexible work arrangements provided part-time work for teachers as specialists, and, in one case, allowed two teachers (one in the morning and the other in the afternoon) to share a single classroom. Efforts to match teacher talents to the variety of school-level opportunities available encouraged teacher interest. Friday project scheduling enabled teachers to have entire mornings available for complex and interesting instructional projects in the classroom and to take classes into the community. This flexibility and support for teacher interests facilitated an environment of continued growth for all teachers.

MULTIPLE AND ENDURING RELATIONSHIPS.   Project Fridays and abundant cross-classroom activities thrust children into multiple and enduring relationships with teachers and fellow students. All students had the opportunity to learn from older children and to mentor younger children. Over the course of their elementary-school years, children also could continue relationships with previous teachers and work with all of the teachers. They also interacted meaningfully with the principal and many parents through the daily opening ceremony and schoolwide activities.

Commitments to Coherence and Accountability

A PRINCIPAL POSITIONED FOR INPUT.   The principal—through teaching (in this case, computer science) and observing in classrooms, Friday lunches with students, and informal meetings with parents—was able to routinely gather information about what was working and not working at all levels of the school community. This excerpt, in the principal's words, captures one such classroom visit:

> I take the time to glance into each classroom as I go by. In the fifth grade, I am never sure what desk arrangement I will find, since seating patterns shift regularly . . . reflecting the teacher's most recent solution to problems of social dynamics or a student's academic progress . . . The fifth grade teacher enjoys talking about her children, particularly when she feels she has made a breakthrough, so we have periodic conversations, as she stops by the kitchen for a cup of coffee while her class is with a specialist teacher. . . . Teachers view this as a time to plan and organize. For me, this is a moment for quiet talk, to discuss issues on my mind, to find out what is needed, or to listen. Recognizing our conflicting expectations for this "free time," I try to intrude with care.

The principal also ate lunch regularly with a mixed-grade group of students, ultimately reaching all students each year, not only to deepen relationships but also to gain valuable feedback from children about their school environment:

> Friday afternoon begins with lunch at my house with one child from each class (we brown-bag it), a time to talk informally about school and give all students a more personal time with the principal. I and the "Friday lunch bunch" return just before one o'clock to find a group of my student employees gathered on the porch waiting for their weekly paychecks. As I write out their checks, we discuss how the job is going and if either of us is having a problem with how the job is being done. The biggest obstacle for

many students is simply remembering their responsibility, so we discuss ways to set routines or build in a system of reminders with either a parent or teacher.

There were both formal and informal ways that the principal kept in touch with parents. Parents were organized as PAL (Parents at Landmark), parent representatives sat on the governing board of the school, and the principal held a monthly tea for parents. She also spent time before and after school greeting parents, poised for input regarding the needs of students and the school: "At three o'clock, I lounge at my office door, chatting with parents sitting on the bench waiting for the stream of students that will shortly round the corner, finally released from their classrooms for the day. It is a time to be open for feedback, to talk about jobs that need doing, in the hopes that someone will volunteer, to tell a parent about an interaction I had with his or her child today. Knowing that parents often feel uncomfortable making formal appointments with me, I am there to be 'caught' for a quick interchange."

SUBSTANTIVE WEEKLY STAFF MEETINGS. Two-hour weekly staff meetings, held Thursdays after school and facilitated by the principal, were devoted to the collaborative development of instructional programs that would be effective for all students. (The principal prepared for this meeting by taking a not-to-be-interrupted preparation period on Thursday mornings.) In the staff meeting, issues of coherence were tackled by framing integrated grade-level curricular goals. Here also the progress of individual students was monitored and appropriate interventions were planned, enhanced by the collective knowledge the staff members had about the children in varied contexts and by consultation, when needed, with a learning-disabilities specialist.

NEWSLETTERS TO BUILD COMMUNITY AND ACCOUNTABILITY. The principal wrote a letter for families each Wednesday, and teachers sent home monthly newsletters about class activities. Because students played key roles in the publishing activities of the school, they became invested in these newsletters, as well as in their monthly newspaper and twice-yearly literary journal. Students were asked to read these communications aloud to and with their parents. These shared communications from the school made parents accountable for knowing what was happening at school and reinforced the values of the school culture at multiple levels.

EFFORTS TO ADDRESS INTERDEPENDENCE AND BALANCE. Both policy formulation and interpersonal interventions by the principal were guided by the need to reinforce a coherent vision as well as to allow for change where needed. As the consequences of decisions rippled throughout the system, the interdependence of the parts was revealed, an interdependence that could be conflictual or mutually reinforcing. The principal anticipated the consequences of change, envisioned how the resources, programs, and decisions would fit together, and worked toward a coherent and mutually reinforcing school environment that would accomplish its goals and sustain its members.

One example of how policies can create coherent and mutually reinforcing effects at multiple levels of the institution is Landmark's Birthday Book tradition. This tradition reinforced the value of reading inside and outside of the classroom. Each child's birthday was marked by the gift of a book to the school library—a tradition that was ritualized at the morning opening ceremony. By design, the financial differences between families were minimized. The money that children earned in the school economy could be used to buy birthday books from the student-run bookstore, and the supply of books was regularly replenished by family and community donations. Another example included the expansion of the afterschool program during half-day school closings, so that all children could be constructively cared for during times set aside for parent-teacher conferences and staff development.

The principal also carefully monitored how resources in the school were used to liberate, conserve, and balance the energy of its participants. By recognizing individual differences in interest or talent, the use of resources was more effective. The energy of teachers, parents, and students was also renewed through positive feedback and appreciation. The tradition of having fifth-grade students and parents host a graduation dinner for sixth-grade students, families, and teachers was one such celebratory ritual that expressed appreciation and also prepared the next generation. The pressure to participate was enormous on many counts: the fifth-grade students planned the menu and led the cooking effort; further, they and their parents were to be the recipients the following year. All sixth-graders gave graduation speeches at the dinner, which certainly drew their own parents to the event. Fifth-graders, meanwhile, learned how to make a speech about their elementary school education so that they would be ready when faced with the same challenge the following year.

Conservation of energy, in schools as elsewhere, meant attending to scheduling, coordination, and bureaucratic requirements in order to provide an environment in which teacher efforts were not drained by tasks tangential to teaching. It also meant protecting the teaching staff from excessive parent demands while encouraging teachers to anticipate and prevent problems by communicating directly and regularly with parents. Maintaining balance in energy use meant recognizing that new demands, particularly on teacher time and responsibility, needed to be compensated for by reducing other demands or by adding new resources. For example, for the teacher who had the extra responsibility of producing the literary magazine, a parent was found to do the typing and another to do the xeroxing so that the teacher could focus on helping the students with editing and layout. Marshalling resources, spreading responsibility, and keeping the system in balance are important roles for the principal to play. Flexibility for how jobs got done—in roles, methods, and time frame—increased energy within the system and the degree to which participants saw the whole school as a domain for their activities and loyalties. Building a system that is responsive to the needs of students, families, and staff requires looking at the system as a whole, anticipating the consequences of actions for all parts of the system, and balancing the need for formalized routines and policies (the pillars of the system) with the need for flexible responses. The tension between flexibility and structure, responsiveness and routinization is constant. The principal must balance these pressures so as to model and maintain an environment that is lively and risk-taking, yet secure and predictable.

Toward What Kinds of Outcomes?

What kinds of outcomes were valued by a school culture such as this? High on the list, for all, was a motivation to learn as well as a growing intellectual and social-emotional mastery that exceeded skills proficiency. Landmark School sought to create passionate and avid readers, writers, historians, scientists, and linguists who would continue to hone their abilities and deepen their inquiry. While performance on standardized tests was monitored by the school staff, it was not a primary criterion of program effectiveness. Critical benchmarks for Landmark School were the degree of participation and the growing talents of all of its members.

Staff turnover across many years had been virtually nil, despite lower salaries than in the public schools. Teachers told the school board that their commitment to the school came from the shared vision, the flexibility of their roles, the opportunities for continued growth, and the warm friendships among staff and with families. Parental participation was exceptionally high. In one year, the parent association reported that thirty-six parents (representing 39 percent of families) served as coordinators of various school activities; this did not include the scores of parent volunteers also participating in each event. The principal's *Wednesday Letter* told of contributions to annual fundraising by 73 percent of the families. Not surprisingly, positive parental feeling about the school was strong, and many parents reported that when their children graduated, they experienced a sense of loss of the intimate connection to their children's schooling.

Finally, drawing from observations of my own children as well as the children of others, I would describe student engagement as high, from early in the morning before school opened to late in the day in the afterschool program. Because children were strongly encouraged to become involved, they often tried things they would not have attempted ordinarily and then worked hard to meet the goals set by the staff and themselves. The fall election results reported in the principal's *Wednesday Letter* listed nineteen students chosen to serve as mayor, vice-mayor, social chairman, treasurer, secretary, and class representatives. Given the requirement of a campaign manager as well as twice-yearly elections, seventy-six students (68 percent) prepared and delivered speeches during the course of one school year, in addition to having the opportunity to vote. Athletic talent was discovered or developed when all students were accepted to be on the school basketball team. That students wrote for the school newspaper and literary magazine created a responsive audience in fellow students and parents for their growing efforts in communication. Parents complained with humor that their children were never ready to go home and that they would not willingly miss a day of school or their place on a job when sick. A waiting list for admission to this school attested to its local reputation. Years later, an acknowledged overrepresentation of the school's graduates on the city's youth council suggested the motivating force of an active school government.

As a parent of fraternal twin sons, each of whom had found numerous areas of success within this same small but diverse environment, I came to believe that more types of students did well here in part because of the diversity of opportunities that stretched and supported their development. I saw both my children develop new talents as well as overcome stumbling blocks in their learning. Adam, the son with dyslexia whose story was told in Chapter 1, learned to read here and he thrived as a budding actor, singer, writer, and scientist, willing to work hard on his reading and spelling skills while engaged in a challenging curriculum. My other son, whom I described as a quick study, developed his passion for community service, history, and government—by learning how to debate, design policy, and address social problems. Like the other students, they became autonomous learners, developed a keen sense of efficacy about their own schooling, and took enormous pride in their school. Not surprisingly, peer friendships ran deep, crossed racial and socioeconomic lines, and have persisted for years. Both help-giving and help-receiving were normative events for the children, as they struggled to reach higher levels of mastery in such varied subject-matter domains.

Talent Development and Positive Self-Fulfilling Prophecies

In its emphasis on talent development, how did Landmark School avoid negative self-fulfilling prophecies, and more importantly, foster positive self-fulfilling prophecies for its students? First, Landmark School set high expectations for the achievement of all children across a broadened range of competencies that were equally valued as evidence of full human development. In this elementary school, the requirement of a second language for all students and the incorporation of the arts and of civic responsibility into the teaching program clearly diminished the higher status commonly assigned to the English language and to linguistic and mathematical skills over other kinds of skills. The second-language requirement thrust all children into the role of a language learner. Not only is bilingualism important in our increasingly diverse country and globalized society but such dual immersion approaches strengthen the status and abilities of linguistically different children, as well as of all children.

The strong appeal of Howard Gardner's (1983) theoretical work on multiple intelligences lies in the important but often ignored valuing of other abilities such as the artistic, interpersonal, and bodily kinesthetic. Schools report that in recognizing such varied talents in children, the motivation to strengthen other abilities is increased (Krechevsky, Hoerr, and Gardner 1995). As noted earlier, lessons and assessments that engage a variety of abilities improve school performance (Sternberg, Torff, and Grigorenko 1998). Most importantly for expectancy theory, in valuing a broader range of talents, the opportunities for stereotypically applied negative expectations are dramatically diminished. Evidence from social psychology laboratory experiments shows that the increased certainty and chronic accessibility of expectations most evident around narrowly defined skill areas enhance the probability that perceivers will act on expectations in ways that promote confirmation (Snyder and Stukas 1999). The work of Elizabeth Cohen and Rachel Lotan (1997) on status equalization in classroom interaction also emphasizes that, unless learning tasks are made complex in ways that highlight myriad component abilities, schoolwork will continue to create the same narrow band of winners and losers.

Second, high and broadened expectations were accompanied by varied and complex opportunities to learn, perform, and celebrate accomplishments—opportunities that engaged the whole range of abilities. At Landmark School, all children received plentiful and enriched educational opportunities despite variation in rates of learning and ease with the varied skills involved in reading, writing, math, and so on. Talent development rests upon challenge, sustained effort over long periods of time, the use of alternative learning strategies when roadblocks appear, and opportunities to apply and celebrate increasing skill levels. This is seen clearly outside of schooling, where accomplishments in sports, the arts, and the sciences usually come from sustained effort, alternative learning strategies, guided coaching, and long hours. Yet what we most often see in schools is exactly the opposite. Segregation and repetition become the primary remedial strategy. Beliefs about smartness (as being fast) and about effort (as indicating a lack of ability) lead children, when confronted with obstacles, to avoid trying in order to save face (Covington 1992). And scarcity of enriched learning opportunities limits the exposure of children to challenge.

In this school, obstacles to skill development were overcome with flexible grouping practices across grades, the assignment of students as tutors and tutees, the use of alternative teaching strategies, and afterschool help. But most importantly, exposure to challenging curricula continued. Getting help was not stigmatizing, because all children gave and received help under a variety of circumstances. The diversity and complexity of these learning opportunities gave all children some experience with struggle, provided success in one domain or another for all children, and broadened what otherwise would be very limited contexts for the evaluation of achievements. What was conveyed to all students was that talents are malleable—that they will improve as children grow older and as children work on them.

Third, at Landmark, the development of student agency and responsibility was at the heart of learning. Children were empowered to regulate their own behavior and to evaluate their own work and progress. Indeed children were engaged as key resources to create the broad array of enriched learning opportunities. And student mentoring of the younger students became the primary means of sustaining the complexity of the whole-school programs. From an expectancy perspective, increasing children's self-reliance minimizes the power of a single teacher's feedback. Self-fulfilling prophecies require both powerful perceivers and powerless targets of others' perceptions and actions (Copeland 1994; Madison 1993).

Giving children voice and agency in their educational experience fosters patterns of choice and self-appraisal that are not only important in their own right but also may leave children less vulnerable to negative expectancy effects. In a cross-cultural study of high school students participating in a writing exchange, Sarah Freedman (1994) noted a striking difference between British and U.S. cultures in the purpose of and audience for student writing instruction. As one American student put it, "When I was reading the stories from England . . . it seemed like they . . . write for themselves, like for other kids and us, more than they write for the teacher which you know I do" (p. 162). Writing for the teacher may similarly place students at heightened risk for confirming teachers' expectations. Mark Snyder and Arthur Stukas (1999) suggest that strong acquiescence findings in laboratory studies may result from "the impoverished situation that targets are placed in"— a situation with diminished power (p. 281). Such laboratory studies also show that targets who actively resist limiting expectancies can overcome the negative prophecies.

Fourth, the investment at Landmark in resource development and in deep relationships among the principal, teachers, students, and parents means that stereotypic thinking about limits in the potential of children to learn does not develop easily nor is it allowed to persist. Children's capabilities are appreciated by many individuals who observe children across a diversity of contexts and get to know them well. Because not every interaction is with a single teacher or the same group of peers, the potential for negative self-fulfilling prophecies is lessened.

Finally, because Landmark strove for a coherence of goals and programs within the school as well as accountability for effective instruction and learned accomplishments, all participants—the principal, teachers, parents, and importantly, the children—held themselves accountable for the continued improvement of the school environment. Such structural conditions reduce the overloading of teachers and motivate them to gain an accurate and comprehensive understanding of their students. In social psychology laboratory settings, these structural conditions have been found to minimize the creation of negative self-fulfilling prophecies (Neuberg 1989).

A More Complex View of Higher Expectations

In stark contrast to the morning opening at Landmark School, I watch another ritual inside a vastly different elementary school where the community gathers only in crisis. The school is under lockdown because of a threatened drug-related shooting in the streets, apparently a routine occurrence in the neighborhood. The police had ordered the doors locked and all occupants of the building away from the windows. The events that unfolded demonstrated this school's valuing of order and discipline above student understanding and participation. Three hours passed, with lunch and recess missed, and children gathered in the hallways, seated on the floor outside classrooms. Efforts were made to keep the children orderly and quiet during the long wait. When it was over, I saw child after child, mostly African American boys, brought to the principal's office for misbehavior, parents called to pick up their youngsters for suspensions, many threats by parents for further punishment at home, and more than a few tears as well as anger.

Here, the expectations for, and the behaviors of, children were radically different. Children were not called on to play meaningful roles, not given a means of participation or an opportunity to express their feelings. The expectation that active youngsters, particularly boys, could sit still for such a long period of time without cognitive and physical stimulation or food is far from reasonable in light of what we know about developmental needs. Tight discipline and monitoring was in place because students were expected to be uncontrollable. Yet the use of tight discipline and punishment likely exacerbated the ensuing infractions that, under different conditions, might have been avoided. Were there other ways to think about the opportunities presented here? What about children's fears that it might be a brother, sister, or themselves shot next time? What about relationships between these real-world events and the subject-matter learning that happens in classrooms? Are there lessons to be drawn, opinions to be sought, and student leaders to be developed?

Plentiful Opportunities for Challenge and Support

Landmark was a school where one child's success did not lie in another child's failure. Scarcity of opportunity and scarcity of appreciation did not rule the day. A commentary in *Education Week* (Mlawer 1994) calls our attention to the message underlying this bumper sticker ("My kid beat up your honor student"), which has arisen in response to the ever-popular "My child made honor roll at X School." This emphasis on "being on top" of an increasingly narrow pyramid has intensified during the past two decades. Economists Robert Frank and Philip Cook (1995) write about the dangerous spread of "winner-take-all" markets where small performance differences are accompanied by increasingly bigger reward payoffs. What was true for the sports and entertainment industry is spreading rapidly across markets and increasingly invading the realm of education—indeed accelerating the demand for "elite" and differential credentials earlier and earlier in schooling. While scarcity of prized resources drives inequality in distribution, it is our conception of resources and opportunities in schooling that in part makes them scarce or plentiful. As Manus Midlarsky (1999) writes in his book *The Evolution of Inequality,* inequality at the extremes "fuels the desire for gain by the disadvantaged, by whatever means" (p. 273). As the diversity of the children who come to school increases—in means, language, cultural background, and preparation—such differences between the players, when placed in contexts of scarce resources, further widen the inequality.

While individuality and individual accomplishment were recognized at Landmark, such recognition was more equitably distributed. If attainments are judged and enjoyed based upon absolute standards regarding the quality of performance (not on relative distinctions between students), if opportunities to learn and perform make accommodations for the diverse pathways and supports needed by students to respond to their limitations and disabilities, if attainments recognize a broad array of abilities across the spectrum of human talent, then perhaps this recognition is fairly and squarely open to all. But most importantly to a development-focused achievement culture, accomplishment brings intellectual and affective pleasure to the entire community. Accomplishments create beautiful artifacts, performances, and events that are open to the whole community to celebrate. The values are focused on mastery and on high-quality work, on collaborative and mentoring relationships, and on innovation and creativity across all the fields of study, including the arts. Are these not the values that we want for an institution concerned with the development of human talent?

Landmark was also a school where participation was demanded, accommodations were natural, and problems were addressed forthrightly. These are precisely the conditions under which capability can be more fully developed. There are other examples of schools that broaden opportunities for students. An article in the *San Francisco Chronicle* (Wheeler 1991) told the story of a Plainville, Indiana high school that adopted the shocking innovation of allowing any student who wanted to play to join the football team and allowing any interested student to train as a cheerleader. The weekly games involved shifting the team members on the field so that all could play and all could cheer. The most notable part of the story was that the school reported the highest ever attendance of parents at football games and the greatest amount of money raised for school programs. Although not studied, one wonders at the new talent that may have been developed by this widening of opportunity to learn.

The broadening of opportunities can be seen in another article in the *San Francisco Chronicle* (Aug. 26, 1996, p. C1), which described a federal court ruling that officials of a youth baseball league had failed to follow anti-discrimination laws in refusing an eleven-year-old with cerebral palsy the opportunity to play in the league. The league had argued that if accommodations were made, "the child might hurt himself or other players with his crutches" and might "embarrass himself." But another league responded very differently and allowed him to play. The welcoming coach was quoted as saying: "When he is at bat, he discards one of two crutches and leans on one when he swings. For two seasons, he played tee-ball in a league for athletes two or three years younger. . . . His motivation and drive—they were amazing . . . He swung the bat like anyone else and he could run pretty fast when he hit the ball . . . He never wanted to be treated any differently than anyone else." When schools accommodate, support, and continue to challenge children, they create conditions in which children can overcome obstacles to their mastery. A study by Mary Lee Smith and Lorrie Shepard (1988) on teachers' beliefs about kindergarten retention lends support to these more fluid conditions for children. These researchers found that "in schools with few retentions, teachers dealt with individual differences in more fluid and less permanent ways than teachers did in high-retaining schools" (p. 328). That is, they made accommodations and provided supports without permanently reducing the level of challenge.

A final example is reflected in the editorial "Student Protest" (p. A26) and in the Michael Taylor and Teresa Moore story "Two Communities Kept Their Cool" (p. A 12–13) in the May 5, 1992 issue of the *San Francisco Chronicle.* These stories report on the day of the Rodney King trial verdict and illustrate the routine and the unusual in encouraging participation and defusing tension in the community. One school in the San Francisco area suspended all the students who led a protest march across the Bay Bridge. In contrast, another school lauded student participation and invited the students to hold an assembly to discuss the events with fellow students and teachers. One community shored up their law enforcement officers and increased patrols, expecting rioting and getting it. Another community opened City Hall and invited citizens in for discussion: there were no incidents reported. These examples all speak to the importance of broadening educational opportunities that challenge as well as connect communities. The research of David Galloway and his colleagues (1982) in England demonstrates that differences between schools in rates of expulsion and exclusion can be linked to classroom and school practices that either escalate, defuse, or ameliorate the behavior problems of students.

A Narrowing of Opportunities in Standards-Based Reforms

As currently framed, our national effort to raise educational standards and to hold schools accountable through high-stakes testing ultimately narrows rather than broadens opportunities for challenge. The curricular standards speak to subject matter knowledge alone—not to lifelong motivation and creativity, nor to self-efficacy, self-regulation of behavior, social competence, and social responsibility, even though we know that these outcomes are critical to achievement. These broader purposes for schooling, important for the promotion of human development, are especially critical for encouraging positive prophecies of student achievement. The showcasing of a broader range of human talent (rather than the limited heralding of discrete linguistic and mathematical skills as measured on standardized tests) enables more children to engage in schooling as competent and interesting human beings and most importantly, to use their strengths to better master the core academic skills. Further, the challenge at hand is to teach processes of inquiry and continuing learning across disparate domains to ensure adaptability in the face of changing facts. Yet evidence is growing that under high-stakes accountability, teaching has become focused on test preparation, accommodations are not being made for differences in language and disability, children are being excluded, and cheating is occurring (Natriello and Pallas 1999).

Further limiting visions are found in our underutilization of school and community contexts as additional sites for learning. In contrast to the voluminous literature on learning that happens inside classrooms, remarkably less attention has been directed to learning outside of "encapsulated" classrooms (McLaughlin, Irby, and Langman 1994; Sarason 1990). In many elementary schools, opportunities to participate outside of classrooms are relatively rare. As described by children, they are limited to serving as monitors or message-carriers, and are seen as special privileges reserved for those who finish their work fast. While the world of middle and high school expands to include sport teams, interest clubs, and student government, the hallmark of these school-level activities (themselves under increasing budgetary threat), is similar scarcity of opportunity and exclusivity of membership. A narrow segment of the student population, the already talented, are most likely to participate in these activities. Research underscores the importance of engagement in school activities and identification with school as critical factors in reducing the risks of school failure and dropping out and in encouraging more children to develop their talents (Finn 1989). Further still, limiting visions of learning undercut the importance of deep and enduring relationships among teachers and students and among a community of learners (Brown 1997).

Finally, current national reforms narrowly focus on accountability for the standards, using behavioral principles of reward and punishment to meet the goal of creating a challenging learning environment for all. By failing to fully invest in teacher and principal development or the transformation of the school culture, we disappoint students who deserve unlimited opportunities for challenge and ensure that schools will continue to develop low expectations for children who do not learn in the limited ways in which they are taught. We need to discard notions of scarcity and make substantial changes in the structural arrangements of schooling to expand resources, foster reflection time, and widen opportunities for more complex learning.

Obstacles to reaching higher lie in contradictions between classroom efforts and the larger culture of the school, as well as within and between classrooms. Discrepancies also exist between what teachers are asked to do and how they are helped to do it. Implementing challenging expectations for students cannot happen unless teachers are provided with opportunities to prepare themselves to teach to those standards. In addition, interest in teaching the harder-to-reach youngsters cannot be fostered if higher status is given to teachers who teach the top performers. An important feature of principal leadership is to nurture coherence and mutual reinforcement between all levels of the system, for students, teachers, and parents. By doing so, a development-focused achievement culture is created that promotes positive educational prophecies.

Challenges for Public Schools

There are some public schools in disadvantaged neighborhoods where expectations focus on the development of talent and agency in children. That there is power in children's ideas is reflected in the title of Deborah Meier's (1995) stirring book about Harlem's Central Park East Elementary School, where under her leadership as principal, such a vision of teaching was fostered; 90 percent of its students went on to graduate from high school and attend college. There are "opportunities to learn" to be found everywhere when they are seen and capitalized upon. Children who are provided with opportunities for exploration as well as responsibility can, and often do, respond accordingly. Meier writes: "It won't come as a surprise that I think the conditions that foster good teaching are . . . small schools, schools of choice, school autonomy over the critical dimensions of teaching and learning, lots of time for building relationships and reflecting on what's happening, along with a culture of mutual respect for others and a set of habits of mind that fosters inquiry as well as responsibility" (p. 184).

There also exists a growing number of school reform models that are being implemented, evaluated, and scaled up, spurred by the business-led nonprofit organization New American Schools and by the 1997 passage by Congress of the Comprehensive School Reform Demonstration Program. This program offers funds to schools willing to adopt a research-based model of instruction and school organization (Berends 2000; Datnow and Castellano 2000; Schorr 1997). Among these models are Success for All (Slavin et al. 1996), Accelerated Schools (Levin 1987), Coalition of Essential Schools (Sizer 1992), the Comer School Development Program (Comer et al. 1996), and the Child Development Project (Solomon et al. 2000). These designs vary—in their relative emphasis on prescriptive versus process and collaborative approaches, in whether they address elementary or secondary school levels, and in the school organizational components and child outcomes targeted for change, with some focused on achievement test score gains, others on inquiry learning, and others on social-emotional and prosocial development. On balance, when the principal and teachers choose to participate, and when new practices are implemented, the outcomes are promising regarding the capacity for schools to improve the performance of their students (at least some schools, and in some of the areas targeted for change) and to reduce special education placements and retentions (Cook et al. 1999; Cook, Murphy, and Hunt 2000; Jones, Gottfredson, and Gottfredson

1997; Slavin et al. 1996; Solomon et al. 2000). But with regard to raising academic expectations for a diverse student population, none of these models have yet targeted the multiple and interwoven components necessary to create and sustain a development-focused achievement culture in classrooms and schools.

Is the achievement culture described at Landmark possible in public schools, at both the elementary and secondary levels? Absolutely. While there are critical differences between public and private schools (most often in student selection, parental choice, and small size), it must be underscored that the student population at Landmark was more diverse by design than that of the local public school district. The conceptual choices made by Landmark that extended and diversified opportunities for learning and garnered the extraordinary engagement of students, teachers, and parents could be made at other schools.

Yet the public school setting poses challenges to this model that render the changes described more difficult (but not impossible) to achieve—the increased size of public schools, the greater child-to-adult ratio, the greater heterogeneity of the school population, and the increased and conflicting external demands (in particular, funding and program forces that dictate differentiated pathways rather than a common curriculum and a schoolwide culture). A staff meeting and a schoolwide morning assembly are experienced differently as the numbers of participants grow. More students per adult means that close relationships, monitoring, and follow-through are more difficult to develop in most public schools. The greater heterogeneity among students, parents, as well as staff (not only along racial and economic lines, but also with regard to learning problems, learning styles, teaching philosophies, and cultural beliefs) multiplies the niches needed and increases the difficulty of reaching consensus. Competing and frequent district, state, and federal mandates put pressure on reform and accountability, setting the agenda for schools and leaving little breathing room to determine priorities and to plan creatively.

It must be emphasized, however, that at Landmark School, the niches available for development and the staff time available for planning were created by design. Money was spent for part-time specialist teachers; the principal taught classes; parents and students ran programs; Friday schedules allowed schoolwide, across-classroom, and block programming; and every activity maximized involvement by tapping a variety of interests and talents and by increasing participation opportunities using the principle of "underpeopled" settings. In some ways, the structure of Landmark elementary school reflected features of the more complex high school model in its use of specialist teachers and a wide array of schoolwide activities. Landmark offered what Valerie Lee and Julia Smith (2001) have described as a communal rather than a bureaucratic form of school organization: "Communally organized schools . . . are more likely to define a common set of academic needs as appropriate for all students, regardless of cognitive capacity . . . although the means for arriving at the goal might be responsive to students' skill levels" (p. 11).

In their studies of the restructuring of high schools for greater equity, Lee and Smith (2001) found that school size has an independent but indirect effect on student learning and on the equitable distribution of educational opportunities—achieved primarily through more frequent, personalized interactions in smaller settings. Some of the benefits of a small school can be obtained by designing "schools within schools," which enable morning assemblies and close mentoring of students. The principal, rather than serving at the hub of all activity, can delegate and share responsibility for leadership—creating a collective responsibility for assessing, anticipating, and resolving issues that pertain to resource use and balance within the system. Yet the same principles hold true: motivated engagement must be encouraged at all levels for teachers, students, and parents. And the activities must be broken down in ways that fully demand participation. The research of Robert Felner (2000) documents how such smaller settings can substantially alter teacher-student relationships in large high schools.

Lee and Smith (2001) found that remarkably few high schools take advantage of cutting-edge practices that have been documented to increase the learning of more children, such as "using parent volunteers, focusing on cooperative learning, teaming their teachers across disciplines, offering mixed-ability classes in mathematics and science, providing teachers with common planning time, offering flexible times for classes, or keeping students in homeroom classes over several years" (p. 157). Rarer still was the utilization of more than one of these practices.

Principal vision and leadership are key. The principal must set priorities and free time from external demands for these internal processes of resource development, niche creation, and monitoring. Central to the constraints are the demands for differentiating instruction according to perceived ability or need and the rules against giving students and parents meaningful responsibilities in schools (rules that are fueled by fears of liability). How the principal values equity, strengthens administrative leadership, and conceptualizes the constraints on the system (as given, fixed, or malleable) determines whether a unifying, coherent, and inclusive vision can be created for the school (Riehl 2000; Sarason 1971)—and whether an achievement culture can be fashioned that will provide "for the fullest measure of development" (Merton 1942/1973, p. 270).

CHAPTER 10

Achievement Cultures for University Faculty

There is the further question of the ratio of scientific achievement to scientific potentialities. Science develops in various social structures, to be sure, but which provides an institutional context for the fullest measure of development?

—Robert K. Merton, 1942

In this chapter, I look at my own house, the modern research university and its achievement culture for the faculty. Indeed, the faculty are themselves learners—as scholars uncovering new knowledge in their fields and as teachers seeking to improve instructional effectiveness. Further, the university is a setting where the student pipeline is directed, the products of the K–12 educational system are taught, teachers are prepared, and disciplinary knowledge is discovered as well as certified through the selection, development, and appraisal of faculty. These functions, while discrete, reflect interdependent spheres of expectation and influence. Can we see parallels in the achievement culture of the university for faculty and that of classrooms and schools in the K–12 educational system? Are there also variations in the qualities of university cultures that might afford different opportunities for achievement? And which institutional context, in Robert Merton's terms, affords "the fullest measure of development" for all in its midst?

Here, I draw from the research literature as well as from my own experiences as a faculty member—in particular, my service on two faculty senate committees: SWEM (status of women and ethnic minorities) and the Budget and Interdepartmental Relations Committee (which reviews faculty appointments and performance). Having the vantage points of both the judged and the judge gave me the chance to see how academic expectations were affected by gender, race, and simply "difference" in the development and the appraisal of faculty talent.

There is an oft-repeated joke about university professors that their fervor over small stakes stems from having been the nerdy children who were least likely to be picked for school sports teams. Attending just one faculty meeting concerned with hiring or promotion would convince most that the fervor over decisions is indeed high. But to depict the stakes as "small" is to miss the powerful role that universities play in framing what constitutes achievement in our society and who has attained it. In each decision about hiring, advancement, and tenure, the winnowing of who is "in" or "out" and "moving up" or "staying in place" shapes the professoriate—which people and intellectual contributions are more or less valued. Similarly, in the development and application of admission criteria for entering students and for differentiated programs, the university serves as a gatekeeper in deciding who may come in and who must stay out, and thereby determines the opportunities and ranks of the college-educated and professional class.

But what we most often forget is that access to each successive step (that is, the selection decision), while heatedly debated, is only one part of an ongoing process. The conditions we offer to support or hinder the work on which future judgments will be based are also crucial. Ultimately, it is both these selection and development choices that shape what we come to identify as ability in individuals and as knowledge in science. In minding the gate, to what extent do we also help open doors?

After formulating the dynamics of the self-fulfilling prophecy, Robert Merton saw similar processes influencing how science was conducted and appraised. His studies of these processes pioneered a new field that came to be called the sociology of science. Merton (1968/1973) described the Matthew effect as "the accruing of greater increments of recognition for particular scientific contributions to scientists of considerable repute and the withholding of such recognition from scientists who have not yet made their mark" (p. 446). His description drew from the Gospel according to Saint Matthew where it is said, "For unto every one that hath been given, and he shall have abundance: but from him that hath not shall be taken away even that which he hath" (p. 445). Merton argued that this very aspect of the faculty reward system not only affected the appraisal of talent but also provided differential access to scientific resources such as grants and laboratories that would enable further scientific production. In this conceptualization are the very elements that Merton identified earlier as critical to self-fulfilling prophecies—a false belief as well as critical actions taken. Thus, the consequences that flow from the judgment of worth, that is, greater recognition and greater resources, could ultimately confirm the initial appraisal. Merton called this the principle of "cumulative advantage" (p. 457).

This phenomenon can well explain the particular difficulties that women and ethnic minority scholars have had in forging careers in the mainstream academic marketplace, where their numbers are fewer and their ranks lower, relative to their distribution in the population and to their proportion of earned doctorates. As reported in the 1999 almanac issue of the *Chronicle of Higher Education,* across all institutions of higher education, including two-year colleges, 86.8 percent of full-time faculty are white and 32.5 percent are female. While affirmative action policies have proved critical for diversifying the overall face of the professoriate, there are still many fields (especially math, physics, and engineering), certain ethnic minority groups (especially African Americans, Hispanics, and Native Americans), and some areas of the professoriate and administration (namely, the upper echelons) that do not show much progress in the diversification of faculty (Brush 1991; Sonnert and Holton 1996; Zuckerman, Cole, and Bruer 1991). Identified trouble spots speak to a lack of fit and to differential opportunities for development. These include the collision of tenure review with the biological clock of child-bearing and child-rearing, a geographical boundedness to marriage, family, and community, demands for and deep commitments to teaching and service, scholarship often different from mainstream disciplines, an uneven playing field in access to mentors, exposure to differential treatment, and conflicts between ethnic or female identity and academic identity—all of which narrow the chances of survival for women and ethnic minorities seeking an academic career.

The sociologist Arlie Hochschild (1975) describes the discomforting lack of fit between women and academe in a provocative paper titled "Inside the Clockwork of Male Careers." She writes:

> To ask why more women are not full professors, or "full" anything else in the upper reaches of the economy, we have to ask first what it means to be a male professor—socially, morally, and humanly—and what kind of system makes them what they become. The academic career is founded on some peculiar assumptions about the relationship between doing work and competing with others, . . . getting credit and building a reputation, . . . doing it while you are young and hoarding scarce time, . . . minimizing family life and leaving it to your wife—the chain of academic experiences that seems to anchor the traditional academic career. (p. 49)

Similarly, psychologist Jacquelyn Mitchell (1983) describes a mismatch between university culture and the experience of African American faculty: "We are assumed to be less competent, yet we are also expected to replicate our white colleagues' output both in quantity and quality. We are chastised for spending excessive time with our students, but we are also relied on to reduce their isolation and cultural shock. We are criticized for participating in ethnically related community events, and we are given little recognition for our service contributions, but at the same time we are viewed as a critical link with the ethnic community" (pp. 21–22).

The qualities of the university achievement culture not only clash with the cultural views of women and ethnic minority scholars but also make it difficult to see these scholars as talented. Fellowships and honors, access to publication outlets, and reputation are all still handed to close associates by judges who perceive value in the work and respond to the accolades already garnered, as Merton noted in his depiction of the Matthew effect in science. A study by Christine Wenneras and Agnes Wold (1997) of the peer review of biomedical postdoctoral fellowships in Sweden underscores the importance of personal connections and the difficulty of perceiving talent in women, even given equal publication records. Their findings showed that female applicants had to be 2.5 times more productive than the average male applicant to receive the same score. Further, there existed a friendship bonus whereby associates of committee members scored higher. These investigators noted that "being of female gender and lacking personal connections was a double handicap . . . that could hardly be compensated by scientific productivity alone" (p. 342). These are some of the elements that in university settings made and continue to make kinship with and the recognition of talent in women and ethnic minority scholars so very difficult.

These examples all speak to how we perceive achievers and value their accomplishments—and to the consequences that flow from such judgments and from the conditions we provide for development. In ways not unlike those we saw in K–12 classrooms, differences from the norm (in gender, ethnicity, socioeconomic background, and learning style) prove difficult to successfully integrate into the culture of the university setting as it is commonly understood. My experiences as a faculty member mirror in many ways what I have observed in my research. I teach as do the teachers I study. I learn and I live under continuous evaluation for my achievements as do the children I interview. Perhaps not surprisingly, I see remarkable continuity in definitions of and contexts for achievement, for both faculty and first-graders. I also see tremendous variations in achievement cultures among universities, similar to the variations in classroom culture that children have identified as creating strikingly different opportunities to develop ability and to be labeled as able. These variations in achievement culture are particularly crucial to the fate of those who are different in any way from what are held as normative standards. Just as a look beneath the averages identified classrooms that differed in culture—some emphasizing equity and development and some emphasizing differentiation and selection—so too does a look beneath the averages illuminate vastly different university cultures. Are we missing out on reducing the gap between "scientific achievements and scientific potentialities"? Are there environmental contexts that more successfully provide for "the fullest measure of development"? If so, what can be learned from them?

Our examination of the university culture of achievement is especially critical given the belief that reform of K–12 schools cannot take place without the participation of higher education (Gifford 1986; Haycock 1998). Such arguments are made because higher education both sets the academic standards for college admission toward which the K–12 educational system gears its preparation of students as well as houses the disciplinary experts who are seen as essential to curricular improvement. Scores of school-university partnerships have emerged to improve math and science education, to align standards, and with the demise of affirmative action, to strengthen opportunities to learn in order to increase diversity in the college applicant pool. There is a touch of irony here given that the very university faculty who themselves are roundly criticized for neglecting teaching in favor of research are being pressed into urgent service to improve the teaching of other professionals. Yet the question of which values, policies, and practices of the university culture best serve the reform of K–12 education is rarely if ever discussed. An exception is found in an editorial by Kati Haycock (1998), director of Education Trust, who cautions about a possible mismatch in vision between schools and universities: "If all universities are as ignorant of the difference between real education reform and SAT preparation classes—if they're interested in ever-finer sorting just when the rest of us are trying to sort more students in—why would anyone even want to partner with such myopic arrogance?" (p. 38).

Also critical is that although research has looked to qualities of schools of education and their preparation of teachers as causal links to what happens in classrooms (see Goodlad 1990), we have yet to seriously examine how the achievement culture of universities may shape our thinking about teaching and about students in K–12 settings. As Seymour Sarason (1996) has underscored, we teach the way we have been taught: "The characteristics and force of the school culture have many sources and chief among them is how educators are *prepared* to live in that culture" (p. 380). So too, do we cultivate and evaluate attainment the way our own accomplishments have been fostered and judged. Here, the cultural ethos of the university and its views about and nurturing of achievement are especially telling.

Star Wars versus Growing Our Own

The Ability Grouping of Faculty

Who becomes and who remains a faculty member, where and for how long, and at what rank of the professoriate? These outcomes are shaped in part by individual choice and in part by processes of appraisal and treatment. The social influence processes are in some ways like those that children face when they are assigned to, ranked within, and moved among ability-based groups and academic tracks. These same sorting and cultivating processes ultimately shape the composition and pecking order of the professoriate. Issues of who can apply to a position, how one's achievement will be measured, what kinds of resources and support one will achieve, and what venues will be offered for demonstrating competence prove to be critical elements (beyond individual choice) in determining who passes each hurdle of the professoriate from assistant to associate to full professor. Distinctions made among faculty within university settings—in perceptions about talent and in opportunities allocated—can create very different environments for professional socialization, development, and advancement. While this is a time of intense "star wars" on all university campuses, with troubling and increasing gaps in reputations, salaries, and perks between the have and have-not faculty (much like what Frank and Cook [1995] have described in the world of sports and business and similar to ability-based reading groups and tracks), universities do differ in how deeply they participate in such differentiation of advantage.

LIMITED MOBILITY WITHIN AND THE BEST GET MORE.   In selection-driven universities, movement into the highest group (that is, into a tenured professorship) is extremely limited. A pyramidal structure is usually in place where the tenured slots are scarce relative to the untenured slots and nu-merous junior hires compete for a single tenured professorship. Recruitment for tenured slots is made from the outside, rather than from within, in order to engage the very best individual in the field. This lets other universities do the critical work of faculty development. A January 29, 1999 article in the peer review section of the *Chronicle of Higher Education* captured this practice by declaring that a certain university "is notorious for snubbing its own peo-ple" (p. A56). Further, differentiation among faculty in opportunity, reward, and salary is very large. Perceptions of need as well as response to demands lead to different perks and treatment—such as salaries, course load, teach-ing relief, equipment allowances, research help, and research leaves of ab-sence—which in turn contribute to differential climates for development.

PROMOTION FROM WITHIN AND A COMMITMENT TO EQUITY. In contrast, there are university cultures where the conceptual underpinnings of the system for faculty hire and advancement are largely nonpyramidal and development-focused. Once appointed at the bottom rung of the fac-ulty, movement into the highest group (that is, a tenured professorship) is open to all, provided that absolute standards of excellence are met. Salary scales are set for each level of the professoriate and made public. Merit in-creases in salary are advanced on an absolute basis (when judged as earned, with no limit set on number of merit advances received), rather than on a relative basis (based on a rank ordering of faculty within the university). The expectation that all must grow is reinforced by a continual review, with multiple promotion junctures beyond the associate and full professor levels. Efforts are made to provide equitable supports for faculty development, all while recognizing that equity sometimes means unequal treatment, such as in the opportunity to delay the tenure clock for women and men who need to do so for child-bearing and child-rearing reasons. In addition, greater out-reach efforts might be made when advertising faculty positions in order to broaden the diversity of candidates considered. These university cultures of-ten have strong faculty leaders who monitor the diversity in gender and eth-nicity of the faculty and ensure equitable treatment.

The Informal Curriculum

Many begin their faculty careers with the belief that if they do their work well, they will be advanced and tenured—but what work, with what resources, how well, for how long, and in whose eyes? The socialization of university faculty for the tenure process involves access to and successful mastery of an implicit curriculum (Tierney and Bensimon 1996). While graduate school prepares aspiring faculty members for conducting their scholarship, it ill-prepares them for the marketplace in which their work, on multiple fronts, has to be balanced, nurtured, marketed, and appraised.

ON YOUR OWN: DIFFERENTIAL ACCESS. In selection-driven cultures, merit is seen as the only issue (the best will win), achievement is perceived to be an individual accomplishment, and the social factors that affect how scholarly achievement is appraised and nurtured are rarely illuminated. In such cultures, it is more likely to be considered irrelevant (and indeed, irreverent) to teach young faculty about what is expected of them and how it might best be achieved. Research in the sociology of science shows that faculty members have differential access to this critical but hidden curriculum, depending on whether they have mentors (particularly, acclaimed mentors) who help them through the ranks and provide critical opportunities for development and recognition (Zuckerman 1998). Ethnic minority and female faculty have been at a great disadvantage in finding mentors among predominantly white, male faculty and in gaining access to more prestigious institutions. Like-minded have always gravitated toward like-minded in the mentoring process. Access to this information and to these opportunities affect how successful junior faculty become.

WITH HELP: EQUALIZING ACCESS. A development-focused university culture works to make explicit the hidden curriculum and to provide all faculty with informational resources and mentoring opportunities. Actual and early assignments of mentors to incoming faculty is one way to increase the knowledge and support of new professors. Tenure survival manuals also attempt to level the mentoring playing field: they teach women and ethnic minority faculty, in particular, about the tenure review process, how to prepare for it, the special obstacles that they face as minorities in the university, and the resources available to help. This curriculum of the higher tracks, differentially allocated, can play an important role in the relative success of different groups of aspiring individuals. One example of such a survival manual has been issued by the National Education Association (1994) to promote academic justice and excellence.

The Incentive Structure: Motivational and Evaluative Systems

What are the qualities of the incentive structure that inform faculty about the criteria important for appointment, tenure, advancement, and marketability? I look here at what we conceptualize and reward as scholarship, how we measure productivity, and the goals we embrace in academe. With the advent of government funding for research in the post–World War II era, there has been a meteoric rise in the size of research universities and a shifting of mission (Graubard 1993). Scholarship has increasingly overshadowed teaching and service in the evaluation of faculty and their judged worth to the institution (Boyer 1990; Boyer Commission 1998). Rarely examined, however, is that research universities differ in their policies and practices concerning which kinds of scholarship are valued more.

NARROWLY PERFORMANCE-DRIVEN CULTURES SEEK SUPERIORITY. Selection-driven cultures offer faculty "relief" from teaching more liberally as well as differentially through research grants, prestigious "chairs," and negotiated research professor positions. Rewards for teaching and service accomplishments are few and far between in the ascent from assistant to full professor.

Judgments about faculty achievement more routinely rest upon speed in completing work, quantifiable indices of production (number of publications, research dollars, citations in the literature and so on), and relative rankings (best, top quartile). Similar to the elementary school culture where smartness is defined as getting the work done fast and first, for university faculty, first, fast, uninterrupted, and sustained ("what have you done lately") production is what is rewarded. Robert Merton (1968/1973) called this the race for "priority": "it is to the swift, to him who gets there first with his contribution in hand" (p. 302). It is not uncommon for selection-focused departments to create a yearly ranking of faculty production based on the just-mentioned indices, weighted according to the prestige of the journals in which publications appear, as a means of determining merit increases.

This pressure to produce and achieve a high rank shifts motivational goals increasingly toward performance and appearance rather than the challenges of knowledge development and task mastery. Like in many elementary classrooms, too much time is spent on *how* one is doing rather than *what* one is doing: "For as rewards are meted out, they can displace the original motive: concern with recognition can displace concern with advancing knowledge" (Merton 1968/1973, p. 338). Further, the rewards are for individual attainment and besting others, rather than for collaborative efforts. Although the actual scholarship may rest on contributions from multiple individuals, particularly in the sciences, appraisal procedures encourage faculty to identify individual products, for example by distinguishing first-authored and sole-authored papers from multiple-authored works and by indicating the percentage contribution of each author in multiple-authored publications.

BROADLY LEARNING-DIRECTED CULTURES PURSUE SUBSTANTIVE EXCELLENCE. A development-focused university culture, while promoting scholarship, also holds all faculty accountable for teaching, for equitable teaching loads, and for excellence in teaching: even administrators teach, teaching relief is not to be bargained for, and travel time is monitored. Greater value is placed on teaching and on service—to the university, the profession, and the community. Excellence in teaching and service is celebrated with awards and recognition, as well as factored into merit reviews and raises. Such cultures support active programs for the improvement of faculty teaching, by even offering special teaching fellowships and professorships with perks to support innovation in teaching.

In development-focused cultures, judgments about faculty achievement also reflect substantive faculty involvement at multiple levels and rest upon a careful reading and analysis of the work, with feedback as one important byproduct. With this depth of faculty review, while outside opinions are important, inside assessments prove equally critical. Use of comparative and across-campus standards sensitizes reviewers to the pitfalls of equating excellence with research dollars, citations, and current popularity, and alerts them to issues of equity in opportunity. Faculty appraisal in such cultures is likely more supportive of the value of research synthesis and application as well as interdisciplinary scholarship, more appreciative of varying pathways and speeds in creative output, and more open to second chances, such as in tenure reviews. Such cultures are more likely to embrace learning goals by emphasizing substantive issues in scholarship rather than the performance of the scholar.

Faculty Agency in Governance

The faculty role in the university carries with it a freedom to investigate and cultivate independent ideas that is protected by the tenure system. But beyond autonomy and voice in individual scholarship, the faculty role in university governance varies greatly with regard to how it is framed and actualized.

ADMINISTRATIVE DIRECTION. Under incentive structures where the concern for recognition overshadows the doing of academic work, faculty members are reluctant to invest in the university—through peer review, curriculum planning, or campus committee work. By giving more weight to external rather than local judgments of faculty achievement and by devaluing teaching and campus service, the faculty allegiance shifts toward national and international disciplinary groups and away from local departments and campuses. Simultaneously, attention shifts toward individual entrepreneurialship and toward the improvement of conditions for oneself. Policies that direct the overhead received from research grants to individuals, departments, or schools reinforce individual and discipline-based aggrandizement. And when faculty members are unwilling to govern themselves, increasingly the administrative arm of such university cultures steps in to direct faculty work and faculty appraisal.

FACULTY SELF-GOVERNANCE. In more development-focused cultures, there is evidence of strong faculty involvement and governance around every dimension of university life, including the appraisal of faculty achievement. Faculty play critical roles at multiple levels in the advancement and promotion decisions. Policies direct overhead funds to a central pool so that they may be shared for common goals. Concerns abound about equity among faculty and about the implications of growth in one unit for expansion elsewhere. Such cultures embrace a university policy of "meeting outside offers" only rarely for fear that doing so will undermine general excellence and the closely held value of equity. Faculty members debate issues such as how the university can reward overall excellence while differentially rewarding the stars and whether to tithe departments or groups that generate substantial external funds for contributions to cash-poor but vital disciplines and programs.

Faculty Climate

What are faculty relationships like within these disparate university cultures? Do faculty members develop close or distant relationships with colleagues? Do they forge a strong or weak identification with their universities?

INDIVIDUAL ABOVE COMMUNITY ALLEGIANCE. In selection-focused university cultures, where faculty allegiances more likely lie with the discipline, where differentiation between faculty and competition over scarce slots is high, and where initiative stems largely from the administration, there is little psychological sense of community. In such cultures, policies are likely to funnel resources to those who bring them in, differentiating the rich and the poor programs and reducing incentives for cross-disciplinary collaboration. Where the well-being of an individual faculty member counts more than an appreciation of the communal mission, relationships among faculty reflect castes of stars and isolates, much like the peer structures found in the unidimensional and high-differential-treatment classrooms described earlier. Bonds of affection and trust among coworkers are eclipsed by the need to compete and win.

INDIVIDUALITY AND COMMUNITY. Development-focused university cultures find ways to celebrate and appreciate the individuality of diverse faculty yet build a strong sense of community, continuity, and institutional loyalty. Through centralized but faculty-driven review of available faculty slots, program development and evaluation, and use of research overhead funds, opportunities are created for collaboration and for those rich in resources to share with others. Friendships among faculty, including junior faculty, likely run deeper, the faculty presence on the campus is greater, and feelings about the institution are perhaps more positive and strong.

The Institutional Consequences
of Differing Achievement Cultures

In bold strokes, I have speculated about contrasting visions of university cultures for faculty achievement that are not dissimilar to the different classroom environments that elementary school children have identified. I will also speculate about the consequences. On one side, we have an achievement culture that emphasizes selection, with marked scarcity at the top and much faculty differentiation—a culture that also defines scholarship more narrowly, favors scholarship over teaching and service, values performance and ego above the mastering of problems, supports self-interest over communal concerns, and covets winners as defined by speed, quantity, relative ranking, and solo performance. On the other side, there exists an achievement culture that emphasizes development, with unlimited places at the top once hired and greater faculty equity—a culture that bases evaluations upon absolute rather than relative standards, is more encouraging of teaching and service, and supports faculty governance, collaborative work, unusual pathways, and multiple chances. The same disparate implicit theories about intelligent behavior and its malleability, about knowledge development and the structural and affective conditions that best nurture it, and so on, have shaped these disparate university cultures for faculty achievement.

For the sake of the argument, the cultures described here are more starkly contrasted and more coherently linked across the domains of the achievement culture than likely exists in practice. There are, of course, contradictions and variations within universities as well as differences among universities in the policies embraced and in how well such policies are implemented across departments and throughout the organization. While some of these identified differences may be seen as reflecting the privileges and different accountabilities of private and public institutions, I suggest that some private institutions more heavily emphasize development-driven practices and some public institutions, selection-driven practices. Similarly, historian David Hollinger (2001) contrasts the strong faculty governance system of the University of California, Berkeley, with its more modest counterpart at the University of Michigan. He notes that the "core of the Berkeley system is the power of the faculty as a corporate, campus-wide body to influence decisions about faculty salaries, as well as appointments and promotions at all ranks in all schools and colleges" (p. 31). He goes on to say that "these 'I'll pull my oar' folks at Berkeley were often the same kinds of people who at Michigan were more inclined to say, 'Administrators are paid to do this, so let them do it'" (p. 31). We need research about such qualities of the faculty achievement culture and about how, through policy and practice, they are implemented in research universities, both public and private, and with what institutional consequences. Historian Steven Graubard (1993) decries the absence of this knowledge: "The real nature of the U.S. research enterprise is so rarely explored in any depth. The conditions that create learning . . . a learned profession, a professoriate, . . . are too rarely examined" (p. 376).

"Growing Our Own": The University of California System

Among other examples, the common lore of the University of California system and its nine research campuses depicts a development-driven culture for faculty. It has been affectionately noted that University of California faculty are chosen "at the starting gate, not the finish line" and are "grown." At the core of this tradition is a strong faculty role in university governance—through service on faculty senate committees (Douglass 2000a; Fitzgibbon 1968; Stadtman 1970). An academic senate was first established as part of the original charter that created the University of California in 1868, and broad authorities over admissions and courses were given to the senate by the regents. These authorities were further extended after the faculty revolt of 1919–1920 to even greater self-governance in creating and operating its own committees. The senate was reshaped again in 1964 to include a federated model of faculty governance with separate but coordinated senate divisions on each campus.

As Graubard (1993) suggests, California is well known for its pioneering higher education system (the California Master Plan of 1960)—a tripartite vision that became a model for the nation. The plan called for a differentiation of functions between three coordinated levels of public higher education (community colleges, state universities, and research universities), which enabled both democratic opportunity as well as high distinction in scholarship. With transfer rights between these levels given to students, opportunities for upward mobility were secured. As Clark Kerr (1994), former Berkeley chancellor, former University of California president, and a chief architect of this plan has described it, the vision is "egalitarian in access and meritocratic in advancement" in these four ways (p. 82):

1. It puts more emphasis on equality in admissions in the earlier stages of higher education than in the later—at entrance to lower division rather than upper division. Merit becomes more important in admissions the more advanced the work.

2. Equality in admissions is more emphasized in nonacademic technical training institutions than in occupational, and in the occupational more than in the professional and scientific institutions, where merit is more nearly supreme.

3. It puts more emphasis on merit at more advanced levels of academic work and in more academically oriented institutions, but also in each situation at points of completion of studies rather than at points of entry.

4. It encourages transfer from one level of institutions to another, based on the aspirations, aptitudes, and past records of accomplishment of students, so that there may be second and third and fourth chances.

These principles highlight that for students, emphasis on merit comes later in the trajectory, enabling greater access to learning opportunities as well as multiple chances to try again and to move up in the educational system. In his history of the factors that shaped this vision, John Douglass (2000b) points to the relative absence of tradition in a state that was geographically removed from the eastern establishment of scholars and that needed to respond innovatively to the land-grant mission of the university. These conditions may have similarly shaped the need for California's public higher education to "grow" and empower its faculty.

There are similar principles of equity that underlie the treatment of faculty. While hiring and advancement decisions are based upon merit, the conditions under which merit is judged and the conditions provided to faculty for development and reward are highly egalitarian. The regular involvement of the faculty in peer review, and in all matters of university function, reflects these cultural values. Faculty are appraised for advancements and promotions against an absolute standard and once hired, tenured slots and merit increases (on a largely common salary scale) are unlimited, if such standards are met. Serious faculty review occurs throughout an individual's career, a model that has been the topic of much discussion in higher education because of what has been perceived as too much "dead wood" in faculty scholarship. The university maintains up to seven levels of review—beginning with the candidate's self-appraisal (an important exercise in and of itself), and moving up to a departmental committee, a chairperson, a dean, an ad hoc committee of faculty relevant to the field (for tenure and promotion to professor), and a campuswide committee of faculty (the budget committee) that makes recommendations to the chancellor—with a heavy reliance on substantive critique and the advice of internal reviewers. Overrides of these decisions by the chancellor are rare, attesting to the strength of faculty governance (Hollinger 2001). But most important for our purposes, this layered review process promotes a serious investment in the development of faculty and provides multiple opportunities, indeed second chances, because the many reviewers at various levels may well differ in their appraisals.

Excellence Achieved within a Development-Focused Culture

This commitment to development pays off, even in the currency of performance indicators. The National Research Council rankings of research-doctorate programs in the United States (1995), for example, placed the

University of California, Berkeley, among the top ten in thirty-five of thirty-six graduate programs. Further, 57 percent of Berkeley's departments ranked in the top three with regard to faculty quality, as compared to 37 percent at Harvard, 30 percent at Yale, and 26 percent at Stanford—universities that have been satirized as chasing the stars and letting others develop the talent.

Further, the Hugh Graham and Nancy Diamond study (1997), which relied on quantitative indices of productivity adjusted for size, also emphasized the leading research excellence of all of the University of California research campuses. In particular, they noted the surprising rise of the newer and smaller campuses: "UC campuses occupied three of the first four positions among public universities and six of the top fifteen" (p. 212). Graham and Diamond argued that the "unmatched success of California's tripartite system posed its own challenge to the traditional state posture of flagship protection and aggrandizement" (p. 212). They attribute this success first to the Master Plan adopted by the California state legislature in 1960, which limited the research and graduate training mission to the University of California system rather than the state and community college campuses, and second, to a systemwide faculty senate and the adoption of common practices (such as a salary scale, promotion criteria, and graduate training standards).

I suggest that it is the commitment to developmental and equitable policies in faculty treatment—a nonpyramidal system of promotion, absolute standards, largely one salary scale, continuous lifetime peer review by colleagues, and strong faculty governance—that is the critical factor for increasing faculty strength ("raising all boats") both within campuses as seen in the National Research Council rankings and across campuses as seen in the Graham and Diamond study (1997). Selection-driven cultures seem less likely to both recognize as well as develop the talent of all faculty, particularly faculty who differ in critical ways from those who provide the appraisals and determine the conditions for development. Indeed, such cultures likely support some, not all scholars, and some, not all departments, in their development, with highly differential treatment and differential rewards. This culture may be reflected by policies that rank faculty (and departments) in order of research dollars and number of publications garnered, with salary raises (and departmental support) commensurate with one's place in the hierarchy. In such university settings, reputations are individually rather than departmentally won and some individuals and some departments thrive while others perish—in stark contrast to the spread of excellence across the University of California system.

Implications for the Nature of Scholarship

There are perhaps further implications that extend to qualities of scholarship and teaching in these disparate achievement cultures. Selection-driven achievement cultures may lessen room for the untried, encourage hyperspecialization of fields, and discourage integration of knowledge. Such cultures may also more readily exclude a diversity of perspectives and scholars.

When emphasis is placed on performance indicators (such as publications, dollars, and citations garnered) rather than on a substantive analysis of the questions asked and the quality of the contribution, room for new ideas marginal to the disciplines is severely constrained. Such constraints are poignantly described by Pat Shipman (1995) in "One Woman's Life in Science": "I am the trickster . . . We are the women in men's fields, the people of color in white-dominated fields, the immigrants from other fields who come in and look at a subject with naive eyes . . . Is there room for tricksters within American Science? . . . Would it benefit our society and our science to expand definitions, loosen our borders, make room for the serendipitous, the quirky, and the untried?" (p. 302).

Similarly, Lisa Delpit (1986) captures the failure of her discipline of education to incorporate her experience, and how she was forced to adapt: "I remember asking myself in the first few months of my graduate school career, 'Why is it these theories never seem to be talking about me?' But by graduation time many of my fellow minority students and I had become well trained: we had learned alternate ways of viewing the world, coaxed memories of life in our communities into forms which fit into the categories created by academic researchers and theoreticians, and internalized belief systems that often belied our own experiences" (p. 379).

Preoccupation with distinguishing oneself in numbers of publications, research money earned, and rank—in a culture of increasing competition—may also be associated with hyperspecialization within disciplines and with a failure to synthesize knowledge. So much superiority is only possible among increasingly smaller circles of judges. Thus, fewer people read each other's work but it becomes easier to say that one is the best in the field (Smith 1990). This press for superiority rather than excellence greatly undermines the integrity and progress of science. The currency of faculty production has become so inflated that faculty are publishing an absurd number of papers and books and are striving to become famous *even faster* than before. English professor Wayne Booth, in a parable about "Upwardly Mobile Research College," captured the decreasing time between the conception of a new scientific possibility and the milking of credit by quipping, "One specialist in chaos theory managed to get publicity for his idea even before he had it" (as quoted in Desruisseaux 1990, A17). These pressures focus increasingly on the most recent work—neglecting historical underpinnings and interdisciplinary contributions, rediscovering what was discovered before, and failing to build upon, replicate, and systematically extend our understanding. And these values undermine the synthesis and application of knowledge—which take longer, cross disciplines, require collaboration, move outside university walls, build on practitioner understanding, and are ultimately harder to judge.

Heavy reliance on performance indicators rather than substantive contributions lessens opportunities for the inclusion of diverse perspectives in the academic pipeline. By contrast, development-focused achievement cultures, which emphasize multilayered and continuous internal faculty evaluation and campuswide absolute standards over external indices, enable far more attention to be directed to substantive excellence, and far greater support for interdisciplinary and disciplinarily marginal work and work on applied problems. The mismatch in needs and desires, and the failure to recognize and develop the talent of those who are different, are exacerbated in selection-driven cultures, which over-emphasize appraisal over development, embrace narrow performance goals and visions of scholarship, and reify time with ability. In such settings, doing it in less time and uninterrupted time equals smartness and motivation—the same lesson we saw in elementary school classrooms. In contrast, development-focused cultures broaden possibilities for equity in access and treatment, for breadth in definitions of and values about scholarship, and for multiple chances.

Implications for Teaching

These elements of the university achievement culture for faculty also shape our beliefs about and our investments in students and teaching. When the work of development is left to others—that is, when we, at every level, focus on identifying the best and the brightest for selective opportunities—the importance of educational contexts in nourishing the development of talent is too often forgotten. Walter E. Massey, a physicist and former director of the National Science Foundation, reminds us about promising educational conditions in his 1992 *Science* article:

Back in the 1950s, a sixteen-year-old student from a predominantly black high school in Hattiesburg, Mississippi, was considered promising enough to be sent off to college—Morehouse, a historically black college in Atlanta, Georgia—two years ahead of his time. He wasn't planning to become a scientist. He had never heard of physics nor had he taken a high school course in chemistry or trigonometry, much less advanced algebra . . . He probably would have flunked out of Morehouse long before graduation—had it not been for a physics teacher there who took the youngster under his wing, guided him, challenged him, and wouldn't leave him alone until he graduated . . . in physics! (p. 1177)

There were to be two more such mentors at different stages of his graduate work, mentors who made the difference between success and failure; all three mentors were white. Massey then suggests: "Few minority students can count on encounters with such giving individuals, black or white. Too often, faculty members look at boys and girls with backgrounds like mine and assume they are inadequate, mistaking lack of confidence and / or poor performance with lack of intelligence. Too many discount the minority student's potential for growth, too few have time even to determine if the potential is there" (p. 1177).

While Massey highlights the mentorship, I emphasize the elements of positive self-fulfilling prophecies: a belief in the potential for growth and actions taken that make growth possible, such as challenging conditions for learning, strategies and support for overcoming obstacles, close relations, and a simple unwillingness to give up. Selection-focused and performance-driven cultures are less likely to value and invest in teaching. An ironic example can be found in one university's gift of time off from teaching for the winners of campuswide teaching awards. In such achievement cultures, the status of teaching is diminished and as Bruce Wilshire (1990) argues, feminized: "The oedipal situation in the patriarchical home reproduces itself in the professionalized university, the messy work of caring for students and 'staying at home with them' being construed as 'women's work.' The prestige of the professionalized professor is directly proportional to the duration and profitability of travel beyond the university, to getting established in the more important outside world of publishing and conventioneering, of pure research and exclusive relationship with peers" (p. 271). Indeed, as the historian Patricia Graham (1978) has suggested, during this century women faculty lost ground in their numbers as universities shifted their emphasis from teaching toward a more entrepreneurial research enterprise. And these changes have led, increasingly, to less time spent on teaching.

But tinkering with the reward structure to better reflect the value of teaching will fail to address the underlying interdependent relationship between the achievement cultures for both faculty and students. The very values that undergird the evaluation and nurturing of our own scholarship are carried over to our appraisals of students and our visions of the teaching and learning process, thereby enhancing or limiting our capacity to develop talent in students.

I suggest that the heavy emphasis on differentiation among faculty is associated with similar differentiation among students. As one example, after a highly selective entry into a prestigious university, students are given the proverbial warning by deans and presidents: "Look to your left and look to your right." To the undergraduates, it is said, "only one of you will be in the top tier of your cohort" and to the graduate students, "only one of you will survive." The message given is that these students are strong enough to be selected but not to finish or be in the top group. Associated practices include seeking out the identified talent—the graduate students, advanced undergraduates, and the bright students in each class—leaving the neophytes and the as yet professionally uncommitted students to be taught by junior faculty, visiting faculty, and graduate student instructors.

When excellence is defined in relative terms (that is, along a normal curve), not all top performers who gained entry can, of course, place at the top. But when absolute standards are held about the quality of performance, indeed all can achieve to these standards. When the goal is to uncover and develop talent in all the students who come our way, the messages we give and the ways we teach are very different. At other prestigious universities, for example, it is said, "Once here, we will do everything to help you do well here"—the perspective of door-openers, not gatekeepers.

Just as the achievement values for faculty stress performance over task mastery, products over processes, relative rankings over absolute standards, so too does the design of undergraduate courses reflect these values in envisioning curriculum, instructional methods, and evaluation requirements. The didactic and distant lecture is perfected as a primary format for learning, akin to the tightly woven, stripped-down research article that leaves out the messy processes, the collaboration, and the missteps taken in the path toward discovery—precisely the elements that students might see as akin to their struggle and that might inspire hope of problem resolution. Teaching is more likely to be characterized as the brilliance of subject matter knowledge distilled in a lecture rather than as opportunities and support offered to students engaged as active learners, for example as a fellow historian or writer, in an appreciative community of peers, with a guide and resources. And evaluation is likely relative, graded on a curve rather than on the degree of success in meeting absolute standards. These qualities of teaching (distant, comparative, and passive) are especially problematic for ethnic minority and female students in fields where they have been historically underrepresented.

Implications for K–12 Educational Reform

The Research University under Assault

The research university has come under increasing assault (see Cole, Barber, and Graubard 1993; also American Academic Profession, special fall 1997 issue of *Daedalus*). The academy has been taken to task for the narrow definition of faculty scholarship embraced as well as for its limited investment in and vision for undergraduate teaching. The problem is argued to lie with the faculty reward structure. In *Scholarship Reconsidered: Priorities of the Professoriate,* the late Ernest Boyer (1990) imaginatively argued: "The most important obligation now confronting the nation's colleges and universities is to break out of the tired old teaching versus research debate and define, in more creative ways, what it means to be a scholar. It is time to recognize the full range of faculty talent and the great diversity of functions higher education must perform . . . It is time to ask how the faculty reward structure can enhance these efforts" (p. xii).

Further still, the Boyer Commission on Educating Undergraduates in the Research University (1998) concluded that "the state of undergraduate education at research universities is such a crisis, an issue of such magnitude and volatility that universities must galvanize themselves to respond . . . Baccalaureate students are the second-class citizens who are allowed to pay taxes but are barred from voting, the guests at the banquet who pay their share of the tab but are given leftovers . . . This report hopes to . . . define in more creative ways what it means to be a research university committed to teaching undergraduates" (pp. 24–25).

Taken together, these reports argue for a radical shift in university culture: first, to broaden our conceptions of scholarship to include not only discovery but also integration, application, and teaching; and second, to promote a more active, research-involved educational experience for undergraduates, one fully integrated with the research mission of faculty. Importantly, both reports implicate the reward structure for faculty as a causal element that must be changed: "Research universities must commit themselves to the highest standards in teaching as well as research and create faculty reward structures that validate that commitment" (Boyer Commission 1998, p. 21). But changing the reward structure for teaching and service would speak to only a slice of the problem; it would not address the particular obstacles that women and ethnic minorities face as learners at all levels of the university.

As I have argued, the achievement values that undergird evaluation of faculty scholarship and the conditions provided to nurture that scholarship shape how we ourselves develop, what we create as knowledge, whom we accept as knowledge producers, and how we come to appraise and teach students. There are parallels between conditions that foster intellectual potentiality in faculty and those that do so for students. Most importantly, there exist important variations among universities in the degree to which development-focused cultures are embraced and fostered. These values of the achievement culture for faculty and students have critical implications for how well we develop talent in the face of diversity among learners, at whatever level.

The judgments of "repute" and "potential" are those that prove problematic on so many grounds, especially for ethnic minority and women scholars, whose access and opportunity have been severely restricted and whose life experiences do not match prevailing world views. The closer one fits the image and the ideals of those doing the appraising and those providing the educational conditions, the easier it is to be perceived as worthy. So too for undergraduates—as well as elementary, middle, and high school students— have differences between teachers and students in gender, culture, and socioeconomic background made recognition of ability difficult.

Making the Commitment to Development

As Robert Merton (1960/1973) has emphasized, far less attention has been paid to the development side of the equation—to the conditions of social institutions that contribute to the realization of intellectual potential:

> It is a matter of demonstrable fact that far more work by far more investigators has been devoted to the problem of identifying individual differences in capacity than to the correlative problem of identifying differences in social

environments that evoke or suppress the effective development of identifiable aptitudes . . . Yet the psychological investigations on the first set of problems will have little significance for enlarging the fulfillment of individual promise unless it is connected with sociological investigations on the second set of problems. It is only so that we shall come to understand the frequent gap between individual promise and individual achievement. (p. 424)

In similar terms, Bernard Bloom (1982) pleaded for a redirection of research efforts, yet to be embraced: "First, that we . . . have a more positive, and more accurate concept of human potential . . . Human potential for learning is best estimated only under the most favorable learning conditions . . . My second wish is for us to reduce our efforts devoted to predicting and classifying humans and for us to make more central in our research the variables, processes, and concepts that make a vast difference in the teaching and learning of students" (pp. 12–13). And Seymour Sarason (1990) has long argued that education reforms will continue to fail unless they take seriously what we know to be productive contexts for learning, for both teachers and students.

The evidence becomes harder to ignore: selection-driven cultures provide diminishing returns and "enabling" environments help enormously to develop human potential. Many of our cherished tests, for example, the Graduate Record Examination, do not predict "meaningful" success beyond first-year grades (e.g., Sternberg and Williams 1997). Evidence grows that quality education can influence intelligence (Neisser et al. 1996), that access to more challenging courses, to college, and to quality education can reduce the black-white achievement gap (Myerson et al. 1998), and that the ethnic diversification of the student population enriches and benefits society without impairing the quality of graduates of medical schools (Davidson and Lewis 1997) or elite undergraduate schools (Bowen and Bok 1998). Similar diversification of faculty by ethnicity and gender has led to productive new knowledge across the disciplines. As one example, until this greater diversification, much of the science of psychology rested upon studies of white male undergraduates (Gilligan 1982; Guthrie 1976; Sue 1999; Trickett, Watts, and Birman 1994). As William Tierney (1997) points out, throughout the twentieth century, public higher education has been viewed "as a central vehicle for increasing equity in society" (p. 173). He suggests as examples the GI bill in 1994, which offered financial assistance and lowered admission requirements, and the Master Plan for Higher Education in California (1960), which, as mentioned earlier, created a network of community colleges, state universities, and research universities for everyone, with transfer rights, and thereby enabled a far broader constituency to attend college and most importantly, to do well.

Yet despite mounting evidence of the relatively poor predictions of many selection criteria and of the importance of "enabling" environments, our societal concern with the selection process and selection criteria continues to intensify. David Labaree (1997) notes that over history, three different goals for American education (social equality, social efficiency, and social mobility) have competed for priority. He argues that we are increasingly threatened by "the growing domination of the social mobility goal, which has reshaped education into a commodity for the purposes of status attainment and has elevated the pursuit of credentials over the acquisition of knowledge" (p. 39). This selection- and performance-driven achievement culture can be seen in the competition among parents of young children for spaces in elite preschools, parents' holding boys back a grade to give them an edge, overscheduled afterschool activities to make résumés distinctive, and excessive enrollment in tutoring, including preparation classes for SAT examinations.

This pursuit of "credentials over knowledge" is evident as well among university faculty. Alexander Astin (1990, 1997) points to what he calls our obsession with demonstrating intellect, rather than cultivating it, evident in how we rank our institutions of higher education: "The institutions perceived to have the smartest faculty members and students receive the highest rankings for quality, and a disproportionately large share of public and private funds" (1997, p. A60). Astin calls on higher education to take the lead in shifting our value system toward assessing the effectiveness of how we develop knowledge and understanding in both faculty and students, and away from simply applauding our capacity to entice stars.

In this climate, development-focused achievement cultures for faculty are under increasing threat. The University of California's commitment toward "growing its own" shows some signs of erosion in the face of the "star wars" competition for faculty. Because the university is responding more to outside job offers for faculty, it has to contend with greater inequities in terms and compensation within the professoriate, which threatens the largely common salary scale and the solidarity among coworkers (Hollinger 2001). In addition, the regents and the California voters have recently overridden aspects of faculty governance by eliminating race and gender as criteria in admission and hiring decisions. Yet despite these threats, the strong tradition of faculty governance and a commitment to equity remain. Further, faculty committees and the university administration are working on alternatives to affirmative action through K–12 outreach programs and more differentiated admissions criteria.

Even so, development-focused universities have not gone far enough in the wake of performance-driven societal values. There is important work yet to be done—in further reducing our obsession with quantity, time, and rankings, in more generously rewarding collaborative, synthetic, interdisciplinary, and applied work as well as teaching and administration, and in creating productive contexts for faculty development—in short, in strengthening the commitment to "grow our own." How can we help transform our own university cultures for achievement and contribute to the reform of education in ways that affirm and promote such development?

In the university, we can take the lead by allowing only three to five publications (that is, one's best and most reflective work) to be evaluated at every juncture, which would likely enable greater attention to substance and quality. We can reduce our responsiveness to outside offers for faculty and tithe money-making units to share their wealth with other departments or fields that are not yet considered market-worthy. And we can recognize the absurdity of forced distributions and relative rankings in appraising faculty when the highest standards are met.

We can also pay attention to the fact that the criteria of first, fast, continuous, and solo cannot do justice to all the ways in which discoveries of scholarship are made—and reward accordingly. We can learn from case studies about the conditions for scientific discovery and create them inside as well as outside universities. In the discovery of high-temperature superconductivity, Gerald Holton, Hasok Chang, and Edward Jurkowitz (1996) argue that the conditions that supported this work depended "on a mixture of basic and applied research, on interdisciplinary borrowing, on an unforced pace of work and on personal motivations that lie beyond the research of the administrator's rule book" (p. 364). Greater advances are sometimes made by collaborative efforts. In a *New York Times Magazine* article about Nancy Wexler, who was awarded the Albert Lasker Public Service Award for spearheading an effort to identify the gene for Huntington's disease, Mary Murray (1994) underscored the uniqueness of this team effort: "In a style virtually unknown in the conduct of modern science, researchers at six laboratories in the U.S., England, and Wales cooperated for ten years to find the fatal culprit" (p. 28).

We can see as injustice the judgment of tenurability "so early" and without taking into account the collision of the tenure review period with the biological time clock of female faculty, the judgment about "continuous" production without taking seriously time for bearing and caring for family, and the judgment that a level playing field is provided for faculty development and appraisal while ignoring the differential treatment of female and ethnic minority faculty. Making changes such as these, assessing what we do for faculty development, will enable us to shift from focusing on the appearance of our work to doing our work in the most favorable conditions.

Needed Leadership: A University and K–12 Partnership

A partnership with K–12 education can be forged, but guided by what values? To the extent that university achievement cultures are heavily selection-driven, we must ask whether this is what we want replicated in schools. There is much to learn from the variation among universities in the degree to which they embrace a development-focused culture—how such values are aligned through policy and practice that interdependently affect faculty and students alike, how they are threatened, and how they might be further supported.

If we are to apply our understanding of "conditions for the fullest development" in our work with K–12 education, we must move beyond the simple equating of human worth and human potential with grades, test scores, number of publications, and citation score. We must shift to substantive assessments and evaluations—a deep reading of faculty scholarship or student portfolios to examine the quality of thinking. We must broaden conversations among ourselves, with schools, and with the public about the conditions that nurture intellectual accomplishment—to include multiple aspects of discovery, to celebrate ideas and process of discovery, and to chart the uneven, the messy, and the serendipitous in creative efforts. Further, we must change our ways of teaching to highlight active learning, whereby students take on the roles of historian, writer, and scientist as they learn the process of doing scholarship, not simply the changing facts of scholarship. We must examine the balance between selecting students on the basis of ability and providing broader opportunities for development.

We might highlight that there are late bloomers and second chances, that problems are solved after much time and passion spent working on them, that people from less prestigious educational settings and with wildly different trajectories often make it just as far, and that one's trajectory is shaped by the supports found and the actions taken.

How does one teach with potential in mind? How does one develop relationships with students where one's passion for the subject is communicated, where students collaborate in "doing" scholarship, and where both challenge and support are provided? The answers lie not with teaching contact hours and test scores but rather with what happens when teaching goes spectacularly well. The nation was entranced by a book called *Tuesdays with Morrie* (1997), which recounted the weekly seminar between a faculty member at Brandeis University, Professor Schwartz, and a former undergraduate student who returned as this professor faced death. The author, Mitch Albom, concluded the book with a question and vision: "Have you ever really had a teacher? One who saw you as a raw but precious thing, a jewel that, with wisdom, could be polished to a proud shine? If you are lucky enough to find your way to such teachers, you will always find your way back. Sometimes it is only in your head. Sometimes it is right alongside their beds" (p. 192). It is in the seeing of the "precious" and in the shared processes of "polishing" human potential that positive expectancy effects likely prevail.

Some may respond that the development of talent among students—and especially among faculty—is *not* the business of universities. Unlike the K–12 educational system, which takes all children, universities are, by definition, highly selective for students and, of course, for faculty. And universities are themselves hierarchically tiered, with scarce, coveted places for both students and faculty at the elite rung. Critics may well argue that selection of the already talented is sufficient: let them sink or swim.

I suggest, however, that these highly selection-focused achievement cultures in the university poorly serve women and ethnic minority scholars, thus limiting diversity in the population of scholars and teachers produced and retained. That such cultures neglect the multiple challenges of knowledge development, narrowing ways of knowing as well as what we know. And that such cultures inadequately train diverse next generations by failing to deeply invest in the kind of teaching that is inclusive and supportive of difference. On the side of development-focused cultures, there is growing evidence that many of the current criteria for appraising achievement are not predictive of the most critical outcomes and that conditions that nurture talent pay off substantially. These are important lessons for universities as well as for the reform of K–12 schooling.

Conclusion

The normal distribution, the bell curve—beautifully symmetric and statistically pleasing as it may be—is a picture neither of quality or equality nor of the reality of human potential. Half our children below average is not an image of educational excellence. Disproportionate numbers of specific groups of children at one or the other end of this distribution is not an image of educational equity. And human potential is not a single, fixed attribute that can be carved into the image of a bell-shaped curve.

—Kenneth Sirotnik, 1990

How we define a problem frames the actions we take to resolve it (Seidman 1983). Social action based on existing explanations for educational self-fulfilling prophecies will likely fail to prevent negative effects or to fully capitalize on positive ones. In addition, our reliance on the achievement score as the standard for predicting future achievement and our favoring of practices that select talent rather than develop it undermine a more positive view of human potential (Sirotnik 1990).

Dead-end thinking spurred by our reliance on averaged effects also blinds us to variation in outcomes and varied possibilities for intervention. The evolutionary biologist Stephan Jay Gould argues in his book *Full House: The Spread of Excellence from Plato to Darwin* (1996) that we must "recognize the central [Platonic] fallacy in our tendency to depict populations as average values" (pp. 3–4). He suggests that "in Darwin's post-Platonic world, variation stands as the fundamental reality and calculated averages become abstractions. But we continue to favor the older and opposite view, and to regard variation as a pool of inconsequential happenstances, valuable largely because we can use the spread to calculate an average, which we may then regard as a best approach to an essence" (p. 41). Gould applies this understanding of variation to his own experience with cancer. In 1982, his condition was described as incurable with a "verdict of eight months median mortality" (p. 48), yet his evolutionary training alerted him to the error of assuming this prognosis applied to any one person. Instead, he reasoned that factors such as point of detection, degree of support, and the specific parameters of the treatment all combine to predict outcomes above or below the median. He also reasoned that "the right tail [of the distribution] has no necessary limits but the maximal human life span" (p. 50) and thus can be pushed.

There are similar lessons here for education and the workings of self-fulfilling prophecies. Researchers have wrongly focused on averaged effects, which tell us little about individual children, the variation with which expectancy effects are accentuated or minimized in a complex world, and the potential for better outcomes. Further, researchers and educators have become so fixated on predicting how much (or little) students will achieve that we have generally neglected to provide the optimal conditions for development—conditions that could alter the distribution of schooling outcomes. Where children are now in the achievement distribution, both in rank and level, best predicts where they will be in the future only when we do nothing but sort on the basis of their differences and provide inferior and limiting opportunities to those for whom we expect less. But if we shift this pattern of underestimating the capability of children, if we change the circumstances of instruction through access to high-quality learning environments, early detection of problems, the adoption of positive and empowering attitudes, and the provision of optimal and nonstigmatizing interventions, the distribution may alter and the median may be raised. The choice is ours.

What We Learned

Using an ecological lens to examine the dynamics of expectancy effects in schooling, what have we learned from different players such as children, teachers, principals, and scholars; from different levels of education such as elementary, secondary, and postsecondary; from the interactive worlds of family and school; and from a longitudinal perspective across children's school careers?

First, we have seen that children know: they are privy to the differential expectations that teachers may hold for students within the same classroom. They are cognizant of subtle differences in treatment that favor high over low achievers. Even first-graders, even so-called low achievers, are deeply sensitive observers of the classroom reality (indeed the world) and have much to teach us about the kinds of experiences in which they and their peers thrive or in which they suffer shame and withdraw from learning. Children's reports direct us not only to differential interactions, verbal and nonverbal, between teachers and students, but also to the institutional basis in the broader achievement culture of classrooms. Further, children tell us that teachers differ in the degree to which they favor some children over others with higher expectations. These reports of classroom differences by elementary-school-age children demonstrate both construct validity (they match in broad strokes what teachers tell us about their beliefs and practices as well as what observers see) and criterion validity (they predict different patterns in children's development). That children know whether we think them smart or dull should give us pause. Such awareness constitutes a critical pathway for the workings of self-fulfilling prophecies—through the internalization of the expectations of others as we frame our own expectations. Such knowledge by children must also inform our understanding and our actions.

Second, with regard to the workings of self-fulfilling prophecies, it matters a great deal in what classroom and in what school children find themselves. There is more variability than we had assumed. Classrooms and schools differ in institutionalized beliefs about ability and about its nurturance, in policies and practices that flow from such beliefs, and in the opportunities provided children to learn and be (and be seen as) competent. Individual differences between children are handled quite differently in these varying contexts. In achievement cultures where beliefs and practices are primed to select out the talented children for different educational pathways, small differences between students loom large and treatment favoring the highs over the lows is more prevalent. In achievement cultures where beliefs and practices develop talent in each child, differences between students inform but do not constrain or stratify instruction, and treatment is more equitable and inclusive.

Trying to understand the differentiation among students within the same classroom as well as among classrooms is akin to distinctions we make in the study of families. Although siblings share the same family, they live different lives within their families (what has been termed the nonshared environment); further, families vary in the degree to which they hold different expectations for siblings and differentiate their child-rearing practices. That such variability exists (within and between settings) cautions us about the measurement of classroom, school, and family climates and about the averaging of influences and effects without a consideration of context. That there are examples of more positive and potentiating achievement cultures gives us hope and a direction.

Third, the elements of expectancy processes are remarkably similar whether they occur in classrooms or in schools, at elementary or secondary levels, or for students, teachers, or university faculty. The experiences of children who are tracked into high- or low-ability reading groups in elementary classrooms greatly resemble those of teachers who are tracked into the instruction of honors or remedial classes in high schools, and those of university professors who are recruited and nurtured as star or as average faculty members. While the dynamics of such expectancies may become manifest in interpersonal interactions, they are always driven and reinforced by institutional arrangements. Such expectancy processes occur both within and across social systems because differential exposure to instruction and labeling of ability precludes otherwise. Similarly, downward generalization of practices reflects shared assumptions about learning and its nurturance. Such institutionalized reinforcement can turn fleeting expectations into entrenched beliefs—which over time can shape children's school careers and even the careers of faculty. Expectancy processes do not reside solely "in the minds of teachers" but instead are built into the very fabric of our institutions and our society.

Fourth, beyond preexisting differences between students, simply being in a classroom environment that sharply differentiates expectations and treatment is associated with greater and growing gaps between children for whom more or less is expected. In such classrooms, children's expectations and their hopefulness for success mirror the expectations of their teachers, perceptions of peers and actual friendship patterns diverge along the lines of academic winners and losers, and the gap between students widens in achievement and in vigilance about teachers' expectations. The achievement culture of the classroom, a public and inherently social situation, frames not only academic growth but also affective and social development in children. Opportunities to be competent across multiple domains become severely constrained in settings that highly differentiate expectations for students.

Fifth, the influence of the achievement culture on children's competence development depends on the balance of risk and protective forces in place in children's lives. Because of societal stereotypes, different learning needs, and relative position in the middle or bottom of a particular achievement hierarchy, differences among students—for example in race, culture, language, socioeconomic means, gender, or learning profile—can heighten the risk for the formation of low academic expectations. While for each of these populations we have accrued distinct bodies of research and advocacy, there is much to be gained by looking across groups. Not only are the processes of lowered expectations and diminished opportunities to learn remarkably similar, but also differing social contexts can cast any child into a disadvantaged role, as we saw with Adam and as has been documented in the special education literature (Singer et al. 1989).

Risk can be further heightened when stereotypes about different groups' capacity to learn coexist with school policies that increase performance anxieties through high-stakes testing and widen performance differences through differential exposure to challenging educational curricula—and with classroom cultures and teacher behavior that signal that less is expected from some than from others. Resilience in the face of the risk of low expectations is also possible with support and when parents, other teachers, and children themselves take action: negative expectations can be discounted, new educational opportunities that challenge and support can be found, and stronger motivation can be forged to prove others wrong in their limiting beliefs. These resilient pathways, while best known to us in novels and newspaper first-person accounts, are ones about which scant research has been done. We need to learn more about how negative expectations can be overcome in these ways, and at what costs.

Finally, we need to understand that expectancy phenomena involve linked psychological, social, institutional, and societal processes. Changing beliefs without changing policies and practices will fail to eradicate the effects of negative prophecies. The successful harnessing of positive self-fulfilling prophecies in schooling will involve far more than simply disproving negative expectancies. What is required is a shift from a selection-driven achievement culture to a development-focused one. The task at hand is to build on newer theories about learning and to change (in coordinated ways) the multilayered and progressive institutional arrangements that narrowly define ability and frame opportunities for growth for students, parents, and peers.

By our overemphasis on appraising achievement and sorting children, we fail to create conditions in classrooms and schools that substantially develop ability. We fail to meet all learners with a challenging curriculum accompanied by differentially appropriate, nonstigmatizing, and flexible educational supports. Thus, from the very beginning, we rule out truly valid tests of our predictions by offering neither the best nor varied conditions for learning for all children. In these ways, unfairly so, we confirm our own beliefs. To make substantive headway in these changes, not only the students, the targets of expectancy effects, but also the perceivers, teachers and principals, will need to be supported as learners of a new philosophy of teaching that develops talent in all children, regardless of their strengths and weaknesses.

Beyond Current Controversies

New demographic realities—an increasingly diverse population of students in our schools, a diminished safety net of support, a decreasing ratio in the population of children to longer-living adults, and increasingly stratified and bureaucratized conditions in schooling—spell trouble in numerous ways. That we have not been effective in teaching students with diverse needs means that we are undermining the numbers of academically and ultimately economically successful children we produce, thereby further reducing the ratio of productive child to longer-living adult. We cannot afford to waste even a drop of academic talent.

Psychological research on self-fulfilling prophecies in schooling, as noted earlier, has been a highly volatile pursuit, subject to enduring skepticism. Our assessment of the state of evidence has much to do with a positivist paradigm of science—a set of assumptions about the rules of evidence and causal inference that has come under increasing siege (Gage 1989; Stewart 2000; Sue 1999). Other paradigms of doing science such as constructivist and relativist models have challenged positivism for privileging numbers over a qualitative understanding of participant voice and language, and for heralding the randomized experiment over all other research designs. Without an understanding of participant voice, without an integrative consideration of all the evidence, conclusions about the strength of a phenomenon are likely suspect.

Researchers continue to debate the methodological flaws of a single study (Rosenthal and Jacobson's *Pygmalion in the Classroom*) as evidence that the phenomenon has not yet been proven (see Spitz 1999). They continue to aggregate results across child populations, classrooms, and schools, to sample thin slices of time, and, as Thomas Good and Elisha Thompson (1998) point out, to study expectations apart from the treatment provided to students. And researchers continue to argue about the direction of effects, be they student-driven versus teacher-driven. Stalled by these arguments, we fail to capture the specific conditions or risk factors that maximize or minimize the potential for negative self-fulfilling prophecies. We fail to question the so-called accuracy of teacher expectations, which may itself result from the workings of expectancy processes, and the appropriateness of a differential treatment that favors highs over lows. We rarely raise the philosophical and moral argument that the "potential to learn" is hardly a measurable entity, is certainly not commensurate with a narrow band of skills as assessed in timed and high-stakes settings, and can only be achieved through optimal conditions for learning (Weinstein and McKown 1998).

These controversies about the existence of self-fulfilling prophecies stifle research and bind us to questions of proof. In this climate, researchers fail to invest in the design and evaluation of interventions in the real world of schools—interventions that might reduce the harm of negative self-fulfilling prophecies and indeed promote positive effects. To move ahead requires taking action based upon current knowledge of possible causal mechanisms. There will be no single experiment that can illustrate the pervasive negative effects of low expectations in schooling and all of its underlying root causes. The institutional embeddedness of these processes at multiple levels defy a simple linear relationship between cause and effect. Conclusions will have to be drawn from hundreds of studies both in psychology and in other disciplines, and across a variety of research designs (including experimental, quasi-experimental, correlational, and meta-analytic) as well as methods of inquiry (quantitative as well as qualitative).

As Lee Cronbach (1982) argued, "Progress in causal knowledge consists partly in arriving gradually at fuller formulations" (p. 139). And indeed, this has happened. These fuller formulations reflect a more complex theory of causes, effects, and multiple pathways, opening the door for more varied interventions (Masten and Coatsworth 1998; Talbert and McLaughlin 1999; Wachs 2000). This theoretically coherent picture points to multiple and multilayered risk factors—for both perceiver and target, across levels of the educational system, across educational opportunities as well as human relationships, and across domains such as family, school, and community—that together shape the formation, expression, and effects of differential expectations. Thus, in the real world of schooling, the full power of expectancy effects lies at this interface. It is this complex vision that must frame preventive action.

Medicine and public health have relied on consistent and strong correlative associations (associations that are also theoretically plausible, temporally consistent, and dose-response dependent) to make a case, for example, for the prevention of lung cancer through the eradication of smoking and of heart disease through changes in diet and exercise (Weed 1997). Further, preventive trials are "considered strong (and scientific) tests of a causal hypothesis, examining the impact of removing or reducing exposure to a potential cause under controlled conditions" (Weed 1997, p. 1137). Similarly, as Donald Campbell (1969) argued in his classic paper on "social reforms as experiments," both experimental and quasi-experimental studies will not only offer the possibility of doing good but also provide stronger evidence about the phenomenon in question.

We have similar evidence to frame the case for the prevention of negative self-fulfilling prophecies in schooling, and philosophical and moral reasons compel us to act. Arguments that teachers are accurate in their expectations for students and appropriate in their treatment rest upon a bankrupt view that the test score represents all that a child is and can be, and that teaching practices favoring high achievers are cutting-edge. But in applying our research-derived understanding of this problem, we will need to supplement our experimental designs with ecological approaches, including quasi-experimental designs, collaborative methods of social change, and rich descriptions of program implementation over long periods of time (Kelly et al. 2000; Lipsey and Cordray 2001).

Given the complex institutional context of expectancy effects, we need to do far more than implant a "false" belief and far more than deceive teachers with the results of a fabricated test. As expectancy researchers of business organizations and social psychology laboratories have also noted, our intervention efforts have to move beyond first-time encounters with strangers and short-lived interventions, in order to have an enduring effect in the real world. In complex settings like educational systems, where expectations are fueled by beliefs, practices, and policies from multiple levels, researchers need to collaborate with teachers and principals in applying new knowledge about motivation and agency, intelligence and its multiple components, the malleability of human abilities under optimal conditions, and the danger of normal curve conceptions of children's abilities—so that they can generate and sustain positive beliefs about each child and his or her potential to learn. And most often forgotten, we need also to put in place conditions in classrooms and schools that provide effective instruction to help a diverse population develop their talents. This means capitalizing on what could be and recognizing that change is possible.

What Kind of Expectations Are Best?

Common versus Differentiated

Where does our new understanding of expectancy effects leave us with regard to the historical struggle over a common versus a differentiated education? The danger of a significantly differentiated curriculum is that such individualized treatments rest most often on perceptions about ability—perceptions that can reflect societal prejudices about race, gender, class, language, and disability; societal beliefs about the nature of intelligence, motivation, and subject-matter learning, as well as about intrapsychic determinism. As William Ryan (1971) suggests, we are prone to pin the cause of most characteristics or behaviors on the individual, blaming the victim rather than questioning the adequacy of our assessment tools or the conditions provided for learning. The existing policies and practices of most schools make it virtually impossible to appreciate and meet the needs of the individual differences that children bring with them to school.

Yet the danger of a common curriculum and common methods is that the individual differences of children (in learning style, pace of learning, and interests) are likely disregarded, ultimately leading to greater rates of school failure. Equity in opportunities to learn lies somewhere in the middle—that is, with access to the most challenging educational experience but implemented with varied methods of instruction and assessment, as well as adequate time to learn. By meeting individual needs while educating toward common goals, one helps learners succeed at the highest level; the focus is ultimately on the development of capacity rather than the selection of the already capable.

Yet for how long should we encourage common goals coupled with a diversity of method and pace? If one indeed embraces the goal of lifelong learning as a primary purpose of schooling, such a perspective should persist at every turn, in work as well as educational settings. Ultimately students would choose a vocation on the basis of individual interest and drive, rather than because an educator guided them to or away from certain careers. This scenario fits well with what we know about the development of talent. Research on the exceptionally talented paints a picture of enormous individual effort applied to that talent, suggesting that interest and drive are critical factors in reaching exceptional performance (Csikszentmihalyi, Rathunde, and Whalen 1993; Simonton 2001).

It is important to underscore that commitment to a core curriculum with diverse methods of instruction does not preclude individuals' moving beyond common goals; it does not mandate equal outcomes. If some grow at faster rates, then the gap would be even wider, if indeed we met all needs well and held all to national standards (Goodlad 1990). But as John Goodlad argues, it is critical to shift the argument away from the gap per se to the reaching of grade-level norms for all. And most importantly, given evidence of multiple abilities, such proficiencies should encompass a broad domain of competencies. It is also critical to ensure that any performance gap does not reflect bias on the basis of race, class, gender, language, disability, age, or relative achievement level. Is there a common core of knowledge and of inquiry processes that we can expect for all? Are there ways that we can train teachers and organize schools so that a diversity of methods and flexibility in timing are provided to students without the penalties of labeling and failure? We must confront these questions if we are to take a preventive and promotive rather than a remedial stance with regard to solving the achievement problem.

Much has gone awry with the values of our educational institutions. An enormous sense of entitlement accompanies high GPAs and high SAT scores, so much so that negligible point differences on these measures spell the difference between the qualified and the unqualified in the scramble for the most competitive university slots (Lemann 1999). So much so that D. L. Stewart of "Being a Dad" writes "in praise of kids who are 'just' good" (1993, p. B4). The score has become the person and the person has become the score. Actual and varied accomplishments in real contexts are ignored in favor of quantitative scores because judges cannot judge quality and make the appropriate differentiations. The parents of students who make it into the higher reading groups and tracks, gifted programs, and select universities hold tightly to this apparent privilege. They fervently believe that their children are better than those who do not make the cut, and further, that there is nothing to learn from interactions with those "less able" students who will only slow their children down. The belief that these achievements result from individual qualities is consonant with the core values of our society. Yet it ignores important information about the conditions for learning and the relationship between individual and environmental factors in the nurturing of achievement. And it settles for simply mirroring or reproducing the status quo through schooling rather than embracing the higher goal of bringing out the best in each child (Bowles and Gintis 1976).

Too High versus Too Low

Some warn of the danger of expectations that are too high and cannot be met. This issue has been raised with regard to the expectations of parents for children with developmental delays; Joan Goodman (1992), for example, has argued that too much has been expected in too short a time for such children. Research on Asian American families points to the high pressure for academic achievement placed on children with possible negative as well as positive outcomes (Lui et al. 1990). Literary works also depict the costs to the individual of expectations that cannot be reached. Parents are sometimes described as engendering in children an enormous sense of failure, a sense of never being "good enough." Pat Conroy in *Beach Music* (1995) writes of Shyla's father who as her piano teacher pushed her too hard: "As she mastered concertos he declared beyond her competence . . . he raised the ante higher and higher, knowing that she did not possess the range and the fluency that greatness in art required . . . when she finally snapped . . . her fingers played noiseless sonatas against her blanket" (p. 392).

While these issues need further study, at least in schools, the evidence seems to suggest overwhelmingly that we have greatly underestimated human ability by holding expectations that are too low for too many children, and by holding differential expectations where such differentiation is not necessary. As Hugh Price, president of the National Urban League, argues in an *Education Week* commentary, "Successful schools produce successful pupils, not a smattering of superstars per building but the bulk of the student body" (1999, p. 44). It is also important to look more closely at what we mean by high expectations—which should involve believing in the potential of all children to learn to grade-level standards by the end of high school, save a small proportion of children due to severe mental retardation. This does not mean obtaining perfect scores and placing first in the class. The expectation that a child will exceed his or her current understanding means believing in the child's capacity to learn, and expecting, as well as bringing about, improvements in the mastery of skills. What underlies these two sides to high expectations—as seen in some grown children being grateful to their parents for holding them to such high standards and others bemoaning their parents' unreachable standards? I suspect that when high expectations are framed in ways that always value the child, support reachable goals on the way to cherished dreams, and provide children with strategies that help overcome obstacles in their path, such expectations can inspire children to grow.

Further, the research literature on children's resilient outcomes in the face of risk is somewhat reassuring about the role of psychological resources and environmental support in helping to overcome disadvantage (Masten and Coatsworth 1998). Newspaper accounts and documentary films, for example, provide us with cases of heroic victories against all odds—of "different" individuals who succeeded in obtaining a college education, advanced graduate training, or critical acclaim despite multiple obstacles and barriers in their path. A common theme underlying all of their stories is the presence of someone important who continued to believe in them. In an interview with Claudia Dreifus in the *New York Times* (2000, p. D7), Dr. Benjamin Carson, an internationally recognized pediatric neurosurgeon who is African American, was quoted as saying, "Even as late as my first year in medical school, my faculty advisor advised me to drop out. He said I wasn't medical school material. I was fortunate in that I had a mother who believed in me and kept telling me that I was smart."

But what happens to children with failure anxiety or poor self-images, who even in the face of high expectations from teachers fail to respond positively, and indeed become frustrated? Earlier, I had highlighted some individual and group differences in our findings about responsiveness to teacher expectations; for example, by fifth grade, students were more resistant to teachers' expectations, and African American children as members of a stigmatized ethnic minority were more responsive than European American children to negative than to positive teacher expectations. But the responsibility for helping children reach higher lies with teachers. Given teachers' understanding of their students' attitudes and fears, strengths and weaknesses, it is the intervention by teachers (who themselves need to be effectively supported) that makes the difference in overcoming obstacles to learning.

Promoting Positive Expectancy Effects in Schooling

Although policy makers have been engaged in raising academic expectations on a societal scale, reform efforts have made little use of research findings about self-fulfilling prophecies in complex social settings. The reforms have tinkered with aspects of education outside of classrooms and schools—

namely, the setting of standards and the close monitoring of outcomes. This vision has narrowed an already constrained view of the purposes for schooling. And the dangling of rewards and punishments, not surprisingly, has failed to engage or support all players in creating a school culture that effectively nurtures the learning of a diverse community of children. To do so would require a radical shift in the achievement culture of schools.

We have struggled on both sides of the three educational antimonies that Jerome Bruner (1996) has identified as underlying the complex aims of education. These are what Bruner calls "pairs of large truths, which though both may be true, nonetheless contradict each other" (p. 66). In the face of a more diverse and economically unequal society, and given what we have learned about optimal conditions for learning, Bruner urges us to risk embracing one side of these truths—that we work to realize human potential, to provide enabling tools to all children, and to value the diverse realities and local knowledge of each and every classroom setting. At stake is our capacity to maintain our social order, to recognize native talents, and to integrate what is unique into a fabric of interconnected people. Yet Bruner argues that the research evidence is compelling: Human learning is best when "it is participatory, proactive, communal, collaborative, and given over to constructing meanings rather than receiving them" (p. 84) and in such cultures of mutual learners, "being natively good at something implies, among other things, helping others get better at that something" (p. 82).

Reforms that do not give such voice and opportunity to children, teachers, and parents fail to engage their motivation and mutual learning. A *New York Times* article on July 8, 2001 reported, "In its strongest stance against standardized testing, the National Education Association has voted to support any legislation that permits parents to let their children skip the tests . . . Dozens of high school students at a New York City school boycotted the state Board of Regents exam in English, saying that the time spent preparing for the exam could be better used for other school projects" (p. 19). Indeed, the sheer costs of annual testing of children from grades three to eight—testing that does not lead to more effective instruction but rather drives a more narrow education—will take funding away from the support of ongoing work to create and sustain optimal conditions for learning for both teachers and students.

Where does this ecological understanding of expectancy effects in schooling take us with regard to opportunities for preventive intervention? Let me briefly emphasize three avenues for thinking about the task at hand. The first concerns a cultural shift in perspective regarding which conditions best nurture the achievements of a diverse citizenry in a complex and changing society. This means refashioning instruction and policy to follow newer and more positive theories about intelligence, motivation, agency, subject-matter learning, and community. It involves embracing an enabling culture that values multiple abilities across varied intellectual, physical, and social-emotional competencies; fuels intrinsic motivation, learning goals, and co-operative learning; engages student choice as well as responsibility; develops scholarship as well as skill; and creates an inclusive community of mutual learners.

Creating such an achievement culture requires shattering myths about relative comparisons, scarcity of opportunities, single methods, and differentiated pathways. Instead, we must work toward appreciating the uniqueness in each child and striving for progress against absolute, not relative, standards. We must create plentiful opportunities to stretch the capacities of children. We must offer multiple methods in varied modalities of instruction and assessment the first time around, drawing from the knowledge of special education teaching but, importantly, placing it in the context of regular classrooms. And we must move away from rigid and highly differentiated pathways toward fluid, responsive, defusing, and accommodating interventions that effectively help children to overcome obstacles in their path while never losing their place as scholars in a community of learners.

The second avenue concerns issues of resource development and deployment. Shifting from a culture of scarce chances to one of plentiful opportunities requires the development of underutilized resources such as in children, parents, and the community. The children themselves are important resources who are largely untapped by schools as currently constituted. Children's voices have too long been ignored in our understanding of what works in education. Children's partnership in the educational enterprise has been similarly dismissed. For example, Yumi Wilson wrote in the *San Francisco Chronicle* (1999), "An eleven-year-old boy who wanted to dress up as the Reading Wizard and introduce preschoolers to the joy of books at his local San Francisco Library" was turned down by officials who explained "that trained staffers were given the task of reading to preschoolers" (pp. A1, A12). When brought to the attention of the mayor and the media, the library changed its tune and promised to launch a summer program called "Kids Read to Kids at the Library," which would give this child and other youths an opportunity to read to preschoolers. In such ways do we routinely dismiss what children have to offer. Rarely do we ask children about their schooling, solicit their ideas and opinions, assess teaching in part through student evaluations, or respond in caring and meaningful ways to student concerns and ideas.

In most schools today, the development of student agency and leadership are the extra perks for working fast and doing well on school tasks, rather than the prioritized way of working for all children from the first days of formal schooling, as they become partners in their own learning and give to others who will follow. We seem surprised when we see how few of our citizenry vote in elections or take initiative in the community and workplace. We seem taken aback by how rough the transition is between high school and college, between undergraduate and graduate education, and between worker and manager, as individuals move from passive roles toward independent initiative. Yet we do not consistently and in increasingly larger ways prepare children to take initiative in their own and their peers' education. In fact, even young elementary school students have more independent opportunities than students in middle and high school, where the developmental need for autonomy clashes with increased emphasis on control (Eccles, Lord, and Buchanan 1996).

Enhancing children's roles as partners in the educational enterprise has a number of clear benefits. Children who can overcome negative self-fulfilling prophecies are those who turn to themselves for evaluation rather than relying solely on the opinions of teachers—and who can develop their own learning strategies to surmount obstacles to learning. We also learn best when we have to act on our growing knowledge, for example, by teaching it to someone else. Children's energy and capacity to teach themselves and others extend the teaching resources available in schools, expand the number and range of learning opportunities for children, and free teachers to individualize and facilitate learning.

The third and final avenue suggests multiple and varied points for preventive intervention. Working from a risk and resilience model of expectancy effects, interventions might target whole-school reforms to nurture and more fully align policies and practices to promote positive prophecies. Interventions might also create "buffering" opportunities and close relationships for children inside and outside of schools—relationships that can instill high expectations, teach strategies for reaching them, and advocate for unmet needs. For teachers and principals to create such enabling achievement cultures, they themselves need to be provided conditions that support their learning of effective pedagogical strategies. For parents to advocate for and instruct their children, they need to develop a comprehensive understanding of the factors that influence their children's learning. They also need the support to challenge unfavorable educational environments. Such interventions will require changes in public understanding, in educational policy and practice, and in the relationship between families and schools. They also require recognizing the importance of collaborative partnerships among all players, including the university, so that all can work together in a culture of mutual learning and continued improvement.

The Will to Harness the Positive

Scattered throughout these pages are examples of teachers, principals, parents, and children who would not be stopped by negative expectations about academic achievement. They believed that learning was possible and found ways to both overcome obstacles to learning and seek ever higher levels of challenge. They created protective educational settings and teaching moments that nurtured talent and fostered resilience in children as they struggled to achieve academic and social-emotional mastery. Such exemplars, however, are likely in the minority, judging from research findings that continue to show a large overrepresentation of children of color, poor children, non-English-speaking children, and children with special needs in the lower tracks of our educational system, as well as glass ceilings for the achievement of female students, especially in math and the sciences. If we want to harness positive self-fulfilling prophecies in schooling, we will need to create, nurture, and scale up far more of these kinds of settings, relationships, and buffering influences. We indeed know which qualities of educational systems nurture a broader array of talent among more students. But, as scholars have underscored, there are strong political and ideological forces that keep the system as it is, preserving a system of differentiated education and thereby privileging some over others.

Yet there are pockets of hope that we must seize and build upon. A commitment toward the improvement of education continues at the top of the national agenda. There are efforts under way, both privately and publicly funded, for research-driven designs that scale up whole-school reforms—many of which seek to sustain high expectations for all children. There are also positive signs that psychology as a field might take more seriously the importance of early and K–12 education and strengthen its contribution to the creation of challenging and nurturing contexts for learning (APA 1997; Short and Talley 1997). One such example is the effort by clinical psychologist Martin Seligman, who in his recent presidency of the American Psychological Association made a commitment to increasing research and intervention regarding a positive psychology of optimal functioning (see a January 2000 special issue of *American Psychologist*). Seligman wrote about a more positive psychology in the March 17, 2000 issue of the *Chronicle of Higher Education*, as it applied to parenting his five-year-old daughter: "Raising children, I realized, is vastly more than fixing what is wrong with them. It is about identifying and nurturing their strongest qualities, what they own and are best at, and helping them find niches in which they can best live out these strengths" (p. B10).

There are important similarities between effective parenting and effective schooling. This lesson that Seligman shared is equally true for the teaching of children. Author Howard Good (2000) wrote a moving epitaph for his twelfth-grade advanced placement English teacher of more than thirty years ago. He noted that Mr. Thompson "wasn't the most brilliant or stimulating teacher I ever had, just the most influential . . . and an inspiring example to all of us who are responsible in one way or another for educating the young." He describes one failed effort, a paper on Arthur Miller's play *Death of a Salesman*, which garnered a "see me" in red ink. In the face of Mr. Thompson's lengthy critique and his own great effort for this paper, young Howard dissolved into tears, born of "frustration and shame":

> I have had some teachers earlier in my school career that would have turned cruelly sarcastic at that moment. I have had others who would have remained indifferent. Not Mr. Thompson. He stopped in midsentence, the expression on his face alternating between surprise and concern. He didn't know me well. He didn't know about my literary ambitions. But he made it his business to find out. He became the first adult beside my parents to ever show any real interest in me. Over the next year, I brought him my awful poems, and he lent me good books. He encouraged my writing, nurtured my imagination, and protected my dreams. I was just an average student, but he gave me the confidence to be more . . . The week he died, he received as a gift a copy of my newest book. I might never have written it or any of my previous books if he hadn't gathered me up all those years ago. (p. 38)

The art of knowing, appreciating, and learning from children's unique and diverse talents has been all but lost from a culture of schooling that focuses narrowly on the point differences on standardized tests. We can and must do better if we wish to take seriously the essential tenet at the heart of education: helping each child become all that she or he can become.

References

Albom, M. 1997. *Tuesdays with Morrie*. New York: Doubleday.

Alexander, K. L., D. R. Entwisle, and S. L. Dauber. 1993. "First-Grade Classroom Behavior: Its Short- and Long-Term Consequences for School Performance." *Child Development* 64: 801–814.

Allport, G. W. 1954. *The Nature of Prejudice*. New York: Doubleday Books.

Alvidrez, J., and R. S. Weinstein. 1999. "Early Teacher Perceptions and Later Student Academic Achievement." *Journal of Educational Psychology* 91: 731–746.

Ambady, N., and R. Rosenthal. 1992. "Thin Slices of Expressive Behavior as Predictors of Interpersonal Consequences: A Meta-Analysis." *Psychological Bulletin* 111: 256–274.

American Psychological Association (APA). 1997. *Bringing to Scale Educational Innovation and School Reform: Partnerships in Urban Education*. Conference Proceedings. Washington, D.C.

Ames, C. 1992. "Classrooms, Goals, Structures, and Student Motivation." *Journal of Educational Psychology* 84: 261–271.

Anastasiow, N. J. 1964. "Frame of Reference of Teacher Judgments: The Psychophysical Model Applied to Education." *Psychology in the Schools* 1: 392–395.

Aronson, E. 1978. *The Jigsaw Classroom*. Beverly Hills, Calif.: Sage.

Ashton, P. T., and R. B. Webb. 1986. *Making a Difference: Teachers' Sense of Efficacy and Student Achievement*. New York: Longman.

Astin, A. 1990. "Educational Assessment and Educational Equity." *American Journal of Education* 98: 458–478.

———. 1997. "Our Obsession with Being 'Smart' Is Distorting Intellectual Life." *Chronicle of Higher Education*, Sept. 26, p. A60.

August, D., and K. Hakuta. 1997. *Improving Schooling for Language-Minority Children: A Research Agenda*. Washington, D.C.: National Academy Press.

Babad, E. 1990. "Measuring and Changing Teachers' Differential Behavior as Perceived by Students and Teachers." *Journal of Educational Psychology* 82: 683–690.

———. 1993. "Pygmalion: Twenty-five Years after Interpersonal Expectations in the Classroom." In P. D. Blanck, ed., *Interpersonal Expectations: Theory, Research, and Applications*. Cambridge: Cambridge University Press.

———. 1998. "Preferential Affect: The Crux of the Teacher Expectancy Issue." In J. E. Brophy, ed., *Advances in Research on Teaching: Expectations in the Classroom.* Vol. 7. Greenwich, Conn.: JAI.

Babad, E., F. Bernieri, and R. Rosenthal. 1987. "Nonverbal and Verbal Behavior of Preschool, Remedial, and Elementary School Teachers." *American Educational Research Journal* 24: 405–415.

———. 1989a. "Nonverbal Communication and Leakage in the Behavior of Biased and Unbiased Teachers." *Journal of Personality & Social Psychology* 56: 89–94.

———. 1989b. "When Less Information Is More Informative: Diagnosing Teacher Expectations from Brief Samples of Behaviour." *British Journal of Educational Psychology* 59: 281–295.

———. 1991. "Students as Judges of Teachers' Verbal and Nonverbal Behavior." *American Educational Research Journal* 28: 211–234.

Babad, E., J. Inbar, and R. Rosenthal. 1982. "Pygmalion, Galatea, and the Golem: Investigations of Biased and Unbiased Teachers." *Journal of Educational Psychology* 74: 459–474.

Babad, E., and P. J. Taylor. 1992. "Transparency of Teacher Expectancies across Language and Cultural Boundaries." *Journal of Educational Research* 86: 120–125.

Baker, E. T., M. C. Wang, and H. J. Walberg. 1994. "The Effects of Inclusion on Learning." *Educational Leadership* 52: 33–35.

Banaji, M. R., and R. Bhaskar. 2000. "Implicit Stereotypes and Memory: The Bounded Rationality of Social Beliefs." In D. L. Schacter and E. Scarry, eds., *Memory, Brain, and Belief.* Cambridge, Mass.: Harvard University Press.

Bandura, A. 2001. "Social Cognitive Theory: An Agentic Perspective." *Annual Review of Psychology* 52: 1–26.

Bandura, A., C. Barbaranelli, G. V. Caprara, and C. Pastorelli. 2001. "Self-Efficacy Beliefs as Shapers of Children's Aspirations and Career Trajectories." *Child Development* 72: 187–206.

Barker, R. G. 1968. *Ecological Psychology: Concepts and Methods for Studying the Environment of Human Behavior.* Stanford, Calif.: Stanford University Press.

Barker, R. G., and P. V. Gump. 1964. *Big School, Small School: High School Size and Student Behavior.* Stanford, Calif.: Stanford University Press.

Barker, R. G., et al. 1978. *Habitats, Environments, and Human Behavior.* San Francisco: Jossey-Bass.

Baron, R. M., D. Y. H. Tom, and H. M. Cooper. 1985. "Social Class, Race, and Teacher Expectations." In J. B. Dusek, ed., *Teacher Expectancies.* Hillsdale, N.J.: Lawrence Erlbaum.

Barr, R., and R. Dreeben. 1983. *How Schools Work.* Chicago: University of Chicago Press.

Bar-Tal, Y. 1989. "Can Leaders Change Followers' Stereotypes?" In D. Bar-Tal, C. F. Graumann, A. W. Kruglanski, and W. Stroebe, eds., *Stereotyping and Prejudice: Changing Conceptions.* New York: Springer-Verlag.

Bear, G. G. 1998. "School Discipline in the United States: Prevention, Correction, and Long-Term Social Development." *School Psychology Review* 27: 14–32.

Berends, M. 2000. "Teacher-Reported Effects of New American School Designs: Exploring Relationships to Teacher Background and School Context." *Educational Evaluation and Policy Analysis* 22: 65–82.

Biddle, B. J. 1979. *Role Theory, Expectations, Identity, and Behaviors.* New York: Academic Press.

———. 1986. "Recent Developments in Role Theory." *Annual Review of Sociology* 12: 67–92.

Blanck, P. D., ed. 1993. *Interpersonal Expectations: Theory, Research, and Applications.* Cambridge: Cambridge University Press.

Block, J., and J. H. Block. 1980. "The Role of Ego-Control and Ego-Resiliency in the Organization of Behavior." In W. A. Collins, ed., *The Minnesota Symposium on Child Psychology.* Vol. 13. Hillsdale, N.J.: Lawrence Erlbaum.

Bloom, B. 1976. *Human Characteristics and School Learning.* New York: McGraw-Hill.

———. 1982. "The Future of Educational Research." *Educational Researcher* 11: 12–13.

Blumenfeld, P. C., P. R. Pintrich, J. Meece, and K. Wessels. 1982. "The Formation and Role of Self-Perceptions of Ability in Elementary Classrooms." *Elementary School Journal* 82: 401–420.

Botkin, M. 1985. "Perceived Competence and Friendship Choice as a Function of Differential Teacher Treatment." Master's thesis, University of California, Berkeley.

———. 1990. "Differential Teacher Treatment and Ego Functioning: The Relationship between Perceived Competence and Defense." Ph.D. diss., University of California, Berkeley.

Boutte, G. S. 1992. "Frustrations of an African-American Parent: A Personal and Professional Account." *Phi Delta Kappan* 72: 786–788.

Bowen, W. G., and D. Bok. 1998. *The Shape of the River: The Long-Term Consequences of Considering Race in College and University Admissions.* Princeton, N.J.: Princeton University Press.

Bowles, S., and H. Gintis. 1976. *Schooling in Capitalist America: Educational Reform and the Contradictions of Economic Life.* New York: Basic Books.

Boyer, E. L. 1990. *Scholarship Reconsidered: Priorities of the Professoriate.* Princeton, N.J.: The Carnegie Foundation for the Advancement of Teaching.

Boyer Commission on Educating Undergraduates in the Research University. 1998. *Reinventing Undergraduate Education: A Blueprint for America's Research Universities.* Stony Brook: State University of New York at Stony Brook.

Bransford, J. D., A. L. Brown, and R. R. Cocking. 2000. *How People Learn.* Washington, D.C.: National Academy Press.

Brattesani, K. A. 1984. "The Role of Initial Self-Evaluation in Student Susceptibility to Teacher Expectations." Ph.D. diss., University of California, Berkeley.

Brattesani, K. A., R. S. Weinstein, and H. H. Marshall. 1984. "Student Perceptions of Differential Teacher Treatment as Moderators of Teacher Expectation Effects." *Journal of Educational Psychology* 76: 236–247.

Braun, C. 1973. "Johnny Reads the Cues: Teacher Expectations." *Reading Teacher* 26: 704–712.

———. 1976. "Teacher Expectations: Socio-Psychological Dynamics." *Review of Educational Research* 46: 185–213.

"Bridging the K–12/Postsecondary Divide with a Coherent K–12 System." 2000. *CPPRE Policy Briefs.* Graduate School of Education, University of Pennsylvania, RB-31-June 2000.

Bronfenbrenner, U. 1979. *The Ecology of Human Development: Experiments by Nature and Design.* Cambridge, Mass.: Harvard University Press.

———. 1986. "Ecology of the Family as a Context for Human Development." *Developmental Psychology* 22: 723–742.

Bronfenbrenner, U., and P. A. Morris. 1998. "The Ecology of Developmental Processes." In W. Damon and R. M. Lerner, eds., *Handbook of Child Psychology.* 5th ed., vol. 1. New York: John Wiley and Sons.

Brophy, J. E. 1983. "Research on the Self-Fulfilling Prophecy and Teacher Expectations." *Journal of Educational Psychology* 75: 631–661.

———. 1985. "Teacher-Student Interaction." In J. B. Dusek, ed., *Teacher Expectancies.* Hillsdale, N.J.: Lawrence Erlbaum.

———. 1998a. "Classroom Management as Socializing Students into Clearly Articulated Roles." *Journal of Classroom Interaction* 33: 1–4.

———, ed. 1998b. *Advances in Research on Teaching: Expectations in the Classroom.* Vol. 7. Greenwich, Conn.: JAI Press.

Brophy, J. E., and T. L. Good. 1970. "Teachers' Communication of Differential Expectations for Children's Classroom Performance: Some Behavioral Data." *Journal of Educational Psychology* 61: 365–374.

———. 1974. *Teacher-Student Relationships: Causes and Consequences.* New York: Holt, Rinehart, and Winston.

Brown, A. L. 1997. "Transforming Schools in Communities of Thinking and Learning about Serious Matters." *American Psychologist* 52: 399–413.

Bruner, J. 1990. *Acts of Meaning.* Cambridge, Mass.: Harvard University Press.

———. 1996. *The Culture of Education.* Cambridge, Mass.: Harvard University Press.

Brush, S. G. 1991. "Women in Science and Engineering." *American Scientist* 79: 404–419.

Butterworth, B., and R. S. Weinstein. 1996. "Enhancing Motivational Opportunity in Elementary Schooling: A Case Study of the Ecology of Leadership." *Elementary School Journal* 97: 57–80.

Campbell, D. T. 1969. "Reforms as Experiments." *American Psychologist* 24: 409–429.

———. 1993. "Systematic Errors to be Expected of the Social Scientist on the Basis of a General Psychology of Cognitive Bias." In P. D. Blanck, ed., *Interpersonal Expectations: Theory, Research, and Applications.* Cambridge: Cambridge University Press. Quoting F. Bacon. 1620. *Novum Organum.* Trans. in J. Devey. 1853. *The Physical and Metaphysical Works of Lord Bacon.* London: Henry G. Bohn.

Cappella, E., and R. S. Weinstein. 2001. "Turning Around Reading Achievement: Predictors of High School Students' Academic Resilience." *Journal of Educational Psychology* 93: 758–771.

Caprara, G. V., C. Barbaranelli, C. Pastorelli, A. Bandura, and P. G. Zimbardo. 2000. "Prosocial Foundations of Children's Academic Achievement." *Psychological Science* 11: 302–306.

Carnegie Council on Adolescent Development. 1989. *Turning Points: Preparing American Youth for the Twenty-first Century.* Washington, D.C.

Casanova, U. 1994. "A Conversation with the Assistant Secretary for OERI." *Educational Researcher* 23: 22–28.

Catterall, J. S. 1987. "On the Social Costs of Dropping Out of School." *High School Journal* 71: 19–30.

Chasin, G., and H. M. Levin. 1995. "Thomas Edison Accelerated Elementary School." In J. Oakes and K. H. Quartz, eds., *Creating New Educational Communities.* Ninety-Fourth Yearbook of the National Society for the Study of Education. Chicago: The University of Chicago Press.

Claire, T., and S. T. Fiske. 1998. "A Systemic View of Behavioral Confirmation: Counterpoint to the Individualist View." In C. Sedikedes, J. Schopler, and C. A. Insko, eds., *Intergroup Cognition and Intergroup Behavior.* Mahwah, N.J.: Lawrence Erlbaum.

Clark, K. 1963. "Educational Stimulation of Racially Disadvantaged Children." In A. H. Passow, ed., *Education in Depressed Areas.* New York: Teachers College Press.

Clark, R. M. 1983. *Family Life and School Achievement: Why Poor Black Children Succeed or Fail.* Chicago: University of Chicago Press.

Cohen, E. G. 1982. "Expectation States and Interracial Interaction in School Settings." *Annual Review of Sociology* 8: 209–235.

———. 1986. *Designing Groupwork: Strategies for Heterogeneous Classrooms.* New York: Teachers College Press.

Cohen, E. G., and R. A. Lotan, eds. 1997. *Working for Equity in Heterogeneous Classrooms: Sociological Theory in Practice.* New York: Teachers College Press.

Cole, J. R., E. G. Barber, and S. R. Graubard, eds. 1993. *The Research University in a Time of Discontent.* Baltimore: Johns Hopkins Press.

Coleman, J. S. 1987. "Families and Schools." *Educational Researcher* 16: 32–38.

Collins, F. A. 1988. "A Teacher's Reflections on the Collaborative Process: Benefits and Obstacles." Paper presented at the American Educational Research Association meeting, New Orleans, April.

Comer, J. P., N. M. Haynes, E. T. Joyner, and M. Ben-Avie, eds. 1996. *Rally the Whole Village: The Comer Process for Reforming Education.* New York: Teachers College Press.

Committee on the Changing Nature of Work. 1993. Human Capital Initiative Report. *APS Observer* October: 9–24.

Committee on Training. 1931. *Essays on Research in the Social Sciences.* Washington, D.C.: The Brookings Institution.

Cone, J. 1988. "Supports beyond the Classroom: School and Parental Links." Paper presented at the American Educational Research Association meeting, New Orleans, April.

Conners, L. J., and J. L. Epstein. 1995. "Parents and School Partnerships." In M. H.

Bornstein, ed., *Handbook of Parenting: Applied and Practical Parenting*. Vol. 4. Hillsdale, N.J.: Lawrence Erlbaum.

Conroy, Pat. 1995. *Beach Music.* New York: N. A. Talese.

Cook, T. D., F. Habib, M. Phillips, R. A. Settersen, S. C. Shagle, and S. M. Degirmencioglu. 1999. "Comer's School Development Program in Prince George's County, Maryland: A Theory-Based Evaluation." *American Educational Research Journal* 36: 543–597.

Cook, T. D., R. F. Murphy, and H. D. Hunt. 2000. "Comer's School Development Program in Chicago: A Theory-Based Evaluation." *American Educational Research Journal* 37: 535–597.

Cooper, H. M. 1979. "Pygmalion Grows Up: A Model for Teacher Expectation Communication and Performance Influence." *Review of Educational Research* 49: 389–410.

Cooper, H. M., and T. L. Good. 1983. *Pygmalion Grows Up: Studies in the Expectation Communication Process.* New York: Longman.

Cooper, H. M., and P. Hazelrigg. 1988. "Personality Moderators of Interpersonal Expectancy Effects: An Integrative Research Review." *Journal of Personality & Social Psychology* 55: 937–949.

Copeland, J. T. 1994. "Prophecies of Power: Motivational Implications of Social Power for Behavioral Confirmation." *Journal of Personality and Social Psychology* 67: 264–277.

Corno, L. 1993. "The Best-Laid Plans: Modern Conceptions of Volition and Educational Research." *Educational Researcher* 22: 14–22.

Corno, L., and M. M. Rohrkemper. 1986. "The Intrinsic Motivation to Learn in Classrooms." In C. Ames and R. E. Ames, eds., *Research on Motivation in Education: The Classroom Milieu.* New York: Academic Press.

Covington, M. V. 1992. *Making the Grade: A Self-Worth Perspective on Motivation and School Reform.* Cambridge: Cambridge University Press.

———. 1999. "Caring about Learning: The Nature and Nurturing of Subject-Matter Appreciation." *Educational Psychologist* 34: 127–136.

Cowan, P. A. 1970. "The Nature of Psycho-Educational Diagnosis." In D. B. Carter, ed., *Interdisciplinary Approaches to Learning Disorders.* Philadelphia: Chilton Books.

———. 1978. *Piaget with Feeling: Cognitive, Social, and Emotional Dimensions.* New York: Holt, Rinehart, and Winston.

Cowan, P. A., C. P. Cowan, M. S. Schulz, and G. Heming. 1994. "Prebirth to Preschool Family Factors in Children's Adaptation to Kindergarten." In R. D. Parke and S. G. Kellam, eds., *Exploring Family Relationships with Other Social Contexts.* Hillsdale, N.J.: Lawrence Erlbaum.

Crano, W. D., and P. M. Mellon. 1978. "Causal Influence of Teachers' Expectations on Children's Academic Performance: A Cross-Lagged Panel Analysis." *Journal of Educational Psychology* 70: 39–49.

Cremin, L. A. 1976. *Public Education.* New York: Basic Books.

Cronbach, L. J. 1982. *Designing Evaluations of Educational and Social Programs.* San Francisco: Jossey-Bass.

Csikszentmihalyi, M. 1990. *Flow: The Psychology of Optimal Experience*. 1st ed. New York: Harper & Row.

Csikszentmihalyi, M., K. Rathunde, and S. Whalen. 1993. *Talented Teenagers: The Roots of Success and Failure*. Cambridge: Cambridge University Press.

Cuban, L. 1990. "Reforming Again, Again, and Again." *Educational Researcher* 19: 3–13.

Darley, J. M., and R. H. Fazio. 1980. "Expectancy Confirmation Processes Arising in the Social Interaction Sequence." *American Psychologist* 35: 867–881.

Darling-Hammond, L. 1996. "The Right to Learn and the Advancement of Teaching: Research, Policy, and Practice for Democratic Education." *Educational Researcher* 25: 5–17.

Datnow, A., and M. Castellano. 2000. "Teachers' Responses to Success for All: How Beliefs, Experiences, and Adaptations Shape Implementation." *American Educational Research* 37: 775–799.

Dauber, S. L., K. L. Alexander, and D. R. Entwisle. 1993. "Characteristics of Retainees and Early Precursors of Retention in Grade: Who Is Held Back?" *Merrill-Palmer Quarterly* 39: 326–343.

———. 1996. "Tracking and Transitions through the Middle Grades: Channeling Educational Trajectories." *Sociology of Education* 69: 290–307.

Davidson, R. C., and E. L. Lewis. 1997. "Affirmative Action and Other Special Consideration Admissions at the University of California, Davis, School of Medicine." *JAMA* 278: 1153–1158.

Delpit, L. D. 1986. "Skills and Other Dilemmas of a Progressive Black Educator." *Harvard Educational Review* 56: 379–385.

Desforges, D. M., C. G. Lord, S. L. Ramsey, J. A. Mason, and M. D. Van Leeuwen. 1991. "Effects of Structured Cooperative Contact on Changing Negative Attitudes toward Stigmatized Social Groups." *Journal of Personality and Social Psychology* 60: 531–544.

Desruisseaux, P. 1990. "Cheney Sparks Further Debate on Core Curricula: A Parable on Upward Mobility." *Chronicle of Higher Education,* Jan. 24, p. A17.

Dewey, J. [1899] 1976. *The School and Society.* Carbondale: Southern Illinois University Press.

Deyhle, D., and K. Swisher. 1997. "Research in American Indian and Alaska Native Education: From Assimilation to Self-Determination." *Review of Research in Education* 22: 113–194.

Douglass, J. A. 2000a. "A Tale of Two Universities of California: A Tour of Strategic Issues Past and Prospective." *Chronicle of the University of California* 3: 93–118.

———. 2000b. *The California Idea and American Higher Education: 1850 to the 1960 Master Plan.* Stanford, Calif.: Stanford University Press.

Doyle, W. 1983. "Academic Work." *Review of Educational Research* 53: 159–200.

Dreifus, C. 1994. "Chloe Wofford Talks about Toni Morrison." *New York Times Magazine,* Sept. 11, p. 73.

———. 2000. "A Pioneer at a Frontier: The Brain of a Child." *New York Times,* Jan. 4, p. D7.

Dusek, J. B. 1985. *Teacher Expectancies.* Hillsdale, N.J.: Lawrence Erlbaum.

Dusek, J. B., and G. Joseph. 1983. "The Bases of Teacher Expectancies: A Meta-Analysis." *Journal of Educational Psychology* 75: 327–346.

———. 1985. "The Bases of Teacher Expectancies." In J. B. Dusek, ed., *Teacher Expectancies.* Hillsdale, N.J.: Lawrence Erlbaum.

Dweck, C. S. 2000. *Self-Theories: Their Role in Motivation, Personality and Development.* Philadelphia: Psychology Press.

Dweck, C. S., and E. L. Leggett. 1988. "A Social-Cognitive Approach to Motivation and Personality." *Psychological Review* 95: 256–273.

Eccles, J. S., S. E. Lord, and C. M. Buchanan. 1996. "School Transitions in Early Adolescence: What Are We Doing to Our Young People?" In G. A. Graber and J. Brooks-Gunn, eds., *Transitions through Adolescence: Interpersonal Domains and Context.* Mahwah, N.J.: Lawrence Erlbaum.

Edelman, M. W. 1981. "Who Is for Children?" *American Psychologist* 36: 109–116.

Eden, D. 1992. "Leadership and Expectations: Pygmalion Effects and Other Self-Fulfilling Prophecies in Organizations." *Leadership Quarterly* 3: 271–305.

Eden, D., D. Geller, A. Gewirtz, R. Gorden-Terner, I. Inbar, M. Leberman, Y. Pass, I. Salomon-Segev, and M. Shalit. 2000. "Implanting Pygmalion Leadership Style through Workshop Training: Seven Field Experiments." *Leadership Quarterly* 11: 171–210.

Eden, D., and Y. Zuk. 1995. "Seasickness as a Self-Fulfilling Prophecy: Raising Self-Efficacy to Boost Performance at Sea." *Journal of Applied Psychology* 80: 628–635.

Elashoff, J. D., and R. E. Snow. 1971. *Pygmalion Reconsidered.* Belmont, Calif.: Wadsworth.

Elder, G. H., Jr. 1974. *Children of the Great Depression: Social Change in Life Experience.* Chicago: University of Chicago Press.

Elias, M. J., J. Zins, R. Weissberg, et al. 1997. *Promoting Social and Emotional Learning: Guidelines for Educators.* Alexandria, Va.: Association for Supervision and Curriculum Development.

Elmore, R. F. 1996. "Getting to Scale with Good Educational Outcomes." *Harvard Educational Review* 66: 1–26.

Entwisle, D. R., and K. L. Alexander. 1988. "Factors Affecting Achievement Test Score Marks Received by Black and White First Graders." *Elementary School Journal* 88: 449–471.

Entwisle, D. R., K. L. Alexander, and L. S. Olson. 1997. *Children, Schools, and Inequality.* Boulder, Colo.: Westview Press.

Entwisle, D. R., and L. A. Hayduk. 1978. *Too Great Expectations: The Academic Outlook of Young Children.* Baltimore: Johns Hopkins University Press.

Epstein, J. L. 1985. "After the Bus Arrives: Resegregation in Desegregated Schools." *Journal of Social Issues* 41: 23–43.

Federal Interagency Forum on Child and Family Statistics. 1999. *America's Children: Key National Indicators of Well-Being.* Washington, D.C.: U.S. Government Printing Office.

Felner, R. D. 2000. "Educational Reform as Ecologically Based Prevention and Promotion: The Project on High Performance Learning Communities." In D. Cicchetti, J. Rappaport, I. Sandler, and R. P. Weissberg, eds., *The Promotion of Wellness in Children and Adolescents.* Washington, D.C.: CWLA Press.

Ferguson, R. F. 1998. "Teacher Perceptions and Expectations and the Black-White Test Score Gap." In C. Jencks and M. Phillips, eds., *The Black-White Test Score Gap.* Washington, D.C.: Brookings Institution.

———. 2001. "Test-Score Trends along Racial Lines, 1971–1996: Popular Culture and Community Academic Standards." In N. J. Smelser, W. J. Wilson, and F. Mitchell, eds., *America Becoming: Racial Trends and Their Consequences.* Vol. 1. Washington, D.C.: National Academy Press.

Finley, M. K. 1984. "Teachers and Tracking in a Comprehensive High School." *Sociology of Education* 57: 233–243.

Finn, C. E., A. J. Rotherham, and C. R. Hokanson, Jr., eds. 2001. *Rethinking Special Education for a New Century.* Washington, D.C.: Thomas B. Fordham Foundation and the Progressive Policy Institute.

Finn, J. D. 1989. "Withdrawing from School." *Review of Educational Research* 59: 117–142.

Finn, J. D., and D. A. Rock. 1997. "Academic Success among Students at Risk for School Failure." *Journal of Applied Psychology* 82: 221–234.

Fischer, C. S., M. Hout, M. Sanchez Jankowski, S. R. Lucas, A. Swidler, and K. Voss. 1996. *Inequality by Design: Cracking the Bell Curve Myth.* Princeton, N.J.: Princeton University Press.

Fitzgibbon, R. H. 1968. *The Academic Senate of the University of California.* Berkeley, Calif.: Office of the President, University of California.

Flanagan, C. A., and N. Faison. 2001. "Youth Civic Development: Implications of Research for Social Policy and Programs." *Social Policy Report* 15: 3–14.

Frank, R. H., and P. J. Cook. 1995. *The Winner-Take-All Society.* New York: Penguin.

Fraser, B. J. 1998. "Classroom Environment Instruments: Development, Validity, and Applications." *Learning Environments Research* 1: 7–33.

Freedman, S. W. 1994. *Exchanging Cultures, Exchanging Writing: Lessons in School Reform from the United States and Great Britain.* Cambridge, Mass.: Harvard University Press.

Freedman, S. W., E. R. Simmons, J. S. Kalnin, A. Casareno, and the M-Class Teams. 1999. *Inside City Schools: Investigating Literacy in Multicultural Classrooms.* New York: Teachers College Press.

Gage, N. L. 1989. "Paradigm Wars and Their Aftermath: A Historical Sketch of Research on Teaching since 1989." *Educational Researcher* 18: 4–10.

Galloway, D., T. Ball, D. Blomfield, and R. Seyd. 1982. *Schools and Disruptive Students.* Essex, Eng.: Longman Group.

Gamoran, A., M. Nystrand, M. Berends, and P. C. LePore. 1995. "An Organizational Analysis of the Effects of Ability Grouping." *American Educational Research Journal* 32: 687–715.

Garcia, E. E. 1990. "Language-Minority Education Litigation Policy: The Law of the Land." In A. Barona and E. E. Garcia, eds., *Children at Risk: Poverty, Minority Status, and Other Issues in Educational Equity.* Washington, D.C.: National Association of School Psychologists.

———. 1993. "Language, Culture, and Education." *Review of Research in Education* 19: 51–98.

Gardner, H. 1983. *Frames of Mind: The Theory of Multiple Intelligences.* New York: Basic Books.

Gifford, B. R. 1986. "The Evolution of the School-University Partnership for Educational Renewal." *Education and Urban Society* 19: 77–106.

Gilligan, C. 1982. *In a Different Voice.* Cambridge, Mass.: Harvard University Press.

Gohm, C. L., L. G. Humphreys, and G. Yao. 1998. "Underachievement among Spatially Gifted Students." *American Educational Research Journal* 35: 515–531.

Goldenberg, C. 1989. "Parents' Effects on Academic Grouping for Reading: Three Case Studies." *American Educational Research Journal* 26: 329–352.

Goleman, D. 1995. *Emotional Intelligence.* New York: Bantam.

Good, H. 2000. "Epitaph for an English Teacher." *Education Week.* Oct. 18, p. 38.

Good, T. L., and J. E. Brophy. 1974. "Changing Teacher and Student Behavior: An Empirical Investigation." *Journal of Educational Psychology* 66: 390–405.

Good, T. L., and E. K. Thompson. 1998. "Research on the Communication of Performance Expectations: A Review of Recent Perspectives." *Advances in Research on Teaching: Expectations in the Classroom.* Vol. 7. Greenwich, Conn.: JAI Press.

Goodlad, J. I. 1990. *Teachers for Our Nation's Schools.* 1st ed. San Francisco: Jossey-Bass.

Goodlad, J. I., and P. Keating, eds. 1994. *Access to Knowledge: The Continuing Agenda for Our Nation's Schools.* Rev. ed. New York: College Board.

Goodman, E. 1994. "The 95 Percent Solution." *San Francisco Chronicle,* July 14, p. A21.

Goodman, J. F. 1992. *When Slow Is Fast Enough: Educating the Delayed Preschool Child.* New York: Guilford.

Gottfredson, D. C., E. M. Marciniak, A. T. Birdseye, and G. D. Gottfredson. 1995. "Increasing Teacher Expectations for Student Achievement." *Journal of Educational Research* 88: 155–163.

Gould, S. J. 1981. *The Mismeasure of Man.* New York: Norton. Quoting L. M. Terman, 1916. *The Measurement of Intelligence.* Boston: Houghton Mifflin.

———. 1996. *Full House: The Spread of Excellence from Plato to Darwin.* 1st ed. New York: Harmony Books.

Graham, H. D., and N. Diamond. 1997. *The Rise of American Research Universities: Elites and Challengers in the Postwar Era.* Baltimore: Johns Hopkins University Press.

Graham, P. A. 1978. "Expansion and Exclusion: A History of Women in American Higher Education." *Signs: Journal of Women in Culture and Society* 3: 759–773.

Grant, C. A., and C. E. Sleeter. 1986. "Race, Class, and Gender in Education Research: An Argument for Integrative Analysis." *Review of Educational Research* 56: 195–211.

Graubard, S. R. 1993. "Notes toward a New History." In J. R. Cole, E. G. Barber, and S. R. Graubard, eds., *The Research University in Time of Discontent.* Baltimore: Johns Hopkins University Press.

Graue, M. E. 1993. *Ready for What? Constructing Meanings of Readiness for Kindergarten.* Albany: State University of New York Press.

Gutek, G. L. 1991. *An Historical Introduction to American Education.* 2d ed. Prospect Heights, Ill.: Waveland Press.

Guthrie, R. V. 1976. *Even the Rat Was White: A Historical View of Psychology.* New York: Harper & Row.

Harris, M. J., and R. Rosenthal. 1985. "Mediation of Interpersonal Expectancy Effects: Thirty-one Meta-Analyses." *Psychological Bulletin* 97: 363–386.

———. 1986. "Counselor and Client Personality as Determinants of Counselor Expectancy Effects." *Journal of Personality and Social Psychology* 50: 362–369.

Hart, S. N. 1991. "From Property to Person Status: Historical Perspectives on Children's Rights." *American Psychologist* 46: 53–59.

Haycock, K. 1998. "What Should K–12 Expect from Higher Education?" *Education Week,* Apr. 29, pp. 38, 40.

Hazelrigg, P. J., H. Cooper, and A. J. Strathman. 1991. "Personality Moderators of the Experimenter Expectancy Effect: A Reexamination of Five Hypotheses." *Personality & Social Psychology Bulletin* 17: 569–579.

Heath, S. B. 1983. *Ways with Words: Language, Life, and Work in Communities and Classrooms.* Cambridge: Cambridge University Press.

Herrnstein, R. J., and C. Murray. 1994. *The Bell Curve: Intelligence and Class Structure in American Life.* New York: Free Press.

Hilton, K. L., and J. M. Darley. 1985. "Constructing Other Persons: A Limit on the Effect." *Journal of Experimental Social Psychology* 21: 1–18.

Hochschild, A. R. 1975. "Inside the Clockwork of Male Careers." In F. Howe, ed., *Women and the Power to Change.* New York: McGraw-Hill.

Hoge, R. D., and T. Coladarci. 1989. "Teacher-Based Judgments of Academic Achievement: A Review of the Literature." *Journal of Educational Psychology* 59: 297–313.

Holahan, C. J. 1986. "Environmental Psychology." *Annual Review of Psychology* 37: 381–407.

Hollinger, D. A. 2001. "Faculty Governance, The University of California, and the Future of Academe." *Academe* 87: 30–33.

Holton, G., H. Chang, and E. Jurkowitz. 1996. "How a Scientific Discovery Is Made: A Case History." *American Scientist* 84: 364–375.

Hrabowski, F. A., K. I. Maton, and G. L. Greif. 1998. *Beating the Odds: Raising Academically Successful African American Males.* New York: Oxford University Press.

Huxley, A. [1932] 1946. *Brave New World.* New York: Modern Library.

Ingstad, B., and S. Reynolds White. 1995. *Disability and Culture.* Berkeley: University of California Press.

Jackson, P. W. 1968. *Life in Classrooms.* New York: Holt, Rinehart, and Winston.

———. 1986. *The Practice of Teaching.* New York: Teachers College Press.

Jastrow, J. 1900. *Fact and Fable in Psychology.* Boston: Houghton Mifflin.

Jencks, C., and M. Phillips, eds. 1998. *The Black-White Achievement Gap.* Washington, D.C.: Brookings Institution.

Jimerson, S., B. Egeland, and A. Teo. 1999. "A Longitudinal Study of Achievement

Trajectories: Factors Associated with Change." *Journal of Educational Psychology* 91: 116–126.

Jones, E. M., G. D. Gottfredson, and D. C. Gottfredson. 1997. "Success for Some: An Evaluation of a Success for All Program." *Evaluation Review* 21: 643–670.

Jones, L. 1989. "Teacher Expectations for Black and White Students in Contrasting Classroom Environments." Master's thesis, University of California, Berkeley.

Jones, R. A. 1977. *Self-Fulfilling Prophecies.* Hillsdale, N.J.: Lawrence Erlbaum.

Jussim, L. 1989. "Teacher Expectations: Self-Fulfilling Prophecies, Perceptual Biases, and Accuracy." *Journal of Personality and Social Psychology* 57: 469–480.

Jussim, L., and J. S. Eccles. 1992. "Teacher Expectations II: Construction and Reflection of Student Achievement." *Journal of Personality and Social Psychology* 28: 281–388.

Jussim, L., J. S. Eccles, and S. Madon. 1996. "Social Perception, Social Stereotypes, and Teacher Expectations: Accuracy and the Quest for the Powerful Self-Fulfilling Prophecy." *Advances in Experimental Social Psychology* 28: 281–388.

Jussim, L., A. Smith, S. Madon, and P. Palumbo. 1998. "Teacher Expectations." In J. Brophy, ed., *Advances in Research on Teaching: Expectations in the Classroom.* Vol. 7. Greenwich, Conn.: JAI Press.

Keillor, G. 1985. *Lake Wobegon Days.* New York: Viking.

Kelly, J. G. 1968. "Toward an Ecological Conception of Preventive Intervention." In J. W. Carter, Jr., ed., *Research Contributions from Psychology to Community Mental Health.* New York: Behavioral Publications.

———. 1969. "Naturalistic Observations in Contrasting Social Environments." In E. P. Willems and H. L. Raush, eds., *Naturalistic Viewpoints in Psychological Research.* New York: Holt, Rinehart, and Winston.

———. 1979. *Adolescent Boys in High School: A Psychological Study of Coping and Adaptation.* Hillsdale, N.J.: Lawrence Erlbaum.

Kelly, J. G., A. M. Ryan, B. E. Altman, and S. P. Stelzner. 2000. "Understanding and Changing Social Systems: An Ecological View." In J. Rappaport and E. Seidman, eds., *Handbook of Community Psychology.* New York: Kluwer Academic/Plenum Publishers.

Kerman, S. 1979. "Teacher Expectations and Student Achievement." *Phi Delta Kappan* 60: 716–718.

Kerr, C. 1994. *Higher Education Cannot Escape History: Issues for the Twenty-first Century.* Albany: State University of New York Press.

Kids Count Data Book. 2001. *State Profiles of Child Well-Being.* Baltimore: Annie E. Casey Foundation.

Kirsch, I., ed. 1999. *How Expectancies Shape Experience.* Washington, D.C.: The American Psychological Association.

Knitzer, J. 2000. "Helping Troubled Children and Families." In J. Rappaport and E. Seidman, eds., *Handbook of Community Psychology.* New York: Kluwer Academic/Plenum Publishers.

Kohn, A. 1993. *Punished by Rewards.* Boston: Houghton Mifflin.

Kozol, J. 1992. *Savage Inequalities: Children in America's Schools.* New York: Harper Perennial.

Krechevsky, M., T. Hoerr, and H. Gardner. 1995. "Complementary Energies: Implementing MI Theory from the Laboratory and from the Field." In J. Oakes and K. H. Quartz, eds., *Creating New Educational Communities*. Ninety-fourth Yearbook of the National Society for the Study of Education. Part 1. Chicago: University of Chicago Press.

Krishna, D. 1971. "The Self-Fulfilling Prophecy and the Nature of Society." *Annual Sociological Review* 36: 1104–1107.

Kuklinski, M. R. 1992. "The Longitudinal Impact of Differential Teacher Treatment." Master's thesis, University of California, Berkeley.

Kuklinski, M. R., and R. S. Weinstein. 2000. "Classroom and Grade Level Differences in the Stability of Teacher Expectations and Perceived Differential Treatment." *Learning Environments Research* 3: 1–34.

———. 2001. "Classroom and Developmental Differences in a Path Model of Teacher Expectancy Effects." *Child Development* 72: 1554–1578.

Labaree, D. F. 1997. "Public Goods, Private Goods: The American Struggle over Educational Goals." *American Educational Research Journal* 34: 39–81.

Lee, V. E., with J. B. Smith. 2001. *Restructuring High Schools for Equity and Excellence: What Works*. New York: Teachers College Press.

Lemann, N. 1999. *The Big Test: The Secret History of the American Meritocracy*. New York: Farrar, Straus, and Giroux.

Levin, H. 1987. "Accelerated Schools for Disadvantaged Students." *Educational Leadership* 44: 19–21.

Levine, J. M., and M. C. Wang. 1983. *Teacher and Student Perceptions: Implications for Learning*. Hillsdale, N.J.: Lawrence Erlbaum.

Lewin, K. 1935. *A Dynamic Theory of Personality: Selected Papers*. New York: McGraw-Hill.

Lieberman, A. 1992. "The Meaning of Scholarly Activity and the Building of Community." *Educational Researcher* 21: 5–12.

Lightfoot, S. L. 1978. *Worlds Apart: Relationships between Families and Schools*. New York: Basic Books.

Lipsey, M. W., and D. S. Cordray. 2001. "Evaluation Methods for Social Intervention." *Annual Review of Psychology* 52: 345–375.

Little, J. W. 1993. "Teachers' Professional Development in a Climate of Educational Reform." *Educational Evaluation and Policy Analysis* 15: 129–151.

Lui, W. T., E. S. Yu, C. Chang, and M. Fernandez. 1990. "The Mental Health of Asian American Teenagers: A Research Challenge." In A. R. Stiffman and L. E. Davis, eds., *Ethnic Issues in Adolescent Mental Health*. Newbury Park, N.J.: Sage.

Luthar, S. S., C. Cicchetti, and B. Becker. 2000. "The Construct of Resilience: A Critical Evaluation and Guidelines for Future Work." *Child Development* 71: 543–562.

Macrae, C. N., and G. V. Bodenhausen. 2000. "Social Cognition: Thinking Categorically about Others." *Annual Review of Psychology* 51: 93–120.

Maddux, J. E. 1999. "Expectancies and the Socio-Cognitive Perspective: Basic Principles, Processes, and Variables." In I. Kirsch, ed., *How Expectancies Shape Experience*. Washington, D.C.: American Psychological Association.

Madison, S. M. 1993. "Pathways to the Disconfirmation of Teacher Expectations." Master's thesis, University of California, Berkeley.

Madon, S., L. Jussim, S. Keiper, J. Eccles, A. Smith, and P. Palumbo. 1998. "The Accuracy and Power of Sex, Social Class, and Ethnic Stereotypes: A Naturalistic Study in Person Perception." *Personality and Social Psychology Bulletin* 24: 1304–1318.

Maehr, M. L., and C. Midgley. 1991. "Enhancing Student Motivation: A Schoolwide Approach." *Educational Psychologist* 26: 399–427.

———. 1996. *Transforming School Cultures.* Boulder, Colo.: Westview Press.

Marshall, H. H., and R. S. Weinstein. 1982. *Classroom Dimensions Observation System.* Department of Psychology, University of California, Berkeley.

———. 1984. "Classroom Factors Affecting Students' Self-Evaluations: An Interactional Model." *Review of Educational Research* 54: 301–325.

———. 1986. "Classroom Context of Student-Perceived Differential Teacher Treatment." *Journal of Educational Psychology* 78: 441–453.

———. 1988. "Beyond Quantitative Analysis: Recontextualization of Classroom Factors Contributing to the Communication of Teacher Expectations." In J. L. Green and J. O. Harker, eds., *Multiple Perspective Analyses of Classroom Discourse.* Norwood, N.J.: Ablex.

Marx, D. M., J. L. Brown, and C. M. Steele. 1999. "Allport's Legacy and the Situational Press of Stereotypes." *Journal of Social Issues* 55: 491–502.

Mason, D. A., D. D. Schroeter, R. K. Combs, and K. Washington. 1992. "Assigning Average-Achieving Eighth Graders to Advanced Mathematics Classes in an Urban Junior High." *Elementary School Journal* 92: 587–599.

Massey, W. E. 1992. "A Success Story amid Decades of Failure." *Science* 258: 1177–1180.

Masten, A. S., and J. D. Coatsworth. 1998. "The Development of Competence in Favorable and Unfavorable Environments: Lessons from Research on Successful Children." *American Psychologist* 53: 205–220.

McCaslin, M., and T. L. Good. 1992. "Compliant Cognition: The Misalliance of Management and Instructional Goals in Current School Reform." *Educational Researcher* 21: 4–17.

———. 1996a. "The Informal Curriculum." In D. C. Berliner and R. C. Calfee, eds., *Handbook of Educational Psychology.* New York: Macmillan.

———. 1996b. *Listening in Classrooms.* New York: HarperCollins.

McCaslin, M., and T. Murdock. 1991. "The Emergent Interaction of Home and School in the Development of Children's Adaptive Learning." In M. Maehr and P. Pintrich, eds., *Advances in Motivation and Achievement.* Vol. 4. Greenwich, Conn.: JAI Press.

McGill-Franzen, A., and R. L. Allington. 1991. "The Gridlock of Low Reading Achievement: Perspectives on Practice and Policy." *Remedial and Special Education* 12: 20–30.

McKown, C., and R. S. Weinstein. 2002. "Modeling the Role of Child Ethnicity and Gender in Children's Differential Response to Teacher Expectations." *Journal of Applied Social Psychology* 32: 159–184.

McLaughlin, M. W. 1990. "The RAND Change Study Revisited: Macro Perspectives and Micro Perspectives." *Educational Researcher* 19: 11–16.

McLaughlin, M. W., M. A. Irby, and J. Langman. 1994. *Urban Sanctuaries: Neighborhood Organizations in the Lives and Futures of Inner-City Youth.* San Francisco: Jossey-Bass.

McLoyd, V., and B. Lozoff. 2001. "Racial and Ethnic Trends in Children's and Adolescents' Behavior and Development." In N. J. Smelser, W. J. Wilson, and F. Mitchell, eds., *America Becoming: Racial Trends and Their Consequences.* Vol. 2. Washington, D.C.: National Research Council.

McNatt, D. B. 2000. "Ancient Pygmalion Joins Contemporary Management: A Meta-Analysis of the Result." *Journal of Applied Psychology* 85: 314–322.

Meece, J. L., and B. Kurtz-Costes. 2001. "Introduction: Schooling of Ethnic Minority Children and Youth." *Educational Psychologist* 36: 1–7.

Mehan, H., I. Villanueva, L. Hubbard, and A. Lintz. 1996. *Constructing School Success: The Consequences of Untracking Low-Achieving Students.* Cambridge: Cambridge University Press.

Mehlhorn, M. 1988. "The Role of Research in Collaboration." Paper presented at the American Educational Research Association meeting, New Orleans, April.

Meier, D. 1995. *The Power of Their Ideas: Lessons for America from a Small School in Harlem.* Boston: Beacon Press.

Meier, K. L., J. Stewart, and R. E. England. 1989. *Race, Class, and Education: The Politics of Second-Generation Discrimination.* Madison: University of Wisconsin Press.

Melton, G. 1987. "Children, Politics, and Morality: The Ethics of Child Advocacy." *Journal of Child Clinical Psychology* 16: 357–367.

Merton, R. K. [1942] 1973. "Science and Technology in a Democratic Order." *Journal of Legal and Political Sociology* 1: 115–126. Reprinted in R. K. Merton, *The Sociology of Science.* Chicago: University of Chicago Press.

———. 1948. "The Self-Fulfilling Prophecy." *Antioch Review* 8: 193–210.

———. [1960] 1973. "Recognition and Excellence: Instructive Ambiguities." In A. Yarmolinsky, ed., *Recognition of Excellence: Working Papers.* New York: Free Press. Reprinted in R. K. Merton, *The Sociology of Science.* Chicago: University of Chicago Press.

———. [1968] 1973. "The Matthew Effect in Science." *Science* 159: 56–63. Reprinted in R. K. Merton, *The Sociology of Science.* Chicago: University of Chicago Press.

———. 1973. *The Sociology of Science: Theoretical and Empirical Investigations.* Chicago: University of Chicago Press.

Midlarsky, M. I. 1999. *The Evolution of Inequality: War, State Survival, and Democracy in Comparative Perspective.* Stanford, Calif.: Stanford University Press.

Miller, L. S. 1995. *An American Imperative: Accelerating Minority Educational Advancement.* New Haven: Yale University Press.

Mitchell, J. 1983. "Visible, Vulnerable, and Viable: Emerging Perspectives of a Minority Professor." In J. H. Cones III, J. K. Noonan, and D. Janha, eds., *New Directions for Teaching and Learning.* San Francisco: Jossey-Bass.

Mitman, A. L., and A. A. Lash. 1988. "Students' Perceptions of Their Academic Standing and Classroom Behavior." *Elementary School Journal* 89: 55–68.

Mitman, A. L., and R. E. Snow. 1985. "Logical and Methodological Problems in

Teacher Expectancy Research." In J. B. Dusek, ed., *Teacher Expectancies.* Hillsdale, N.J.: Lawrence Erlbaum.

Mlawer, M. A. 1994. "My Kid Beat Up Your Honor Student." *Education Week,* July 13, p. 39.

Moll, A. 1898. *Hypnotism.* 4th ed. New York: Scribner.

Moos, R. H. 1973. "Conceptualizations of Human Environments." *American Psychologist* 28: 652–665.

Mueller, C. G. 1979. "Some Origins of Psychology as a Science." *Annual Review of Psychology* 30: 9–29.

Murray, M. 1994. "Nancy Wexler." *New York Times Magazine,* Feb. 13, pp. 28–31.

Myerson, J., M. R. Rank, F. Q. Raines, and M. A. Schnitzler. 1998. "Race and General Cognitive Ability: The Myth of Diminishing Returns to Education." *Psychological Science* 9: 139–142.

Nakanishi, D. T., and T. Y. Nishida. 1995. *The Asian American Educational Experience.* New York: Routledge.

Namir, S., and R. S. Weinstein. 1982. "Children: Facilitating New Directions." In L. R. Snowden, ed., *Reaching the Underserved: Mental Health Needs of Neglected Populations.* Beverley Hills, Calif.: Sage.

National Center for Education Statistics. 1995. *Dropout Rates in the United States: 1995.* Washington, D.C.: U.S. Department of Education, Office of Educational Research and Improvement.

National Commission for Excellence in Education. 1983. *A Nation at Risk.* Washington, D.C.: United States Department of Education.

National Commission on Children. 1991. *Beyond Rhetoric: A New American Agenda for Children and Families.* Final Report. Washington, D.C.: U.S. Government Printing Office.

National Education Association. 1994. *Entering the Profession: Advice for the Untenured.* Washington, D.C.: National Education Association.

National Educational Goals Panel. 1991. *The National Educational Goals Report: Building a Nation of Learners.* Washington, D.C.: U.S. Government Printing Office.

National Research Council. 1995. *Research-Doctorate Programs in the United States.* Washington, D.C.: National Academy Press.

Natriello, G., E. L. McDill, and A. M. Pallas. 1990. *Schooling Disadvantaged Children: Racing against Catastrophe.* New York: Teachers College Press.

Natriello, G., and A. M. Pallas. 1999. "The Development and Impact of High Stakes Testing." Cambridge, Mass.: Harvard Civil Rights Project, Harvard University.

Neisser, U., G. Boodoo, T. J. Bouchard, A. W. Boykin, N. Brody, S. J. Ceci, D. F. Halpern, J. C. Loehlin, R. Perloff, R. J. Sternberg, and S. Urbina. 1996. "Intelligence: Knowns and Unknowns." *American Psychologist* 51: 77–101.

Neuberg, S. L. 1989. "The Goal of Forming Accurate Impressions during Social Interactions: Attenuating the Impact of Negative Expectancies." *Journal of Personality & Social Psychology* 56: 374–386.

Nicholls, J. G. 1976. "When a Scale Measures More than Its Name Denotes: The Case of the Test Anxiety Scale for Children." *Journal of Consulting and Clinical Psychology* 44: 976–985.

———. 1989. *The Competitive Ethos and Democratic Education*. Cambridge, Mass.: Harvard University Press.

Noddings, N. 1992. *The Challenge to Care in Schools: An Alternative Approach to Education*. New York: Teachers College Press.

Nucci, L. P., and H. J. Walberg. 1981. "Psychological Models of Educational Growth." In F. H. Farley and N. J. Gordon, eds., *Psychology and Education: The State of the Union*. Berkeley, Calif.: McCutchan.

Oakes, J. 1985. *Keeping Track: How Schools Structure Inequality*. New Haven: Yale University Press.

Oakes, J., and K. H. Quartz, eds. 1995. *Creating New Educational Communities*. Ninety-Fourth Yearbook of the National Society for the Study of Education. Chicago: University of Chicago Press.

Oakes, J., A. S. Wells, M. Jones, and A. Datnow. 1997. "Detracking: The Social Construction of Ability, Cultural Politics, and Resistance to Reform." *Teachers College Record* 98: 482–510.

O'Connell, E. J., J. Dusek, and R. J. Wheeler. 1974. "A Follow-Up Study of Teacher Expectancy Effects." *Journal of Educational Psychology* 66: 325–328.

O'Day, J. A., and M. S. Smith. 1993. "Systemic Reform and Educational Opportunity." In S. H. Furhman, ed., *Designing Coherent Educational Reform*. San Francisco: Jossey-Bass.

Olson, J. M., and M. P. Zanna. 1993. "Attitudes and Attitude Change." *Annual Review of Psychology* 44: 117–154.

Olszewski, L. 1999. "Third of Oakland Students Must Go to Summer Schools." *San Francisco Chronicle*, June 30, p. A1.

Orfield, G., and J. T. Yun. 1999. *Resegregation in American Schools*. Cambridge, Mass.: Harvard Civil Rights Project, Harvard University.

Oz, S., and D. Eden. 1994. "Restraining the Golem: Boosting Performance by Changing the Interpretation of Low Scores." *Journal of Applied Psychology* 79: 744–754.

Pagani, L., R. E. Tremblay, F. Vitaro, B. Boulerice, and P. McDuff. 2001. "Effects of Grade Retention on Academic Performance and Behavioral Development." *Development and Psychopathology* 13: 297–315.

Page, R. N. 1991. *Lower-Track Classrooms: A Curricular and Cultural Perspective*. New York: Teachers College Press.

Pallas, A. M., D. R. Entwisle, K. L. Alexander, and M. F. Stluka. 1994. "Ability-Group Effects: Instructional, Social, or Institutional?" *Sociology of Education* 67: 27–46.

Pallas, A. M., G. Natriello, and E. L. McDill. 1995. "Changing Students, Changing Needs." In E. Flaxman and A. H. Passow, eds., *Changing Populations, Changing Schools*. Ninety-Fourth Yearbook of the National Society for the Study of Education. Part 2. Chicago: University of Chicago Press.

Patterson, J. T. 2001. Brown v. Board of Education: *A Civil Rights Milestone and Its Troubled Legacy*. New York: Oxford University Press.

Pedersen, E., T. A. Faucher, and W. W. Eaton. 1978. "A New Perspective on the Effects of First-Grade Teachers on Children's Subsequent Adult Status." *Harvard Educational Review* 48: 1–31.

Peterson, P. L., S. J. McCarthey, and R. F. Elmore. 1996. "Learning from School Restructuring." *American Educational Research Journal* 33: 119–153.

Pfungst, O. [1911] 1965. *Clever Hans (The Horse of Mr. Von Osten): A Contribution to Experimental, Animal, and Human Psychology.* Trans. C. L. Rabin. New York: Holt,
Rinehart and Winston.

Phillips, M., J. Crouse, and J. Ralph. 1998. "Does the Black-White Test Score Gap
Widen after Children Enter School?" In C. Jencks and M. Phillips, eds., *The Black-
White Test Score Gap.* Washington, D.C.: Brookings Institution.

Pianta, R. C. 1994. "Patterns of Relationships between Children and Kindergarten
Teachers." *Journal of School Psychology* 32: 15–31.

———. 1999. *Enhancing Relationships between Children and Teachers.* Washington, D.C.:
American Psychological Association.

Porter, R. P. 1990. *Forked Tongue: The Politics of Bilingual Education.* New York: Basic
Books.

Pressley, M., R. L. Allington, R. Wharton-McDonald, C. C. Block, and L. M. Morrow.
2001. *Learning to Read: Lessons from Exemplary First-Grade Classrooms.* New York:
Guilford.

Price, H. B. 1999. "Urban Education: A Radical Plan." *Education Week,* Dec. 8,
p. 44.

Proctor, C. P. 1984. "Teacher Expectations: A Model for School Improvement." *Elementary School Journal* 84: 469–481.

Rappaport, M. M., and H. Rappaport. 1975. "The Other Half of the Expectancy
Equation: Pygmalion." *Journal of Educational Psychology* 57: 531–536.

Ratnesar, R. 1998. "Lost in the Middle." *Time Magazine,* Sept. 14, pp. 60–64.

Raudenbush, S. 1984. "Magnitude of Teacher Expectancy Effects on Pupil IQ as a
Function of the Credibility of Expectancy Induction: A Synthesis of Findings
from Eighteen Experiments." *Journal of Educational Psychology* 76: 85–97.

Ravitch, D. 1983. *The Troubled Crusade.* New York: Basic Books.

Reice, S. R. 1994. "Nonequilibrium Determinants of Biological Community Structure." *American Scientist* 82: 424–435. Quoting C. Elton. 1927. *Animal Ecology.*
London: Sidgwick and Jackson.

Reynolds, A. J., and B. Wolfe. 1999. "Special Education and School Achievement:
An Exploratory Analysis with a Central-City Sample." *Educational Evaluation and
Policy Analysis* 21: 249–269.

Richardson, J. G. 1994. "Common, Delinquent, and Special: On the Formalization of
Common Schooling in the American States." *American Educational Research Journal* 31: 695–723.

Riehl, C. J. 2000. "The Principal's Role in Creating Inclusive Schools for Diverse Students: A Review of Normative, Empirical, and Critical Literature on the Practice
of Educational Administration." *Review of Educational Research* 70: 55–81.

Rist, R. 1970. "Student Social Class and Teacher Expectations: The Self-Fulfilling
Prophecy in Ghetto Education." *Harvard Educational Review* 40: 411–451.

Rosenholtz, S. J. 1989. *Teachers' Workplace: The Social Organization of Schools.* New
York: Longman.

Rosenholtz, S. J., and C. Simpson. 1984. "The Formation of Ability Conceptions: Developmental Trend or Social Construction?" *Review of Educational Research* 54: 31–64.

Rosenthal, R. 1956. "An Attempt at an Experimental Induction of the Defense Mechanism of Projection." Ph.D. diss., University of California, Los Angeles.

———. 1963. "On the Social Psychology of the Psychological Experiment: The Experimenter's Hypothesis as Unintended Determinant of Experimental Results. *American Scientist* 51: 268–283.

———. 1973. *On the Social Psychology of the Self-Fulfilling Prophecy: Further Evidence for Pygmalion Effects and Their Mediating Mechanisms.* New York: MSS Modular Publications.

———. 1989. "The Affect/Effort Theory of the Mediation of Interpersonal Expectation Effects." D. T. Campbell Address. Paper presented at American Psychological Association meeting, New Orleans, August.

———. 1993. "Interpersonal Expectations: Some Antecedents and Some Consequences." In P. D. Blanck, ed., *Interpersonal Expectations: Theory, Research, and Applications.* Cambridge: Cambridge University Press.

Rosenthal, R., and K. L. Fode. 1963. "Psychology of the Scientist: Three Experiments in Experimenter Bias." *Psychological Reports* 12: 491–511.

Rosenthal, R., and L. Jacobson. 1968. *Pygmalion in the Classroom: Teacher Expectation and Pupils' Intellectual Development.* New York: Holt, Rinehart and Winston.

Rosenthal, R., and D. B. Rubin. 1978. "Interpersonal Expectancy Effects: The First 345 Studies." *Behavioral & Brain Sciences* 3: 377–386.

———. 1982. "A Simple General Purpose Display of Magnitude of Experimental Effect." *Journal of Educational Psychology* 74: 166–169.

Ross, S. I., and J. M. Jackson. 1991. "Teachers' Expectations for Black Males' and Black Females' Academic Achievement." *Personality and Social Psychology Bulletin* 17: 78–82.

Rothbart, M., and O. P. John. 1985. "Social Categorization and Behavioral Episodes: A Cognitive Analysis of the Effects of Intergroup Contact." *Journal of Social Issues* 41: 81–104.

Rothbart, M., and B. Park. 1986. "On the Confirmability and Disconfirmability of Trait Concepts." *Journal of Personality & Social Psychology* 50: 131–142.

Routh, D. K. 1996. "Lightner Witmer and the First Hundred Years of Clinical Psychology." *American Psychologist* 51: 244–247.

Rury, J. L., and J. E. Mirel. 1997. "The Political Economy of Urban Education." *Review of Research in Education* 22: 49–110.

Ryan, W. 1971. *Blaming the Victim.* New York: Pantheon.

Sadker, M., and D. M. Sadker. 1994. *Failing at Fairness: How America's Schools Cheat Girls.* New York: Scribner's.

Safford, P. L., and E. J. Safford. 1996. *A History of Childhood and Disability.* New York: Teachers College Press.

Sanders, M. G. 1997. "Overcoming Obstacles: Academic Achievement as a Response to Racism and Discrimination." *Journal of Negro Education* 66: 83–93.

Sarason, S. B. 1971. *The Culture of the School and the Problem of Change.* Boston: Allyn and Bacon.

———. 1990. *The Predictable Failure of Educational Reform.* San Francisco: Jossey-Bass.

———. 1996. *Revisiting the Culture of the School and the Problem of Change.* New York: Teachers College Press.

———. 2001. *American Psychology and Schools: A Critique.* New York: Teachers College Press and Washington, D.C.: American Psychological Association.

Sarason, S. B., and M. Klaber. 1985. "The School as a Social Situation." *Annual Review of Psychology* 36: 115–140.

Schmidt, W. H., C. C. McKnight, G. A. Valverde, R. T. Houang, and D. E. Wiley. 1997. *Many Visions, Many Aims: A Cross-National Investigation of Curricular Intentions in School Mathematics.* Vol. 1. Dordrecht, The Netherlands: Kluwer Academic.

Schofield, J. W. 1995. "Review of Research on School Segregation's Impact on Elementary and Secondary Students." In J. A. Banks and C. A. McGee Banks, eds., *Handbook of Research on Multicultural Education.* New York: MacMillan.

Schoggen, P. 1989. *Behavior Settings: A Revision and Extension of Roger G. Barker's Ecological Psychology.* Stanford, Calif.: Stanford University Press.

Schorr, L. B. 1997. *Common Purpose: Strengthening Families and Neighborhoods to Rebuild America.* New York: Anchor Books.

Schunk, D. H., and J. L. Meece. 1992. *Student Perceptions in the Classroom.* Hillsdale, N.J.: Lawrence Erlbaum.

Seidman, E. 1983. "Unexamined Premises of Social Problem Solving." In E. Seidman, ed., *Handbook of Social Intervention.* Beverly Hills, Calif.: Sage.

Shaw, B. [1912] 1940. *Pygmalion.* New York: Dodd Mead.

Shepard, L. A. 2000. "The Role of Assessment in a Learning Culture." *Educational Researcher* 29: 4–14.

Shepard, L. A., and M. L. Smith, eds. 1989. *Flunking Grades: Research and Policies on Retention.* London: Falmer Press.

Shipman, P. 1995. "One Woman's Life in Science." *American Scientist* 83: 300–302.

Short, R. J., and R. C. Talley. 1997. "Rethinking Psychology and the Schools: Implications of Recent National Policy." *American Psychologist* 52: 234–240.

Simontacchi, K. 1988. "Collaborative Development of Curricular and Instructional Innovations in the Classroom." Paper presented at the American Educational Research Association meeting, New Orleans, April.

Simonton, D. K. 2001. "Talent Development as a Multidimensional, Multiplicative, and Dynamic Process." *Current Directions in Psychological Science* 10: 39–43.

Singer, J. D., J. S. Palfrey, J. A. Butler, and D. Klein Walker. 1989. "Variation in Special Education Classification across School Districts: How Does Where You Live Affect What You Are Labeled?" *American Educational Research Journal* 26: 261–281.

Sirotnik, K. A. 1990. "Equal Access to Quality in Public Schooling." in L. I. Goodlad and P. Keating, eds., *Access to Knowledge: An Agenda for Our Nation's Schools.* New York: The College Board.

Sizer, T. R. 1992. *Horace's School: Redesigning the American High School.* New York: Houghton Mifflin.

Skiba, R. J., R. S. Michael, A. C. Nardo, and R. Peterson. 2000. *The Color of Discipline: Sources of Racial and Gender Disproportionality in School Punishment.* Policy Research Report #SRS1. Bloomington: The Indiana Education Policy Center, Indiana University.

Skinner, E. A., and M. J. Belmont. 1993. "Motivation in the Classroom: Reciprocal Effects of Teacher Behavior and Student Engagement across the School Year." *Journal of Educational Psychology* 85: 571–581.

Slavin, R. E. 1983. *Cooperative Learning.* New York: Longman.

Slavin, R. E., N. A. Madden, L. A. Dolan, and B. Wasik. 1996. *Every Child, Every School: Success for All.* Thousand Oaks, Calif.: Corwin Press.

Smith, A. E., L. Jussim, and J. Eccles. 1999. "Do Self-Fulfilling Prophecies Accumulate, Dissipate, or Remain Stable over Time?" *Journal of Personality and Social Psychology* 77: 548–565.

Smith, M. 1980. "Teacher Expectations." *Evaluation in Education* 4: 53–55.

Smith, M., and L. Shepard. 1988. "Kindergarten Readiness and Retention: A Qualitative Study of Teachers' Beliefs and Practices." *American Educational Research Journal* 25: 307–333.

Smith, P. 1990. *Killing the Spirit: Higher Education in America.* New York: Viking.

Snyder, M. 1992. "Motivational Foundations of Behavioral Confirmation." In M. P. Zanna, ed., *Advances in Experimental Social Psychology.* Vol. 16. New York: Academic Press.

Snyder, M., and A. A. Stukas, Jr. 1999. "Interpersonal Processes: The Interplay of Cognitive, Motivational, and Behavioral Activities in Social Interaction." *Annual Review of Psychology* 50: 273–304.

Solomon, D., V. Battistich, M. Watson, E. Schaps, and C. Lewis. 2000. "A Six-District Study of Educational Change: Direct and Mediated Effects of the Child Development Project." *Social Psychology of Education* 4: 3–51.

Solomon, D., M. S. Watson, K. L. Delucchi, and E. Schaps. 1988. "Enhancing Children's Prosocial Behavior in the Classroom." *American Educational Research Journal* 25: 527–554.

Sonnert, G., and G. Holton. 1996. "Career Patterns of Women and Men in Science." *American Scientist* 84: 63–71.

Soulé, C. R. 1993. "Predictors of Children's Susceptibility to Teacher Expectations: Developmental, Classroom, and Child Perception Factors." Ph.D. diss., University of California, Berkeley.

Spitz, H. H. 1999. "Attempts to Raise Expectations." In M. Anderson, ed., *The Development of Intelligence.* Hove, Eng.: Psychology Press/Taylor & Francis.

Stadtman, V. 1970. *The University of California, 1868–1968.* New York: McGraw-Hill.

Steele, C. M., and J. Aronson. 1995. "Stereotype Threat and the Intellectual Test Performance of African Americans." *Journal of Personality and Social Psychology* 69: 797–811.

Sternberg, R. J. 1999. "The Theory of Successful Intelligence." *Review of General Psychology* 3: 292–316.

———. 2000. "Implicit Theories of Intelligence as Exemplar Stories of Success: Why Intelligence Test Validity Is in the Eye of the Beholder." *Psychology, Public Policy, and Law* 6: 159–167.

Sternberg, R. J., E. L. Grigorenko, and D. A. Bundy. 2001. "The Predictive Validity of IQ." *Merrill-Palmer Quarterly* 47: 1–41.

Sternberg, R. J., B. Torff, and E. L. Grigorenko. 1998. "Teaching Triarchically Improves School Performance." *Journal of Educational Psychology* 90: 374–384.

Sternberg, R. J., and W. M. Williams. 1997. "Does the Graduate Record Examination Predict Meaningful Success in the Graduate Training of Psychologists?" *American Psychologist* 52: 630–641.

Stevenson, H. W., and J. W. Stigler. 1992. *The Learning Gap.* New York: Touchstone.

Stewart, D. L. 1993. "In Praise of Kids Who Are 'Just' Good." *San Francisco Chronicle,* June 11, p. B4.

Stewart, D. W. 1993. *Immigration and Education: The Crisis and the Opportunities.* New York: Lexington Books.

Stewart, E. 2000. "Thinking through Others: Qualitative Research and Community Psychology." In J. Rappaport and E. Seidman, eds., *Handbook of Community Psychology.* New York: Kluwer Academic/Plenum Publishers.

Stipek, D. J., and D. H. Daniels. 1988. "Declining Perceptions of Competence: A Consequence of Changes in the Child or in the Educational Environment?" *Journal of Educational Psychology* 80: 352–356.

Stipek, D. J., and J. H. Gralinski. 1996. "Children's Beliefs about Intelligence and School Performance." *Journal of Educational Psychology* 88: 397–407.

Stodolsky, S. S. 1995. "The Impact of Subject Matter on Curricular Activity: An Analysis of Five Academic Subjects." *American Educational Research Journal* 32: 227–249.

Stokols, D. 1992. "Establishing and Maintaining Healthy Environments: Toward a Social Ecology of Health Promotion." *American Psychologist* 47: 6–22.

Stromquist, N. P. 1993. "Sex-Equity Legislation in Education: The State as a Promoter of Women's Rights." *Review of Educational Research* 63: 379–407.

Sue, S. 1999. "Science, Ethnicity, and Bias." *American Psychologist* 54: 1070–1077.

Swann, W. B. 1987. "Identity Negotiation: Where Two Roads Meet." *Journal of Personality & Social Psychology* 53: 1038–1051.

Talbert, J., and M. McLaughlin. 1999. "Assessing the School Environment." In S. Friedman and T. D. Wachs, eds., *Measuring Environment across the Life-Span.* Washington, D.C.: American Psychological Association.

Terman, D. L., M. B. Larner, C. S. Stevenson, and R. E. Behrman. 1996. "Special Education for Students with Disabilities." *The Future of Children* 6: 4–24.

Tharp, R. G., and R. Gallimore. 1988. *Rousing Minds to Life.* Cambridge: Cambridge University Press.

Third International Mathematics and Science Study (TIMMS). 1999, 2001. *Benchmarking Highlights: A Bridge to School Improvement.* http://isc.bc.edu.

Thomas, W. I. 1931. "The Relation of Research to the Social Process." In Committee on Training, ed., *Essays on Research in the Social Sciences*. Washington, D.C.: Brookings Institution.

Tierney, W. G. 1997. "The Parameters of Affirmative Action: Equity and Excellence in the Academy." *Review of Educational Research* 67: 165–196.

Tierney, W. G., and E. S. Bensimon. 1996. *Promotion and Tenure: Community and Socialization in Academe*. Albany: State University of New York Press.

Trent, J. W., Jr. 1994. *Inventing the Feeble Mind: A History of Mental Retardation in the United States*. Berkeley: University of California Press.

Trickett, E. J., and D. Birman. 1989. "Taking Ecology Seriously: A Community Development Approach to Individually Based Interventions." In L. Bond and B. Compas, eds., *Primary Prevention in the Schools*. Hanover, N.H.: University Press of New England.

Trickett, E. J., R. J. Watts, and D. Birman, eds. 1994. *Human Diversity: Perspectives on People in Context*. San Francisco: Jossey-Bass.

"Two Communities Kept Their Cool." 1992. *San Francisco Chronicle*, May 5, p. A13.

Tyack, D. B., and L. Cuban. 1995. *Tinkering toward Utopia: A Century of Public School Reform*. Cambridge, Mass.: Harvard University Press.

Tyack, D. B., and E. Hansot. 1990. *Learning Together: A History of Coeducation in American Schools*. New Haven: Yale University Press.

Valencia, R. R., ed. 1991. *Chicano School Failure and Success*. London: Falmer Press.

Vernon, P. A. 1971. *The Structure of Human Abilities*. London: Methuen.

Vincent, T. A., and E. J. Trickett. 1983. "Preventive Interventions and the Human Context: Ecological Approaches to Environmental Assessment and Change." In R. D. Felner, L. Jason, J. Moritsugu, and S. Farber, eds., *Preventive Psychology: Theory, Research, and Practice in Community Interventions*. New York: Pergamon.

Vispoel, W. P., and J. R. Austin. 1995. "Success and Failure in Junior High School: A Critical Incident Approach to Understanding Students' Attributional Beliefs." *American Educational Research Journal* 32: 377–412.

Vygotsky, L. 1978. *Mind in Society: The Development of Higher Psychological Processes*. Cambridge, Mass.: Harvard University Press.

Wachs, T. D. 2000. *Necessary But Not Sufficient: The Respective Roles of Single and Multiple Influences on Individual Development*. Washington, D.C.: American Psychological Association.

Wang, J. 1998. "Opportunity to Learn: The Impacts and Policy Implications." *Educational Evaluation and Policy Analysis* 20: 137–156.

Weed, D. L. 1997. "On the Use of Causal Criteria." *International Journal of Epidemiology* 26: 1137–1141.

Weinstein, J. A. 1994. "Growing Up Learning Disabled." *Journal of Learning Disabilities* 27: 142–143.

Weinstein, R. S. 1976. "Reading Group Membership in First Grade: Teacher Behaviors and Pupil Experience over Time." *Journal of Educational Psychology* 68: 103–116.

———. 1983. "Student Perceptions of Schooling." *Elementary School Journal* 83: 287–312.

———. 1986. "The Teaching of Reading and Children's Awareness of Teacher Expectations." In T. Raphael, ed., *The Contexts of School-Based Literacy.* New York: Random House.

———. 1989. "Perceptions of Classroom Processes and Student Motivation: Children's Views of Self-Fulfilling Prophecies." In R. A. Ames and C. Ames, eds., *Research on Motivation in Education.* Vol. 3. New York: Academic Press.

———. 1993. "Children's Knowledge of Differential Treatment in School: Implications for Motivation." In T. M. Tomlinson, ed., *Motivating Students to Learn: Overcoming Barriers to High Achievement.* Berkeley, Calif.: McCutchan.

———. 1996. "High Standards in a Tracked System of Schooling: For Which Students and with What Educational Supports?" *Educational Researcher* 8: 16–19.

———. 1998. "Promoting Positive Expectations in Schooling." In N. M. Lambert and B. L. McCombs, eds., *How Students Learn: Reforming Schools through Learner-Centered Education.* Washington, D.C.: American Psychological Association.

Weinstein, R. S., S. M. Madison, and M. R. Kuklinski. 1995. "Raising Expectations in Schooling: Obstacles and Opportunities for Change." *American Educational Research Journal* 32: 121–159.

Weinstein, R. S., H. H. Marshall, K. A. Brattesani, and S. E. Middlestadt. 1982. "Student Perceptions of Differential Teacher Treatment in Open and Traditional Classrooms." *Journal of Educational Psychology* 74: 678–692.

Weinstein, R. S., H. H. Marshall, K. A. Brattesani, and L. Sharp. 1980. "Achieving in School: Children's Views of Causes and Consequences." Paper presented at American Psychological Association meeting, Montreal, September.

Weinstein, R. S., H. H. Marshall, L. Sharp, and M. Botkin. 1987. "Pygmalion and the Student: Age and Classroom Differences in Children's Awareness of Teacher Expectations." *Child Development* 58: 1079–1093.

Weinstein, R. S., and C. McKown. 1998. "Expectancy Effects in Context: Listening to the Voices of Students and Teachers." In J. Brophy, ed., *Advances in Research on Teaching: Expectations in the Classroom.* Vol. 7. Greenwich, Conn.: JAI.

Weinstein, R. S., and S. E. Middlestadt. 1979. "Student Perceptions of Teacher Interactions with Male High and Low Achievers." *Journal of Educational Psychology* 71: 421–431.

Weinstein, R. S., C. R. Soulé, F. Collins, J. Cone, M. Mehlhorn, and K. Simontacchi. 1991. "Expectations and High School Change: Teacher-Researcher Collaboration to Prevent School Failure." *American Journal of Community Psychology* 19: 333–364.

Wells, A. S., and R. L. Crain. 1994. "Perpetuation Theory and the Long-Term Effects of School Desegregation." *Review of Educational Research* 64: 531–555.

Wenneras, C., and A. Wold. 1997. "Nepotism and Sexism in Peer-Review." *Nature* 387: 341–343.

West, C. K., and T. H. Anderson. 1976. "The Question of Preponderant Causation in Teacher Expectancy Research." *Review of Educational Research* 46: 613–630.

Wheeler, L. 1991. "The School Where Nobody Gets Cut." *San Francisco Chronicle,* Nov. 11, p. D3.

Wheelock, A. 1992. *Crossing the Tracks: How Untracking Can Save America's Schools.* New York: New Press.

Wilshire, B. 1990. *The Moral Collapse of the University.* Albany: State University of New York Press.

Wilson, K., and B. Daviss. 1994. *Redesigning Education.* New York: Teachers College Press.

Wilson, W. J. 1996. *When Work Disappears: The World of the New Urban Poor.* New York: Knopf.

Wilson, Y. 1999. "Library's About-Face on Boy's Idea." *San Francisco Chronicle,* May 13, pp. A1, A12.

Wineburg, S. S. 1987. "The Self-Fulfillment of the Self-Fulfilling Prophecy." *Educational Researcher* 16: 28–44.

Witmer, L. [1907] 1996. "Clinical Psychology." *American Psychologist* 51: 248–251. Reprinted from *Psychological Clinic* 1: 1–9.

Wolff, E. N. 1995. *Top Heavy: A Study of the Increasing Inequality of Wealth in America.* New York: Twentieth Century Fund.

Zebrowitz McArthur, L., and R. M. Baron. 1983. "Toward an Ecological Theory of Social Perception." *Psychological Review* 90: 215–238.

Zhou, M. 2001. "Contemporary Immigration and the Dynamics of Race and Ethnicity." In N. J. Smelser, W. J. Wilson, and F. Mitchell, eds., *America Becoming: Racial Trends and Their Consequences.* Vol. 1. Washington, D.C.: National Academy Press.

Zimiles, H. 1986. "The Changing American Child." In T. M. Tomlinson and H. J. Walberg, eds., *Academic Work and Educational Excellence: Raising Student Productivity.* Berkeley, Calif.: McCutchan Publishing.

Zuckerman, H. 1998. "Accumulation of Advantage and Disadvantage: The Theory and Its Intellectual Biography." In C. Mongardini and S. Tabboni, eds., *Robert K. Merton and Contemporary Sociology.* New Brunswick, N.J.: Transaction.

Zuckerman, H., J. R. Cole, and J. T. Bruer, eds. 1991. *The Outer Circle: Women in the Scientific Community.* New York: W. W. Norton.

Zuroff, D. C., and J. B. Rotter. 1985. "A History of the Expectancy Construct." In J. B. Dusek, ed., *Teacher Expectancies.* Hillsdale, N.J.: Lawrence Erlbaum.

Acknowledgments

I am deeply indebted to The Spencer Foundation for funds to support the reflective work of this book—a precious gift of time that has been critical to my development. Earlier research grants from The Spencer Foundation, the U.S. Department of Education, the National Institute of Mental Health, and the University of California at Berkeley (including the School-University Partnership for Educational Renewal project in the School of Education) also enabled the collection of data presented here. While appreciative of this support, I bear sole responsibility for the conclusions drawn.

Excerpts from the article "Growing Up Learning Disabled," by J. A. Weinstein, which appeared in the *Journal of Learning Disabilities* 27 (1994): 142–143, are reprinted here with the permission of PRO-ED Inc. Excerpts from the commentary "Epitaph for an English Teacher," by H. Good, which appeared in *Education Week*, October 18, 2000, p. 38, are reprinted with the permission of Copyright Clearance Center. I am also especially grateful to the Museum of Modern Art and the Jacob and Gwendolyn Lawrence Foundation for permission to reprint on the cover of this book panel 58 from *The Migration of the Negro* (1940–1941) by Jacob Lawrence. Lawrence's image and his words "In the North the Negro had better educational facilities" beautifully capture the theme of "reaching higher." Even beyond the hope expressed in this painting, Lawrence's own story speaks to the important role of an influential teacher. During a troubled period in his youth, his mother enrolled him in an after-school program. There he was able to work with the noted art teacher Charles Alston, who saw potential in young Lawrence and helped nurture this talent.

Scores of individuals have been helpful to me in pursuing this work over many years, more than I can name, and I remain ever grateful. These include collaborator Hermine Marshall, whose classroom observation instrument and understanding of teaching proved pivotal to my learning; Peggy Moffett, whose efficient grace helped us through periods of data collection and analysis; and the many graduate students whose research inspired as well as contributed substantively to this effort (Jennifer Alvidrez, Meryl Botkin, Karen Brattesani, Elise Cappella, Kathleen Donahue, Anne Gregory, Lauren Jones, Margaret Kuklinski, Sybil Madison, Clark McKown, Susan Middlestadt, Lee Sharp, Charles Soulé, and Carol Sullivan). Collaborations with Barbara Butterworth, Florence Collins, Joan Cone, Nina Gabelko, Michelle Mehlhorn, and Karen Simontacchi especially nurtured this work. To the children, teachers, parents, and principals whose voices echo through this book, I offer my deepest gratitude.

I also acknowledge wonderfully constructive and supportive feedback from the graduate students of seminars I taught in 1997 and 2000, and from dear colleagues Philip and Carolyn Cowan, Martin Covington, Sarah Freedman, Arnold Leiman, Seymour Sarason, and Sheldon Zedeck. Sarah Freedman was a lifeline in helping me see as well as seize the story. I am indebted to Jessica Black, Nicole Yee, Marge Johnson, Barbara Glendenning, and Paulette Comeau for their contributions to the final phases of manuscript preparation, to Ted Crum and Eric Eichorn who at a moment's notice kept my computers operative, and to the staff of the Psychology Department at Berkeley, who provided essential support and cheered when the manuscript was finally in the mail.

Elizabeth Knoll, my editor at Harvard University Press, has been a thoughtful and empathic reader of this manuscript from the start, and a champion of its message. Julie Carlson has served expertly as my most literal reader, working to polish the manuscript to a high sheen. The staff at Harvard University Press, among them Kirsten Giebutowski, Christine Thorsteinsson, Jill Winitzer, and Marianne Perlak, have worked mightily and creatively to produce the final product. The book is far stronger as a result of their contributions and I am most appreciative.

I owe a substantial intellectual debt to a number of extraordinary mentors. The late M. Sam Rabinovitch, who founded the McGill University–Montreal Children's Hospital Learning Center, spearheaded a movement in Canadian schools to recognize that children with learning disabilities were indeed of normal intelligence and could learn when given appropriate instructional opportunities. His methods, developed over a career cut short by his premature death in 1977, underscored the importance of listening to children, capitalizing on their strengths, linking assessment to pedagogical interventions, and holding all accountable for good teaching. Seymour B. Sarason founded one of the first settings for community psychology at the Yale Psycho-Educational Clinic. His work as a staff psychologist in 1942 at the Southbury Training School for the mentally retarded opened his eyes to the ways in which the qualities of social settings can limit the unfolding of human potential. From Seymour Sarason, I developed a passion for prevention, a curiosity about the culture of schools, and an enduring interest in the ways in which educational settings can lessen the gap between potential and performance. At Yale University, I also had the good fortune to work with N. Dickon Reppucci, who chaired my long-ago doctoral dissertation on reading groups in first-grade classrooms. He helped me find my own voice in the doing of research and of teaching—a precious gift indeed. At the University of California, Berkeley, I was blessed with and recently lost an intellectual soulmate, the late Arnold Leiman, whose passion about higher education drove him to create programs and settings that would replicate for generations of students "the special things that happened with teachers that shaped paths to success."

I want also to acknowledge the important contributions of my late parents, Alex and Lotte Strasberg. My passion for the issues raised in this book is rooted in the immigrant experience of my father and my mother, and the denial of educational opportunity—thankfully overturned for my father, but not so for my mother. Both my parents steadfastly nurtured my intellectual curiosity and supported my ambitions to become a university professor at a time when women were greatly in the minority. And finally, I express my deepest appreciation to my husband Harvey and our sons, Jeremy and Joshua, who allowed this book to have a place in their lives for far too many years. They proved to be visionary as well as helpful readers, but most importantly, they have encouraged me at every turn in this journey. They are my cheering section, and I am truly blessed to call them mine.

Index

ability-based grouping, 34–35, 70–71, 83, 104, 182, 207; reading group assignments, 3, 20, 22, 49, 52–54; mobility between groups, 49, 52–54, 77, 119–120, 140, 142, 155–156, 265–266; of university faculty, 265–266. *See also* grouping; reading group assignments; tracking

accommodation, 171–173

accountability: for effective instruction, 142–144, 243–246, 250; in educational reforms, 196, 197, 254

achievement culture, 10–11, 73–76, 114–116. *See also* classroom culture; development-focused achievement cultures; school culture; selection-focused achievement cultures; university achievement culture

achievement gap, 53, 160–162, 167–168, 177, 194, 282, 290, 296

adaptation, 63, 76

administration, 211, 213, 215–216, 223–225, 228, 230, 270

admissions policies, 264, 273

advocacy, 35, 91, 190–191, 301–302

African American students, 177, 211; as targets of low expectations, 163–166; stereotypes of, 171, 184, 298; resilience, 191, 193. *See also* racial/ethnic differentiation

afterschool programs, 236, 237, 245

agency, 170–171, 207, 219–221, 301; in classroom culture, 103, 107–108, 132–

135; of teachers, 213, 269–270; in development-focused school culture, 236, 237–238, 249–250

Albom, Mitch, 286

Allport, Gordon, 5

Alvidrez, Jennifer, 84, 178–180

American Psychological Association, 82, 303

Anastasiow, Nicholas, 84

anxiety, 2, 163, 165, 171

Asian students, 74, 83, 297

assemblies, 234–235

Astin, Alexander, 263

athletic participation, 247, 253

averaged effects, 57–58, 73–75, 110, 287–288

Babad, Elisha, 6, 39, 45–46, 51, 55, 56, 57, 58, 60, 111–112, 204

Bacon, Francis, 39–40, 41

Baltimore School Study, 74

Bandura, Albert, 40, 113, 142, 193

Barker, Roger, 61, 63

Beach Music (Conroy), 297

Beginning School study, 176–177

behavior, observable sequences of, 47–49

behavioral principles, 38, 139, 255

beliefs about learning, 1–6, 41, 81, 170–171, 207; leading to behavior, 47–48; actions and, 50–51; carryover and, 190–191. *See also* capability; expectancy effects; self-fulfilling prophecies